Lewisburg, Arkansas

an anthology of articles and newspaper clippings

Bob Crossman, Editor

"The town of Lewisburg... gave up its life to nourish the young *Morrilton*. As a hen broods its young, it sheltered its sturdy sons until they left it for better fields, and then deserted by all, it sank peacefully from existence leaving nothing to mark its resting-place, but a few crumbling ruins."
Daily Arkansas Gazette, Friday, September 26, 1884 ·Page 2

"The City of Lewisburg 1852" by Susan Gordon Stout
This image is the original painting before professional restoration.
The image on this book's cover is a 2008 replica that is on display at the Conway County Historical Museum.

Explore the BUTTERFIELD OVERLAND NATIONAL HISTORIC TRAIL that passes through Lewisburg, Arkansas by reading these books by Bob Crossman:

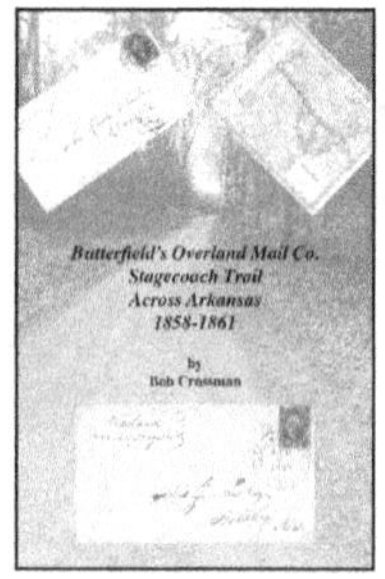

Butterfield's Overland Mail Co. STAGECOACH TRAIL Across Arkansas
in color, 266 pages

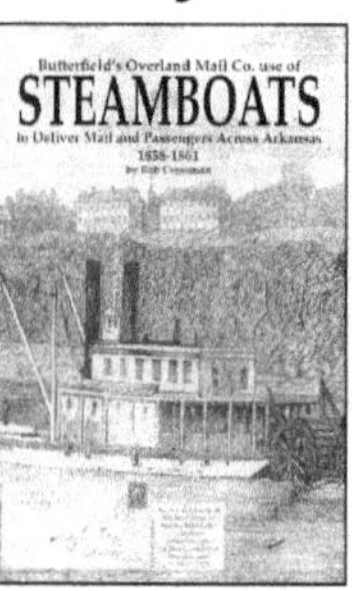

Butterfield's Overland Mail Co. use of STEAMBOATS to Deliver Mail and Passengers Arkansas
460 pages

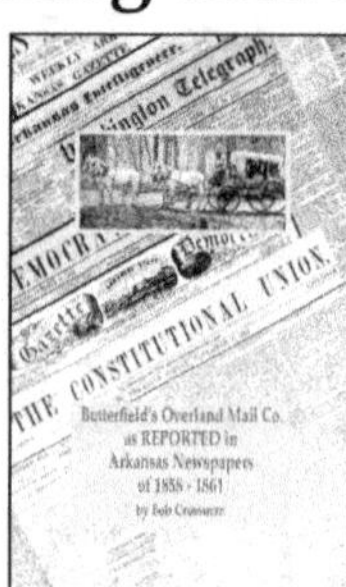

Butterfield's Overland Mail Co. as REPORTED in Arkansas Newspapers of 1858-1861
632 pages

POSTAL HISTORY of John Butterfield's Overland Mail Co. on the Southern & Central Routes including Butterfield's Pony Express
in color, 354 pages

Butterfield Overland National Historic TRAIL PASSENGER DIARIES & STORIES Across Oklahoma, Arkansas and Missouri
460 pages

Butterfield Overland National Historic Trail Through FAULKNER County, Arkansas
in color, 144 pages

Butterfield Overland National Historic Trail Through Arkansas' POPE & CONWAY Counties
in color, 236 pages

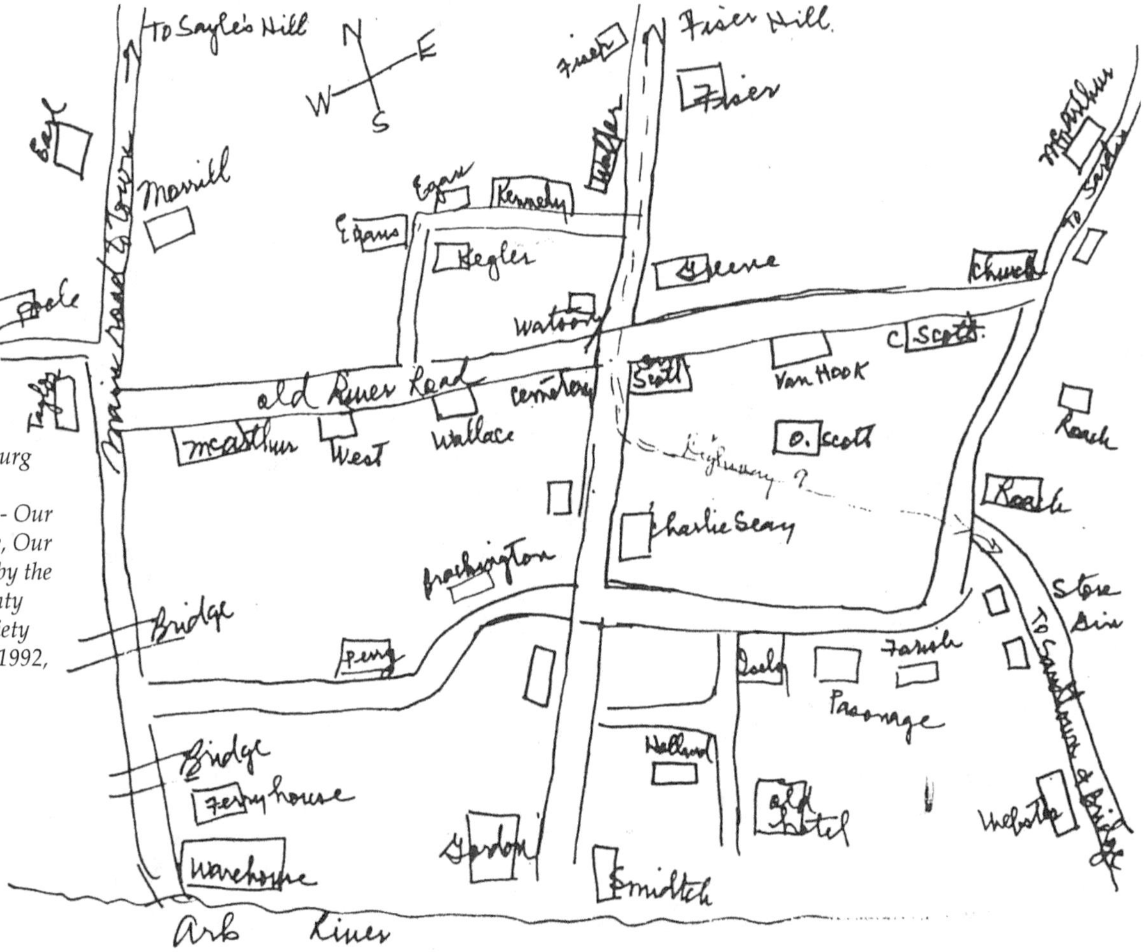

Map of Lewisburg Source: Conway County - Our Land, Our Home, Our People compiled by the Conway County Historical Society Second Edition, 1992, page 13

Map of Old Lewisburg

© 2024 Robert O. Crossman
Ingram Spark Press
ISBN 979-8-9885900-8-8 Paper Cover

August, 2024

Table of Contents

The Town of Old Lewisburg

Photo by Grissom
Close up of the upper left corner of a 1907 photo-postcard.
This post card was mailed from Morrilton on March 25, 1907, addressed to Atkins, Arkansas.
Retired Corp of Engineer employee, Jack Johnson, reports: *"Lewisburg, like Ozark Arkansas, never flooded because it was on high-ground overlooking the Arkansas River."*
Image courtesy of Sharon Hamilton

"Lewisburg, Arkansas: an anthology of articles and newspaper clippings" by Bob Crossman, editor, contains four articles on the general history of this steamboat landing on the Arkansas River, and two articles on its role in the Civil War. The editor also examined sixteen Arkansas newspapers from the 1830's to the 1870's, and selected hundreds of articles with a significant mention of Lewisburg or its people.

*Front of the 1907 photo-postcard
from the collection of Sharon Hamilton.*

*Back of the 1907 photo-postcard
from the collection of Sharon Hamilton.*

HISTORY OF LEWISBURG & MORRILTON, ARKANSAS
Marcia Swain Crossman, Editor

Introduction

For those interested in the **history of the Morrilton area** from it's earliest beginnings, I have included parts of a paper by **Mary Ellen Guffey Brents** from Morrilton, Arkansas, **Encyclopedia of Arkansas** and revised, **2022**, and by **David Sesser, Henderson State University**. Information from **Rachel Silva**, employed by the **Arkansas Historic Preservation Program** wrote, *"Walks through History: A History of Morrilton"* in **2014**. Other information came from the book, *"Butterfield Overland Mail Through Conway and Pope Counties in Arkansas"* by author **Bob Crossman** published in **2024**. *Thanks so much to all of these educators for their research and writing that informs us today. I hope you enjoy this!* **Edited by Marcia Swain Crossman, 2024.**

The Geography of Conway County

Located in the Arkansas River Valley, Conway County's geography ranges from the ridges of the Ozark foothills, in the extreme northwest, to the rich lowlands near the Arkansas River — a quite varied topography. The ***Arkansas River divides the county into two unequal parts***, the largest being to the north. To the south is Petit Jean Mountain *(elevation 1,207 feet)*, the county's highest summit.

Pre-European Exploration

Spears and darts dating from very early periods have been found at the **Travis Moreland Site**, which was perhaps a camp for the butchering of animals. Other sites dating from more recent prehistoric periods have been located in Conway County, including the **Alexander Site**, which some archaeologists believe was a satellite community for the larger **Toltec Mounds Site** in Lonoke County. More than 700 pictographs are located on or near Petit Jean Mountain. Ancestors of the **Quapaw Indians** may have lived in the county.

Louisiana Purchase through Early Statehood

Conway County's early settlers came by way of the **Arkansas River** and included **trappers, traders, and fugitives**. Most of the earliest settlements were along the **Arkansas River** and in the valley of **Cadron Creek**, which forms part of the county's east boundary. The county was under **French and Spanish** rule before the **Louisiana Purchase** put it under American control, though there were no permanent French or Spanish settlements in the area. A few Americans had settled in the area before the Louisiana Purchase, such as the family of **Benjamin Standlee**, who lived above the mouth of Cadron Creek from **1777** to **1780**.

The Trail of Tears

From **1817** to **1828**, the **Western Cherokee occupied a reservation in Arkansas** that included a great deal of Conway County. In **1828**, the **Cherokee in Arkansas** signed a treaty swapping this reservation for lands west of the territorial border. *This coincided with the **1820's** and **1830's** removal of Cherokee and other Indians from the southeast United States to Indian Territory (present-day Oklahoma) on what is known as **"The Trail of Tears."*** The **Arkansas River** was a much-used water route for **Indian removal**, with **Point Remove** in **Conway County** being a stop along the route. The **Via Dolorosa** road was built from the east of the White River and west through **Springfield** to transport these Indian refugees.

Creation of Conway County

Conway County was **created by the Arkansas General Assembly on October 20, 1825** from land taken from Pulaski County. It was **named for Henry Wharton Conway**, from of the Arkansas Territory's delegation to Congress. *At the time, it comprised 2,500 square miles and included most of the present Conway, Faulkner, Van Buren, White, Cleburne, and Perry counties and part of Yell County.*

The town of **Cadron**, which was then located centrally in **Conway County,** was made a temporary county seat. In **1829**, the territorial legislature moved the county seat to **Harrisburg** *(then the house of Stephen Harris in Welborne Township).* In **1831**, the county seat moved again after Dr. Nimrod Menifee donated a plot of land in **Lewisburg** for the building of a courthouse. **Lewisburg** remained the county seat until **1850.**

On December 11, 1840, when **Lewisburg** was still the county seat, a steamboat named **"Cherokee"** **exploded** after leaving the dock from Lewisburg. The incident led to the deaths of at least twenty people.

The county seat then moved to **Springfield** because of that town's more central location. The **first post office** for the county was at **Peconery**, an early settlement on the Arkansas River between **Lewisburg** and **Cadron.**

Secession of Arkansas and The Civil War

Dr. S. J. Stallings went to the **Secession Convention** held in Little Rock *(Pulaski County)* in **March, 1861** with instructions to **vote against Arkansas leaving the Union**. After the **firing upon Fort Sumter,** the following month, most **Conway County citizens supported secession.** *(Stallings owned six enslaved people at the time of the 1860 census).* The county recorded **5,895 white residents in 1860** and **802 enslaved persons,** showing that about **twelve percent of the population was held in bondage**. The county produced 3,181 bales of **cotton in 1860** and almost 35,000 pounds of **tobacco.**

The **first Confederate Civil War company** in the county was organized by **Robert W. Harper** of **Lewisburg**. Other companies were subsequently raised at **Lewisburg** and **Springfield. About 900 men from Conway County fought in the Civil War, primarily in Arkansas but also in Tennessee and Kentucky; only 200 men returned home from the war. *There were no major actions fought in Conway County, although numerous minor engagements took place.***

The Third Arkansas Cavalry, *from the Union side*, was partially **recruited in Conway County. They patrolled from a base in Lewisburg**. Operations in the county included scouts to locate Confederate cavalry in June **1864** and anti-guerrilla operations in August **1864**, and an expedition into Johnson County in November **1864**. A skirmish fought at **Lewisburg on February 12, 1865, saw the end of most military operations in the Conway County.**

Note: Some of these war solders are buried at the Lewisburg Missionary Baptist Church Cemetery and others at the Elmwood Cemetery in Morrilton. In 2024, a new Internet home page was created for the Elmwood Cemetery population which includes the names of Civil War solders buried there.

Conway County Seat was moved to Morrilton

In 1873, the county seat was returned to **Lewisburg** from **Springfield**. In **1883**, it again was taken from Lewisburg and established at **Morrilton**, where it remains to this day. It's original parent county was **Pulaski**. The current courthouse was constructed in **1929**.

Transportation In the Mid 1800's

In its early days, beginning in **1828**, the Conway County area thrived due to its **location on the Arkansas River.** Travel on the river was the best transportation for crops and business. In that day **Lewisburg**, *(which is almost nonexistent today)* on the Arkansas River, boasted over **80 businesses**, including two sawmills, two gristmills, a flour mill, cotton gin, hotels, two newspapers, saloons and numerous stores. The location of the county seat which, was at **Lewisburg** for many years, brought this commerce there.

Before the railroad in the **1870's, stagecoach** and **horse drawn** vehicles were the main means of travel by the people of the area. **Persons** and the **United States Mail** were delivered by the **Butterfield Overland Mail Company**, a popular but slow line of travel. **Steamboats** also carried mail and people across the state. When the **railroad tracks** were laid through Conway County, it quickly became the major mode of transportation.

In **1867**, surveyors for the **coming of the Little Rock and Fort Smith Railroad** were looking at land outside of **Lewisburg**. The progress of the railroad was interrupted by the Civil War.

About **1870,** actual construction of the railroad began after the war. The railroad company invited the residents of **Lewisburg** to provide $3,000 to defray costs. The residents of **Lewisburg declined the invitation**.

Edward Henry Morrill and **James Miles Moose** were forward thinking businessmen in the area. They **donated land for railroad track to run through their property about a mile north of Lewisburg.** *The area along the tracks grew quickly.* The twenty-four miles of **Missouri Pacific Railroad** tracks were completed through the county. In **1872.** *Residents of Conway County could see that the area around the new track was better for business.* **Many Lewisburg residents disassembled their houses and businesses and moved these one mile north to be near the new tracks.** *James Miles Moose bought*

Lewisburg's Markham Tavern and moved it to **Morrilton** as his new home.

The **first bona fide rail depot** in that area was established in **1873**. The land for the depot was given by **E. H. Morrill**. The first station agent, was **Capt. J.W. Boot**. With a **flip of a coin, between Morrill** and **Moose, choose the town to be named after Mr. Morrill. Morrilton** was first spelled with two "l's" like its namesake. The population of the **Lewisburg area slowly moved to Morrilton**. The new town of **Morrilton** was incorporated in **1835** with a **population of 800**.

In **1874**, the **Springfield-Des Arc Bridge was completed**, spanning the north fork of Cadron Creek connecting Conway County with the newly created Faulkner County. *It is now on the National Register of Historic Places.*

Newspapers in the Town of Morrilton

The **earliest newspaper** to be published in Conway County was the *Wide Awake*, established in **Lewisburg** in January **1872**. In May of that year, the *Western Empire* also began publication in **Lewisburg**. Neither paper lasted more than a few years. A number of papers have been based in Conway County since that time, but the only one surviving today is the *Petit Jean Country Headlight,* which was **founded on April 8, 1874,** by the **Reverend W. C. Stout**, an Episcopalian minister, as the *Weekly State*.

In the News:

In **1889**, Conway County attracted national attention when **John Middleton Clayton,** brother of former governor Powell Clayton, was **assassinated** at **Plumerville** *(Conway County)*. John Clayton ran as a Republican candidate in the **1888** congressional election against Democratic incumbent **Clifton Rhodes Breckinridge**, losing narrowly in what was one of the most **fraudulent elections** in Arkansas history. **Clayton had the support of black Republican voters,** and **in Conway County, four white masked men armed with guns had stolen a ballot box at a predominately black precinct**. Clayton contested the election and came to Plumerville to investigate missing votes.

On January 29, **1889, Clayton** was **shot through the window** of his boarding house and died instantly. The **murderer was never brought to justice**, probably due in some part to a great antipathy in the county to the **Republican Party and their black allies.** One man who offered to turn state's evidence in the case was murdered by his brother, though the **coroner ruled the death an accident.** In **1893**, a man named **Hickey** was tried for Clayton's murder, but though he admitted his guilt in the Conway County court, the jury deliberated for only a few minutes before returning a **not guilty verdict.** Clayton's murder was only one incident of violence that was perpetrated in the county from 1886 to 1892 **related to politics**, with the period being known as the **Plumerville Conflict of 1886–1892**.

The newspapers reported **multiple incidents of racial violence within the county**, with at least four African American men lynched from the late nineteenth to the early twentieth centuries. At least three **lynchings** followed the alleged murder of law enforcement officials. The body of **William Rice** was discovered hanging near Plumerville on November 7, **1891. Flanigan Thornton**, accused of killing a constable, was lynched on April 19, **1893**. A crowd lynched **John Williams** on July 4, **1912,** for the alleged killing of a citizen serving as a temporary deputy. The most recent lynching took place on December 9, **1922**, when **Less Smith** was lynched for the alleged killing of a deputy.

Later in the news: Conway County **sheriff, Marlin Hawkins,** played an out sized role in the **politics of the state** in the **1950-60's.** Local newspaper **publisher Gene Wirges** helped expose **corruption in the county.**

Agriculture and Economic Life

Agriculture has long been a mainstay of Conway County's economic life. Many farmers cleared land to plant **cotton.** In the **1930s,** local farmers, like those throughout the South, were trying to plant more cotton to offset their losses due to the perpetually low price for cotton.

Many people became concerned with the number of **acres left abandoned** after the demise of cotton farming and sought ways to put abandoned acres back into production. Eventually, the **Central Valley Soil Conservation District** — *comprising Conway, Faulkner, and Van Buren counties, as well as parts of Pope and Cleburne counties* — was formed to encourage soil and water conservation. This was one of the first districts in Arkansas; it was granted a state charter on February 16, **1938.**

As time went on, the county's native **hardwood and pine forests** have been a resource for the timber and recreation industries. **Cotton** had been grown in the early days of the county, but now the dominant agriculture products became **soybeans and hay,** as well as **poultry** and **livestock.** In modern days, Conway County's northwest corner became the site of **natural gas deposits** deep underground.

Two Civilian Conservation Corps (CCC) camps operated in Conway County during the **Depression years. Company 1781** was active at **Petit Jean Mountain,** from **1933** to **1938.** They built and maintained the facilities at what was Arkansas' first state park. **Company 3789** carried out work such as terracing and sodding pastures under the supervision of the **Soil Conservation District.** The camp was closed in **1937.**

Despite its rural nature, Conway County did have some **limited industry** in the **early twentieth century.** The **Morrilton Cotton Mill** was built in **1901** and operated for more than **forty years, it later becoming Crompton-Arkansas Mills. John B. Richard** started a **soda bottling company** in Morrilton in **1919.** In **1929,** the **Coca-Cola Company** established a bottling plant in the same town. Other smaller industries were also present, most of them concentrated in Morrilton. The first **hospital in Conway County** opened in **1920.**

Conway County's most famous resident, **Winthrop Rockefeller** of the famous Rockefeller family, bought a large amount of land on Petit Jean Mountain in the early **1950's.** He established a showplace home there. In **1964,** he founded the **Museum of Automobiles** atop the mountain. In **1966, Rockefeller became the first Republican elected governor since Reconstruction.** *He served two terms and was widely recognized as the standard bearer of a new progressive* **Spirit in Arkansas.**

World War II and Korea

Many Conway County men served in World War II. Lieutenant Nathan Gordon of Morrilton received the **Medal of Honor** in 1944 for using his Catalina patrol plane to rescue personnel shot down in combat over Kavieng Harbor on February 15, **1944**. *Gordon would go on to serve as lieutenant governor from 1947 to 1967, the longest tenure of anyone to hold the office in Arkansas' history.* Plumerville native **John Yancey** received a battlefield commission as a second lieutenant in the Marine Corps along with the **Navy Cross** during the **Battle of Guadalcanal**. During the **Korean War**, Yancey received a **second Navy Cross** for his actions at the Battle of **Chosin Reservoir**.

Education Prospered

The first recorded school in Conway County was a **small log house at Lewisburg** sometime before **1836**. In **1867, the Male and Female Academy** was operating at **Lewisburg**. Morrilton's first public **school for white children** appeared in **1881**. Its first **school for black children** was built in **1895**. Soon, every community had a small school, many of only one room. The **Springfield Male and Female Collegiate Institute** operated for a number of years in the late nineteenth century.

In **1889**, Morrilton founded the **Male and Female College**, which lasted until the late **1890's**. It later became part of the public school system. **Arkansas Christan College** was established in Morrilton in **1922**. Two years later, it merged with a college in Harper, Kansas, and changed its name to **Galloway Female College** in Searcy, Arkansas later becoming **Harding College**.

On May 26, **1965**, the **Morrilton School Board abolished the black Sullivan High School**, transferring the black students to the city's predominately white junior and senior high schools. At the present time, **Conway County has four higher education schools and five elementary schools**. It is also the home of the **University of Arkansas Community College in Morrilton**.

Modern Era

In the **1960's**, Conway County became home to **four of Arkansas's eighteen Titan II Missile silos**. *The Titan II was an intercontinental ballistic missile (ICBM) placed in five Arkansas counties, as well as sites in Arizona and Kansas. The program was decommissioned in the early* **1980's**. Launch Complex 374-1 **near Blackwell** was **deactivated** on August 19, **1985**; 374-3 near **St. Vincent** on August 6, **1986**; 374-4 near **Springfield** on August 28, **1986**; and 374-2 near **Plumerville** on September 16, **1986**.

In **1968, Interstate 40 was completed**, creating a main thoroughfare through previously rural Conway County. *Some will remember that the Morrilton High School Band performed in the middle of the Interstate the day it was officially opened.* In **1966**, construction began southwest of Morrilton on **Lock and Dam No. 9**, part of the McClellan-Kerr Arkansas River Navigation System. Finished in **1969**, it was renamed the **Arthur V. Ormond Lock and Dam** at a dedication ceremony on November 17, **1986**. The dam has aided transportation and flood control on the Arkansas River.

Modern-day Conway County has twenty-one townships and three incorporated cities, as well as one incorporated town. Today, the **county seat of Conway, County is Morrilton**. It was established October 20, **1825**. The population in **2020** was **20,715**. That census also showed the area to be **551.92** square miles.

Attractions

One point of interest in Conway County is the state park on **Petit Jean Mountain**; it was the **first state park in Arkansas** and is the most visited. Petit Jean State Park holds many attractions for tourists such as the **Museum of Automobiles, Cedar Falls** *(one of the highest waterfalls in the South)*, and many hiking trails with scenic vistas of the river valley and mountains beyond. The **Winthrop Rockefeller Institute** is also located on Petit Jean Mountain. The Arkansas Sky Observatories operate two sites on the mountain.

The **Depot Museum in Morrilton** opened in **1981** and houses a collection of Conway County memorabilia. An old **Missouri Pacific depot** that closed in **1954**, it was later purchased by the **Conway County Historical Preservation Society** and remodeled. Another attraction in the area is the **Conway County Library**, one of the few Carnegie Libraries remaining in the state. **The Great Arkansas Pig Out**, a two-day festival, is held in Morrilton each August. Also, the downtown **Rialto Theatre**, closed for many years, has been refreshed and opens for plays and special events.

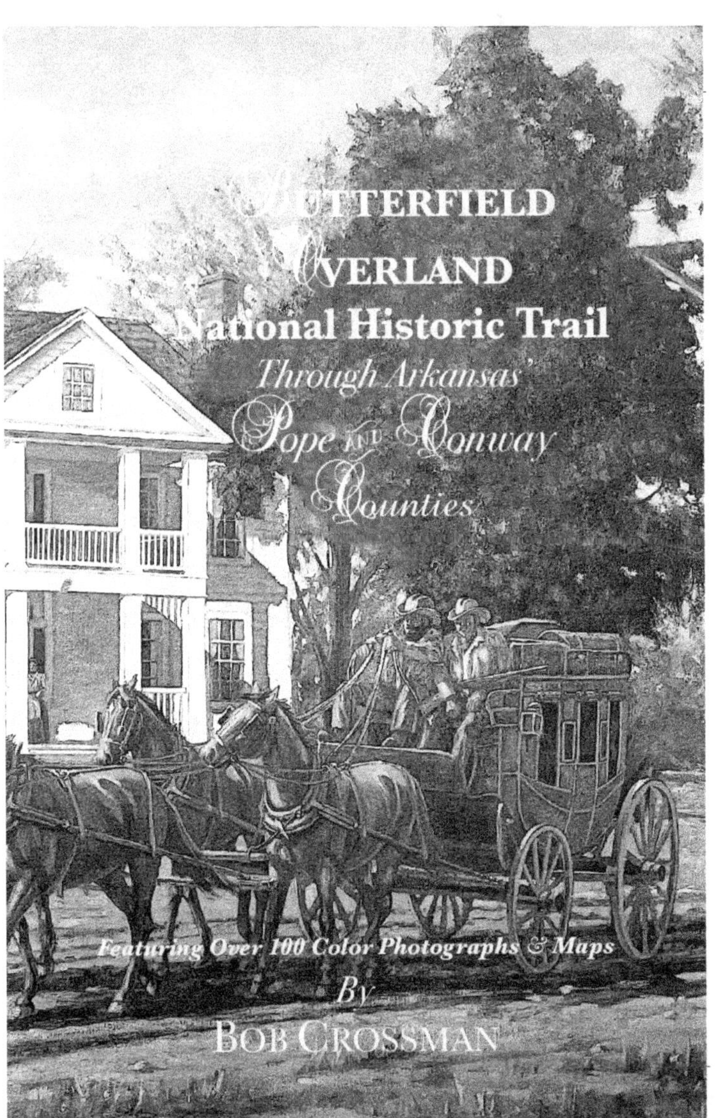

Would you like to know more history about Conway and Pope Counties?

Check out the newest book, finished in 2024, from Bob Crossman, author of several historical books on the Butterfield Overland National Historic Trail through Arkansas.
bcrossman@arumc.org

Would you like to see historical photos of Morrilton?

Euna Wood Beavers is the administrator of the Facebook page, "REMEMBER MORRILTON" where you can find hundreds of historical photos of people and places around Conway County and Morrilton, Arkansas.

About the painting on the cover:
"City of Lewisburg 1852" by Susan Gordan

Arkansas Democrat-Gazette/STATON BREIDENTHAL

Jackie Guccione of Russellville (pictured) and her sister, Carol Fly, found this oil painting in the garage of Fly's former home in Batesville. The two later learned the painting of the old Conway County river town of Lewisburg was a piece of Arkansas' history.

Batesville garage yields bit of history

Sisters find lost art tied to state, family's past in Conway County town

BY DEBRA HALE-SHELTON
ARKANSAS DEMOCRAT-GAZETTE

Jackie Guccione had no idea a bit of both Arkansas and family history lay tucked away in a corner of her sister's garage when she suggested the two check out an oil painting they found covered with cobwebs and dirt-dauber nests.

The sister, Carol Fly, was pre-paring to move from Batesville to Dallas last May when she and Guccione came across the 20-by-30-inch canvas.

"I think she had stuck $5 on it [for a garage sale], but thought it would probably wind up in the trash," Guccione recalled in a telephone interview earlier this month from her home in Rus-sellville. "I said, 'Let's set this aside, and let me play on Google a little while before we decide to toss it.'"

That night, Guccione went to the Internet search site and punched in the painting's title, *Old Lewisburg 1852.*

A black-and-white photograph of the more-than-century-old work popped up, prompting

See **PAINTING**, Page 3B

⊙ ⊙ TUESDAY, JANUARY 16, 2007 ⊙ 3B

Arkansas Democrat-Gazette/STATON BREIDENTHAL

This oil painting, *Old Lewisburg 1852,* is signed by Susan Gordon, who was the daughter of a Conway County merchant and plantation owner.

Painting

◦ Continued from Page 1B

Guccione to call her friend, Paula Stobaugh of Russellville, a fellow member of the Conway County Genealogical Society.

Accompanying the picture on the Web page was text taken from the 1989 book, *Conway County: Our Land, Our Home, Our People,* which Stobaugh helped compile. According to Stobaugh, the book says the painting's location was unknown.

Lewisburg, once the Conway County seat between Morrilton and the Arkansas River, was home to roughly 2,000 residents in the 1850s. The river-bluff town boasted a bustling shipping port, even an opera house, but was hit hard by the Civil War. By the 1880s, little more than a ghost town remained and, eventually, Lewisburg disappeared altogether, according to Guccione.

Guccione read further on the Web page and learned her great-grandfather, a dentist named Ruben T. Markham, owned a Lewisburg hotel that served as a stagecoach stop and a place for riverboat travelers to rest.

"So, now [the painting is] not a piece of trash," Guccione said. "It's a historical treasure and a family heirloom all in one minute."

The painting's artist, Susan Gordon, signed the work. A daughter of Anderson Gordon, a merchant and cotton plantation owner, Susan was born in 1851. That raised the question of how she could have done a painting in 1852.

Guccione ventured an explanation: Gordon probably "painted what she imagined the town

> "So, now [the painting is] not a piece of trash. It's a historical treasure and a family heirloom all in one minute."
> — Jackie Guccione

to have looked like but incorporated people from her present."

Indeed, the artwork depicts such sites as the Gordon home shaded by white magnolia trees; Anderson Gordon's General Store; the Griffin General Store, owned by an uncle of Susan Gordon; and a drug store owned by another uncle.

The painting portrays people on porches as others walk up Sayle's Hill toward a small church. Also shown are four steamboats, among them the New Orleans Packet: Eclipse, which is mentioned in Mark Twain's *Life on the Mississippi.*

Guccione said an essay found in the University of Arkansas Libraries' Special Collections quoted a nephew of Susan Gordon as saying she painted the work in about 1870.

Gordon, who died five days short of her 23rd birthday in 1874, is buried in a cemetery on a cliff along the Arkansas River. Stobaugh and Guccione found the grave shortly after their garage discovery.

"I tripped over a broken rock, looked up and picked up a piece of Susan Gordon's headstone," Guccione said.

According to Guccione, Fly didn't know how the painting came to be in Batesville until she located the former homeowner. Fly then learned the work had once belonged to that woman's mother.

"Turns out, she [the former homeowner] is the great-granddaughter of Dr. Frank Gordon, Susan's younger brother," Guccione said.

Although the former owner had not intended to leave the painting, she was unaware of its history and was excited it was in the hands of someone who could research it and share it with the community, both Guccione and Stobaugh said. The two also said the Conway County Historical Society has applied for a grant to clean and preserve the work.

"It's an absolutely wonderful painting, considering how old it is," Stobaugh said. "There are no cracks, peeling," just some yellowing.

Meantime, Guccione has had several speaking engagements on the history of Lewisburg and the painting.

Morrilton has begun planning an Old Lewisburg celebration for May 12 as part of Arkansas Heritage Month. The date, coincidentally, will mark the first anniversary of the day Guccione found the painting.

"People are getting excited about their history," Guccione said. "This painting is what ignited it."

Fly added, "I think it is a wonderful serendipity that we discovered something with significance to our family as well as to the community. I am eager to participate in Old Lewisburg days and see it successfully continue."

Source: Arkansas Gazetted, January 16, 2007, pages 1B and 3B

Lewisburg
(Conway County)

Encyclopedia of Arkansas
by Kenneth Rorie

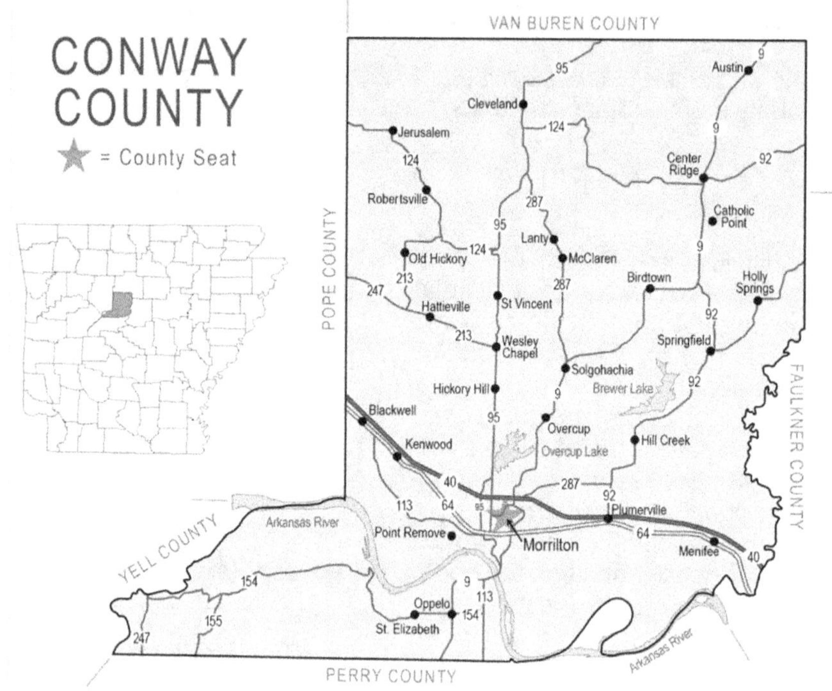

Lewisburg is a former town in Conway County. It was a vibrant community from 1831 until 1883, when it ceased being the county seat of Conway County, replaced by Morrilton. An important town on the Arkansas River, Lewisburg played a significant role in the Civil War. But following the war, the town was bypassed by the railroad, which favored the development of Morrilton.

Lewisburg was founded as a trading post and steamboat landing along the Arkansas River in 1825 by Stephen D. Lewis—hence the name Lewisburg. (Some later sources also credit Lewis's father, General William Lewis, although he died in January 1825.) The town was an important stagecoach stop and played a part in the Indian Removal along the Trail of Tears.

Historical marker in the Lewisburg Cemetery in Lewisburg

Lewisburg was located about one mile southeast of what would become Morrilton. Incorporation as a town occurred in 1844 with a sizable population and numerous businesses. Strategically located on the Arkansas River, Lewisburg gained the reputation as being one of the best transportation routes for people and products of the day. (However, the steamboat Cherokee did experience a boiler explosion at Lewisburg on December 11, 1840.) By the mid-nineteenth century, Lewisburg claimed over eighty businesses, including two sawmills, two gristmills, a flour mill, a cotton gin, hotels, saloons, several stores, and even an opera house. Lewisburg became the county seat in 1831, lost that title to Springfield (Conway County) in 1850, and then regained it in 1873.

A Mr. McNabb established the first ferry at Lewisburg about 1848. The ferry passed through several hands until W. P. Wells and John Ward took possession in 1866. The Lewisburg ferry was used until 1920, when the bridge across the Arkansas River was built.

The Little Rock and Fort Smith Railroad began surveying for a route through Lewisburg in 1850, but the Civil War intervened. Following the war, the railroad asked Lewisburg citizens for a monetary contribution to aid in the construction of the railroad. This never happened because Lewisburg had been hard hit by the war and money was scarce in the town.

Lewisburg was a significant river port town, located about fifty miles west of Little Rock (Pulaski County) on the way to Fort Smith (Sebastian County) and Indian Territory, which made it vulnerable to attack by the Union army. The town fell to the Union on September 28, 1863, and was occupied until August 1865. A Union refugee camp was established in the town under very harsh conditions involving food shortages, disease (including smallpox), and poor sanitation. Many men, women, and children died there. Too, there was significant local division between those who favored the South and others who favored the North.

The occupation army was led by Colonel Abraham H. Ryan, who commanded the newly formed Third Arkansas Regimental Cavalry. Confronting Colonel Ryan was a guerrilla assortment of soldiers led by Colonel Allen R. Witt and his Quitman Rifles, a division of the Tenth Arkansas Cavalry. Colonel Ryan was in association with Williams's Raiders commanded by T. Jeff Williams. Both Williams and Witt were local, and thus the rivalry was intense and personal. A showdown took place on February 12, 1865, on the road from Lewisburg to Dover (Pope County) and became known as the Skirmish of Lewisburg. Colonel Ryan and his troops prevailed, but Witt and about thirty members of his guerrilla force escaped and rode north to the Center Ridge (Conway County) community to the residence of Captain Williams, called him out, and shot him as he stood in his front doorway. The Williams family retaliated by killing more than half of Witt's band.

A Freedmen's Bureau office opened in June 1866 to aid freed people with labor contracts and to run a school. A Male and Female Academy opened in Lewisburg in 1867. However, as elsewhere in the state and in the South in general, law and order continued to break down, with outlawry, thievery, and killings carrying over into the days of Reconstruction. In 1868, the town became embroiled in conflict between the Ku Klux Klan and the Republican militia during voter registration. Parts of Lewisburg were burned twice during December, and Governor Powell Clayton declared martial law in Conway County on December 8, 1868. The militia that patrolled the county was composed of one company of freedmen and three white companies. Governor Clayton replaced the militia with federal soldiers until martial law was ended in 1869.

A notorious act of lawlessness in Lewisburg following the war was Frank M. Hill's murder of prominent Lewisburg physician S. W. Crittenden in June 1874. The motive was never ascertained, but robbery was suspected. Fugitive Hill hid out with his brother-in-law George Looney at the Smith Williams house near Lewisburg. Deputy Sheriff Dickerson took a small posse to surround the Williams residence, hoping to flush out Hill. In the shootout that followed, a member of the posse, John Absalom Rorie, was killed; a fellow posse member and friend to Dr. Crittenden, Louis McClure, was wounded but survived; and fugitive Hill was wounded in his hip but lived to stand trial.

Many of the town leaders believed erroneously that the railroad had no choice but to go through Lewisburg because of its strategic location. The Little Rock and Fort Smith Railroad was, however, given a choice when two leading businessmen, Edward Henry Morrill and James Miles Moose, donated land about a mile north of the river town; thus the tracks by-passed Lewisburg, and Morrill's Town was begun, incorporated in 1879 with a population of about 800. It is said that the first station agent, Captain J. W. Boot, flipped a coin and Morrill-town (original spelling for Morrilton) won out over Moosetown. In 1883, Morrilton was designated the new county seat and remains as such in the twenty-first century.

In 1880, Lewisburg still had a population of 356 and several businesses. But more families began to move out as the nearby town of Morrilton developed with the stimulus of the railroad. By 1930, not much was left of the historic community on the bluffs overlooking the Arkansas River. It is today a part of Morrilton, with a few old cisterns and two cemeteries the only remnants of a once thriving riverboat town in north-central Arkansas.

For additional information:

Barnes, Kenneth C. "The Williams Clan: Mountain Farmers and Union Fighters in North Central Arkansas." Arkansas Historical Quarterly 52 (Autumn 1993): 286–317.

The Biographical and Historical Memoirs of Western Arkansas: Yell, Pope, Johnson, Logan, Scott, Polk, Montgomery, and Conway Counties. Easley, SC: Southern Historical Press, 1978.

Conway County Historical Society. Conway County: Our Land, Our Home, Our People. Little Rock: Historical Publication of Arkansas, 1992.

Finley, Randy. From Slavery to Uncertain Freedom: The Freedmen's Bureau in Arkansas, 1865–1869. Fayetteville: University of Arkansas Press, 1996.

Historical Reminiscences and Biographical Memoirs of Conway County, Arkansas. Chicago: Goodspeed Publishing Co., 1890.

Shinn, Josiah H. Pioneers and Makers of Arkansas. Baltimore: Genealogical Pub. Co., 1967.

Trelease, Allen. White Terror: The Ku Klux Klan Conspiracy and Southern Reconstruction. New York: Harper, 1971.

Civil War historical marker in the Lewisburg Cemetery in Lewisburg (Conway County)

Conway County, Arkansas Genealogy and History

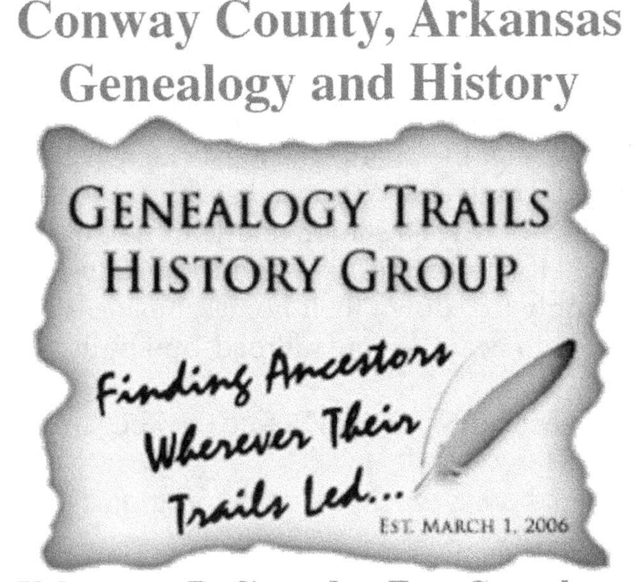

Volunteers Dedicated to Free Genealogy

Town Histories

Lewisburg

About 1820, Major Wm. Lewis, his son, Stephen D. Lewis and Dr. Nimrod settled near the Arkansas River and Point Remove Creek. Stephen D. Lewis established the first trading post in Conway County in 1825, and called it "Lewisburg". In 1831, Padford Ellis, Sr. And Thomas Mathers were appointed commissioners to select two acres of ground belonging to Nimrod Menifee upon which to locate a courthouse and jail, and take deed from Menifee for same. Dr. Menifee donated the ground, and he and Stephen Lewis built a crude log house of small dimensions which served as the courthouse of Conway County till 1850, when the county seat was moved to Springfield. In 1873, Lewisburg donated $5,000 to erect a courthouse when the county seat was returned to Lewisburg. Conway County Court, on October 10, 1873, appointed W. H. Burrow, W. P. Egan, and D. B. Russell commissioners to let the contract, supervise the work and receive the building on completion. This served the county till 1884 when the county seat was moved to Morrilton. In the meantime, a substantial stone jail was erected in Lewisburg, which cost about $10,000.

Business Establishments

In 1840, the mercantile firm of Mason and Morrill was established. It was conducted till 1844, when Mr. Morrill bought his partner's interest and built up a thriving trade. He also kept a hotel, and continued both till all trade was suspended by the Civil War. Dr. Dudley Mason was the first hotel keeper, having opened a hotel about 1840. The town of Lewisburg was incorporated in 1844. Aldermen and town council members were E. Morrill, Edward I. Morrill, George W. Lemoyne, Henry Hamilton, Benedict Beyer, and Harrison H. Higgins. By 1850, Lewisburg had grown into a thriving town, and from then until the Civil War, it was one of the best business points in the state. It derived its trade from remote interior settlements and was the shipping and receiving point, via the Arkansas River, for all the produce shipped and supplies received for a large territory, even to the north border of the state. Some of the people in business here in 1850 were A. Gordon, L. O. Breeden, E. J. Morrill, M. Whistler, W. W. Adams, Levi Mitchell, William Balls, Dudley Mason, Stagman and Ward, Dr. W. W. Adams and Ragsdale. A. C. Well entered business here in 1855.

In 1851, many extensive firms were engaged in business here, all of whom were compelled to close their doors within the next year on account of the war. Some of these were Thomas Henry, L. O. Breeden, A. C. Wells, J. M. Gordon, Anderson Gordon, Griffey and Alron, Joseph Rodgers, Sayle & Morill. These large stores were closed on the arrival of the federal troops, which made the town a barracks until the close of the war. Some business was conducted by the federal camp settlers. The town experienced several years of excitement of war, but when peace was declared many former citizens returned from war and resumed their previous occupations.

The first firms to open for business were Howard & Wells, Burrow, Rankin & Co., James Gordon, Anderson Gordon, and W. P. Egan. Of the later merchants the most extensive were Kaufman & Black, D. W. Mason, Thomas & Russell, Hugh and Wilson Gibson.

Lewisburg continued to grow and prosper until 1875, when a station on the Little Rock & Ft. Smith railroad was instead of building a good road to the station, as is done nowadays, and enlarging the town in that direction, the people simply tore down their homes, business houses, churches, school, etc. and moved them over the hill near the new railroad, and built the new town of Morrilton.

Many of the pioneers of Lewisburg were the pioneers of Morrilton. Before they began moving, Lewisburg had a population of 1800 or about 2000.

There were two sawmills, two grist mills, an opera house, where the same programs were given as were given in Little Rock and Ft. Smith.

There were two dentists, Rev. Hereford and Dr. R. T. Markham, who also owned a hotel, two druggists - Mr. Drake (1870) and Dr. Wm. Scarborough, who opened a drug store in Lewisburg in 1872. He moved it to Morrilton in 1880.

There were two livery stables – run by Jim Dillon and George Wilbanks two black-smiths, Tom Laws and Sam Collins; two saddlery stores, L. O. Breeden and W. L. Wood – moved to Morrilton. Dick Cobb was drayman.

Some of the merchants at that time were Straughan & McClung, Dan Thomas, Hugh Gibson, Wilson Gibson, W. P. Egan, Major Mason, Tom Hill, Anderson Gordon, Jim Gordon, H. W. Burrow, Gran Burrow, William Howard, Peter Fahy, Conley, Pompt Breeden, D. B. Henry, jack Breeden, and many others - about eighty business establishments in all.

The first ferry at Lewisburg was run by a Mr. McNabb, and was established about 1848. This was an important crossing. Mr. McNabb was followed by John Willis then, Grary and Hines, who sold to Thomas S. Haynes. In 1866, it fell into the possession of A. C. Wells, and John Ward. The Lewisburg ferry was used until 1920, when the bridge across the Arkansas River was built.

Newspapers of Lewisburg

The first newspaper in Conway County of which we have any record was the "Wide Awake", established at Lewisburg in January1872, with Charles E. Isham as editor and H. P. Barry as proprietor, who continued its publication about two years. About the first of May 1872, C. C. Reid commenced the publication of another paper in Lewisburg Called the "Western Empire". Later Sam T. Watson and B. F. Kerney became editor and proprietor for a short time. On the eighth of April, 1884, the "Weekly State" was ushered into life at Lewisburg by the Rev. W. C. Stout. With the Issue of the third volume, Mr. Stout transferred the paper to Edward H. Feltus as publisher and James J. Stout as Editor. In 1878, Mr. Feltus moved his office to the new town of Morrilton.

Lawyers of Lewisburg

The first resident lawyer of which we have any account was C. W. Lemoyne, a man of considerable ability. A. F. Woodward came from Little Rock about 1870, was elected county judge in 1873. He lived in Lewisburg until his death in 1878. He was considered a good lawyer. C. C. Reid came to Lewisburg about 1869. He was considered a brilliant attorney. He died here about 1879. His son, C. C. Reid, Jr. was later congressman from this district B. C. Coblentz, 1873 to 1884 - Mayor Lewisburg - E. B. Henry, 1875 - earlier a merchant of Lewisburg, later of Morrilton. His father, Thomas F. Henry, was reared near Lewisburg and raised a company for the Confederate Army at the outbreak of the war. His grandfather, James Henry - a cousin of Patrick Henry - settled near Lewisburg in 1826. He died in 1855. P. H. Evans was a later attorney of Lewisburg.

Lodges

Lewisburg Lodge No 105, A. F. And A. M. was organized at Lewisburg November 5, 1857. Dr. E. W. Adams was first master, J. M. Moose, senior warden, and J. F. Porter junior warden. Medical doctors Dr. Nimrod Menifee, first physician of Conway County, Came in 1820, before the county or town was founded. Dr. E. W. Adams came in 1844 and practiced medicine until 1859, then retired and entered the mercantile business. His son. Dr. R. J. Adams was born in Lewisburg in 1850. After finishing his education he located in Lewisburg and practiced there, and later in Morrilton, many years. He married Lydia Gordon, a native of Lewisburg, in 1876. Dr. C. M. Green came to Lewisburg in 1861. In 1862, he joined the confederate army. A few years after the war closed, he came back and followed his profession here and in Morrilton for many years. He died in Morrilton in October of 1907. Dr. W. A. C. Sayle came to Lewisburg in 1859 as a young physician, where he practiced until he moved to Morrilton, where the Brannons now live. In 1879, he built the first brick building in Conway County at Morrilton. Dr. Cowden practiced medicine in Lewisburg from 1874 until he moved to Morrilton about 1879, where he continued his practice. Dr. G. W. Taylor came about 1878 - later went to Morrilton for many years. Dr. Stallings came in 1843, practiced many years in Lewisburg, where he also ran a boarding house. Dr. Pankey practiced medicine here from 1845 until the civil war, then again several years after the war. Dr. Frank Gordon, son of Anderson Gordon, was born in Lewisburg in 1853. After finishing his education, he located in Lewisburg and started in his chosen profession in 1874. He was the last of the pioneers to desert the old town, as he did not move to Morrilton until 1904.

Churches of Lewisburg

It is believed that the Methodist church had itinerants here as early as 1825. J. M. Moose, who came to Lewisburg in 1838, said that there was an organized body of Methodists here before that time, and they held their services in an old log school house. This was the first church of any denomination in Conway County. John J. Simmons was Sunday school superintendent, Lewis Stocton class leader in the church, and rev. John Harris, whose circuit extended from Argenta (now North Little Rock) to Galla Rock, preached in Lewisburg once a month. About 1843, this church was moved to Sardis camp grounds, and then located at what is now the north end of St. Joseph Street in Morrilton. The Lewisburg Methodist church south was organized in 1869, with rev. Abel C. Ray as circuit rider. Some of the original members were Mrs. Mary E. Bentley and daughters, Addie l. And Jennie, J. M. Moose and wife, Mrs. Mary T. McClung, Mrs. Mary E. Umphlet. In the same year Rev. L. L. Burrow located in Lewisburg, as teacher in the academy, and in August he held a revival meeting which added forty - five members to the recently organized church. This organization erected a church building costing about $2,500, which was dedicated in 1872. It was removed to Morrilton in 1880. This memorial marker is on the old church grounds. There was a union church in Lewisburg in the early 1850's which was sold to Dr. Stallings and moved away by him. Some way the Methodist church was built at the same place.

The Missionary Baptist church of Lewisburg was organized in 1860 with about fifteen members by elder W. M. Lee and Rev. B. H. Bearden. Some of the original Members were Dr. W. A. C. Sayle, Jonathan Wells, E. F. Wills, John and Jennis Wills, Fred and Annie Wellborn. They had no pastor prior to the war and became nearly defunct during the war. In about 1868, this society was reorganized by the Rev. M. Bledsoe, who held services for them once a month in the school house. They had about twenty members. This church was removed to Morrilton about 1878.

The Cumberland Presbyterian church was organized in Lewisburg in 1869 by Rev. Talkington, with D. B. Russell, P. O. Breeden, Moses Baker, Mrs. Addie L. Russell, and Mrs. M. J. Breeden as members. They erected a church in 1871 which cost about $ 2,000. In 1879, this edifice was removed to Morrilton.

The primitive Baptists of Lewisburg held their services in the courthouse - later moved to Morrilton, where they built a church.

Schools

The first school house in Conway County was built in Lewisburg prior to 1836, and William Watson taught school here at that time. There were no free schools in the state at that time. Soon after the Civil War the citizens of Lewisburg induced Rev. I. L. Burrow of Tennessee to accept the principal ship of the male and female academy of Lewisburg, which prospered under his direction for four years. After that the school was run by a Mr. Rayburn, Mr. Malone, Mr. Mason, and others until the school was moved To Morrilton.

Farmers

There were many outstanding farmers and planters of Lewisburg who meant much to the up building of Conway County. Some of these were the Bentleys, who settled here Before Arkansas was made a territory, the Henrys, who came about the time the county was formed, the Lewises, W. E. Green and T. H. Hervey, who came together in 1844, G. W. Howard, who came earlier, the Mooses, Col. Burrow, D. B. Russell, the Armstrong brothers, Carroll and Robert, Josh Maratta, who was county surveyor, C. Stout, who bought five thousand acres of land here in 1856, Jesse Gray, Sleeper, the Wells, and the Gays, Stallings, and many Others. Most of them are still represented in the community by their descendants.

This article is reprinted from the website of the Genealogy Trails History Group with the permission of Veneta McKinney. To see their web site: **http://genealogytrails.com**

Northwest Arkansas Democrat
October 1, 2023

Union cavalry helped secure Arkansas during Civil War

by - Ronnie A. Nichols and Mark K. Christ

Col. Abraham H. Ryan of the Third Arkansas Cavalry (U.S.) (Courtesy of the Butler Center for Arkansas Studies, Central Arkansas Library System)

The Third Arkansas Cavalry was organized in October 1863 at Little Rock, becoming one of four Union cavalry regiments raised in Arkansas during the Civil War. Led by Col. Abraham Ryan, the Third Arkansas was vital for securing the state for the Union, especially along some of the lawless stretches of the Arkansas River Valley.

Abraham Ryan was born in New York on Feb. 16, 1837, and moved to Illinois as a child. When the Civil War began in 1861, he helped organize Company A of the 17th Illinois Infantry Regiment, mustering in as first lieutenant in May; he was soon made the regiment's adjutant. In the chaotic fighting at Shiloh, Tenn., in April 1862, Ryan commanded a brigade for several hours after its colonel was killed in action, leading to his promotion to captain.

May 1862, Ryan became chief of staff for Brigadier Gen. Leonard F. Ross. After the Confederate defenders of Vicksburg, Miss., surrendered on July 4, 1863, Ryan was attached to the staff of Major Gen. Frederick Steele during the campaign that led to the Union capture of Little Rock that September. On Oct. 26, 1863, Steele authorized Ryan to begin raising the Third Arkansas Cavalry. Ryan mustered in as colonel of the Third Arkansas Cavalry on Feb. 10, 1864.

On April 5, 1864, Special Order No. 6 commanded Colonel Ryan to take charge of all the troops at **Lewisburg**, Dardanelle, and the vicinity. **Lewisburg**, a small town located on the north bank of the Arkansas River, became the station for the Third Arkansas Cavalry.

– 21 –

Before the war, **Lewisburg** had some 300 inhabitants, but lawlessness coupled with retributions carried out by small bands of guerrillas caused most of these citizens to leave the area.

The Third Arkansas Cavalry saw very strenuous service from the beginning. During the months of November and December 1864, they had traveled 100 miles on picket duty, 300 miles on escort duty and 400 miles on scouts. The regiment was composed of 888 farmers, 19 blacksmiths, three physicians, two mechanics, two shoemakers, two carpenters, one miller and one merchant.

This regiment was armed with 880 of Starr's carbines (.54 caliber) and 993 Remington revolvers (.44 caliber), as well as a few sabers. The carbines had been in the hands of the men for a short time, yet were in bad condition. On the other hand, the pistols were in tolerable firing order. Ryan's Third Arkansas was aided in part by local Union captain Jeff Williams and his independent infantry company. They attacked forces led by Confederate colonel Allen R. Witt. Witt had originally organized men from Conway and Van Buren counties into the Quitman Rifles, later known as the 10th Arkansas. Captain Williams and the "Williams' Raiders," along with Witt's guerrillas, turned north-central Arkansas into a no-man's land in which the Third Arkansas Cavalry had to try to maintain civil law and military order.

First Lt. Frank Pease of Company "H" Third Arkansas Cavalry supplied an insight into the operations of the regiment to the adjutant general of Arkansas: "On the organization of the regiment, two battalions were sent up the Arkansas River to hold a large scope of territory infested by numerous guerilla bands, who were robbing and murdering Union families in the most barbarous manner that human depravity could invent. Territory held by these marauders was soon wrested from their hands by the 3rd Cavalry and comparative quiet restored."

During the final years of the Civil War, the Third Arkansas participated in more than 40 different engagements and operations against Confederate forces. The Third Arkansas was mustered out of service on June 30, 1865.

Ryan went into business in Little Rock following the war, serving as the general manager of the Little Rock, Mississippi River and Ouachita Railroad for a number of years. While vacationing on Cape Cod, Mass., in 1873, Ryan rescued two women who were in a boating accident and recovered the bodies of three others who drowned.

In 1880, Ryan moved to East Orange, N.J., where he was active in public and business life. He was president of the Savings Investment and Trust Company and cashier of the People's Bank, with a newspaper proclaiming that "the universal esteem and honor" in which Ryan was held was responsible for the bank's success. He also served on the local school board, was on the Town Committee and did a stint as president of the Orange Art Association.

Ryan was heading home from New York on Dec. 29, 1903, when he died while aboard a train. He is buried at Oak Grove Cemetery in Falmouth, Mass.

-- Ronnie A. Nichols and Mark K. Christ

Skirmish at Lewisburg, by Larry Taylor
Encyclopedia of Arkansas

Location:	Conway County
Campaign:	Union effort against guerrillas in the Arkansas River Valley
Date:	February 12, 1865
Principal Commanders:	Colonel Abraham H. Ryan (US); Colonel Allen R. Witt (CS)
Forces Engaged:	Third Arkansas Cavalry Regiment, Fiftieth Indiana, Eleventh U.S. Colored Infantry (US); Tenth Arkansas Infantry (CS)
Casualties:	Unknown
Result:	Union victory

Lewisburg (Conway County), a thriving town in the 1860s, was the site of a significant occupation force of Union troops during the Civil War. Located about fifty miles west of Little Rock (Pulaski County), it was the first and most significant river port along the way to Fort Smith (Sebastian County) and Indian Territory. Federal troops under the command of General Frederick Steele raised the U.S. flag there on September 28, 1863, and remained there as an occupation force until August 1865.

As Conway County had divided interests and loyalties, two Union companies were raised there soon after the Rebels abandoned their relatively unprotected positions in late 1863. These units were assigned to the newly formed Third Arkansas Regimental Cavalry Regiment and the command of Colonel Abraham H. Ryan, who led the occupation to its completion. During the period, there was considerable guerrilla activity in the area, resulting in savage killings and brigandage along the roadways near Lewisburg. Many of these engagements were associated with a Confederate scouting group led by Colonel Allen R. Witt and his Quitman Rifles, a unit of the Tenth Arkansas Cavalry.

Associated with Col. Ryan's Third Arkansas Cavalry Regiment were those local Union troops under the command of Captain T. Jeff Williams. Known as an Independent Union Company of Scouts and Spies, they were sometimes called Williams' Raiders. This unit was used to patrol local areas and to escort supply trains and troop movements in the area. There were frequent conflicts and skirmishes between the Witt and Williams forces. Being local, both groups knew the major roadways and the smaller connectors that were used for both ambush and escape.

While these "run-ins" had taken place since early in the war, things changed dramatically on February 12, 1865. A routine encounter along the Lewisburg-Dover Road became a full skirmish, as a reinforced Union force, supported by the Fiftieth Indiana and the Eleventh U.S. Colored Infantry at Lewisburg and led by Col. Ryan, destroyed the main elements of the Tenth Arkansas Infantry. However, Col. Witt and about thirty of his men escaped and rode north to the Center Ridge (Conway County) community and fulfilled their final objective of the war. They rode to the residence of Capt. Williams, called him out, and shot him as he stood in his front doorway. After the Williams family took their revenge on the Witt group by killing more than half of the remaining members, the conflicts of the Civil War in Conway County finally ceased.

For additional information:

Barnes, Kenneth C. "The Williams Clan: Mountain Farmers and Union Fighters in North Central Arkansas." In Civil War Arkansas: Beyond Battles and Leaders, edited by Anne J. Bailey and Daniel E. Sutherland. Fayetteville: University of Arkansas Press, 2000.

Dirck, Brian. "Witt's Cavalry: An Arkansas Guerilla Unit." Faulkner Facts and Fiddlings 36 (Fall/Winter 1994): 63–76.

Goad, Michael. "Impact of the Civil War on the Farmers of the Arkansas River Valley and Northwest Arkansas." stellar-one.com. http://stellar-one.com/civil_war/impact_of_civil_war_on_ar_river_valley_farmers.htm (accessed May 13, 2022).

The War of the Rebellion: A Compilation of the Official Records of the Union and Confederate Armies. Series I, Vol. 48, Part I, p. 111. Washington DC: Government Printing Office, 1896.

1850 Survey of Lewisburg

Showing Route of the Old 1828 Military Road from Little Rock to Fort Smith

5N 16W

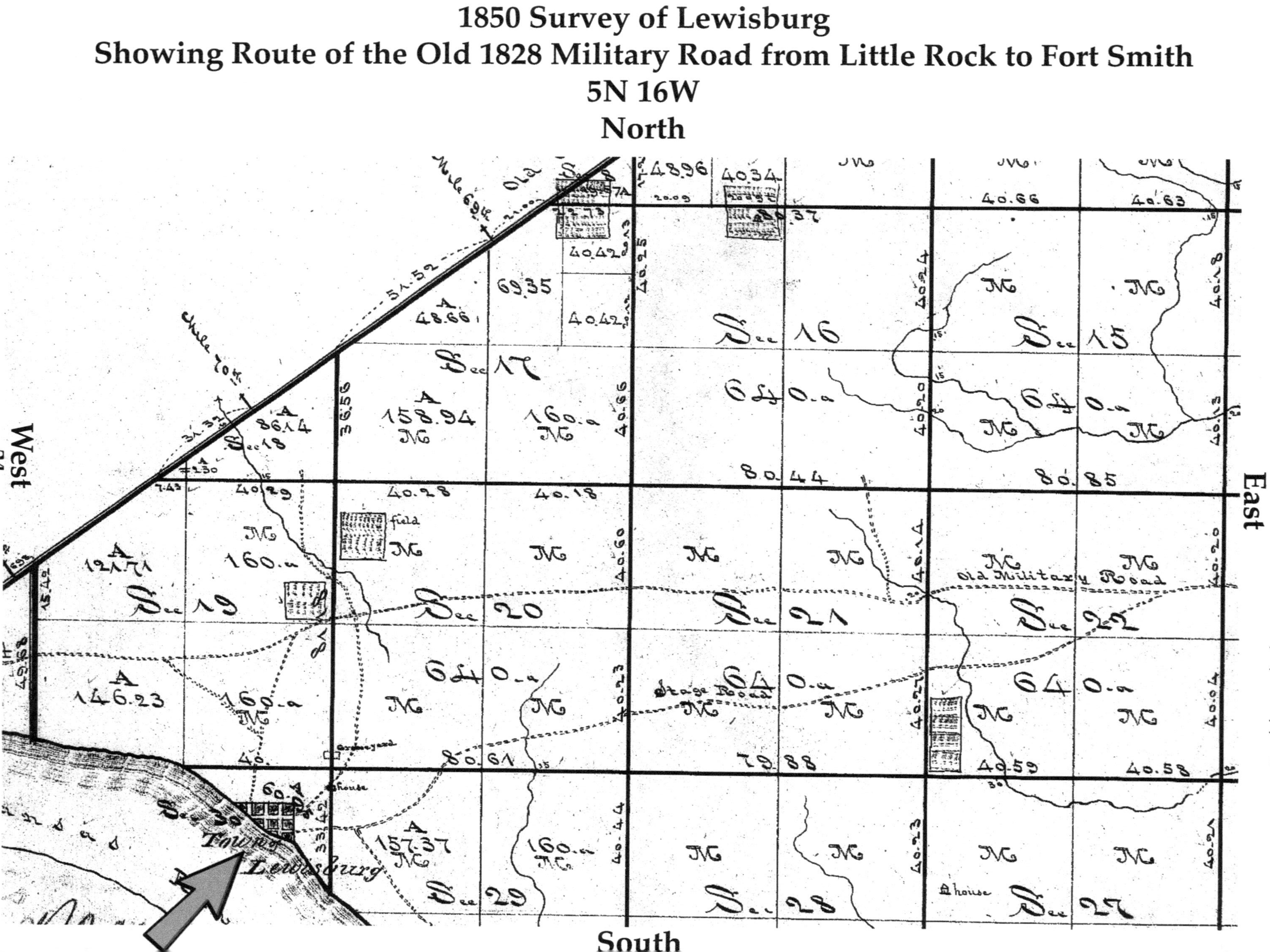

Lewisburg, Arkansas

文A **Add languages** ∨

Article   Talk

Read   Edit   View history   Tools ∨

From Wikipedia, the free encyclopedia

Coordinates: 35°08′31″N 92°44′07″W

Lewisburg, Arkansas was a town in southern Conway County, Arkansas. Founded as a trading post in 1825 by William Lewis, it served as the original county seat of Conway County from 1831 until 1883, when it ceded its role to Morrilton.[1]

While thriving as a town of nearly 2,000 residents along the Arkansas River up to the 1860s, the community was the site of significant Union troop occupation during the Civil War, from September 1863 through August 1865.[2] Lewisburg witnessed several guerrilla killings in the area, also common in surrounding communities throughout the river valley. A skirmish in early 1865 effectively ended war activity in the county, ahead of the surrender that would conclude the overall war.

In the years immediately following the war, the community became unsettled amid conflict between local militia and the Ku Klux Klan in 1868, leading to major fires in town and a declaration of martial law by Governor Powell Clayton in December 1868.[3]

Lewisburg Ghost Town in Arkansas

Desirability of Lewisburg as a ferry site along the river was superseded as years passed, first by the Little Rock and Fort Smith Railroad bypassing the town in 1875, and later with a bridge constructed in 1919 to carry traffic onward to Oppelo and other points south of the river.

The approximate area of Lewisburg is a neighborhood in the southeast portion of modern-day Morrilton.

References [edit]

1. ^ "Lewisburg - FranaWiki" ↗. *honors.uca.edu.* Retrieved September 27, 2019.
2. ^ "Encyclopedia of Arkansas" ↗. *Encyclopedia of Arkansas.* Retrieved September 27, 2019.
3. ^ "Lewisburg in the Civil War" ↗. *www.arkansascivilwar150.com.* Retrieved September 27, 2019.

The source of the article on this page is FranaWiki, developed by the Honors College at the University of Central Arkansas. The site can be found at:
https://honors.uca.edu/wiki/

Lewisburg

Lewisburg was the original county seat of Conway County, Arkansas. The county seat later moved to Morrilton.

Major William Lewis, his son Stephen Lewis, and Dr. Nimrod Menifee founded Lewisburg as a trading post in 1825. It was the first such trading post in the county. The community became the county seat in 1831, and a post office opened the next year. A courthouse was established in a log cabin. The town was formally incorporated in 1844, and by 1850 held approximately two thousand residents and eighty businesses. The town once supported two newspapers, the *Western Empire* and the *Wide-Awake*.

Lewisburg located on c. 1864 map by Helmuth Holtz.

Located on the Arkansas River the town witnessed the arrival of numerous steamboats. A number of steamboats were constructed at the town site prior to the Civil War. The first ferry across the river at the town was established by a man named McKnobb in 1848. A steam ferry owned by R. D. Morgan replaced this early ferry in 1882. Markham Tavern served as a relay station on the Butterfield Stage Route between Little Rock and Fort Smith. The town also had an opera house.

In 1875 the Little Rock and Fort Smith Railroad bypassed the town when local citizens refused to pay $2,000 to have the rails pass through town. By 1880 many townspeople and businesses had moved a mile north to Morrilton to be close to the vital rail connection. The last ferry operator was Charles Isley Sr., who continued to provide the service until a bridge was constructed in 1919.

Additional Notes from FranaWiki:

William Lewis was the earliest European settler on land that would become the city of Little Rock. Lewis made his living by trapping and trading along the Arkansas River beginning in 1812. He registered his claim in the Nashville, Tennessee, land office. He sold the claim two years later to Elisha White. The certificate was later resold to group of investors led by St. Louis land speculator William Russell.

The Lewisburg Western Empire was the second newspaper started in Lewisburg, Conway County, Arkansas. The paper was established in May 1872 by Charles C. Reid Sr.. In 1874 the newspaper was sold to Sam T. Watson and B. F. Kerney. In May 1874 it was sold again to editor Eugene F. Henry. The paper ceased publishing in June 1874.

Markham Tavern in Lewisburg, Arkansas, served as a relay station on the Butterfield Stage Route between Little Rock and Fort Smith in the nineteenth century. The tavern, owned by former Alabaman Ruben T. Markham, had a bar and hotel accommodations. Sam Houston is reputed to have stopped at the tavern.

Markham Tavern in Lewisburg, Arkansas, served as a relay station on the Butterfield Stage Route between Little Rock and Fort Smith in the nineteenth century. The tavern, owned by former Alabaman Ruben T. Markham, had a bar and hotel accommodations. Sam Houston is reputed to have stopped at the tavern.

Lewisburg Related Newspaper Articles 1832 to 1882

Compiled by Bob Crossman

The date of each of these articles is listed immediately below each clipping.

An attempt was made to include any article with more than a passing Lewisburg content. In the 1870's, the editor of Lewisburg's *The Weekly State*, was involved in state politics, and was frequently quoted by the Little Rock papers - only a few of those editorials appear here as they do not contain any reference to Lewisburg.

The town of Lewisburg had several home-town newspapers through the years, including:
The Western Empire, 1872-1874;
The Lewisburg Wide-Awake, 1871-1873; and
The Weekly State, 1875-1882.
Regretfully, only one or two copies of these newspapers have survived.
Fortunately, on occasion the Little Rock papers reprinted stories of interest from the Lewisburg papers.

Many of the advertisements on the following pages were reprinted dozens of times, but only one copy is shown here.

One Hundred and Fifty years ago, newspaper printing presses were primitive by today's standards. This resulted in over-inking, and off-set that is evident in the smeared, faint, or out-of-focus appearance of many of the newspaper clippings below.

A few of the articles were over-inked to the point of making them almost unreadable. In those instances the editor of this volume substituted a transcription of the article.

Newspaper Clippings

Several of the newspaper clippings were so smeared, light or offset that the author has inserted a transcription. Examples below.

ORIGINAL	TRANSCRIPTION
"In referring to the proposed telegraph line from Ft. Smith to Little Rock and Van Buren, Ozark, Clarksville, Dardanelle and Lewisburg, in our issue of the 13th inst., we inadvertently omitted to mention Van Buren as one of the	In referring to the proposed telegraph line from Ft. Smith to Little Rock and Van Buren, Ozark, Clarksville, Dardanelle and Lewisburg, in our issue of the 13th inst., we inadvertently omitted to mention Van Buren
but another mode for suicide. They are easily begun, but it is difficult to quell them; and, I tell you, it is rare that those who begin them ever suffer; but the innocent and unoffending do suffer. I have witnessed two in my life, and they are the most terrible displays of force that we know of; storms, whirlwinds and the convulsions of nature are trifles, compared with these popular outbreaks. They are the most	but another mode for suicide. They are easily begun, but it is difficult to quell them; and I tell you, it is rare that those who begin them ever suffer. I have witnessed two in my life, and they are the most terrible displays of force that we know of storms, whirlwinds and convolutions of nature are trifles, compared with these popular outbreaks. They

---

Lewisburg articles were found in the following 17 Arkansas newspapers:

THE ARKANSAS ADVOCATE.
VOL. III. LITTLE ROCK, A. T. WEDNESDAY, SEPTEMBER 5, 1832. NO. 22.

The Arkansas Gazette.
LITTLE ROCK, (A. T.) WEDNESDAY, MAY 29, 1833

The Arkansas Intelligencer.

THE ARKANSAS TRUE DEMOCRAT.
LITTLE ROCK, ARKANSAS, THURSDAY MORNING, JANUARY 2, 1862. Number 11.

THE ARKANSAS STATE DEMOCRAT, AND HELENA COMMERCIAL ADVERTISER.

Arkansas State Gazette.
LITTLE ROCK, (Ark's), WEDNESDAY EVENING, MARCH 28, 1838.

DES ARC SEMI-WEEKLY CITIZEN.
TUESDAY, MAY 21, 1861. VOLUME I. NO. 4.

Fayetteville Democrat.

Fort Smith Weekly Herald.
BY JOHN F. WHEELER. [NEW SERIES.] ESTABLISHED JUNE 1847

HELENA WEEKLY CLARION.
VOL. V. HELENA, ARKANSAS, WEDNESDAY, AUGUST 18, 1880. NO. 16.

HOT SPRINGS ILLUSTRATED MONTHLY.
VOL. IV., NO. 1. HOT SPRINGS, JAN. 1880. Price Ten Cents.

The Osceola Times.
VOL. 6. OSCEOLA, ARK., AUGUST 28, 1875. NO. 27.

The Russellville Democrat.

The Southern Shield.
"ONE COUNTRY—ONE CONSTITUTION—ONE DESTINY."

THE SOUTHERN STANDARD.
VOLUME XI. ARKADELPHIA, ARKANSAS, SATURDAY, MAY 11, 1878. NUMBER 12

The Van Buren Press.

Washington Telegraph.

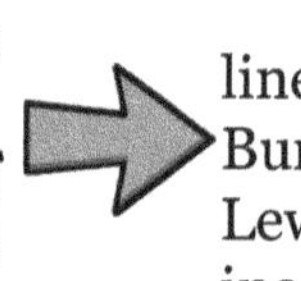

Newspaper clippings begin below in chronological order.

They have been clipped and reproduced exactly as they appeared back in the day.

LOTS
FOR SALE IN THE TOWN OF LEWISBURGH.

A SECOND sale of LOTS in this town will be offered for sale at the next September term of the County Court, commencing on Monday the 17th day of said month, on a credit of six and twelve months, purchasers giving bond and approved security.

Lewisburgh is beautifully situated on the north bank of the Arkansas river, 45 or 50 miles above the Little Rock, and it is believed, unites more advantages in point of locality of situation and the fertility of the adjacent country, than any town in the Territory. It is situated between the two flourishing settlements of Peconery below, and Point Remove above, and a most excellent body of land on the opposite side of the river, including Esq'r Ellis settlement, and extending south-west as far as the prosperous settlement of Fourche-la-Favre. North-east from Lewisburgh, for 8 or 10 miles, the country is gently rolling and interspersed with a few rich prairies, until you reach the rich bottoms of cane and cypress, and the north fork of Cadron and sources of Point Remove; all of which are very fertile and susceptible of extensive settlements.—Further on in the same direction, you strike the very flourishing settlement (the most remote in the county) of Little Red river, known by the name of Rich Woods, or New Kentucky. This picturesque, healthy and fertile section of the country is settling rapidly with an enterprising, industrious class of citizens, who find it greatly to their interest to make Lewisburgh the place of deposite for their imports and exports, being the nearest possible point to navigation, which will, without doubt establish a trade of mutual and lasting benefit between the two places.

Lewisburgh is the permanent Seat of Justice for the county of Conway, the centre of business for the immense regions of fine country above mentioned, which, with the acknowledged healthiness of the situation, will unite in making it a place of no inconsiderable commercial importance.

Within a few hundred yards to the town is a fine bold never-failing chalybeate spring, and also a spring of pure water—building materials of every description are in great abundance on and near the premises, such as clay suitable for brick, an excellent stone quarry, and extensive groves of fine timber.

A court-house and jail will be contracted for and completed in the current year which, together with some private dwellings wanted immediatly, present strong inducements to the mechanic, who will be liberally encouraged.

N. MENEFEE & CO.

Lewisburgh, August 25,   21 3w

Arkansas Times and Advocate
Wed, Sep 05, 1832 ·Page 4

The Arkansas Gazette
Wed, May 29, 1833 ·Page 2

MEDICAL NOTICE.

Dr. J. S. BALL,

HAVING located himself in Lewisburg, Conway county, A. T., intends practising Medicine, in the various branches of his profession.—He will always be found at his residence, except when professionally absent, and hopes to receive general patronage.

June 9th, 1833.   25–3w

The Arkansas Gazette
Wed, Jun 12, 1833 ·Page 3

Drs. Menefee & Pollard,
(LEWISBURG, CONWAY COUNTY.)

HAVING formed a co-partnership in the practice of MEDICINE and SURGERY, offer their professional services to the citizens of Lewisburg and surrounding country. They may at all times be found at their office in Lewisburg, when not professionally absent.

April 13, 1833.   8tf

Arkansas Times and Advocate
Wed, Jul 10, 1833 ·Page 4

Celebration at Lewisburg

CLEBRATION AT LEWISBURG.

The 57th Anniversary of the Declaration of American Independence was celebrated at Lewisburg, Conway county, A. T., on the 4th instant, with great eclat. The Declaration of Independence was read by THOS. MATHERS, Esq., prefaced by a suitable introductory address, by an oration from B. B. Ball, Esq., commemorative of the occasion. About 2 o'clock the company sat down to a plentiful dinner, furnished by Mr. T. S. HAYNES, and the festivities of the evening were closed by a splendid Ball, furnished by the same gentleman, adorned by the fair of Conway and adjoining counties. After the cloth was removed, the following sentiments were given:

1. The day we celebrate—Liberty in despair had retired from earth until the Declaration of Independence brought her again from her heavenly residence to dwell with men.

2. The Congress of '76—The Saviour proclaimed us free from the powers of hell, and the Congress of '76 from the shackles of tyrants.

3. The memory of George Washington.

4. The memory of Adams, Franklin, and Jefferson—Will be revered as long as patriotism has a name on earth.

5. The soldiers and patriots of the Revolution—The rest of heaven is the reward of the brave and good.

6. The United States—The character and safety of the country depend upon it—despots and the nullifiers are opposed to it.

7. Lafayette—France, his native country, will not look on his like again.

8. Christopher Columbus—In all things the most god-like man of the 15th century.

9. Our country, our whole country, and nothing but our country—right or wrong.

10. The President of the United States—May his latter days be as peaceful as his former ones have been glorious.

11. Our country-women—Hail sweet woman—creation would be a blank without you.

VOLUNTEER TOASTS.

By William Carter.—Col. A. H. Sevier—Like pure gold, the more you handle him the brighter he shines.

By H. Matthews.—Arkansas—May science and agriculture continue to improve, until the one shall eclipse that of the States, and the other furnish wealth and happiness to its citizens.

By Wm. Ellis.—Col. Sevier, our faithful Delegate to Congress—He made the Territory of Arkansas during his first term in Congress, the two next he put it in operation, and we will now send him as long as he will serve us.

By Benj. Bryant.—Thomas Jefferson—The 4th day of July, 1776, gave utterance to his speech, and the 4th day of July, 1826, closed it.

By Thos. Mathers.—The Union of the States—not a transient confederacy at the will of the parties, like the agreement of a company of traders—but an eternal band of the people combined to support, with their lives, their fortunes, and their sacred honors, a permanent constitutional government.

By B. B. Ball.—The organization of the Militia of Arkansas Territory.

By Jesse Turner.—The Union of the States—Cemented by the blood of a glorious ancestry, can only be broken by an ignoble posterity.

By S. D. Lewis.—Robt. Crittenden—May he retrieve the character of the people of Arkansas with success to republicanism.

By Thomas Yates.—The four greatest

By Thos. Mathers.—The Union of the States—not a transient confederacy at the will of the parties, like the agreement of a company of traders—but an eternal band of the people combined to support, with their lives, their fortunes, and their sacred honors, a permanent constitutional government.

By B. B. Ball.—The organization of the Militia of Arkansas Territory.

By Jesse Turner.—The Union of the States—Cemented by the blood of a glorious ancestry, can only be broken by an ignoble posterity.

By S. D. Lewis.—Robt. Crittenden—May he retrieve the character of the people of Arkansas with success to republicanism.

By Thomas Yates.—The four greatest Generals in the world are, Gen. Beautiful, Gen. *Satisfaction*, Gen. *Washington*, and Gen. *Jackson*.

By John Couch.—Col. Henderson, of Tennessee, fought, bled, and died for liberty.

By N. H. Buckley.—The Nullifiers, who assail our liberties—May they be treated as the Ides of March did Julius Cæsar.

By J. Chapman.—Robt. Crittenden, the Statesman and Orator—We will hail his elevation to Congress.

By R. J. Blount.—On this day may party-spirit hide her head, and peace and union prevail in our beloved country of Arkansas.

By S. Plumer.—Virtue, Liberty and Independence—May they always exist in our beloved country.

By Wm. A. Logan.—B. B. Ball, Esq., the Orator of the day—His eloquent address deserves publication.

By Dr. John S. Ball.—May the Daughters of America wear their charms as attendants on their virtue, the satellites of their innocence, and the ornaments of their sex.

By Dr. Jesse C. Roberts.—Martin Van Buren, recalled from foreign services by the aristocracy of the Senate of the country, and promoted to the second office on earth by the voice of millions of freemen—When the national tree of our country is worn out by the old age and exhaustion of old Hickory, may Martin Van Buren be grafted on his roots.

By a friend to the Union.—R. M. Johnson—His bravery and patriotism merits one of the first offices within the gift of the American people.

By Mr. Newell.—Col. Sevier—May he shuffle, cut, and deal for Arkansas, for the next fifty years to come.

The Arkansas Advocate
July 24, 1833, page 1

Drs. Menefee & Pollard,
(Lewisburg, Conway County.)

HAVING formed a co-partnership in the practice of MEDICINE and SURGERY, offer their professional services to the citizens of Lewisburg and surrounding country. They may at all times be found at their office in Lewisburg, when not professionally absent.

April 13, 1833.   8tf

Arkansas Times and Advocate
Wed, Dec 18, 1833 ·Page 4

$10 Reward.

STRAYED from the subscriber, at Lewisburg, about the 1st of July last, a SORREL HORSE, 4 years old last spring, near 15 hands high, blaze in his forehead, both hind legs white nearly up to the hock, perhaps some white on one of his fore legs, (not recollected which), and is the same horse that Samuel S. Hall, Esq., bought of John Watson, of Lawrence county, and it is probable he will attempt to return to that county thro' Van Buren and Independence counties. Any person taking up the above horse, and returning him to Samuel S. Hall, Esq., at Little Rock, and producing to me his receipt therefor, shall be entitled to the above reward, or half that sum for information so that I can get him. WM. A. DICKSON.

Aug. 28, 1834.   37-3w

The Arkansas Gazette
Tue, Sep 02, 1834 ·Page 3

Small Pox.—We regret to learn, that this loathsome disease has made its appearance on board the s. b. Compromise, (detained near Lewisburg, by low water and ice), and our informant was told that two deaths had occurred on board her before he passed.

The Arkansas Gazette
Tue, Feb 10, 1835 ·Page 3

Little Rock—sometimes classically termed—ACROPOLIS—is the capital of the Territory, and contains nearly five hundred inhabitants.   There are about twenty families in the Post of Arkansas, fifteen at
Batesville, twelve at Lewisburg, ten at Van
Buren, &c.

The Arkansas Gazette
Tue, Feb 10, 1835 ·Page 2

The day after she left our landing for
Fort Gibson, the steam-boat LITTLE ROCK,
Capt. Smith, ran upon a snag, and is lost.
The accident occurred on Thursday even-
ing, 20th inst., about four miles below
Lewisburg. The snag was under water,
and no break was perceptible on the surface.
When she struck she was in twenty feet
water, but fortunately succeeded in reach-
ing a sand-bar a short distance off, where
she now lies, in six or eight feet water.—
No lives were lost.

The Little Rock is owned by Mr. Emzy
Wilson, of this place, and is insured at $7,-
000. The Clerk passed down a few days
since, on his way to New-Orleans, to inform the underwriters of her loss. All her
freight, save that in the cabin and on deck,
is lost. She had a large lot of public freight
on board, for Fort Gibson.

A letter from a gentleman on board at
the time, says :—

"Most of the freight was insured. Mr.
Wallace, of Washington county, lost all his
goods—no insurance. Mr. Alston, of Spadra Bluffs, and Mr. Wright, of Washington, will lose but little. Their goods were
insured, save about a thousand dollars
worth, belonging to the former. The Captain of the Signal could not take any portion of her freight, but took all her passengers on board."

The Arkansas advocate.
February 28, 1834, page 2

GREEN OAK.

THE noted running horse,
GREEN OAK, sired by
a WHIP PRINTER, owned by me,
will stand the ensuing season at
Lewisburg, Conway county.—
Those who wish to improve the
breed of their horses, will do well to call and
examine this celebrated and excellent animal. Terms made known in handbills.
JAMES STEVENSON.
March 6, 1835.—48tf

Arkansas Times and Advocate
Fri, Mar 20, 1835 ·Page 4

$30 REWARD.

DESERTED, from on board the steam-boat
Lafourche, lying in the Arkansas river, near
Lewisburg, Conway county, on the 4th instant,
JAMES BROWN,
a private Soldier in the 7th Regiment U. S. Infantry.
He is thirty-two years of age, five feet eleven and
a half inches high, blue eyes, brown hair, and fair
complexion; says he was born in Swanton, State
of Vermont, and by profession a farmer, but has
evidently been a soldier, and may pass for a fo-
reigner. He was enlisted by Maj. Stanford, in
New-York, on the 2d January, 1835.

The above reward will be paid for the apprehension and delivery of the above deserter to me, on
board the Lafourche, or any officer of the United
States Army, at any Post in the United States.
CHARLES THOMAS, Capt.
7th Infantry—commanding detachment.
S. B. Lafourche, near Lewisburg, A. T.,
5th April, 1835.   17-3w

The Arkansas Gazette
Tue, Apr 21, 1835 ·Page 3

Steam-boat Register.
May 5.—Lafourche, Gillett, from Lewisburg—
left next day for New-Orleans.

The Arkansas Gazette
Tue, May 12, 1835 ·Page 3

DRY GOODS AND GROCERIES.

THE subscriber having established himself in the
town of LEWISBURG, Conway county, will keep on
hand a large and general assortment of all the articles
sold by dealers in the above line—which will be sold at
low prices and on accommodating terms.
E. W. JOHNSON.
Lewisburg, Conway county, July 12, 1836.—15-tf

The Arkansas Advocate
Aug 12, 1836, Page 4

LAW NOTICE.

B. BALL, Attorney at Law, resides at Lewisburg, Arkansas Territory.

February 1, 1836. 8–tf

The Arkansas Gazette
Tue, Aug 23, 1836 ·Page 4

DRY GOODS AND GROCERIES.

THE subscriber having established himself in the town of LEWISBURG, Conway county, will keep on hand a large and general assortment of all the articles sold by dealers in the above line—which will be sold at low prices and on accommodating terms.

E. W. JOHNSON,

Lewisburg, Conway county, July 12, 1836.–15–tf

Arkansas Times and Advocate
Fri, Sep 02, 1836 ·Page 4

By Mr. Roberts, to open a road from Lewisburg, Conway county, by the way of Thomas Adams', on Crooked creek, in Izard county, crossing the Missouri state line where it crosses the Little North Fork of White river, on the most direct route to Jefferson City, the seat of government of Missouri; by Mr. Fowler, for the appointment

Arkansas Times and Advocate
Fri, Oct 16, 1835 · Page 2

2,200 Creeks
to Rendezvous at Lewisburg

The s. b. John Nelson came up on Thursday, having on board about 900 Creeks, part of Tuckabatchiehadjo's party, under the charge of Lt. J. T. Sprague, U. S. Marine Corps. The whole party of 2200 will rendezvouz at Lewisburg—900 more being to come up the river, and 400 through the prairie.

Capt. Bateman's company, of 2500, and Lt. Sevier's, of 3000, passed 25 miles north of this place for the west, on Thursday of last week. Two parties are still behind—Lt. Dea's, of 2600, and Col. Campbell's, of 2800. These compose the whole nation, except 3000.

We saw the party which came upon the John Nelson. They are filthy looking beasts. Tuckabatchiehadjo is a sullen looking old fellow—ugly but not ungraceful. The inflammable material is pouring fast over our frontier.

Arkansas Times and Advocate
Fri, Nov 11, 1836 ·Page 2

Point Remove Creek
1 Mile from Lewisburg

From the Editor.

Dear P——.

On my way to Crawford I have passed large numbers of the emigrating Creeks. They are scattered along the whole road, camping here and there like gypsies. The way they and their wagons have torn up the road is a caution. Point Remove, which has long been a terror and a nuisance to all travellers, is twenty-five times as bad as ever it was known to be before. I passed through it in great tribulation, and with much fear and trembling. It is a disgrace to Arkansas, and if Uncle Sam won't fix the road in that section, why, the State should do it, and the sooner the better. No man who has not travelled through it, has any idea how bad it is. It is actually dangerous. But of the Indians.— Government is sending them on, under the care of contractors, who have no command of them, and are unable to restrain them or make them go on. They are scattered all along on the road in little predatory bands, killing hogs and stealing as they go. They are a perfect nuisance. One company which numbered 3200 when it started, now only numbers 2000. The remainder has separated into straggling parties, and fallen in the rear. Harsh and unjust as our Government has been to them, it is still not fair that they should be permitted to remain in the State all the winter, committing depredations on the people and their property. I think Governor Conway should order out a company of volunteers to follow in their rear and drive them on— make them leave the State and go to their homes. Tuck-a-batch-i-had-jo has stopped just above Potts', and declares he will go no farther. He says he is west of the Mississippi, and can be compelled to go no further—and when threatened that force would be used to make him remove, he has ridiculed the idea. I saw Milly Francis, daughter of the Prophet Francis, she who saved a white man's life in the Seminole war, 18 years ago. The readers of the Advocate have probably all heard the story. The Prophet Francis was hung at St. Marks. Our Government should have given his daughter a pension. As it is, she is travelling to her new home on foot.

Ever yours, &c. P.

Arkansas Times and Advocate
Fri, Dec 16, 1836 ·Page 2

H. A. Berry, Esq. has been appointed Postmaster at Lewisburg, Conway county, *vice* J. J. Simmons, resigned.

Arkansas Times and Advocate
Fri, Jan 13, 1837 ·Page 2

County Judges.—The following gentlemen have been elected Judges of the county courts of their respective counties, viz:

Wm. T. Gamble.....................Conway county.
John Bowen.......................Madison "

Weekly Arkansas Gazette
Tue, Feb 14, 1837 ·Page 1

Arkansas river. The distance from Batesville is ninety miles, or less, and the most direct eligible route to the Hot Spring, a distance of 43 miles, making the distance from Batesville to the latter place not exceeding 133 miles, which is some 75 miles nearer than the route now usually travelled. For health, Lewisburg is not surpassed by any point on the Arkansas river, if not itself surpassing. Terms liberal, and made known on the day of sale.

N. MENEFEE, } *Proprietors.*
D. THOMPSON, }

Lewisburg, March 10th, 1837.   51-1w.

Arkansas Times and Advocate
Fri, Mar 24, 1837 ·Page 3

New Supply of Goods.

THE Subscirbers have just received, and are now opening and offering to their customers a fresh lot of Dry Goods, Hardware, Cutlery, Tinware, Queensware and Saddlery, together with a choice lot of Groceries, all of which will be sold on the most reasonable terms. We feel thankful for past favors, and earnestly solicit a continuance of the public patronage.

D. D. MASON, & Co.
Lewisburg, April 3, 1837—10--6w.

Arkansas Times and Advocate
Mon, May 01, 1837 ·Page 4

New Supply of Goods.

THE Subscirbers have just received, and are now opening and offering to their customers a fresh lot of Dry Goods, Hardware, Cutlery, Tinware, Queensware and Saddlery, together with a choice lot of Groceries, all of which will be sold on the most reasonable terms. We feel thankful for past favors, and earnestly solicit a continuance of the public patronage.

D. D. MASON, & Co.
Lewisburg, April 3, 1837—10--6w.

Arkansas Times and Advocate
Mon, May 01, 1837 ·Page 4

SALE OF TOWN LOTS.

A SALE of lots will take place in the town of Lewisburg, Conway county, Arkansas, on the 27th inst. It is quite unnecessary to resort to the usual practice, in modern town-making, of portraying the numerous advantages of the site and surrounding country, as it is presumed that persons wishing to make investments in property of that kind, will make the necessary examinations for themselves. Suffice it to say, that Lewisburg is situated on a fine eminence on the north bank of Arkansas river, and is the permanent seat of justice for Conway county—a permanent depot for Van Buren county, and intervening settlements north, and the extensive Fourche LaFave and intervening settlements south of Arkansas river. The distance from Batesville is ninety

---

DRY GOODS AND GROCERIES.

THE subscriber having established himself in the town of LEWISBURG, Conway county, will keep on hand a large and general assortment of all the articles sold by dealers in the above line—which will be sold at low prices and on accommodating terms.

F. W. JOHNSON.
Lewisburg, Conway county, }
July 12, 1836.-15-tf   }

Arkansas Times and Advocate
Mon, May 08, 1837 ·Page 4

Look out for the Thief.

WAS stolen from the Store of the subscribers, on Saturday the 2d inst., a pair of Scissors, made in the form of a Dirk, 15 or 16 inches long; one half of the guard broken off—silver handle, without the Scabbard. We will pay $15 dollars to any person that will apprehend the thief, so that he can be dealt with according to law.

PITTMAN & JOHNSON.

Lewisburg, Conway co., Sept. 15, 1837.—34–3w.

Arkansas Times and Advocate
Mon, Sep 25, 1837 ·Page 4

STOP THE THIEF!
Thirty Dollars Reward.

WE will pay thirty dollars to any person or persons that will apprehend and deliver the body of JOHN LUSK, who runaway from this place on the 17th ult., and stole from the house of Wm. T. Robertson, a large OVERCOAT, belonging to Wm. C. Reaves. The coat is a large overcoat nearly new, made out of blue pilot cloth, with the said Reaves' name wrote in the sleeve. The aforesaid Lusk is a man weighing about 180 pounds, heavy built, fair complexion, blue eyes, fair hair, with much talk, and loud laughter, fond of ardent spirits, gambling, &c. &c.; passes as a shoe maker by trade, says his connections live in Conway county, Arkansas. He left here with a man by the name of Meeks, we suppose for the Cadron Cove, on Ochitaw. In addition to the above, I will give $10 for the coat, delivered here, or at the Times and Advocate Office, at Little Rock.

WM. T. ROBERTSON,
WM. C. REAVES.

Sulphur Springs, Independence county, Sept. 25, 1837—37–4w

Arkansas Times and Advocate
Mon, Oct 16, 1837 ·Page 1

Escape from Lewisburg Jail

"*Glorious uncertainty of the law.*"—WM. G. H. TEEVAULT, late attorney for the State, in this district, who stands charged with *murder*, in Pope co., and is also *indicted* there for an *attempt* to commit *Rape*, or *Sodomy*, some days since escaped from the Lewisburg jail. The attorney, who defended him, and who also is "commorant" up the country, for some similar indecencies, as it is said, was a few days since shot through the suburbs of his "unmentionables." Wound said not to be mortal, although a transformation to the neuter gender may be seriously apprehended. "*Fiat justitia ruat cœlum.*"

Arkansas Times and Advocate
Mon, Feb 12, 1838 ·Page 2

An Ordinance

TO AUTHORIZE THE COMMON COUNCIL OF THE CITY OF LEWISBURG TO ISSUE ONE HUNDRED THOUSAND DOLLARS:

Whereas the shin-plaster system has become in high repute as the "better currency" and in our neighboring city of Little Rock, is considered indispensable as a circulating medium. And whereas our Legislature, in their wisdom, has prohibited individuals from defrauding the Community by issuing change tickets;—and whereas it is thought that *certain* city Corporations are above the laws, and cannot be effected by Legislative acts, but have perfect right and authority to misuse, cheat and swindle the good citizens of this community,—and whereas the city of Lewisburg thinks she has as good right as any other city to defraud the community by issuing shinplasters, and knowing that in this way she will bring thousands of dollars into the city treasury, taken from the earnings of honest industry—therefore:

§ 1 *Be it ordained by the Common Council of the city of Lewisburg*, in convention assembled, That they cause to be issued, in their name, shin-plasters to the amount of one hundred thousand dollars, in denominations from 6¼ cents to ten thousand dollars.

§ 2. *Be it further ordained*, That said shin-plasters shall purport to be redeemable when one thousand dollars is presented.

§ 3. *Be it further ordained*, That the receiving and disbursing officers of the city corporation, shall receive such change tickets in payment of all dues, debts, or demands—or they shall receive nothing.

§ 4. *Be it further ordained*, That whenever one thousand dollars is received for such change tickets, the superintendant of the common council shall deposit the same in his "breeches pockets" and in no case shall any part thereof be removed from said place of deposit, unless as a last resort, to maintain the credit of the Corporation.

§ 5. *Be it further ordained*, That whenever one hundred thousand dollars shall be realized, in clear profit from said shin-plaster trafic; the present Common Council of the Lewisburg city Corporation shall be made to resign, and retire if they please to private life—and another Common Council shall then be elected to supply their places, who shall be, in all cases required to *tread in the footsteps of their predecessors, generally.*.

A true copy of record, S. S. SIMMONS, *Superintendant of said Common Council.*
Attest, DANIEL A. CLARK, *city recorder.*

6—2w.

Arkansas Times and Advocate
Mon, Mar 26, 1838 ·Page 3

SHIN-PLASTERS.

Our merry neighbors of the *city* of Lewisburg, Conway county, have been amusing themselves, lately, by *taking off* the legislation of the Common Council of Little Rock on the issue of shin-plasters. We give the ordinance below. If we had been a member, we should have moved an amendment to the 5th section, authorizing the members of the Council, when *the* $100,000 should be accumulated, to divide it among themselves, retire, and leave the corporation to their successors to tread in their footsteps!!

By the way, why should not *city* corporations *manufacture* money, and, if you will, filch the community, as well as a thousand incorporated *bankrupt* banks? Where is the difference? None of them trade on an

Where is the difference ? None of them trade on an *actual* and *full* capital paid in !—they are nearly all on credit. The Bank of Arkansas is one of the few institutions in the Union, which has as much or more silver in its vaults than notes in circulation. The only difference that we can see, as to the public, between municipal and banking corporations, is, that the profits in the former go to maintain the public order and improvements of a city, (in every other place except Little Rock), and, in the case of banks, the proceeds go into the pockets of a speculating set of Shylocks, who never bring them out again, except for individual aggrandizement. Yet, under right management, banks are excellent institutions, by furnishing, for large sums, a cheaper and more convenient currency ; but, for all small denominations, we go for the *hard money.*

Our neighbors at Lewisburg have a mortal enmity to shin-plasters; and we do not differ from them in the least ; and we give a place to their ordinance, with as much good humor as, wherewithal, it was written.

Weekly Arkansas Gazette
Wed, Mar 28, 1838 ·Page 2

State of Arkansas,
County of Conway.
PROBATE COURT—*January Term,* 1838.

ROBERT TWEEDY, administrator, and Mafida A. Tweedy, administratrix. of the estate of *Lewis S. Tweedy,* deceased, came into open court, and filed their petition in writing, verified to the same, that they did not have sufficient personel estate in their hands to pay the legal demands against said estate : and by motion, it is ordered by the court, that the heirs and legal representatives of said estate appear here and answer said petition, by the second day of our next term, being the first Monday after the 4th Monday in April next, or the court will proceed to hear the same *ex parte*, and order the lot number one, block number three, fronting fifty feet on Main-street, and running back to an alley one hundred and fifty feet, (more or less), situate in the town of Lewisburg, in the county Conway, and State of Arkansas. It is further ordered by the court, that this order be published at least six weeks, in some newspaper published in this State, previous to the next term of this court.

A true copy from the records. Teste :
14-6w[8 75]   JOS. J. SIMMONS, *Clerk.*

Weekly Arkansas Gazette
Wed, Apr 04, 1838 ·Page 3

Valuable Farm and Servants
FOR SALE.

THE subscriber will sell, at private sale, his plantation, situated in the county of Conway and State of Arkansas, one mile from Lewisburg, consisting of 320 acres; one half of which is bottom land of the very best quality; 50 acres of which is well cleared and in good repair, with comfortable dwelling, out houses, &c. The upland is of excellent quality, and has also a comfortable log house, with some cleared land.

I will also sell a likely young Negro Man, with his wife and three children.

Terms—One half Cash in hand, and a credit of twelve months on the balance, secured by note with approved endorsers.

Any person wishing to purchase the above description of property, would do well to call on the subscriber, upon the premises, and examine them.

ELISHA WELBORN.

April 24, 1838—14-3w.

Arkansas Times and Advocate
Mon, Apr 30, 1838 ·Page 3

STEAM-BOAT REGISTER.

June 6. John Jay, Mason, from New Orleans ; left next day for New-Orleans.

——— Oswego, Hart, passed down, from above, for Cincinnati.

——— Cinderella, Stephenson, left for N. Orleans.

———7 Nashville, Buchanan, from Louisville ; left for same place next day.

———8. Mount Pleasant, left for Mouth.

———9. Tecumseh, McCulloh, from Lewisburg, passed down for Mouth.

———10 Fox, Douglass, from Fort Coffee ; left 12th for above, with Seminoles.

———11. Mount Pleasant, Taylor, from Post of Arkansas ; left 12th, to bring up freight from steam-boat Ozark.

Weekly Arkansas Gazette
Wed, Jun 13, 1838 ·Page 3

4th of July
Celebration at Lewisburg

CELEBRATION OF THE FOURTH OF JULY
AT LEWISBURG.

Agreeably to arrangements previously made, a large and respectable number of persons assembled at the late residence of Radford Ellis, Esq., in Conway county, within about one mile of Lewisburg, to celebrate the anniversary of our national independence. The large numbers of the *fair* present gave a zest and spirit to the occasion never before witnessed in this county. The Declaration of Independence was read by JAMES DARLING, Esq., accompanied with appropriate remarks by several gentlemen present. The company, consisting of several hundred persons, then sat down to a sumptuous dinner, got up by Mr. Peter Ellis, in the best style ; after which, JAMES DARLING, Esq., having been appointed President of the day, and D. A. CLARK, Secretary, the following toasts were drank ; and although the company present consisted of persons of all parties in politics, as will appear from the sentiments offered, yet all were well received, as the expressions of free and honest opinion, and passed off with hearty

of free and honest opinion, and passed off with hearty good cheer. A ball in the evening closed the festivities of the occasion. The company then separated, evidently better satisfied with themselves, and with better feelings towards each other, more fully alive to the importance of the occasion that had brought them together, and to the cost and worth of our free institutions, than when they assembled.

REGULAR TOASTS.

1. The day we celebrate.
2. Washington, the father of his country.
3. The Constitution of the United States.
4. The signers of the Declaration of Independence.
5. The patriots of '76.
6. The President of the United States.
7. Thomas Jefferson and John Adams—fellow-laborers in the American Revolution.
8. Patrick Henry—may the patriotism and zeal which animated him in the American Revolution, be present with us on this occasion.
9. Benjamin Franklin—the electricity of his republican principles will thunder down to the remotest ages, and the meteors of his knowledge shine the brighter the nearer we approach them.
10. The State of Arkansas—but yesterday, a wilderness—to-day, inhabited by thousands of independent freemen.
11. The United States—the asylum of the oppressed, and the admiration of the world.
12. The literary institutions of the United States.
13. The fair sex—the last of our toasts, and the first in our affections.

VOLUNTEER TOASTS.

By N. Menefee. The repeal of the specie circular—Producing a vista in the political horizon, through which we may see the dawn of prosperity returning to the western people, who have long been oppressed by its baneful and partial operations.

By Robert Bull. Andrew Jackson—It is glory enough for one man that he has rendered his country more important service than any man living. Health and peace to the evening of his days.

By James Darling. Henry Clay—May his disinterested patriotism and untiring defence of the constitution and rights of the people, against the despotic and tyrannic encroachments of the last and present administration, be rewarded with the Presidential chair in 1840.

By D. A. Clark. Martin Van Buren—Our candidate for the Presidency—he goes in for "lawless intruders," and "western land pirates"—[as the settlers on the public lands in the west are called by HENRY CLAY.]

By James Campbell. Wm. Cummins—The highly gifted, intellectual, and able statesman—present appearances augur, most unerringly, that he will be the choice of the people of Arkansas for a seat in the 26th Congress of the United States

By Mr. Hornbeck. Judge Cross—The people's candidate—he will represent us in the 26th Congress of the United States, unless his defeat be occasioned by

By Cptain Whit---- ----more. The signers of the Declaration of Independence—A phalanx of patriots, numerous and resplendent as the galaxy of the Heavens.

By Judge Carr. The day we celebrate—As it was in '76 so may it remain for ever.

By Capt. Thomas Lawdon. Our delegation in Congress—Well rigged and well mounted.

By Charles Ward. Our candidates for office—We hope they will not deceive us, for God's sake.

By P. J. Pitman. Honor to the brave, success to the lover, and freedom to the slave.

By Cptain Whit---- ----more. The signers of the Declaration of Independence—A phalanx of patriots, numerous and resplendent as the galaxy of the Heavens.

By Judge Carr. The day we celebrate—As it was in '76 so may it remain for ever.

By Capt. Thomas Lawdon. Our delegation in Congress—Well rigged and well mounted.

By Charles Ward. Our candidates for office—We hope they will not deceive us, for God's sake.

By P. J. Pitman. Honor to the brave, success to the lover, and freedom to the slave.

By H. H. Higgins. Adieu to old bachelors—May the single get married, and the married be happy.

By Thomas G. Beeson. The United States Bank—The only obstacle to a general resumption of specie payments and the general prosperity of our country—God deliver us from all such regulators!

By James Hadlock. Our western Indians—We are expecting they will charge on us—we have ourselves and our families to defend, or we will die in the "last ditch."

By B. B. Ball. Henry Clay—The superlatic candidate for the Presidency—may the ides of March meet him at the City of Washington in 1840, as they did Julius Cæsar at the capitol of Rome. *Defunct.*

———

Declaration.—A company of citizens of Harper's Ferry, as we learn from the Alexandria Gazette, have it in contemplation to apply for, an offer to go to the war, and purchase their claims established, at rest of land, part of which is to be divided into a new city, and part into farms—and there is now a respectable show of success.

The President
Visited Lewisburg????

"The President breakfasts, dines, and sups at the public table, and acts in all respects as if he had no station, visiting the ladies and gentlemen, and joining in all the amusements of the place, like any other private gentlemen!"

"The President sits down, and stands up, and walks about. Sometimes he puts his handkerchief to his face, and sometimas he does'nt. When the people saw this, they were very much surprised, and expressed their satisfaction at it· He went last Wednesday to Lewisburg, with Mr. Poinsett, where he was called upon by a large number of citizens, who expresed themselves highly gratified with the interview, being exceedingly well pleased with his amiable deportment, bland and courteous manners., As he passed through the town, every body looked at him—the women, and the children, and the negroes, and all were delighted with manners, and said to themselves with one accord, that he is the man to be president.''

Arkansas Times and Advocate
Mon, Sep 24, 1838 ·Page 2

Steam boat Disaster—We learn, by a passenger on the steam-boat Eagle, which arrived down the river last evening, that the Renown, which left here a few days since, bound up, struck a snag, near Lewisburg, and immediately sunk, with four feet water in the hold. Her cargo was taken on board by the Trident, which passed along soon after the accident. Whether the boat will be saved or not, we have not been able to learn.

Weekly Arkansas Gazette
Wed, Apr 10, 1839 ·Page 2

More Spurious Money.—A friend at Lewisburg, Conway county, gives us information of three men who are traversing that section of country, putting off large quantities of spurious paper, purporting to be on the "*Farmers' and Merchants' Bank of Illinois, at Chicago.*" Large amounts have been passed on the unsuspecting—one individual alone having received ,3300 in payment for a valuable horse. There is no such institution as the above, and the community are warned to be on the look-out for the individuals passing the paper, whose names are given as *McHenry*, *Hughes*, and *Clever.* They are making their way towards Texas, with a drove of horses, probably obtained by money similar to the above. It is to be hoped that some means will be taken to bring these individuals to condign punishment, before they leave the state. The passing of money of this description, is punishable as larceny under the new code.

Weekly Arkansas Gazette
Wed, Jun 12, 1839 ·Page 2

AUCTION SALE.

WILL be sold at public auction, on *Tuesday, the 21st day of April next*, on a credit of 6 months, with interest and approved security, for all sums over five dollars, all the household furniture of the subscriber, viz: Feather-Beds, Mattrasses, Bedsteads, Bedding, Bureaus, Tables, Kitchen Furniture, Crockery and Glass-ware, Iron-ware and many other articles.

Also—A number of full-blooded *Berkshire Pigs*, one Jack and Jenny, a lot of Carpenter's Tools, four Clocks, Window Glass and Sashes, with sundry other goods not mentioned.

Sale to be at my store, Lewisburg, near the court-house.   EARL BUXTON.

March 16, 1840.   15–3w

Weekly Arkansas Gazette
Wed, Apr 08, 1840 ·Page 4

STEAMBOAT EXPLOSION!

It has never before fallen to our lot to record a disaster so melancholy, or one so destructive of human life, as the one we shall now attempt to describe. On Thursday last, about ten o'clock, A. M., the steam boat *Cherokee*, C. Harris, Master, bound for Fort Gibson, stopped at Lewisburg, (about fifty miles above this city,) to land passengers. She had not been at the landing more than ten minutes, before her boilers exploded, sweeping right and left, from midships forward, every part from the guards up. One boiler was thrown into the river, the other on shore, making the most-dreadful havoc of human life, that can be imagined. One man was thrown up in the air two hundred feet, and fell in the town, some distance from the river's bank ; 17 other persons were killed—their blackened corses mangled in the most shocking manner. From 9 to 14 persons known to have been on board, are missing; 18 or 20 persons are severely injured, some burned, some scalded, others with broken legs, heads and arms; presenting, as we are informed by an eye-witness, "a scene too horrid for description." Several ladies were on board at the time of the explosion, all of whom, we are happy to state, escaped unhurt. Capt. W. Armstrong, was also on board, having in his charge a large amount of specie the for payment of Indian annuities, all of which, with the exception of three or four hundred dollars, was saved. The boat and the

four hundred dollars, was saved. The boat and the rest of the cargo are totally lost, she having sunk in fifteen feet water.

From the best infomation we have been able to procure, we make the following list of the names of those killed and wounded:

KILLED.

Mr. Hobson, of Steubenville, Ohio.

Mr. Osgood, of the house of Deiblean & Easton, New Orleans;

Mr. Miles, of Van Buren;

T. Fanning, do. do.;

D. L. Cook, Lewisburg;

P. J. Pitman, do.;

J. L. Budd, watchman;

Capt. Wyman, of steamboat Lady Morgan.

Messrs. Cecil, sr., and Cecil, jr., R Clayton, sr. R. Clayton, jr., and G. W. Glover, are also supposed to have been killed, with five others, firemen and deck hands, whose names we have not learned.

WOUNDED.

Capt. C. Harris, very severely;

Mr. A. V. Brokie, clerk, slightly;

Mr. Clyde, leg broken;

Mr. Smith, of Ky., leg broken;

Mr. Campbell, thigh broken;

Col. B. B. Ball, of Lewisburg, slightly;

Mr. Nathan Keith, of L Rock, slightly;

Mr. Middleton, fireman, leg broken;

Martin Williams, badly;

Tracy Cook, slightly;

— Hammond, steward, badly;

— Smith, do., do.

Capt. Harris and several other wounded persons, were brought to this city on Monday last, on board the steamboat Keystone. We have visited Capt. H., and are happy to state that his hurts are not so serious as was at first apprehended. He states it as his opinion, that the cause of the explosion, was an insufficiency of water in the starboard boiler, and a stoppage of the connection between the two; he himself had a few minutes before the explosion, tried the water in the larboard boiler, and found it full to the upper cock. Added to which, was some inattention to duty by the Engineer.

Weekly Arkansas Gazette
Wed, Dec 09, 1840 ·Page 2

A *disgraceful affray* took place at Lewisburg, on the night of the 10th instant, in which several persons belonging to the steam boat Cherokee and a man named Thompson, a citizen of Lewisburg, were engaged. All of the had been drinking, gambling, and quarreling, which resulted in the death of Jabez Doins, engineer of the boat, who was shot, and in the shocking mutilation of Thompson with a Bowie knife.

The whole matter is, we understand, undergoing a legal investigation, and we forebear to mention the rest of the names, or to make further comment than to express decided disapprobation of the affair, and to wish a speedy application of justice, according to the laws of the land, to all the parties concerned in this and other transactions of a similar character.

Transcribed from the:
Weekly Arkansas Gazette
Wed, Dec 16, 1840 ·Page 2

More Details
on Steamboat Explosion

We subjoin the following detailed account of the explosion of the Steamer Cherokee, in the Arkansas River, the announcement of which we made in our paper two weeks since, at which time, not being apprised of the facts and circumstances attending the melancholy affair, we merely mentioned the occurrence, as told us in conversation, by a friend, who seemed only cognizant of the fact, without the details. Though several deaths resulted form the accident, we are happy to learn, that more of the number who were aboard at the time of the explosion, were not killed or injured. As before stated, we believe this is the first accident of the kind which has occurred in the Arkansas River, since our residence in the State. We learn from other sources than the one from which we take the annexed, that this calamity may be attributed to inattention and negligence on the part of the Engineer, who was on duty at the time. If this be the fact should not efforts be made to bring such a man to condign punishment. Visit three or four of such miscreants with the proper chastisement of the law, and in future we may travel with comparative safety, but otherwise, there is no security for either our persons or property. Such a course has been pursued with effect in the East and North. May we not in Arkansas, hope and strive to protect ourselves against such lawless *butcher* and *murder?*

EXPLOSION OF THE CHEROKEE

It today becomes our painful duty to record the most disastrous explosion which ever occurred on the Arkansas river. The steamer Cherokee which left this place on Thursday evening last, arrived at Lewisburg about sunrise on Friday morning. After stopping at that place about fifteen minutes, and just as the captain had rung the bell to start, the boilers burst with a tremendous explosion, killing fifteen or twenty individuals, and wounding as many more.

Those killed, so far as we have heard, are

Mr. Pittman, of Lewisburg, who had just stepped aboard on business.

David Cook, Esq. also of Lewisburg.

Captain Wayman, of the steamboat Lady Morgan.

Mr. Osgood, of New Orleans.

A small lad by the name of Fanning.

Mr. Miles, of Van Buren, who had a wife and two children on board uninjured.

One body was found 150 years from the wreck, so mutilated that it could not be recognized by anyone.

Fragments of bodies, arms, legs, & c. have been found in every direction.

Captain Harris, the commander of the boat, has his back broke, is badly scalded, and is otherwise injured. He was blown about fifty yards from the boat.

A. V. Brooke, clerk, has lost an eye, and otherwise injured.

Mr. Nathan Keith, of this city, was slightly injured; being thrown ashore amongst wood and rubbish. One of the boilers was blown into the river, and the other on the bank, but a short distance above Mr. Keith.

Captain Armstrong, who was on board with upwards of $140,000 in specie, was slightly injured, but succeeded in saving all the specie with the exception of three or four hundred dollars. The boat commenced sinking so rapidly that nearly all her freight was destroyed or injured. Several Ladies were aboard, all of whom escaped without injury. Of the individuals wounded, it is thought several will die.

This information is derived from several letters received in this city, from Lewisburg, on Saturday night; none of which says anything as to the cause of this distressing calamity. It is probable, however, that it was owning to carelessness in not letting off steam when the boat stopped.

transcribed from the:
Arkansas State Democrat, and Helena Commercial Advertiser, Dec 24, 1840 ·Page 2

DIED

At the residence of Col. C. Ashley, in this city, on the 12th instant, **Capt. *Charles Harris,*** of New York, aged 27 years, of the steamboat Cherokee. In recording the death of our friend, whose exit has occasioned a painful chasm in the circle of his acquaintances, we feel that his friends have lost one from their midst who was plain and unaffected in his manners, in conversation sensible and intelligent, open, kind and generous in his disposition, and possessing a high degree, the virtues that cause a man to be beloved.

At Lewisburg, on the 8th instant, ***William Middleton*** and ***Frederick Kierz.*** The former, a native of Shelby county, Kentucky, a deck hand on board the Cherokee, as the time of the explosion. The latter was a German (deck passenger) recently form his native country.

transcribed from the:
**Weekly Arkansas Gazette
Wed, Dec 16, 1840 ·Page 3**

ADMINISTRATOR'S NOTICE.

LETTERS of Administration were granted to the undersigned, on the 22d day of January, A. D. 1842, by the court of probate of the county of Conway, Arkansas, on the estate of *James Allen,* deceased. All persons having claims against said estate, are hereby notified to exhibit the same for allowance and classification, according to law, within one year from the date of said letters, otherwise they may be precluded from deriving any benefit in said estate; and if said claims are not presented within two years, they will be for ever barred.

All persons indebted to said estate, are requested to pay up. The administrator can be found at his house in Lewisburg, at all times.

  EPHRAIM MORRELL, *Adm'r.*
Lewisburg, Jan. 25. 1842. 8*4w

**Weekly Arkansas Gazette,
Wed, Feb 09, 1842 ·Page 1**

Every year the post office would put out for bids, the various mail routes across the state. Three routes included Lewisburg, indicating its import role at the time. Most Arkansas towns, on the other hand, were fortunate if the mail was delivered once a week.

U. S. MAIL PROPOSALS.

PROPOSALS for carrying the mails of the United States from the 1st of July, 1842, to the 30th of June, 1846, inclusive, in Arkansas, will be received at the contract office of the Post Office Department, in the city of Washington, until 3 o'clock p m of the 14th day of April, 1842, (to be decided by the 30th day of said April), on the routes, and in the manner and time herein specified, viz:

ARKANSAS.

5808 From Little Rock by Lewisburg, Point Remove, Galley Rock, and Dwight, to Scotia, 83 miles and back, twice a week in two horse coaches.

Leave Little Rock every Tuesday and Friday at 4 a m, arrive at Scotia next days by 2 p m

Leave Scotia every Tuesday and Friday at 11 a m, arrive at Little Rock next days by 8 p m

Proposals for tri-weekly service, also for four horse coach service, will be considered.

5836 From Lewisburg by Stell's Mills to Clinton, 45 miles and back, once a week

Leave Lewisburg every Tuesday at 1 p m, arrive at Clinton next day by 4 p m

Leave Clinton every Monday at 7 a m, arrive at Lewisburg next day by 12 m

5837 From Lewisburg to Perryville, 14 miles and back once a week

Leave Lewisburg every Tuesday at 1 p m, arrive at Perryville same days by 6 p m

Leave Perryville every Tuesday at 6 a m, arrive at Lewisburg same days by 11 a m

Weekly Arkansas Gazette
Wed, Feb 23, 1842 ·Page 3

MEDICAL NOTICE.

DR. A. G. BRENT, a graduate of the University of Glasgow, Scotland, having removed from Pope county to Lewisburg, Conway county, tenders his services to the citizens of Conway and Perry counties, and surrounding neighborhoods, in the practice of

PHYSIC, SURGERY AND OBSTETRICS.

Dr. Brent may at all times be found at his office, at Col. B. B. Ball's, near Lewisburg, unless when professionally engaged. Those persons calling upon him, professionally, may depend upon his close attention, and the application of that medical and surgical skill

acquired by upwards of twelve years' successful practice, chiefly in the west, as also from a long course of public studies in the University of Glasgow, and the Royal College of Surgeons, Dublin, with an attendance on their public hospitals.

LEWISBURG, CONWAY CO. ARK.,
March 10, 1842.   13–tf.

Weekly Arkansas Gazette
Wed, Mar 09, 1842 ·Page 3

FALL AND WINTER ARRANGEMENT.

FOR MANDEVILLE, LEWISBURG, MADISON-*ville and Covington.*—The fine, fast running steamer WALKER, Capt. Bonneval, will leave the end of the Pontchartrain Railroad on TUESDAYS, THURSDAYS and SATURDAYS, of each week, on the arrival of the 8 o'clock morning cars, touching at Mandeville, Louisburg and Madisonville, and from thence to Covington, touching at the intermediate landings when required.— Leaves Covington on Mondays, Wednesdays and Fridays of each week, at 7 o'clock; also touching t Madisonville, Louisburg and Mandeville.   o21 tf

The Times-Picayune
Thu, Mar 10, 1842 ·Page 4

Dr. A. G. BRENT,

A GRADUATE of the University of Glasgow, Scotland. Office and residence, one half mile north of Lewisburg.
Oct. 24, 1843.   7–1y

True Democrat
Sat, Dec 02, 1843 ·Page 4

Meeting of the Whig Party at Lewisburg

WHIG MEETING.

At a meeting of the whigs of Conway co., assembled at the Court-house in the town of Lewisburg, on Saturday, the 16th of December, 1843, the meeting being called to order,

On motion, D. D. Mason, Esq., was called to the Chair, and R. Welborne, appointed Secretary.

The object of the meeting being stated by an address from the chair,

On motion of G. W. Lemoyne,

Resolved, That the Chairman appoint a committee of seven persons—one from each township in the county, to draft a preamble

WHIG MEETING.

At a meeting of the whigs of Conway co., assembled at the Court-house in the town of Lewisburg, on Saturday, the 16th of December, 1843, the meeting being called to order,

On motion, D. D. Mason, Esq., was called to the Chair, and R. Welborne, appointed Secretary.

The object of the meeting being stated by an address from the chair,

On motion of G. W. Lemoyne,

Resolved, That the Chairman appoint a committee of seven persons—one from each township in the county, to draft a preamble and resolutions expressive of the views, sentiments and principles of this meeting; and recommend five suitable persons as Delegates to represent the whigs of Conway county, in the WHIG STATE CONVENTION, to be holden at Little Rock in January next;

Whereupon the Chairman appointed Hiram A. Berry, J. J. Lewis, Wm. T. Gamble, N. Phillips, Wm. Roberts, James Holyfield and Ephraim Morrill, said committee; who retired, and in a short time returned, and reported to the meeting the following preamble and resolutions, which were unanimously adopted:

Whereas the whigs of Conway county, feeling a unity of interest and sentiment with their whig brethren throughout the State and Union, in the great cause and *principles*, which did in 1840, and will in '44—and will ever actuate them to move onward, bold and fearless, *with unfurled banners, wafted by pure Democratic Whig breezes*, bearing the inscription, ☞HARRY OF THE WEST—A NATIONAL BANK—A PROTECTIVE TARIFF— sufficient to defray the expenses of Government —rendering us INDEPENDENT OF FOREIGN NATIONS—HONESTY AND QUALIFICATIONS the WATCH-WORD—A JUST CONSTRUCTION OF THE CONSTITUTION—THE PRINCIPLES of WASHINGTON, JEFFERSON, MADISON, HARRISON, AND CLAY—*principles* well calculated to storm the unfortified forts of Locofocoism, and by a unity of determination, zeal and concert of action, we will triumph over all opposition—advance, and plant our standards upon the walls of success, and restore an involved and prostrated Government, to that proud, prosperous and happy position, it occupied in primitive days.

—*Be it therefore resolved*, That we concur in the time and place fixed upon for holding said Convention; and that we will unite heart and hand in the cause, raise our voices in the defence—battle most gallantly in the field— stand up manfully at the ballot box,

"*Voting aloud!*—Harry of the West,
The greatest of all,
With him we are blessed,
Without him, we *fall.*"

Resolved, That we recommend to this meeting Geo. W. Lemoyne, Stephen D. Lewis, Hawkins Gregory, Emzy Wilson, and Ephraim Morrill, as delegates to represent the whigs of Conway county, in the State Convention, to be holden at Little Rock, on the 3d Monday of January next, for the purpose of nominating a suitable person to run on the whig ticket for Governor of the State of Arkansas, a candidate for Congress, Electors for President and Vice President in the National Whig Convention, to be held in Baltimore in May next, and delegates to the Young Men's Convention to be holden at the same time and place,

Be it further resolved, That, having every confidence in the delegates appointed by this meeting, and the honesty, patriotism, and fidelity of every true whig, and feeling well assured that none others will take their seats on that occasion, we pledge ourselves to support the nominees, yielding the *preference* to a majority elect to said Convention.

On motion it was

Resolved, That the proceedings of this meeting be signed by the Chairman and Secretary, and published in the whig papers at Little Rock, and all other whig papers in the State requested to copy.

On motion, the meeting adjourned to meet on the first Monday in May next.

D. D. MASON, *Chairman.*
RUSSELL WELBORNE, *Secretary.*

Weekly Arkansas Gazette
Wed, Jan 03, 1844 ·Page 3

NOTICE.

BY an order of the Court of Probate, for the county of Conway, State of Arkansas, notice is hereby given, that in the spring of 1842, while passing down the Arkansas river, in a canoe, a short distance below the town of Lewisburg the canoe upset and the occupant was drowned; the dead body together with trunks and luggage was taken up by a steamboat, which was lying at shore within a short distance. The body proved to be the body of Dr. IRA ABNEY, from Van Buren, Arkansas, and formerly from Washington county, Texas; lately the books, papers and effects of the deceased was placed in my hands as public administrator. Notice therefore, is given to all persons interested in the estate of the deceased, as heir, legatee, or creditor, to come forward and establish their claims to the same; there being many valuable papers belonging to said Abney, deceased, now in my possession.

JOHN MURRAY, *Sheriff,*
and public Administrator of
Conway county, Arkansas.

February 6, 1844. 22-3w [pr. fee $6 50]
☞The Washington Telegraph, and Texas Inquirer are requested to give the above one insertion,

True Democrat
Tue, Feb 13, 1844 ·Page 3

The River is falling slowly—but is navigable for small boats. The Arkansas Mail from Cincinnati, arrived Thursday and left the same day, on her return to Lewisburg, where she had left a part of her cargo owing to the low stage of the river. The Rolla arrived from Fort Gibson on Friday, and will return for the same place to day.

Arkansas Intelligencer
Sat, Feb 24, 1844 ·Page 2

Dissolution of Co-Partnership.

THE firm heretofore existing under the name of *Theiss & Stegeman* was this day dissolved by mutual consent of both parties. The Store in this place will be continued by Cha's Theiss: and the other store in Lewisburg Conway County, Ark., will be continued by H. Stegeman.

Cha's Theiss is authorized to collect all debts due the concern in this place only. CHAS. THEISS.
H. STEGEMAN.

H. STEGEMAN would inform the people of Conway and the adjoining counties, that he has, and intends continually to keep on hand, at the town of Lewisburg a large assortment of DRY GOODS & GROCERIES. He will sell low for cash or take PELTRIES, HIDES, TALLOW, BEESWAX and all kinds of country produce in exchange at the market prices. He hopes by punctuality and industry in business to receive a full share of custom from those among whom he has concluded to reside.

Weekly Ark. Gazette
Wed, Mar 06, 1844 ·Pg 1

The Steamboat Arkansas Sunk.—On Friday the 29th ult , about day break, this boat struck a stump, as she was crossing Bentley's bar a few miles below Lewisburg, receiving a raking snag from near the bow to abaft of her wheels ; and after having been rounded too, sunk in 8 feet water. The crew took the bright work from her engines, furniture, state-room-doors, and other light fixtures and sent them to Little Rock.

Her cargo consisted of 500 bales of cotton and 800 sacks of corn. The former was shipped by Mr. H. T. Myers of this town and the Messrs. Howell of Norristown, and was insured. The corn by Messrs. Quinn and Titsworth of M'Leans Bottom and was not insured. Nothing was saved but 200 bales of cotton. The corn was a total loss.

The river rose a short time after the "Arkansas" sunk, and now, nothing of her is visible but the chimneys. It is expected that as soon as the river falls, the cylenders and the other parts of her machinery will be saved. She was not insured; and the loss is estimated at about $8,000.

When she struck, one of her hands who was heaving the lead, was thrown into the river; as

soon as Capt. Pennywit learned that fact, prompted by his humane feelings, highly creditable to his heart, devoted his whole attention to save this unfortunate man. He immediately sent out the yawl; and stood on the guards cheering and encourageing him to sustain himself until the yawl could reach him; and not until his humane efforts proved unavailable, did he turn his attention to the boat. Such praiseworthy conduct will receive its reward from a discerning and a generous public.

We understand that the owners of the "Arkansas" have, building at Cincinnati, a boat of greater accommodations which will soon be in the trade between this place and New Orleans.

Arkansas Intelligencer
Sat, Apr 06, 1844 ·Page 2

Uncle Dudley writes me, that he is President of the Clay Club at Lewisburg ; that his Club was organized many weeks ago, at which time *Dick Slaughter*, from *Possum Walk*, (but I don't know where that is,) made quite a good speech. He says, that his Club has not, of late, increased as rapidly as he wished ; and thinks it is on account of not having a good speaker. *Dick*, he says, comes over but seldom, and so they have to depend upon lawyer *Lemoyne*, who, bye-the-by, seems to exhibit more noise than real substance.

He also writes me, that *Encle Emzy*, *Ed. Morrill*, *Ephraim Morrill*, and several other leading men down there, have joined ; and all seem to be doing about the best they can, except *Ed.*, who seems to be getting a little indifferent about the matter.

Arkansas Intelligencer
April 20, 1844, Page 1

Gov. YELL, the Democratic Candidate for Congress, will address the people at the following places—to-wit:

Lewisburg, May 2d, 1844.
Norristown, " 4th, "
Clarksville, " 6th, "
Ozark, " 7th, "
Tucker's, (on Mulberry,) May 8th, 1844.

May 11, Fayetteville,		July	2, Lawrenceville,
" 14, Beatty's Prairie,		"	4, Helena
" 18, Van Buren,		"	6, Marion,
" 20, Fort Smith,		"	8, Osceola,
" 21, Fleming's Store,		"	11, Mount Vernon,
" 22, Boonville,		"	13, Bolivar,
" 23, Winfield,		"	15, Gainsville,
" 25, Mount Ida,		"	17, Pocahontas,
" 27, Murfreesboro,		"	18, Smithville,
" 28, Russey's Store,		"	19, Fulton C. H.
" 29, White Cliffs,		"	20, Athens,
June 1, Washington,		"	22, Batesville,

June 1, Washington,   " 22, Batesville,
"   3, Lewisville,   " 23, Elizabeth,
"   6, Arkadelphia,   " 25, Searcy,
"   8, Ecore a'Fabre,   " 27, Clinton,
" 10, Union C. H,   " 29, Wiley's Cove,
" 12, Warren,   " 30, Lebanon,
" 15, Columbia,   Aug. 1, Yellville,
" 17, Napoleon,   " 2, Crooked Creek,
" 18, Arkansas Post,   " 3, Carrollion,
" 20, Heckatoo,   " 5, Jasper,
" 22, Pine Bluff,   " 7, Huntsville,
" 27, Hot Springs,   " 10, Fayetteville,
" 29, Benton,   " 12, Bentonville.
April 24th, 1844.

True Democrat
Wed, May 01, 1844 ·Page 2

ple. Owing to the high water, which flooded the country, it was impossible for Gov. Yell to reach his first appointments by the land route from this place; and, accordingly, he took the first steam boat which offered, the only one which it was supposed would pass for several days, in order not to be behind his appointment. He spoke at Lewisburg on the 1st instead of the 2nd of May, because a large crowd had assembled to hear him, and because the route, to his next appointment, was rendered difficult and uncertain, by the high water, and required more time than had been anticipated when it was made.

The Arkansas Banner
May 15, 1844, Page 2

THE LAME CAPTAIN.

Upon accepting the nomination of the "Rump Convention" for Congress, Gov. Yell lost no time in running up at the mast-head of the Banner, a long and fearful-looking list of appointments. His first address to the people, as published, was to "come off" at Lewisburg, on Thursday last, (2d inst.) He was informed, before he left here, that GIBSON, the whig candidate for Governor, would meet him at his first appointment, and would not part company with him until he should have the pleasure of introducing him to Mr. WALKER, his whig competitor. When this communication was made to the Governor, he boasted very largely (and modestly), of the manner in which he would *use up* Dr. Gibson. Well, when Gibson reached Lewisburg, on Wednesday night, (1st inst.), he was informed that the Governor had delivered himself on *that day*, and "cut stick" for Norristown. This looks very like the Governor, notwithstanding his boasts, did not care to " *use up*" Gibson in discussion. Did he fear the development of a few *facts*, which might not set easy on his

stomach? A *clean pair of heels* is sometimes useful in such cases.

But it won't do—he cannot escape. At the last accounts, Gibson was in hot pursuit of the *running candidate,* and he is, doubtless, snugly *treed* before now. Let him talk no more about using up his competitors, until he can muster up courage to stand his ground, and face the enemy. He will always play the *lame Captain,* whenever there is a prospect of his being met by either Gibson or Walker.

Weekly Arkansas Gazette
Wed, May 08, 1844 ·Page 2

By the last mail we received the annexed letter from Dr. Chapman, from which it will be seen, that he is perfectly willing to take a hand in coon skinning the whig candidate for Governor. If there is any skin left on that gentleman, after all he has gone through, it must be a very tough one, and will probably be useful only for *stuffing.* **Dr. C. writes in the very highest strain of good spirits and feels assured of his election.**

BATESVILLE, Arkansas, }
May 24th, 1844. }

Dr. S. BORLAND—Dear Sir: May I beg that you will make public the following list of appointments, which I have made for the purpose of meeting my fellow-citizens, and in which I hope Dr. Gibson, the whig candidate for Governor, may find it convenient to join me.

June 14, Lewisburg, Conway county.
"   15, County Seat of Perry.
"   17, Dover, Pope county.
"   18, Clarksville, Johnson county.
"   20, Ozark, Franklin county.
"   22, Van Buren, Crawford county.
"   25, Cane Hill, Washington county.
"   26, Fayetteville, Washington county.
"   29, Bentonville, Benton county.
July 1, Huntsville, Madison county.
"   3, Carrolton, Carroll county.
"   4, Bellar's Store, Carroll county.
"   6, County Seat of Newton.
"   8, Lebanon, Searcy county.
"   10, Yellville, Marion county.
"   12, Maj. Wolf's Izard county.
"   13, Athen's Izard county.
"   15, Salem, Fulton county.
"   22, Batesville, Independence county.
Very respectfully,
Your ob't servant,
D. J. CHAPMAN.

True Democrat
Wed, May 29, 1844 ·Page 2

COL. ASHLEY is absent from the city, on a tour through the northwestern counties. He addressed the people at Lewisburg, on Saturday last, with great power and effect. See his list of appointments to speak, in another column.

The Arkansas Banner
Wed, Aug 28, 1844 ·Page 2

GOVERNOR YELL.

The people of Conway county have received the *refutation* of the false charges which *Davy Walker* made against Gov. YELL, at Lewisburg; and they are perfectly satisfied with it. The Gov. reached there on the 11th, and redeemed the pledge he had made to prove the truth of all he had said, as well as the falsehood of Walker's statement and Drennen's letter.

An intelligent friend, at Lewisburg, writes us, under date of 12th instant, as follows :

"Gov. YELL reached here yesterday, and presented his refutation of Davy Walker's and John Drennen's slander upon him. The people, both *Whigs* and Democrats, are perfectly satisfied with the refutation; and manifest a very just indignation that Walker should have resorted to such a low, and villainous trick to impose upon them. The consequence of this is that YELL's strength is greatly increased in this county, and he will get a good many Whig votes, which would, otherwise, have been given to Walker. Thus, it always has been, and will be—"Old Archy" is invulnerable, and invincible; and every blow his enemies aim at him recoils upon them. They have a great deal to learn yet; and the ensuing election will teach them a lesson, which they will not soon forget. Of one thing be assured that the exposure of this base trick, of Walker and Drennen, has opened the eyes, at least of the people of Conway county, and the remainder of the foul brood of Whig falsehoods between this and the elections, will be *duly appreciated.*—What will they do next?"

True Democrat
Wed, Sep 18, 1844 ·Page 2

FOR PRESIDENT.
JAMES K. POLK,
OF TENNESSEE.
FOR VICE-PRESIDENT
GEORGE M. DALLAS,
OF PENNSYLVANIA.
FOR ELECTORS,
WILLIAMSON S. OLDHAM, *of Crawford.*
CHESTER ASHLEY *of Pulaski.*
MARK W. IZARD, *of St. Francis.*

Col. W. S. Oldham, one of the candidates on the Democratic Electoral ticket, will address his fellow-citizens at the following times and places:

Ozark, on Saturday, 26th inst.

Clarksville, Monday, 28th, inst.

Norristown, Tuesday, 29th, inst.

Lewisburg, Wednesday, 30th, inst.

Gov. Yell will accompany Col. Oldham, and will also address the people.

October 14th, 1844.

Arkansas intelligencer
Oct 19, 1844, Page 2

☞We see by the Little Rock "Age" that a number of boats had left that city for this place; and we learn, by passengers in the stage, who left the "Hatchee Eagle" near Lewisburg, that they are there waiting for high water. We can console them by promising that if we have a warm season, next summer, *the* mountain rise will certainly come.

Arkansas Intelligencer,
Sat, Jan 25, 1845 ·Page 2

☞ The Steamboat 'Panola,' a new boat, is advertised in New Orleans to leave on the 10th inst for the Arkansas river. The 'Eveline' on the 13th inst. The 'Arkansas No 4' is aground near Lewisburg.

Arkansas Intelligencer
May 24, 1845, Page 2

☞The 'Arkansas No. 4,' has at last reached our city. She is certainly the most splendid and well-constructed boat that ever we saw upon this river, and her advent drew out the whole population. She brought up a very large amount of freight, amongst it that which was greatly and unavoidably damaged by the sinking of the keel boat below Lewisburg. Steamboats are always welcome here, but the 'Arkansas No. 4' especially, for it is the fourth boat of the name and owner built for the Arkansas river, and her captain has navigated this river upwards of twenty years, and therefore to us twenty times welcome. She will return from New Orleans in three weeks. Capt. Pennywit has another and new boat—the 'Arkansas No. 5'—which is about the size of the 'Arkansas' No. 3, but draws only 20 inches water. This boat he intends to command himself and run upon this river solely. We trust that she will prove a light craft upon the Arkansas river, but a heavy one in success; she cannot but be so, for Capt. P. has almost invariably been "lucky" the whole long period that he has run the river, and if he does not know it, we should like to know who does?

Arkansas Intelligencer
June 07, 1845, Page 2

For Sale.

I HAVE seven likely negroes, which I will sell for Cash : a *man* of large stature, not surpassed as a *Blacksmith*, in the State; his brother, a good mechanic; *two others*, farm negroes; and three boys large enough for field hands. Also a woman and child, a good house *servant*. I would prefer selling them together . Title indisputable and free from all incumbrance. Any person wishing to purchase, and wanting a bargain will call upon me, or address me through the Post Office, at Lewisburg, Ark.

ELI BENTLY.

October 1 1845   3-tf

True Democrat
Wed, Oct 29, 1845 ·Page 3

WILLIAM DAVIDSON & CO.

COTTON FACTORS

AND

Commission Merchants,

No. 81 CANAL STREET, NEW ORLEANS.

REFER TO—

Scott, White & Co.
Col. John Drennen,   } Van Buren, Ark's.
Hon. G. W. Paschal.
E. B. Alston, Esq., Spadra Bluff, Ark's.
Moreau Rose, Esq., Clarksville, Johnson Co, Ark.
John H. Strong, Esq., Morrison's Bluffs, Ark's.
Joseph B. Terry, Esq., Nortistown, Ark's.
Kirkbride Potts, Esq., Pope Co., Ark's.
Henry Hamilton, Esq., Lewisburg, Ark's.
Messrs. Ringo & Trapnall, Esqrs , Little Rock, Ark.
James De Baun, Esq , Pine Bluffs, Ark's.
Col. James Smith, Esq , Post of Arkansas.
Aug. 29, 1843.—29 tf

Arkansas Intelligencer
Dec 06, 1845, Page 3

Postal Routes For

July 1, 1846 to June 30, 1850

5941. From Lewisburg to Clinton, 45 miles and back, once a week.

Leave Lewisburg every Tuesday at 1 p m, arrive at Clinton next day by 4 p m.

Leave Clinton every Monday, at 7 a m, arrive at Lewisburg next day by 12 m.

5942. From Lewisburg to Perryville, 14 miles and back, once a week.

Leave Lewisburg every Wednesday at 1 p m, arrive at Perryville same day by 6 p m.

The Arkansas Banner
Feb 11, 1846, Page 3

The steamer Swallow struck a snag, on Tuesday last, just above Lewisburg, and sunk in nine feet water. Engine, and a small part of her cargo saved. Boat a total loss.

Weekly Arkansas Gazette
Mon, Mar 02, 1846 ·Page 3

DEMOCRATIC STATE NOMINATION.

For Representative in the 30th Congress, at the ensuing August election:

ROBERT W. JOHNSON,

OF

PULASKI COUNTY.

COL. R. W. JOHNSON, The Democratic candidate for Congress, will address the people at the following times and places :

BENTON,	Monday,	*March* 23rd, 1846.
HOT SPRINGS,	Wednesday,	" 25th, "
MONTGOMERY c. h.	Thursday,	" 26th, "
POLK C. H.,	Saturday,	" 28th, "
MURFREESBORO'	Monday,	" 30th, "
PARACLIFTA,	Wednesday,	*April* 2d, "
WASHINGTON,	Saturday,	" 4th, "
LEWISVILLE,	Monday,	" 6th, "
CAMDEN,	Friday,	" 10th, "
EL DORADO,	Monday,	" 13th, "
CHAMPAGNOLE,	Wednesday,	" 15th, "
WARREN,	Saturday,	" 18th, "
PRINCETON,	Monday,	" 20th, "
ARKADELPHIA,	Wednesday,	" 22th, "
PERRYVILLE,	Tuesday,	*May* 5th, "
LEWISBURG,	Thursday,	" 7th, "
DOVER,	Saturday,	" 9th, "
DANVILLE,	Tuesday,	" 12th, "
CLARKSVILLE,	Friday,	" 15th, "
OZARK,	Monday,	" 18th, "
BRAWLEY's,	Tuesday,	" 19th, "
C. H. of SCOTT co,	Friday,	" 22d, "
FORT SMITH,	Monday,	" 25th, "
VAN BUREN,	Wednesday,	" 27th, "
FAYETTEVILLE,	Monday,	*June* 1st "

The Arkansas Banner
March 04, 1846, Page 2

☞ The Arkansas Mail is lying a few miles below Lewisburg, and we expect will get up on the present swell of water.

Arkansas Intelligencer
March 14, 1846, Page 2

COL. R. W. JOHNSON, the Democratic Candidate for Congress, addressed the people of Conway county, by regular appointment, at Lewisburg, on Thursday last, the 7th inst. An intelligent correspondent, in a letter written the next day, speaks as follows of the speech :

"Col Johnson addressed the people here yesterday. He was personally a stranger to most of us, yet as our candidate, and as a gentleman of whom report had spoken well, he was cordially received. His speech was a fine—a noble specimen of oratory ; compelling even those who differed with him in politics, to acknowledge his ability. As he was well received, before his speech, the good feeling of his democratic brethren rose up to enthusiasm, afterwards. You may judge of the impression he has made here, when I assure you that he will run up with the large vote that has always been cast for Gov. Yell, in this county. The Convention acted wisely in nominating him."

The Arkansas Banner
May 13, 1846, Page 2

Methodist Preacher at
Lewisburg: Rev. L. C. Adams

List of Appointments in the Arkansas M. E. Conference.

Little Rock District—A. HUNTER, P. E.
"   " Station—J. F. Truslow.
Searcy Circuit—To be supplied.
Little Red River Mission—S. Farish.
Smithville Circuit—G. E. Hays.
Batesville Circ't—J. J. Roberts & J. M. Stevenson.
Athens Mission—J. H. Blakely.
Lewisburg Circuit—L. C. Adams.
Perryville Mission—T. Owen.
Benton Circuit—S. Carlisle.
Elizabeth Circuit—J. Cowle.

The Arkansas Banner
Dec 09, 1846, Page 2

NEW ESTABLISHMENT.

JUST RECEIVED, and now opening at the Ware House near the steam-boat landing, a large, and well-assorted stock of GOODS, consisting of every variety of

DRY GOODS:
Ready-made Clothing; Saddlery:
Boots and Shoes
of every size and description:
Hats, Caps, and Bonnets;
Hardware, Queensware, Groceries,
Drugs, Paints, Oils, Dyestuffs,
Confectionaries. &c:
which we will sell low for cash, and in exchange for the produce of the country. We will buy any quantity of corn, from *one peck*, to *ten thousand bushels*, if shelled and delivered; and any quantity of bacon, from 10 to 10,000 lbs·; and every thing raised by the farmer, that we can ship.

G. W. & F. L. LEMOYNE.
Lewisburg, 1847.
I feel under grateful acknowledgments to the citizens of Conway and Perry counties, for the favors received at their hands, and expect to receive their patronage as long as I merit it.

G. W. LEMOYNE.

Weekly Arkansas Gazette
Sat, Apr 24, 1847 ·Page 3

POLITICAL APPOINTMENTS.

VAN BUREN, 11th May, 1848.
The undersigned one of the candidates on the Democratic ticket for Elector for President and Vice President will address the people at the following places and times :
In Bentonville, in Benton County, on Monday, the 15th of May.
In Fayetteville, Washington county, on Monday the 22nd of May.
In Van Buren, Crawford county, on Saturday the 27th of May.
In Ozark, Franklin county, on Tuesday the 30th of May.
In Clarksville, Johnson county on Thursday the 1st day of June.
In Dover, Pope county on Saturday the 3rd day of June.
In Lewisburg, Conway county on Monday the 5th day of June.
In Little Rock, on Saturday the 10th day of June.

JOHN SELDEN ROANE.

Arkansas Intelligencer
May 13, 1848, Page 2

The river is low, but has been *swelling* slowly, since last Monday; and from all prospects, it will soon be navigable for the largest boats: at present none but the smaller class, can run. The *Arkansas No. 5*, from New Orleans, was heard from, a few days ago, lying a few miles above Lewisburg, waiting for water.

Arkansas Intelligencer
May 15, 1847, Page 2

MARRIED,

Near Lewisburg, Conway county, Ark's, on the 27th day of May, by the Rev. Levi Adams, Mr. JAS. MADDUX to Miss SARAH JANE MASON, daughter of Dudley D. Mason, Esq.

Weekly Arkansas Gazette
Sat, Jun 05, 1847 ·Page 3

G. W. & F. L. LEMOYNE,
Commission and Forwarding
MERCHANTS.

Steamboat Landing, Lewisburg, Ark's.
Any consignments made to them, will meet with prompt attention.

Refer to

M. Greenwood, } New Orleans.
J. W. Dodd, }
Tho's J. Dobyns, Memphis, Ten.
Newton, Chase & Co. } Little Rock.
Gov. Adams, }
Paschall & Ogden, Van Buren.
June 12, 1847.   20—tf.

Arkansas Intelligencer
Sat, Jul 03, 1847 ·Page 3

**The Little Rock newspapers
printed arrivals and departures of steamboats on the Arkansas River.
Below, the steamboat Ringgold
arrived in Little Rock on Jan. 21, 1848
from Lewisburg landing.**

STEAM-BOAT REGISTER.

[*Reported by Geo. A. Worthen, Steamboat Landing.*]

ARRIVALS.
20—Ringgold, from New Orleans.
21   "   " Lewisburg.
21—P. H. White, from Napoleon.
22—Medium,   "   "
23—Cashier, from Cincinnati.
22—Alert, from Napoleon.
26—Wm. Armstrong, from Napoleon.
DEPARTURES.
20—Wm. Armstrong, for Napoleon.
20—Ringgold, for Fort Smith.
21—P. H. White,   "   "
23—Medium, for Napoleon.
24—Cashier, for Fort Smith.

**Weekly Arkansas Gazette
Thu, Jan 27, 1848 ·Page 3**

Col. *S. H. Hempstead*, democratic candidate for the vacancy in the United States Senate occasioned by the death of Col. Ashley, will address the people at the following places and times, viz:

Bentonville, Benton co. July July 5.
Fayetteville, Washington co., July 8.
Cane Hill, Washington co., July 10.
Van Buren, Crawford co., July 12.
Fort Smith, Crawford co., July 13.
Ozark, Franklin co., July 15.
Clarksville, Johnson co., July 17.
Dover, Pope co., July 19.
Norristown, Pope co., July 20.
Danville, Yell co., July 22.
Perryville, Perry co., July 24.
Lewisburg, Conway co., July 25.
Clinton, Van Buren co., July 27.
Little Rock, Pulaski co., July 29.

**Arkansas Intelligencer
July 01, 1848, Page 3**

☞ The *River* has fallen two or three feet during the past week, but is yet in a navigable condition for small boats. Considerable rain having fallen during the last twenty-four hours, we may expect another rise shortly.

The *Wm. H. Day* passed down from Fort Gibson to the mouth of the river, on Wednesday.

The *Amazon* is aground near Lewisburg. Some of her passengers came up in Thursday's stage.

**Arkansas Intelligencer
Sat, May 05, 1849 ·Page 2**

**Headed to California for Gold?
Stock up your caravan at Lewisburg!
We must keep the 1828 Old Military Road
in Good Repair for Travelers**

Conway will organize a company, (if the news from their friends be favorable) to proceed early in April next to the gold diggins in California.— Companies coming from other States, who purpose taking the Van Buren and Fort Smith route to California, would do well to call at Lewisburg and vicinity, to complete their outfit for the expedition—for there is no part of the State, in my knowledge, in which they can buy horses, mules, or oxen, cheaper than they can in this county; they can also buy provisions as cheap here as any place in the State. Boats can come to this place at any time that they can reach Little Rock.

I do hope that the citizens of the north side of the river, will, for the future, be more zealous of their interest, than they have been heretofore, and try to use more industry in keeping their public roads in good repair. The citizens of Conway have thrown off their cloak of laziness, and are determined on keeping their roads in good order, so that neither the traveller or emigrant will be stopped *en route* to his place of destination, on account of bad roads within her limits. I think the crisis has come in which the citizens of the north side should be doing, and that their watchword should be, "*thorough improvement of their roads.*" We must not let the south side of our river outstrip us in making good roads. The face of the country on this side is as good, if not better, than that on the south side. But if we do not attend closely to our interest in this matter, what must obviously be the result, it is easy to foresee —the south side of the river will complete her road from Little Rock to Fort Smith, and thereby induce travellers and California emigrants to travel on that side; securing all the valuable trade, which will be no small item in the way of the '*white iron.*'   CONWAY.

Lewisburg, July 27, 1849.

**Arkansas Intelligencer
Sat, Aug 11, 1849 ·Page 2**

Public Meeting in Conway County.

At a meeting of the citizens of Conway county, held at the court-house in the town of Lewisburg, on the 16th day of August, for the purpose of electing Delegates to attend the Memphis convention, on the 22d October next, William Standlee, esq., was appointed chairman, and R. B. Gordan, esq., and Samuel Plumer, vice presidents, and E. Morrill, Secretary.

The object of the meeting being explained by the chairman, the meeting was appropriately addressed, by Messrs. J. S. Morris and D. Maddux, after which upon motion of Jno Murry, esq., a committee of the five following gentlemen were appointed by the chairman, to draft and report resolutions expressive of the sense of the meeting, viz, John Murray, D. Maddux, R. Welborn, J. H. Ward, and Dr. E. W. Adams. The committee reported as follows:

1st. We believe that the general government is properly authorized to carry on such Internal Improvements as the people and the States petition for repectively made and provided by the constitution; having therefore met for the purpose of electing delegates to attend the Memphis convention, to be holden on the 22d October next, for the purpose of construction a rail-road from the Mississippi river to the Pacific Ocean.

2d. For the following reasons to wit, the growing interest and extention of our Union points to Memphis as the most acceptable point for the great utility and advantage of our general government, the Mississippi river being at all times navigable to said point.

3d. Believing the farther South said rail-road should be constructed, the more facility will be given to a continuous communication from ocean to ocean, and from country to country, thereby obviating the snows of the North—the dreaded danger by the Emigrant.

4th. We recommend this meeting to elect ten delegates to attend said convention, said delegates then and there to use their influence for the construction of said rail-road from Memphis to the most suitable point on the Pacific ocean.

5th. Be it further resolved that we duly appreciate the newspaper press in their efforts for the interest of our State, in disseminating correct knowledge to the emigrant of the best and most practicable route to the Pacific ocean; and that it is the duty of every citizen to subscribe and pay for at least one newspaper.

(All of which was unanimously adopted.)

The following persons were elected delegates to the Memphis convention, viz:

Hon. D. Maddux, Dr. E. W. Adams, R. Welborn, Hon. G. W. Lemoyne, R. W. Benedict, Lindsey Breedon, W. L. Ball, Robert E. Wilson, Benjamin H. Murphey, and Hayes J. Isaacs.

WILLIAM STANDLEE, *Chairman.*

E. MORRILL, *Secretary.*

True Democrat
Tue, Sep 11, 1849 ·Page 4

Wm Duval "Decently" buried at Lewisburg

Death of Wm. J. Duval, Esq.—Below will be found an extract from the Fort Smith Herald, of last Wednesday, giving the particulars of the death of Wm. J. Duval, Esq., of Fort Smith, in Point Remove bottom, on the 9th inst. Mr. D. was a gentleman of fine talents and amiable qualities, possessing many friends on this frontier.

Melancholy Death.—We learn from the stage driver, that *Wm. J. Duval* Esq. for many years an Attorney at Law in this place, was found dead near the Little Rock road, in the Point Remove bottom, in the neighborhood of Lewisburg, on Friday last. He left this place a few days since in company with his brother, Marcellus Duval, Esq., Seminole Agent, who was on his way to Florida with a delegation of Seminoles. Wm. J. Duval was on his return home and left Lewisburg on Tuesday, the 9th inst. His horse was found on Wednesday, which excited suspicion that he was dead. Search was made by the citizens of the neighborhood, and his body was found as above related, and decently buried at Lewisburg. He is supposed to have fallen from his horse in a fit of apoplexy.

Arkansas Intelligencer
Sat, Nov 17, 1849 ·Page 2

Mail Route #5904 Left Little Rock Twice a Week to Deliver at Lewisburg, Hurricane (Atkins), Galley Greek (Pottsville), and Norristorn (Russellville)

5904 From Little Rock at 2 p m, twice a week, Monday and Friday;
By Lewisburg, Hurricane, Galley Creek, Norristown, Dwight and Scotia.
To Pittsburg by 12 p m next days. 112 miles;
And back between 10 a m Tuesday and Saturday, and 8 p m next days.
Bids for tri-weekiy service are invited

Washington Telegraph
Wed, Feb 06, 1850 ·Page 3

Mail Route #5961 and #5961 Originated at Lewisburg Twice a Week

5961 From Lewisburg at 2 p m once a week, Tuesday;
by Centreville and Lick Mountain;
to Clinton by 5 p m next day. 49 miles;
and back between 7 a m Monday, and 10 a m next day.
5962 From Lewisburg at 1 p m once a week. Tuesday;
to Perryville by 7 p m, 14 miles;
and back between 6 a m and 12 m same day.

Washington Telegraph
Wed, Apr 10, 1850 ·Page 4

Article below:
Remembering when on the 1838 trail
of a young woman for the murder of
gunman Hiram Shore at Lewisburg.
She was defended by Methodist
preacher John Taylor.
She was found not guilty by the jury.

From the Great West.
JOHN TAYLOR;
THE TIMON OF THE BACKWOODS BAR AND PULPIT.

BY CHARLES SUMMERFIELD.

I can never forget my first vision of John Taylor. It was in the court-house at Lewisburg, Conway county, Arkansas, in the summer of 1838.

The occasion itself possessed terrible interest. A vast concourse of spectators had assembled to witness the trial of a young and very beautiful girl, on an indictment for murder. The judge waited at the moment for the sheriff to bring in his prisoner, and the eyes of the impatient multitude all centered on the door; when suddenly a stranger entered, whose appearance rivited universal attention.

Here is his portrait: a figure, tall, lean, sinewy and strait as an arrow; a face, sallow, billious and twitching incessantly with nervous irritability; a brow, broad, soaring, massive, seamed with wrinkles, but not from age—for he was scarcely forty; eyes, reddish yellow, like the wrathful eagle, as bright and piercing; and finally, a mouth with lips of cast iron, thin, curled, cold, sneering, the intense expression of which looked the living embodiment of an unbreathed curse. He was habited in a suit of new buckskin, ornamented after the fashion of Indian costume, with beads of every color in the rainbow.

Elbowing his way slowly through the crowd, and apparently unconscious that he was regarded as a *phenomenon*, needing explanation, this singular being advanced, and with the haughty air of a king ascending the throne, seated himself within the bar, thronged as it was with the disciples of Coke and Blackstone, several of whom it was known, esteemed themselves far superior to those old and famous masters

The contrast between the outlandish garb and disdainful countenance of the stranger, excited, especially, the risibility of the lawyers; and the junior members began a suppressed titter, which grew louder, and soon swept around the circle.

They doubtless supposed the intruder to be some wild hunter of the mountains, who had never before seen the interior of a hall of justice.

Instantly, the cause and object of the laughter perceived it; turned his head gradually, so as to give each laughter a look; his lips curled with a killing smile of infinite scorn; his yellow eyes shot arrows of lightning; his tongue protruding through his teeth literally writhed like a serpent, and ejaculated its asp-like poison in a single word: "Savages!"

No pen can describe the defiant force which he threw into that term, no pencil might paint the infernal *furor* of his utterance, although it hardly exceeded a whisper.

But he accented every letter as if it were a separate emission of fire that scorched his quivering lips; laying horrible emphasis on the S, both at the beginning and end of the word: "SavageS!"

It was the *growl* of a red tiger in the *hiss* of a rattle-snake.

"*Savages!*"

It cured everybody of the disposition to laugh.

The general gaze, however, was immediately diverted by the advent of the fair prisoner who then came in, surrounded by her guard.

The apparition was enough to drive a saint mad. For her's was a style of beauty to bewilder the tamest imagination, and melt the coldest heart, leaving in both imagination and a heart gleaming picture enameled in fire and fixed in a frame of gold from the stars. It was the spell of an enchantment to be *felt* as well as seen. You might feel it in the flashes of her countenance, clear as a sunbeam, brilliant as the iris; in the contour of her features symmetrical as if cut by the chisel of an artist; in her hair of rich auburn ringlets flowing without a braid, softer than silk, finer than gossamer; in the eyes, blue as the heaven of southern summer, large, liquid, beamy; in her motions, graceful, swimming, like the gentle waftures of a bird's wing in the sunny air; in the figure, slight, etherial—a sylph's or a seraph's; and more than all, in the everlasting smile of the rosy lips, so arched, so serene, so like starlight, and yet possessing the power of magic or of magnetism to thrill the beholder's heart.

As the unfortunate girl so tastefully dressed, so incomparable as to personal charms, calm and smiling, took her place before the bar of the judge, a murmur of admiration arose from the multitude which the prompt interposition of the court by a stern order of "Silence," could

court, by a stern order of "Silence," could scarcely repress from swelling into a deafening cheer.

The judge turned to the prisoner: "Emma Miner, the court has been informed that your counsel, Col. Linton, is sick, have you employed any other?"

She answered in a voice sweet as the warble of the nightingale, and clear as the song of the sky-lark: "My enemies have bribed all the lawyers—even my *own to be sick;* but God will defend the innocent!"

At this response so touching in its simple pathos, a portion of the auditors buzzed applause and the rest wept.

On the instant, however, the stranger, whose appearance had previously excited such merriment, started to his feet, approached the prisoner, and whispered something in her ear.

She bounded six inches from the floor, uttered a piercing shriek, and then stood trembling as if the presence of a ghost from Eternity; while the singular being who had caused her unaccountable emotion addressed the court in his sharp ringing voice, sonorous as the sound of bell-metal:

"May it please your honor, I will assume the task of defending the lady."

"What!" exclaimed the astonished judge, "are *you* a licensed attorney?"

"The question is irrevalent and immaterial,' replied the stranger, with a venomous sneer, "as the recent statute entitles any person to act as counsel at the request of a party."

"But does the prisoner request it?" inquired the judge.

"Let her speak for herself," said the stranger.

"I do," was the answer, as a long drawn sigh escaped, that seemed to rend her very heart strings.

The case immediately progressed; and as it has a tinge of romantic mystery, we will epitomise the substance of the evidence.

About twelve months before, the defendant had arrived in the village, and opened an establishment of millinery.— Residing in a room connected with her shop, and all alone; she prepared the articles of her trade with unwearied labor and consumate taste. Her habits were secluded, modest and retiring; and hence she might have hoped to avoid notoriety; but for the perilous gift of that extraordinary beauty, which too often, and to the poor and friendless always, proves a curse.

poor and friendless always, proves a curse. She was soon sought after by all those glittering fire-flies of fashion, the profession of whose life, every where, is seduction and ruin. But the beautiful stranger rejected them all with unutterable scorn and loathing.

Among these rejected admirers was one of a character from which the fair milliner had everything to fear. Hiram Shore belonged to a family, at once opulent, influential and dissipated. He was himself licentious, brave and ferociously revengeful— the most famous duelist in the Southwest. It was generally known that he had made advances to win the favor of the lovey Emma, and had shared the fate of all other wooers—a disdainful repulse.

At nine o'clock on Christmas night, 1837, the people of Lewisburg were startled by a loud scream, as of some one in mortal terror; while following that, with scarcely an interval, came successive reports of fire-arms, one, two, three—a dozen deafening roars. They flew to the shop of the milliner, whence the sounds proceeded; pushed back the unfastened door, and a scene of horror was presented. There she stood in the center of the room, with a revolver in each hand, every barrel discharged, her features pale, her eyes flashing wildly, but her lips parted with a fearful smile. And there at her feet weltering in his warm blood, his bosom literally riddled with bullets, lay the all-dreaded duelist Hiram Shore, gasping in the last agony!

He articulated but a single sentence: "Tell my mother that I am dead and gone to hell!" and instantly expired.

"In the name of God who did this?" exclaimed the appalled spectators.

"I did it," said the beautiful milliner, in her sweet, silvery accents: "I did it to save my honor!"

As may be readily imagined the deed caused an intense sensation. Public opinion, however was divided. The poorer classes, crediting the girl's version of the facts, lauded her heroism in terms of measurless eulogy. But the friends of the deceased and of his wealthy family, gave a different and a darker coloring to the affair, and denounced the lovely homicide as an atrocious criminal. Unfortunately for her, the officers of the law, especially the judge and sheriff, were devoted comrades of the slain and displayed

voted comrades of the slain and displayed their feelings in a revolting partiality.—The judge committed her without the privilege of bail, and the sheriff chained her in the felon's dungeon!

Such is a brief abstract of the circumstances developed in the examination of witnesses. The testimony closed and the pleading began.

First of all, three advocates spoke in succession for the prosecution; but neither their names nor their arguments are worth preserving. Orators of the blood and thunder *genus*, they about equally partitioned their howling eloquence betwixt the prisoner and her leath-robed counsel, as if in doubt who of the twain was then on trial. As for the stranger he seemed to pay not the slightest attention to his opponents, but remained motionless with his forehead bowed like one buried in deep thought, or in slumber.

When the proper time came, however, he suddenly sprang to his feet, crossed the bar, and took his position almost touching the jury. He then commenced in a whisper, but it was a whisper so wild, so clear, so unutterably ringing and distinct, as to fill the hall from floor to galleries.

At the outset, he dealt in pure logic separating and combining the proven facts, till the whole mass of confused evidence looked transparent as a globe of glass, through which the innocence of his client shone, brilliant as a sunbeam; and the jurors nodded to each other signs of

thorough conviction: that thrilling whisper, and fixed concentration, and language simple as a child's, had convinced everybody; satisfied the demands of the intellect; had accomplished the work, too, in twenty minutes.

He then changed his posture, so as to sweep the bar with his glance; and began to tear and rend his legal adversaries — His sallow face glowed as a heated furnace; his eyes resembled living coals; and his voice became the clangor of a trumpet. I have never before or since, listened to such murderous denunciations. It was like Jove's eagle charging a flock of crows; it was like Jove himself hurling red-hot thunder-bolts among the quaking ranks of a conspiracy of inferior gods! And yet in the highest tempest of his fury, he seemed calm; he employed no gesture save one—the flash of a long, bony forefinger direct in the eyes of his foes. He painted their venality and unmanly mean-

ness, in coalesing for money, to hunt down a poor and friendless woman, till a shout of stiled rage arose from the multitude, and even some of the jury cried 'Shame!''

And thus the orator had carried another point; had aroused a perfect storm of indignation; and this too, in twenty minutes.

He changed his theme once more. His voice grew mournful as a funeral song, and his eyes filled with tears, as he traced a vivid picture of man's cruelties and woman's wrongs, with particular illustrations in the case of his client; till one half the audience wept like children.

But it was in the peroration that he reached his zenith at once of terror and sublimity. His features were livid as those of a corpse; his very hair appeared to stand on end; his nerves shook as with a palsy; he tossed his hands wildly towards heaven, each finger stretched apart and quivering like the flame of a candle; as he closed with the last words of the deceased Hiram Shore: "Tell my mother that I am dead and gone to hell!" His emphasis on the word *hell* embodied the acme and *ideal* of all horror; it was a wail of immeasurable despair. No language can depict the effect on us who heard it. Men groand; females screamed, and one poor mother fainted, and was borne away in convulsions.

The whole speech occupied but an hour.

The jury rendered a verdict of "Not Guilty," without leaving the box; and three cheers, like successive roars of an earthquake, shook the old court-house from dome to corner-stone, testifying the joy of the people.

After the adjournment, which occurred near sunset, the triumphant advocate arose and gave out an appointment: "I will preach in this hall to-night, at 8 o'clock." He then glided through the crowd, speaking to no one, though many attempted to draw him into conversation.

At 8 o'clock the court-house was again thronged, and the stranger, according to promise, delivered his sermon. It evinced the same attributes as his previous eloquence of the bar; the same compact logic, the same burning vehemence, and increased bitterness of denunciation. Indeed misanthropy revealed itself as the prominent emotion. The discourse was a tirade against infidels, in which class the preacher seemed to include every body but himself; it was a picture of hell, such as Lucifer migh have drawn, with a world in flames for his pencil. But one paragraph pointed to heaven, and that only demonstrated the utter impossibility that any human being should ever get there.

a tirade against infidels, in which class the preacher seemed to include every body but himself; it was a picture of hell, such as Lucifer migh have drawn. with a world in flames for his pencil. But one . paragraph pointed to heaven, and that only demonstrated the utter impossibility that any human being should ever get there.

As to effect, the lecture was a failure; the people were not much pleased to hear themselves foredoomed, in advance of the day of judgment! He ended, and left the village immediately, without even sc much as his name being known.

Such was the strange eccentricity of John Taylor. I met him afterwards in Texas, and there learned the skeleton of his remarkable history. At twenty-two years of age he was one of the most promising juniors of the Philadelphia bar and such was the confidence inspired by the integrity of his character, that a distinguished wholesale merchant of the Quaker city engaged him at a high salary to travel in the western states as a collecting agent. Taylor bade a tender adieu to his young and beautiful wife, and his infant boy, and set out on his laborious tour. But from that hour he heard no more from his fickle consort till the end of a year; and then the intelligence came in the letter of a friend with a newspaper enveloped. Shorlty after his departure the false lady had changed her domicil to Mississippi; obtained a divorce by the ac of the legislature; married again: and procured a statute changing the name o Taylor's son to that of Marks, for he second husband!

This was a cruel blow in the most sen sitive of all human hearts; and John Tay lor lost his reason. For several year afterwards he wandered over the wildes regions of the west, a melancholy maniac

At length, however, he recovered fron the shock, professed religion, and join ed the Methodist itinerancy, where hi matchless eloquence must have soon rais ed him to the highest station, could hi restless spirit have brooked restraint. H returned to the bar without forsaking th pulpit: and both as an attorney and preach er his name is now familiar in every fron tier community.

But the strangest part of our narrativ remains to be told. It might be assume that one, who had suffered such merciless crucifixion from the inconstancy of woman, would have exercised great caution in the formation of any new connexions. Unfortunately the very reverse proved to be the fact. John Taylor, without a wife, was always running mad with love, while with a wife, he grew still madder from

jealousy. He wedded half a dozen beautiful young girls in as many different States, and never lived with any longer than six months.

The lovely milliner of Lewisburg vas one of the half dozen. He married her in New Orleans and took her to Natchitoches, where he then resided. Having lost so many bright birds, he determined to make sure of this. He provided iron shutters to all his windows; laid in a plentiful supply of fuel, food and water; locked up his charmer; hung out a sign, inscribed: "This is a private dwelling into which there can be no admittance;" and started for Baton Rouge court, to be absent three weeks.

He returned, and found his beautiful bird gone. She made her way to Arkansas, as has been previously noticed; and an acquaintance passing at the date of her arrest for the homicide, recognized her, and sent the news to Taylor, which accounts for his timely appearance at the trial. Yet I could not learn that he ever attempted to live with her again.

He resides now at Marshall, Harrison county, Texas; though he is scarcely to be found at home once a year, sweeping as he does a circuit as wide as the limits of the State. He never converses but on business; camps out nightly in the open air; thunders now in the *forum*, and anon in the sacred desk; he is a wanderer; a misanthrope; a scorner of the world; a Timon of the woods; but yet, by the unanimous verdict of all hearers, the most eloquent advocate that the sun of heaven ever saw.

Washington Telegraph
Wed, May 15, 1850 ·Page 1

Sale of Lands for Non-Payment of Taxes,

IN THE COUNTY OF CONWAY, AND STATE OF ARKANSAS.

NOTICE IS HEREBY GIVEN,

That the undersigned, Sheriff and Collector of the county of Conway, in the State of Arkansas, will offer for sale, at the Court-house door in the Town of Lewisburg, the Seat of Justice of said county, *on Monday the 4th day of November, A. D.* 1850, the following described tracts or parcels of land, lying and being situate in the said county of Conway, in the State aforesaid, or so much of each tract as will be sufficient to pay the taxes, penalty and costs, due thereon for the years designated opposite each tract, unless the said taxes, penalty and costs, shall be paid on or before the said day of sale.

Sale to take place between the hours of 10 o'clock in the forenoon and 3 o'clock in the afternoon of said. day, and to continue from day to day until the whole are sold.

NOTE.—If a less quantity than eighty acres be stricken off for the taxes, penalty and costs, due on any tract, it will be surveyed off of the south-west corner of the tract; and, if eighty acres or more be struck off, it will be surveyed off of the west side of the tract.

Names of Owners.	¼ or ½ of section.	¼ or ½ of sec.	Section.	Town.	Range.	No. acres.	State Tax and Penalty.	County Tax and Penalty.	Years for which Taxes are due.
Mitchell Mitchell A.		SW	27	8N	9W	160	$1 50	$2 25	1850
same		SE	32	8N	13	160	1 50	2 25	"
same		NE	25	7N	15	160	1 50	2 25	"
Blackburn S. D.	NE	SE	6	6N	17	40	37½	56¼	"
Blasdell Daniel	E½	SE	13	6N	17	80	1 50	1 87½	1849 and 1850
Arnold John		SE	22	7N	14	160	3 00	3 75	" "
same	part	SW	22	7N	14	25	47	59	" "
Case Lovel		SE	22	7N	13	160	3 00	3 75	" "

Name	Pt	Sec	Twp	Rge	Acres	Tax	Total	Years
Case Loyel	SE	29	7N	13	160	3 00	3 75	" "
Sleeker Lewis' heirs	NW	29	7N	13	160	44 75	37 37	1824 to 1850
Manning William	SE	28	7N	13	160	39 75	36 37	1826 to 1850
Cook Thomas' heirs	SW	14	4N	15	160	44 75	37 37	1824 to 1850
Kenedy Daniel	NE	23	4N	15	160	39 75	36 37	1826 to 1850
Dorothy Anthony's heirs	SW	9	4N	14	160	39 75	36 37	1826 to 1850
Pegan William's heirs	NE	4	5N	16	160	34 75	35 37	1828 to 1850
Moreland J. F.	SE	34	7N	13	160	11 25	23 87	1840 to 1850
Collins Orrin's heirs	SW	14	7N	14	160	37 25	36 87	1827 to 1850
Barnes Charles	NE	15	4N	13	160	11 25	23 87	1825 to 1850
Henderson Robert	SE	36	7N	12	160	22 75	29 37	1833 to 1850
Williams James	SW	23	6N	14	160	42 25	36 87	1825 to 1850
Rupell William	NE	36	5N	15	160	42 25	36 87	"
Hart Barnard	NE	13	5N	13	160	42 25	36 87	"
Langton David W.	NW	19	5N	14	160	1 50	2 25	1850
DONATED LANDS								
Brown Eliza A.	SE	33	7N	15	160	1 50	2 25	1850
Echols Larkin	SW	18	6N	11	160	1 50	2 25	"
Young Martha A.	SW	10	6N	11	160	1 50	2 25	"
Young Daniel M.	NW	10	6N	11	160	1 50	2 25	"
Spinks Wm B.	SW	7	6N	11	160	1 50	2 25	"
Gordon James	NE	15	6N	16	160	1 50	2 25	"
Gordon Henry T.	NW	16	6N	16	160	1 50	2 25	"
Williams Eliza	SE	17	6N	16	160	1 50	2 25	"
Tutt Milton B.	SE	6	7N	13	160	1 50	2 25	"
Tutt Wm. P.	NE	7	7N	13	160	1 50	2 25	"
Loveall John	SW	26	7N	13	160	1 50	2 25	"
McIntire John R.	NE	17	6N	13	160	1 50	2 25	"
Philips Amanda J.	SW	26	7N	11	160	1 50	2 25	"
Whitmore Lucius A.	NW	34	7N	11	160	1 50	2 25	"
Graves	SW	27	7N	11	160	1 50	2 25	"
Henry James Augustus	NE	26	7N	11	160	1 50	2 25	"
Hinay Mary P.	NE	24	7N	11	160	1 50	2 25	"
Brady William, sen.	NE	33	7N	11	160	1 50	2 25	"
Judd Daniel C.	NW	36	7N	13	160	1 50	2 25	"
Judd Thomas C.	NE	36	7N	13	160	1 50	2 25	"
Castell Francis L.	NW	24	7N	13	160	1 50	2 25	"
Castell James	SE	33	8N	13	160	1 50	2 25	"
Judd Rachael Jane	SW	33	8N	13	160	1 50	2 25	"
Fleming Robert	SW	27	7N	14	160	1 50	2 25	"
Battenburg John S.	NW	23	6N	13	160	1 50	2 25	"
Battenburg Augustus	SW	23	7N	11	160	1 50	2 25	"
Miller Casper	NW	29	7N	13	160	1 50	2 25	"
George Augustus	NW	26	6N	13	160	1 50	2 25	"
Yerby Casper	SE	34	7N	13	160	1 30	2 25	"
Martin Sebastian	NW	3	6N	13	160	1 50	2 23	"
Nathwang Christean	NE	33	7N	11	160	1 50	2 25	"
Moulder Lewis	NW	33	7N	11	160	1 50	2 25	"
Moulder Cathrine	SE	3	6N	13	160	1 50	2 25	"
Saunders Christean W.	SE	25	6N	13	160	1 50	2 25	"
Link Frederick	SE	27	6N	13	160	1 50	2 25	"
Hasseloff Ferdinand	SW	20	6N	13	160	1 50	2 25	"
Hinke William	NE	10	6N	13	160	1 50	2 25	"
Hinkle Albert	NW	11	6N	13	160	1 50	2 25	"
Hamming Wm.	SW	14	6N	13	160	1 50	2 25	"
Hoffmaster Lewis C.	SW	10	6N	13	160	1 50	2 25	"
Hoffmaster Johanna	NW	15	6N	13	160	1 50	2 25	"
Rinklin George F.	NE	1	7N	13	160	1 50	2 25	"
Simmons J. E.	SE	15	7N	13	160	1 50	2 25	"
Simmons Cathrine	SW	22	7N	13	160	1 50	2 25	"
Large Frederick	NE	23	7N	13	160	1 50	2 25	"
Large William	NW	27	7N	13	160	1 50	2 25	"
Jacobs Greedo	SE	27	7N	13	160	1 50	2 25	"
Schock Julius	NW	33	7N	13	160	1 50	2 25	"
Parker Thomas	SE	31	7N	13	160	1 50	2 25	"
Parker Nancy Ann	NW	1	6N	14	160	1 50	2 25	"
Hibbold William	NE	1	6N	11	160	1 50	2 25	"
Wilson Joel W.	NW	2	6N	9	160	1 50	2 25	"
McPherson Charles	SE	3	8N	9	160	1 50	2 25	"
McPherson Asa	SW	2	8N	9	160	1 50	2 25	"
Schuck Charles	SW	5	7N	13	160	1 50	2 25	"
Hoff George	SE	5	7N	13	160	1 50	2 25	"
Ruck Christian	NE	8	7N	13	160	1 50	2 25	"
Glock Frederick	NW	6	7N	13	160	1 50	2 25	"
Russell Charles	NW	9	7N	13	160	1 50	2 25	"
Theon Peter C.	NW	9	7N	13	160	1 50	2 25	"
Hoemrichousen Henry	NW	10	7N	13	160	1 50	2 25	"
Bassennett John	SE	7	7N	13	160	1 50	2 25	"
Wilson J. G.	NE	18	7N	13	160	1 50	2 25	"
Schuberman Christian	NE	18	7N	13	160	1 50	2 25	"
Schuberman Magdalena	NW	18	7N	13	160	1 50	2 25	"
Pfeffer Frederick	SW	19	7N	13	160	1 50	2 25	"
Hall Thomas	NW	20	7N	13	160	1 50	2 25	"
Spohn George	SE	20	7N	13	160	1 50	2 25	"
Spohn Barbara	NE	34	7N	13	160	1 50	2 25	"
Speyer Conrad	NW	35	7N	13	160	1 50	2 25	"
Keeber Joseph	NE	35	7N	13	160	1 50	2 25	"
Mason Cornelia	NW	29	6N	16	160	1 50	2 25	"
Mason Joseph	NW	21	6N	16	160	1 50	2 25	"
Walker Joseph	NW	26	6N	16	160	1 50	2 25	"
Walker Rebecca	NE	2	6N	16	160	1 50	2 25	"
Walker Isaiah H.	SE	1	6N	16	160	1 50	2 25	"
Walker Joseph J.	NE	23	6N	16	160	1 50	2 25	"
Walker Ann	SE	11	6N	16	160	1 50	2 25	"
Hall Luther A.	NE	12	6N	16	160	1 50	2 25	"
Hall Cyntha	SE	32	8N	14	160	1 50	2 25	"
Hall Isaiah H.	SW	10	5N	14	160	1 50	2 25	"
Hall James	SW	3	7N	13	160	1 50	2 25	"
Hall John	SE	23	6N	13	160	1 50	2 25	"
Hall Albon	SW	9	6N	11	160	1 50	2 25	"
Calvier Wm. H.	SE	35	7N	14	160	1 50	2 25	"
Lambkin Charles	SW	7	7N	14	160	1 50	2 25	"
Lambkin Silvester	SW	22	7N	14	160	1 50	2 25	"
Robertson William	NW	24	8N	13	160	1 50	2 25	"
Witts Isaac	NW	11	8N	13	160	1 50	2 25	"
Chase Hiram	NW	27	7N	12	160	1 50	2 25	"
Stickney Hudson F.	SW	15	7N	11	160	1 50	2 25	"
Stickney Charles	SE	5	7N	11	160	1 50	2 25	"
Littler Anthony	SW	9	7N	11	160	1 50	2 25	"
Wood Garrett B.	SE	35	6N	11	160	1 50	2 25	"
Witzel Theodore	SW	36	7N	14	160	1 50	2 55	"
Ulman Charles F.	NE	2	6N	14	160	1 50	2 25	"
Fowler Daniel B.	NE	10	6N	11	160	1 50	2 25	"
Fowler A. D.	SE	3	6N	11	160	1 50	2 25	"
Coggres Wilson	NW	14	7N	14	160	1 50	2 25	"
Frazier David S.	SW	11	6N	14	160	1 50	2 25	"
Frazier Rebecca	SE	3	6N	14	160	1 50	2 25	"
Stokes Henry F.	NE	5	7N	14	160	1 50	2 25	"
Witson W. F.	NW	4	7N	14	160	1 50	2 25	"
Verbeck Philip	NW	29	7N	11	160	1 50	2 25	"
Gray Edward B.	NW	9	6N	12	160	1 50	2 25	"
Muir Robert	SW	35	7N	12	160	1 50	2 25	"
Gray Wm. Arnold	SW	4	6N	12	160	1 50	2 25	"
Marin Mitchell	SW	23	7N	12	160	1 50	2 25	"
Dougherty John	SE	21	7N	11	160	1 50	2 25	"
Crossdale Eben	SW	22	7N	11	160	1 50	2 25	"
Grealy Joseph	NE	30	7N	11	160	1 50	2 25	"
Williams Robert	NE	29	7N	11	160	1 50	2 25	"
Williamson James	NW	33	7N	11	160	1 50	2 25	"
Obersterffer Elizabeth	NE	36	7N	11	160	1 50	2 25	"
Obersterffer George H.	SW	12	6N	11	160	1 50	2 25	"
Weoss Dorothy	SW	15	6N	11	160	1 50	2 25	"
Frederitz Joseph	NW	36	7N	11	160	1 50	2 25	"
Menning Wm. D.	NE	35	7N	11	160	1 50	2 25	"
Wilson John W.	NW	20	6N	11	160	1 50	2 25	"
Battenfield Joseph	NW	33	8N	14	160	1 50	2 25	"
Battenfield Sarah	SW	33	8N	14	160	1 50	2 25	"
Battenfield Michael	SE	33	8N	14	160	1 50	2 25	"
Battenfield Solomon	SW	32	8N	14	160	1 50	2 25	"
Singleton John	SW	4	5N	14	160	1 50	2 25	"
Obersterffer Reece W.	SW	3	5N	14	160	1 50	2 25	"
Obersterffer Alberton	NW	10	5N	14	160	1 50	2 25	"
Obersterffer Emma L.	NW	2	5N	14	160	1 50	2 25	"
Donnelly Andrew	SE	35	7N	13	160	1 50	2 25	"
Bartlett Dorothy	NW	22	5N	14	160	1 50	2 25	"
Phips Hiram	SE	21	5N	14	160	1 50	2 25	"
Gaines Jackson	NE	14	7N	13	160	1 50	2 25	"
Gaines Andrew	SE	14	7N	13	160	1 50	2 25	"
Torrence Jane H. H.	SW	30	7N	13	160	1 50	2 25	"
Torrence Lawson H.	NE	31	7N	13	160	1 50	2 25	"
Torrence Hughs	SE	30	7N	13	160	1 50	2 25	"
Smith Aribilee	SW	17	7N	13	160	1 50	2 25	"
Smith Benjamin W.	SE	17	7N	13	160	1 50	2 25	"
McFie James, sen.	SE	7	5N	13	160	1 50	2 25	"
McFie William	NE	22	5N	14	160	1 50	2 25	"
McFie John, sen.	SE	15	5N	14	160	1 50	2 25	"
Murray Archable A.	NE	20	7N	13	160	1 50	2 25	"
Palmer Benjamin R.	SE	23	7N	13	160	1 50	2 25	"
Cargell B. V.	SW	1	7N	11	160	1 50	2 25	"
Cargell Mary	SE	1	7N	11	160	1 50	2 25	"
Edwards George	SE	28	7N	11	160	1 50	2 25	"
Murphey S. H.	NW	8	5N	14	160	1 50	2 25	"
Hinkle A.	NW	4	6N	11	160	1 50	2 25	"
Smith Thomas	NE	14	6N	11	160	1 50	2 25	"
Smith James	NW	11	6N	11	160	1 50	2 25	"
Gonel L. B. G. A	SE	22	6N	14	100	1 50	2 25	"

JOHN QUINDLEY, Sheriff and Collector, Conway county, Arkansas.

Lewisburg, Arkansas, Sept. 21, 1850.　[Costs of Advertising, 26¼ cents per tract.]

Weekly Arkansas Gazette
Fri, Sep 27, 1850 ·Page 4

TO THE PUBLIC.

THE undersigned has taken the old and well-known stand at Lewisburg, recently occupied by Messrs. E. & J. Thompson, under the name of the Craig House, and fitted it up in good condition for the reception of the traveling community. His stable will be well supplied and well attended to, and no pains spared to give general satisfaction to all who may favor him with their custom.　WILLIAM CRAIG.

Lewisburg, Nov 19, 1850.—11—2w

The Gazette & Democrat and Fort Smith Herald will please give the above two insertions, and forward their bills to A. Gordon, P. M. of this place.

W. C.

True Democrat
Tue, Nov 26, 1850 ·Page 1

ARREST OF A MURDERER.—In May last a man named James Massey brutally murdered one John Brown, in Meigs county, Tenn. On the 23d ult., two gentlemen, Peter Huff and Chas. Cretcher, arrived at St. Louis, having Massey, whom they had arrested a few days previously in Washington county, Mo., in custody. The circumstances of the murder, as we find them in the St. Louis Intelligencer, are these:

An illicit connection existed between Massey and a woman of bad character in the neighborhood where both he and the murdered man resided, and on account of an intimacy which had sprung up between the latter and this woman, a feeling of jealousy was harbored by Massey. Enticing his intended victim, under some reasonable pretext, to a lonely place in the neighborhood of his own dwelling, he, in the presence of the woman spoken of, offered him a flask of liquor, and, while he was in the act of drinking, struck him a blow on the forehead with a large piece of stone, which knocked him down, when he sprang upon him, and, with the stone, literally mashed in his face and a portion of his skull. He then stamped and otherwise mutilated the body of Brown. After having accomplished the bloody deed the murderer fled. A true bill for murder was found by the grand jury, and a reward of $300 offered for the arrest of the fugitive, who was arrested by Mr. Huff a short time after Christmas, at Lewisburg. Ark., but escaped from custody on the way to Tennessee.

Some time since, Mr. H. learning that Massey was living in Wright county, not far from his (Huff's) place of residence, which is in the adjoining county, again started in pursuit of him in company with Mr. Cretcher, and discovering the place of his concealment, which was in an out-house attached to his dwelling, arrested and secured him. Massey was aware of the pursuit, and had armed himself with a rifle, which he attempted to use, but the assailants closing with him, managed, after a desperate struggle, to wrench the weapon from his hands before he could use it.

Washington Telegraph
April 23, 1851, Page 1

☞The steamer Gen. Shields, which left here last week for Fort Smith, was snagged and sunk near Lewisburg, by which her freight was all damaged. They had, however, succeeded in raising her, and she was under way, proceeding up, when passed by the St. Francis, on Tuesday evening.

Weekly Arkansas Gazette
Fri, Jun 13, 1851 ·Page 2

The Methodist Preacher
at Lewisburg: Rev. John H. Rice

List of Appointments of the Preachers of the Arkansas Annual Conference.

LITTLE ROCK DISTRICT.—John Coule, P. E.
    "   Station—Augustus R. Winfield.
    "   "   Circuit—Stevens Farish.
Benton   "   Wm. T. Anderson.
Hurricane   "   Wm. A. Maples.
Brownsville "   To be supplied.
Lewisburg   "   John H. Rice.
Clinton   "   Jesse M. Boyd.
Perryville Mission—James B Thetford

Washington Telegraph
Nov 19, 1851, Page 3

WOOD CHOPPERS AND LABORERS WANTED AT WILSON'S LANDING.

EMPLOYMENT will be given immediately, to active men willing to engage in this work. The highest prices for such labor will be paid, and the cash ready, when the services are rendered.—
Apply to   **W. O. WILSON,**
      about 4 miles above Lewisburg.
Little Rock, Dec. 16, 1851.   15--4w.

True Democrat
Tue, Dec 23, 1851 ·Page 3

☞The *River Mail* failed again on Friday last, and again on Sunday—but arrived on Monday. It again failed on Wednesday last, but arrived between 10 and 11 yesterday morning. The failures, we understand, are attributed to foggy weather, high winds, *high water*, and drift wood in the river.

The *Western Mail*, due on Saturday evening last, arrived at the opposite bank of the river in proper time, but was unable to cross until the following morning, in consequence of the rapidity of the current. It brought nothing from above Lewisburg— the stages above that point being stopped, it is supposed, by back water from the high stage of the river.

Weekly Arkansas Gazette
Fri, Feb 27, 1852 ·Page 2

Horrible Murder—The Murderer Killed.

One of the most terrible affairs which we have lately heard of, occurred on Tuesday evening, the 23rd ult., in Conway county, in this State. Truly may it be said, condign punishment, though illegal it must be admitted, was speedily visited upon the head of the bloody murderer. We have been furnished with the following account of the terrible affair, which we have no misgivings in endorsing as true, because we believe the writer incapable of doing any man injustice, though that man might be a Murrelite, if his varacity was to suffer thereby:

GALLEY ROCK, Aug. 27th, 1853.
F. N. Coleburn, Esq.:

Learning that the first number of your paper will appear in a few days, we respectfully solicit the publication of one of the most unjustifiable, malignant and unparralled murders ever perpetrated in this State.

John G. Paschall, a merchant, an honorable and very moral citizen of this place, had an unsettled store account against one William O. Wilson, of Conway county, who lived about ten miles below. Paschall called upon Wilson to settle, a few days since, in this place, he refused to pay the account at the time, saying, he had a note of $31 20 cents against Paschall. A slight difficulty ensued, which was quelled; Paschall presenting a receipt against the note. Tuesday evening, the 23rd instant, Paschall went to Wilson's house for a settlement, was seen in his house, and, in a few minutes after the witness left the house, he heard two reports of a gun; a human (naked) body was found in the river, nearly opposite Wilson's house, head off, right leg off, and the body cut open from the throat to the lower part of the abdomen — Upon inquest, it proved to be the body of Paschall. He had a club-foot, which was cut off. He had scars on his left leg, that were recognized by several persons. He was dragged from Wilson's gate to the river, and blood found upon the trail. His pocketbook, with money identified, had been found by one of Wilson's negroes at the river, the next day after the killing. It was proven, the negro that found the pocket-book, had just returned from the woods with a load of new timbers, and had been absent, from Tuesday 1 o'clock until Wednesday 11 o'clock. Wilson's clothes, that he had on at the time of the killing, were found in the river; also the axe, used in opening of Paschall, and severing the head and leg. Upon examination before the justice, he was considered guilty of the charge, and committed. The mare and saddle, that Paschall rode, have never been found. A strong guard took him to Lewisburg—arrived there about nine o'clock p. m. Saturday 26th inst., and about 12 o'clock in the night he was shot by some one unknown and wholly unobserved by the guard. He lived about two hours, made no confession, nor never mentioned the circumstance. We are informed that he was not questioned upon the subject. In his statement, upon examination, he acknowledged Paschall had been at his house, and, when the blood was shown him found on the trail and questioned about it, he replied, 'prove it.' [*Dardanelle Post.*

Washington Telegraph
Wed, Sep 21, 1853 ·Page 3

NEW MAIL ROUTE.

Mr. SEBASTIAN submitted the following resolution; which was considered by unanimous consent, and agreed to:

Resolved, That the committee on the post office and post roads be instructed to inquire into the expediency of establishing by law a mail route from Des Arc bluff on White river, intersecting the military road near the Cadron ferry, in Conway county, by way of Lewisburg, Lemoyne's ferry and Dardanelle, to Fort Smith, all in the State of Arkansas, and report by bill or otherwise.

The True Democrat
May 02, 1854, Page 1

Below is a long article,
"portions of it probably, purely fiction" about Lewisburg's Doctor, John Menefee.

☞ The following is not original in the True Democrat, but was found floating about in our exchanges without any paternity. While it is greatly exagerated, and some portions of it probably, purely fiction, yet it is very interesting, and no doubt will be read with avidity by most of our readers:

JOHN MENEFEE,
THE FIGHTING DOCTOR.

The hero of the following short sketch was a native of Kentucky. His father was a farmer of moderate circumstances, living a few miles from Louisville, who managed by great labor and scrupulous economy, to give his favorite and first born an excellent education, embracing the degree of a doctor of medicine.— Young Menefee was remarkable from the earliest period of his intellectual development, for an intense and burning ambition, such as could brook no rival in whatever he undertook, while the glorious gifts of a magnificent brain and mighty physical constitution, seemed to furnish the surest guarantees for the ultimate reality of

the surest guarantees for the ultimate reality of his every hope. By prodigious exertions, day and night, he stood foremost in all his classes at college, and graduated with an eclat that obscured the fame of all competitors; so that had the rising star of his genius met with no adverse shock to hurl it away from its appropriate and radiant orbit, imagination can scarcely assign a limit to the splendor it might have attained.— But unfortunately, a hostile collision occurred at the very commencement of its career, to arouse the sleeping volcano of his darkest passion, and project the course of his ambition at a dangerous tangent from the circle of a peaceful life.

He had a young and beautiful sister, who was seduced and betrayed by a fashionable villain in Louisville, one James Murray, a lawyer, and universally regarded as the most desperately brave duellist that Kentucky—the land so prodigal of heroes—ever produced.

While the father and mother of the ruined girl were weeping tears of despair, John, then only twenty years of age, armed himself and proceeded in search of his enemy. He found him in the court house, immediately after an adjournment, and without uttering a word, attacked and belabored him dreadfully with a cowhide. Murray, on his part, fought like a fiend, but in vain; for the fiery desperation of fierce and concentrated wrath appeared to have given young Menefee the strength of a dozen men. He blinded his antagonist with quick and countless blows, dashed from his hand every pistol the other succeeded in drawing from his pocket, and flagellated him till he was literally covered with blood.

A challenge was the consequence. Menefee accepted on these conditions: That the meeting should take place at a certain spot the ensuing morning, directly after sunrise. Three pistols were to be loaded—each foe should take one and fire by turns at a mark ten paces distant. Whoever hit nearest the center should then have the remaining pistol, and shoot at his adversary's head. If he missed, the other should be entitled to a shot, and so on by alternation till one of them should fall dead. These ferocious terms were mutally settled, and the principals and seconds met accordingly on the banks of the Ohio river, six miles below the Falls.

The seconds measnred off ten paces and then made a black spot with moistened gunpowder, about as high as a man's heart, on a slender oak tree. They then loaded the three pistols, handed one to each principal and retained the third to be given to the successful marksman. The antagonists then cut a pack of cards for the first shot. Murray drew the queen of diamonds— Menefee the ace of spades, and so won the first fire. He immediately took his stand, turned his right side to the tree, let the hand which grasped the weapon, now at full cock, fall until the dark muzzle reached below his knee, fixed his flashing blue eyes steadily a moment on the mark and then swift as thought, raised and pulled trigger. Unfortunately, the pistol "hung fire," as it is called in the back-woods—that is the flash in the pan was seen, first, and then the explosion of the load in the barrel, sounding long like a double report. Under such circumstances, most persons would have missed the tree; but as it was, Menefee's bullet barely cut the upper edge of the mark. An excellent shot.

Murray now took his position. He was a famous level shooter, having previously slain three men in as many shots, sending his balls directly through their brain. He raised slowly, poised a deliberate aim, stood several seconds motionless as the tree at which the muzzle of his pistol was pointed, and fired. The crack was short and sharp like the pealing of a bell; and when the blue wreaths of curling smoke cleared away, the spot on the oak was not to be seen—the white bullet hole bored into the splintered wood occupied its place.

The seconds then gave Murray the third pistol, and he stationed himself ten steps from his unarmed adversary, who, in the meanwhile, seemed calm and fearless as an unconcerned spectator, without the slightest symptom of either alarm or surprise. According to the terms stipulated, Murray might choose his own time after the elevation of his weapon, to fire; and the thought appeared to cross his soul to torture his antagonist by a cruel and unnecessary delay. He raised his right hand gradually, and fixed a mortal aim at Menefee's head, in which posture he continued for more than two minutes. But Menefee still betrayed no emotion. Not a nerve shook—his face paled not a shade. A bitter smile of scorn writhed on his purple lip, and his gleamy blue eye, gazing fiercely into that of his deadly foe, seemed to the wandering mind like a ball of fire, so intense and revengeful was its glare. At length he called out in a voice piercing and shrill as the shriek of a trumpet:

"Murray, you d——d coward, why don't you shoot? Are you afraid to shoot?"

And whether it was the position of Murray's arm, so long extended, affected the aim or that he became excited by the mocking taunt, or was surprised at the terrible tones of his enemy's voice, or quailed with preternatural dread before the lightning of his burning blue eye, it is impossible to say; but at last, whatever might be the cause, a remarkable change passed over his features. His cheek grew pallid—his pale lips quivered—his hand shook. He fired!— The ball merely grazed Menefee's left temple without injury.

Then the seconds reloaded the pistol and placed it in the hands of Menefee, and the parties again assumed their proper stations. The youthful avenger of a sister's shame waited not an instant. He was in too great a hurry to

an instant. He was in too great a hurry to finish his work for suspense. Quick as the flash of a sunbeam, he elevated his weapon and fired. With the roar of the explosion, without a sigh or groan, Murray dropped dead in his tracks.— His right eye had been shot out!

Menefee fled the country and settled in Conway county, Arkansas. Henceforth the whole current of his thoughts and passions appeared to be changed. The earthquake of moral wrath, which had burst up from the profound abysses of his soul, had plowed out a new passage for the march of ambition—a passage stained with ineffable blood! Before his heart had burned with unquenchable enthusiasm to excel in knowledge, in variety, depth and extent of attainments; now he coveted superiority only in desperate deeds—the cloudy achievements of brute bravery. Nor, to say the truth, could he have selected a more appropriate field in the wide world for his belligerent purposes, than Arkansas then afforded. Political strife raged with incredible fury. No man could be a leader either in the parties of the State, or in those of a county, unless he stood ready at all times to defend his principles at the point of the bowie knife and muzzle of the pistol. To enumerate all the duels fought by opposing chiefs of the different factions during that sanguinary era, would stagger belief. A faint idea of this barbarous state of things may be conceived from the astonishing fact that Arkansas has never to this day had a senator or representative in the councils of the nation, who has not once, if no more, periled his life on the so-called "field of honor." Honorable duels, however, formed scarcely a tithing of the combats waged. Riots, affrays, and deadly rencontres by chance medley, were weekly and sometimes daily occurrences. Dr. Menefee took a hand in all and yet escaped from each without a scar, till his very name grew to be a thing of terror, at the sound of which even brave men trembled.— And thus he had reached the fate of his now false, and at last fatal ambition. As a "famous fighter," he was universally acknowledged to be without a second, and that too, in a country abounding with bold spirits from every quarter of the Union. The Rectors, the Deshas, Wilsons, Conways—the most redoubtable hero was he of the ferocious blue eye.

It would have been a curious thing to analyze the motives and feelings of the terrible duelist at this period. He does not seem to have been actuated by sheer and absolute cruelty. He did not wield the bowie-knife for the sake of inflicting pain; it was only the sharp instrument with which he cleaved his way to notoriety. He fought, not so much to avenge insults as to achieve popularity. To excel, ascend, culminate, formed the end of all his thoughts and wishes, and to do this in his present sphere, but a single path lay open—the path marked by fire and blood. He became a

sent sphere, but a single path lay open—the path marked by fire and blood. He became a monomaniac, hopelessly diseased in the organ of destructiveness. He lived only in a state of extatic dream of bravery—a dream overflowing with the consciousness of surpassing power, the power to make all eyes and all hearts tremble.

He devised extraordinary methods of displaying his courage and contempt of death.—He was known on several occasions, without uttering a word, to approach and spit in the faces of notorious bullies, with whom he had no cause of quarrel, and for the sole end of provoking a fight. One personal advantage, however, resulted from this excessive desperation.

No other physician could be found hardy enough to settle in Conway, where such foe reigned, and as a matter of course Menefee got all the practice. He even attended on his own wounded—would cut a man open with his bowie-knife in the morning, and if called upon, sew him up with needle in the evening.

The old proverb says—"There must be an end to every thing," and an end came at last to the reign of "The Fighting Doctor," as he was christened in blood throughout Arkansas. He had a neighbor named Phillips, a peaceful inoffensive man, who had never previously been engaged in a difficulty with any human being, and hence in that region was generally deemed a coward. From some cause, which never publicly transpired, feelings of hostility arose between the two, and Menefee sought an early opportunity to cowhide the other in the streets of Lewisburg. Phillips bore his chastisement without so much as an effort of resistance.—Indeed, at the moment, he had no other alternative, for he was altogether unarmed, while his enemy had a pistol cocked at his breast.

Immediately afterwards, however, Phillips went and literally loaded himself with murderous weapons, and returned to face his foe on more equal terms. They encountered in the public square, while court was in session, and never did the sun of heaven shine on a more obstinate combat. First of all they fired two rounds with pistols, and at the second round, Phillips was wounded in the loins. But this, instead of checking his furious ardor, only tended to inflame and madden him the more. He unsheathed his knife and bounded upon his enemy, who received his thrusts with a like deadly blade. With clenched teeth, foam on their vivid lips, panting chests, and blazing eyes, they fought like maniacs, till both were bathed in sweat and blood. At length Phillips ventured a desperate manœuvre. He dropped his own knife and seizing the naked blade of his antagonist's, snapped it in two by main strength, cutting at the same time, his own fingers to the bone. He then drew from beneath his vest another knife, and made a plunge at Menefee's heart; but Menefee, in turn, caught the sharp

Phillips was wounded in the loins. But this, instead of checking his furious ardor, only tended to inflame and madden him the more. He unsheathed his knife and bounded upon his enemy, who received his thrusts with a like deadly blade. With clenched teeth, foam on their vivid lips, panting chests, and blazing eyes, they fought like maniacs, till both were bathed in sweat and blood. At length Phillips ventured a desperate manœuvre. He dropped his own knife and seizing the naked blade of his antagonist's, snapped it in two by main strength, cutting at the same time, his own fingers to the bone. He then drew from beneath his vest another knife, and made a plunge at Menefee's heart; but Menefee, in turn, caught the sharp blade in his hand and broke off the point—when Phillips produced a third bowie-knife, much larger than the others and plunged it up to the hilt in his enemy's side, who fell to rise no more. Menefee, as he lay upon the gory ground, looked up with a smile, and gasped in a dying voice—

" Phillips, you are the King of Conway, now, for you have have killed the FIGHTING DOCTOR."

True Democrat
Tue, Jun 13, 1854 ·Page 1

Below, two brief newspaper clippings immediately below, mention Lewisburg within a long article about Faulkner County: Cost of land in Lewisburg & Temperance Society in Lewisburg

Lands in the vicinity of Lewisburg are commanding $20 per acre, and wealthy farmers with negroes are coming in.

The cause of temperance is steadily progressing in Conway. The little village of Lewisburg boasts of a society of 54—*all men*. Intemperance is a theme the sad *realities* of which places at defiance the novelty of *fiction*. To this terrible habit is to be ascribed nine-tenths of the crimes committed,

Weekly Arkansas Gazette
Fri, Feb 09, 1855 ·Page 4

THE UNIVERSITY FAMILY REMEDIES:

ISSUED under the seal, sanction and authority of the university of free medicine and popular knowledge. Chartered by the State of Pennsylvania, April 29, 1853, with a capital stock of $100,000, mainly for the purpose of arresting the evils of spurious nostrums, also for supplying the community with reliable remedies wherever a competent physician cannot or will not be employed, have purchased from Dr. John R. Rowand, his celebrated Rowand's Tonic Mixture, known for upwards of twenty-five years as the only sure and safe cure for Fever and Ague, etc., and his inestimable remedy for Bowel Complaints. Rowand's Compound Syrup of Blackberry root, which highly approved and popular remedies, together with the University's Remedy for Complaints of the Lungs, the University's Remedy for Dyspepsia or Indigestion, the University's Remedy for Costive Bowels.

Also the University's Almanac may be had at the Branch Dispensary, or store of

A. & J. M. GORDON & CO.
Lewisburg, Conway Co., Ark.

May 22, 1855   4t

True Democrat
Tue, Jun 05, 1855 ·Page 4

DISSOLUTION OF PARTNERSIP.

THE partnership existing between the subscribers expires by limitation on the 1st day of September next, (1855,) and we would respectfully request all persons indebted to us to come forward immediately and settle the same with Anderson Gordon, who alone is authorized to receive and receipt for the same; and those having claims against said firm will present them to him for payment, as he hereby agrees to pay all the debts of the late firm.

ANDERSON GORDON,
JAS. M. GORDON,
JOHN A. GRIFFIN.

Lewisburg, Ark., Aug. 8, 1855.

The undersigned, having purchased the interests of James M. Gordon and John A. Griffin, in the firm of A. & J. M. Gordon & Co., will continue the Mercantile Business at their old stand, on his own account—where he will keep on hand a general assortment of **Dry-Goods, Groceries, Hardware, Queensware, Hats, Caps, Boots, Shoes, Drugs, Paints, Oils, Dye-stuffs,** etc., etc., which he will sell low for cash, or exchange.

Feeling thankful for the patronage so liberally extended to the old firm, he hopes to merit a continuation of the same. GENTLEMEN GIVE ME A CALL.

Aug 21, 55 4m   ANDERSON GORDON.

True Democrat
Tue, Aug 28, 1855 ·Page 1

☞ The *river*, after rising several feet, commenced falling. There is now, however, some four feet in the channel below this. The *Lucy Robinson* left for Fort Smith on Tuesday morning, but the Western stage driver reports the river, as having fallen two feet at Lewisburg. The F. K. Jr., a small stern-wheel steamer, arrived on Sunday, from Napoleon, and left on Monday evening for Fort Smith and Van Buren. The Exchange reached here about 1 P. M. on yesterday, being but 5 days out from this port. She reports no yellow fever at Napoleon.

The Fox was to have been here to-night.

Weekly Arkansas Gazette
Fri, Sep 07, 1855 ·Page 2

From Lewisburg, Conway county, we have the following:

"A know nothing meeting was held here to-day, (Sept. 8.) and was addressed by a young champion from Dover. One would suppose, from the manner of the young Sam, that *he* thought he had completely demolished foreigners and Catholics. He proved, to the satisfaction of his know nothing hearers, that the Pope of Rome had shipped an army of foreign Catholics, ready armed, to crush our liberties, and that he himself was on his way to gather up the spoils. He also poured out the vials of his wrath upon what he termed ceceders—which proved to my mind, that, although a man may be seduced into their midnight associations, they do not allow him to withdraw, without placing him under the ban of the order.

After the speaking, they held a meeting with closed doors. Twenty-one remained, two of whom had been democrats.   LEWISBURG."

The True Democrat
Sept 11, 1855, Page 2

THE BOATS.—The river, despite the recent rains, seems fast receding towards low water mark. The "New World" reached our landing last Monday. The "Fox" has been here, and left for Napoleon, since our last. The "Exchange" is below. The "F. K., Jr." got up as high as Spadra, returned here on Wednesday evening, and left, yesterday, for Napoleon. The "Lucy Robinson," we learn, got only as high up as Lewisburg.

Weekly Arkansas Gazette
Fri, Sep 14, 1855 ·Page 2

Letter from Anderson Gordon.

Lewisburg, Ark., Sept. 20th, 1855.

EDITOR TRUE DEMOCRAT—At the speaking here on Wednesday last, Mr. Turner, of Prairie county, stated that the democrats who had joined the know nothings had or would withdraw, and named myself as an instance. When the Hon. G. W. Lemoyne and Dr. Westerfield asserted publicly that I had not withdrawn.— One of these gentlemen, (Mr. Lemoyne) if not both of them knew at the time that I had withdrawn from the American, alias know nothing party. What motive they had in denying my withdrawal I cannot imagine.

I wish it distinctly understood that I have withdrawn, now and forever from the said order, for many reasons:

If there is a single prominent man in the know nothing party in the northern States, who is not either a freesoiler or abolitionist, I have not been able to find him, and I have watched their movements close. The whole party north is anti-Nebraska, without doubt, and pledged to the repeal of the Kansas and Nebraska law. I am opposed to arraying one section of this Union against the other, which seems to be the legitimate fruits of know nothingism. I find the American, alias know nothing party north, unitedly opposed to the extension of slavery, and in favor the restoration of the Missouri restriction, the only thing, in my opinion, that ever did draw a line of north and south in this glorious Union. The know nothing party is sectional and not national. For instance, they set out as strongly anti-Catholic and anti-foreign, and now in Louisiana, Maryland, South Carolina and other States they allow Catholics to be members and their candidates for public office; while in some other States, where the naturalized voters are numerous, they discard the plank proscribing foreigners and naturalized citizens, provided they are Protestants. Here in Arkansas, Capt. Pike says he will not rest until the Catholic test is stricken out.

I find that the platform, published by the Philadelphia convention was, at the time, repudiated by twelve States, and since then several other large States, Pennsylvania and Ohio among them, have joined the bolters.

So you see they cannot possibly make a national party of it. The best that can be said of it, is, that it is various factions, made up of material, according to the climate in which they live. This is demonstrated by the fact, that the national council allowed every State to so arrange their respective platforms as to catch the popular breeze in their particular locality.

So you may consider me safely on board the old ship of democracy. She has rode out many a storm, and will ride out many more. Place me in what capacity you will, I care not where, I am for my country and the good old cause of democracy.   ANDERSON GORDON.

P. S. You may add the name of Henry F. Gordon as having withdrawn from the *great American party*.   A. G.

The True Democrat
Oct 02, 1855, Page 3

NOTICE.

There will be a "mass meeting" of the Conway county democracy and a public dinner at Lewisburg on Saturday the twentieth instant. The public are invited to attend. Able orators will be in attendance.

True Democrat
Tue, Oct 09, 1855 ·Page 2

Healing Sulphur Springs
North of Lewisburg?

LEAP YE LAME FOR JOY.

THE Weathersfield Sulphur Springs, midway between Lewisburg and Springfield, Conway county, Arkansas. They are not inferior to any in the State as many can testify, being situated on the main road between the above places. The proprietor would invite the attention of the public to them.

Sept. 25, 1855 4w   ELI EATON.

True Democrat
Tue, Oct 09, 1855 ·Page 4

Withdrawals from the Know Nothing Party.

For the True Democrat.

LEWISBURG, CONWAY Co., Oct. 19, '55.

MR. EDITOR—You will please inform your readers, that I have withdrawn from the so-called Know Nothings. Having associated myself with them, I soon found that it injured my acceptability as a minister of the gospel. And it has long since been a settled principle with me, that a minister of the gospel should not take any step that would circumscribe his usefulness. You will confer a favor upon a friend by inserting this in your paper, that all may know where I now stand.

J. D. STOCKTON.

True Democrat
Tue, Oct 23, 1855 ·Page 2

A Voice from Conway County !
Mass Meeting of the Democracy.

According to previous notice, a very large meeting of the democracy of Conway county assembled at Lewisburg, on Saturday last, the 20th inst. The capacious room, which had been prepared for the occasion, was densely thronged with ladies and gentlemen, and the windows and doors were crowded with anxious participants. It was really a gala-day for old Conway !

The meeting was organized by calling Dr. S. J. Stallings to the chair, and appointing J. W. Griffin, esq., secretary.

The object of the meeting being briefly explained by the chairman, it was

Resolved, That the chairman appoint a committee of five to draw up suitable resolutions expressive of the sentiments of the meeting.

Whereupon, the chair appointed Messrs. Geo. C. Brooke, William Fryers, Timothy Gay, Stephen Farish, and Doctor T. Bennet, who, after a short recess, reported the following preable and resolutions, which were read by Mr. Brooke, the chairman of the committee, and passed enthusiastically :

Whereas, There has recently sprung up in our midst, upon the ruins of the "old whig party," a secret, oath-bound, political association, which whilst, like the Jacobine clubs of France, they assume the name of friends to the constitution, or America, their avowed principles and purposes are to obliterate and trample upon that sacred instrument ; therefore be it

Resolved, That we, members of the democratic party of Conway county, in mass meeting assembled, venerating the memory of our patriotic ancestors — cherishing their dearest gift, the constitution of the United States, under the sacred guidance of which we have attained our present enviable position as a nation; and, unwilling thus to be robbed thereof, can but look upon the doctrines of this oath-bound, proscriptive order but as at war with every republican principle which should be cherished by us as democrats and true Americans.

Resolved, That if there was nothing in their creed dangerous to republicanism, the meeting in secret, the oaths, the grips, the cry of distress, and other like Jacobin acts, should be sufficient to arouse the apprehension of every true patriot in the land.

Resolved, That the doctrine carefully couched in the eight article of the Philadelphia platform is openly and palpably in violation of the federal constitution, wherein the right to worship God according to individual preference, free and unmolested, is guaranteed to every citizen of the confederacy.

Resolved, That the war made upon our naturalized citizens is in opposition to the liberal principles as recorded in that sacred chart— the foundation of democratic faith, and contrary to the cherished and pursued policy of the *fathers of our country.*

Resolved, That the doctrine as published in the third article of the Know Nothing platform—declaring the maintainence of the Union

to be the paramount political good, is old *federal doctrine*, opposed by the democratic party since the days of Jefferson; and we, as believers in the true republicanism of that great chieftian, as did Jefferson, Madison, and Jackson, take issue on this declaration of federalism; the constitution of the Union, that compact which formed the Union — that sacred instrument which made us what we are, and which, if rigidly adhered to, will preserve us prospering to the end, we hold to be the paramount political good, as well as the primary object of patriotic desire.

Resolved, That the second clause of the fourth article of said platform, carries in its careful words a sentiment inimical to the Nebraska and Kansas act, and as such, should be opposed by every true republican, whether north or south, as it settled the territorial question according to republicanism and requirements of the constitution—obliterating the line of 36 min. 30 deg., that fruitful cause of sectionalism, and not taking from any section the right guaranteed by the constitution. For the passage of said act, Stephen A. Douglas, of Illinois, and his co-democratic workers from the northern States, deserve the thanks of every true American in the Union, and for their manliness in facing and conquering that fanaticism which reigned supreme around them — we, as democrats, would rejoice to vote for the little giant of the west as the next chief magistrate of the nation.

Resolved, That the twelfth article of said platform declares an absolute falsehood, when it declares Know Nothingism to have been reared upon the ruins of the democratic party, as is proved by their recent victories in Virginia, North Carolina, Georgia, Tennessee, Alabama, Texas, Maine and Indiana ; these overwhelming majorities show it not only alive " but KICKING."

Resolved, That Franklin Pierce, our present chief magistrate, deserves the admiration of the nation for his bold and manly administration, and we as democrats fully endorse and approve every act thereof.

Resolved, That the proceedings of this meeting be published in the True Democrat.

Geo. C. Brooke, esq., was then called on to address the meeting, and responded in a beautiful and eloquent speech of about one hour and a half in length. His able exposition and defence of democratic principles was convincing, and his argumentative denunciations of "Know Nothingism" had a telling effect, as was evinced by the enthusiastic manner in which his speech was received.

Chas. A. Carroll, esq., was then called on, and in a happy manner entertained the meeting

Chas. A. Carroll, esq., was then called on, and in a happy manner entertained the meeting for a brief time.

The company then retired on board the splendid steamer Lucy Robinson, which is now lying at the Lewisburg wharf, where a sumptious dinner had been prepared for the occasion. The viands having had ample justice done them, all quietly dispersed, well pleased. The meeting passed off in the utmost harmony, and "showed *old Conway* up" in her true light—democratic to the *back-bone*.

S. J. STALLINGS, *Ch'm.*

J. W. GRIFFIN, *Sec'y.*

True Democrat
Tue, Nov 13, 1855 ·Page 1

GEORGE C. BROOKE,
Attorney at Law,
LEWISBURG, ARKANSAS.
October 5, 1855.   13—26w.

Weekly Arkansas Gazette
Fri, Nov 16, 1855 ·Page 4

Married—In Lewisburg, Conway county, on the 15th inst., by R. Welborn, esq., HENRY T. GORDEN, merchant, to MISS JANE GORDEN, both of Lewisburg.

In this city, on the 27th inst., by the Rev. C. L. Jeffries, Dr. S. J. STALLINGS, of Lewisburg, Arkansas, to MISS ELIZA JANE WATSON, of this city.

True Democrat
Tue, Jan 01, 1856 ·Page 3

Death of George C. Brooke,
Attorney at Law, Lewisburg

WHEREAS, information has been received by the members of this Bar, that our highly esteemed and much beloved brother Geo. C. Brooke, Esq., of Lewisburg, Conway county, Arkansas, has been suddenly removed from our midst by the unseen hand of the fell destroyer, death. Therefore

Resolved, That we deeply deplore the loss of so promising and amiable a member of this Bar, who, by his cautious deportment and gentlemanly bearing, had endeared himself to all who knew him.

Resolved, That we tender to the relatives and friends of the deceased, our sincere condolence and heartfelt sympathy for this sad bereavement, with which the hand of an inscrutable Providence has inflicted them.

Resolved, That the proceedings of this meeting be communicated to the Court by the Chairman, with a request that they be entered upon the records; and further, that they be communicated to the relatives and friends of the deceased by the Secretary of this meeting, and be published in the True Democrat and Gazette and Democrat by request. Whereupon, on motion the meeting adjourned *sine die.*

P. JORDAN, *Ch'n.*

WALTER C. DENT, *Sec'y.*

The foregoing proceedings were accordingly presented and read in open Court, on Wednesday morning, 12th March, 1856, to which Mr. Justice Clendenin made the following response, which, together with the proceedings aforesaid, were on motion ordered to be entered on the records of the Court.

HON. JUDGE CLENDENIN'S RESPONSE.—I had the pleasure of a brief acquaintance with the deceased, the subject of your resolutions, and during that acquaintance, I formed a high opinion of him, both as a lawyer and a man, and thought him to be one, who was eminently qualified to exalt and adorn his profession. I unite with you, gentlemen, in all that you have expressed by your resolutions, and direct that they be entered on the records of this Court.

Weekly Arkansas Gazette
Sat, Mar 22, 1856 ·Page 2

W. W. EDWARDS, Attorney at Law. Lewisburg, Conway county, Ark., will practice in the courts of the counties of Conway, Perry, Pulaski, Prairie, Pope, Saline, Van Buren, White and Yell, and in the Supreme and Federal Courts at Little Rock.

Prompt attention given to the collection of claims, to any and all business pertaining to Land or Taxes.
April 29, 1856.   1y *

RUNAWAY,

FROM the undersigned on Sunday the 6th inst., two negro men, **Sampson** and **Peter,** of the following description: Sampson is about six feet two inches high, copper complexion, and will weigh two hundred pounds. Peter is a mulatto, five feet eight or ten inches high, and will weigh one hundred and seventy-five pounds. They were bought of James Woosley of Crawford county in this State, and may possibly be aiming to get back. A liberal reward will be paid for their apprehension and delivery to me, or confinement in any jail so that I can get them.   THOS. KEESEE, Jr.
Hillsboro, April 15th, 1856.   29—3t

True Democrat
Tue, Apr 29, 1856 ·Page 3

Danley Sneaking Again and Caught.

The editor of the Gazette attempted again to steal a march upon the democrats of Conway county. Instead of publishing a notice that he intended to address the citizens at Lewisburg, he *privately* sent off hand bills to the faithful. He hoped thus to elude discussion with any democrat. It should be remembered that, but a few weeks ago, Danley charged Warren, very unjustly, of being guilty of this very act. In Col. Warren, he thought it an offence deserving the severest reprobation. In himself, he deems it fair Know Nothing tactics.

But with all his cunning, Danley did not escape at Lewisburg. Mr. Arthur Carroll, a young democrat of great talents, happening to be in the neighborhood, met and completely demolished him. There was scarcely any thing left of the Old Bar-Keeper when Mr. Carroll let him off. A correspondent writing about the speeches, said:

"Danley spoke here to-day. Arthur Carroll answered him and made a splendid speech—got Danley down badly. The Know Nothings slipped off very quietly. They are down in the mouth."

True Democrat
Tue, Jul 15, 1856 ·Page 2

Lewisburg, Conway crunty, Ark.,
July 15th, 1856.

EDITOR TRUE DEMOCRAT — Permit me through your paper to announce my withdrawal from the so-called American party; for I have always been a democrat after the old Hickory style, and ever expect to vote that independant vote that every true American should vote; so good bye, coony Sam.
ELISHA HARRIS.

The True Democrat
July 22, 1856, Page 3

ADMINISTRATOR'S SALE.

I WILL sell to the last and best bidder, in the town of Lewisburg, Ark. on the 24th day of January next. A. D. 1857, the following negro girls, viz :— **Harriett,** aged 18 years; **Diey,** aged 16 years, and **Sylva,** aged 14 years—belonging to the estate of Felix and Margarett Farrelly, deceased. The said negroes are all well grown, and likely. Terms of sale **Cash in hand.** JAMES GORDON, Administrator.

Dec 23 '56-5t-Cost of adv $3 00

True Democrat
Tue, Jan 13, 1857 ·Page 1

Minstrel Show
at Lewisburg, May 1st 1857

All of Spalding & Rogers' Shows Coming!

MESSRS. SPALDING & ROGERS, having concentrated all their Circuses, Museums, Minstrel Bands and Steamboats, South and West, for the Season of 1857, respectfully announce that the Season here will commence with the **Banjo Minstrels,** Under the direction of NED DAVIS, consisting of ☞**Fourteen Star Minstrel Performers!** enlarged, revised and improved, so that it is confidently claimed to be the best Band in the United States.

Will be exhibited at **Little Rock,** Monday, Tuesday, Wednesday and Thursday, April **27th, 28th, 29th** and **30th.** Open 2 and 7 o'clock, P M., on board Messrs. S. & R's, beautiful Steamer Banjo, which they have re-fitted in recherche style, with Stage, Music Saloon, Cushioned Seats, etc., etc.

Admission 50 cts., Children and Servants 25 cts.

At LEWISBURG, May 1st; and at DARDANELLE, May 2d, 1857. April 7, 1857 2w

True Democrat
Tue, Apr 07, 1857 ·Page 3

LAND FOR SALE.

A VALUABLE tract of land for sale on the river, six miles below Lewisburg, Conway county—containing 770 acres—one hundred in cultivation—with a good frame house with stone chimneys, and good out houses and well, etc., all in good repair and 50 acres deadened. Apply to

May 26, 1857. 4t HARRIS CROSS, Lewisburg, Ark.

True Democrat
Tue, Jun 09, 1857 ·Page 1

Steamboat
Built at Lewisburg
by A. Gorden & Co.

NEW STEAMBOAT.—By the following extract from a letter received from a gentleman living in Conway county, we learn that a new steamboat is in progress of construction near Lewisburg on the Arkansas river. Such evidences of enterprise in our State are truly gratifying to hear of, and we hope to chronicle many such. Our correspondent says:

"I have just examined the new steamboat that is being built by A. Gorden & Co., five miles below Lewisburg, at the well known place called Harris' Bend, and I do think, if I am a competent judge, that it will be one of the most compact little boats that ever was constructed in slandered Arkansas. It will be constructed to run on 10½ inches light, carrying 150 tons, or thereabouts, drawing not more than 2½ feet, which will enable it to run about the season through. As it is building expressly for the Arkansas trade, I would respectfully recommend the owners to the shipping and traveling community when their boat is completed, which will be in time to carry out the early cotton. The workman engaged in constructing this boat is the well known ship carpenter, Dick Masters, of Little Rock, who built the 'Rock City' and the 'Fox,' and he says it will be far superior to either of the latter, as the timber is of the best selection."

True Democrat
Tue Jul 14, 1857 ·Page 2

Circus At Lewisburg
September 10, 1857

MAMMOUTH
CIRCUS COMING.
FREE EXHIBITION.

TERRIFIC DOUBLE ASCENSION

From the ground adjoining the Tent of L. B. Lent's Mammoth National Circus, immediately before opening the doors for the afternoon performance.

A DOUBLE ASCENSION

will take place OUTSIDE OF THE CANVAS, FREE TO ALL. MLLE. MARIE will walk a TIGHT WIRE from the ground to the top of the Pavilion,

A HEIGHT OF EIGHTY FEET;

and PROFESSOR HEMMING will achieve a similar feat. PROPELLING A WHEELBARROW BEFORE HIM THE ENTIRE DISTANCE.

No one should fail of witnessing this extraordinary display of intrepidity and address. which is

ENTIRELY WITHOUT PARALLEL.

AT LITTLE ROCK,

Saturday Afternoon. Sept. 12th.

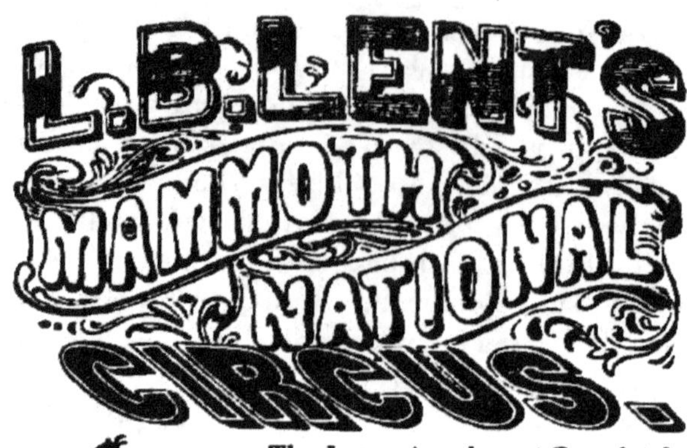

The Largest and most Completely Equipped Equestrian Establishment in the world, comprises the

GREATEST TROUPE
OF
EUROPEAN & AMERICAN
MALE AND FEMALE ARTISTS,
AND THE MOST
MAGNIFICENT COLLECTION
OF WONDERFULLY
TRAINED HORSES AND PONIES,
EVER BROUGHT TOGETHER, AFFORDING FACILITIES FOR THE PRESENTATION OF
MORE NOVEL AND VARIED PERFORMANCES
THAN HAVE EVER BEEN GIVEN IN A TRAVELLING EXHIBITION.

THE GORGEOUS ENTRÉE of the establishment into the various towns of exhibition will be found a spectacle of surpassing grandeur. The brilliant procession will be led by the BAND-CHARIOT, drawn by the Longest Team of Horses ever driven, and managed in pairs by H. LACEY, the modern John, and

FIFTY-HORSE DRIVER.

THE PERFORMANCES will consist of every imaginable variety of

Equestrian, Gymnastic and Acrobatic Feats,

Including many features at once
New and Astounding.

Each Evening's Entertainment will conclude with the GRAND LEGENDARY SPECTACLE of

New and Astounding.
Each Evening's Entertainment will conclude with the GRAND LEGENDARY SPECTACLE of

ST. GEORGE AND THE DRAGON.

WILL EXHIBIT AT

OZARK,

Monday, Sept. 7th.

CLARKSVILLE,

Tuesday, Sept. 8th.

DOVER,

Wednesday, Sept. 9th.

LEWISBURG,

Thursday, Sept. 10th.

LITTLE ROCK,

Saturday, Sept. 12th.

Doors open at 2 and 7 o'clock, performances commence half an hour after.

Admission **50 cents**, Children under 10 years of age and servants **25 cents.**

Sept. 1, 1857   2t

True Democrat
Tue, Sep 01, 1857 ·Page 3

Died—Near Lewisburg, Ark., on the 6th of October, 1857, GEORGE M., infant son of Theodore and Sarah Griffey, aged one year, six months and twelve days.

True Democrat
Tue, Oct 20, 1857 ·Page 3

NOTICE.

ON Sunday, February 14th, 1858, a suspicious looking character made his appearance in this place, riding a mule: offered it so low that several persons present, concluded it was stolen property, and that they would test the matter by attempting to arrest him: in doing so he ran off, leaving the mule, which is now in the hands of H. T. Gordon, where the owner can get it by proving property, paying charges, etc., etc.

DESCRIPTION OF THE MULE.—It is a large Bay Mule, very much shaved with breeching, about 5 years old, no marks or brands perceivable.

DESCRIPTION OF THE MAN.—About 5 feet 10 or 11 inches high, spare made, light complexion, 21 or 2 years old, said his name was Micham, said he was from Van Buren, Arkansas, and that he had an uncle in that place by the name of John Micham.

Lewisburg, Ark., Feb. 16th, 1858.   20-2w.
Gazette and Democrat please copy.

Arkansas True Democrat
March 02, 1858, Page 4

For the True Democrat.

CONWAY COUNTY AS IT WAS, IS, AND WILL BE—1st. "In the good old days of Aadam and Eve," or about 1812, there were a few settlers in this county, or part of the country, who were principally trappers and hunters, that come here for the purpose of reaping the benefits of a pioneer life. At the mouth of Cadron was the grand rendevous for all the hunters and trappers on the upper Arkansas; this was named Cadron; and here annually assembled those restless spirits to procure their ammunition, and indulge frequently in a regular free fight, and drink enough whisky to last them through to the next season.

Emigration still continued to set in this direction until a county was fromed, with the county seat where Col. B. F. Howard now resides. Drinking and fighting was still the road to distinction. Finally, the courts were moved to Lewisburg; and, in a few years, there were a number of outlaws assembled and organized, so they could commit any crime with impunity and go unpunished. The civil portion of the community were awed into silence and submission. But after bearing until forbearance ceased to be a virtue, they elected officers to execute the laws, who were honest and determined to do their duty. So, some have been killed, some punished, and others forced to flee like "true patriots for their country's good."

So this was the end of the "reign of terror." Which brings us to about the year 1850, when the county seat was removed to Springfield.

2d. Since which time the laws have been duly respected and administered, and there is no place in Arkansas where there is less rowdyism than Lewisburg. Indeed the law has become a complete terror to evil doers. In point of fertility of soil, this is one of the best counties in the State. Having a large amount of the richest river bottom, which has never been overflowed only in 1833 and 1844, which

been overflowed only in 1833 and 1844, which is more than any of the western rivers can boast of. The uplands are excellent, producing cotton, corn and wheat, and well adapted to fruit growing. With these superior agricultural advantages, and the Arkansas river, which has never failed but once in fifty years to afford sufficient navigation for all the purposes that have been or will be needed, and far healthier than many counties that make a great boast of their superior health. Indeed, there is no healthier place in Arkansas than Lewisburg; there has never been known an individual, who resided here over twelve months, that had the chills.

With cotton land that will yield 1500 to 2,000 pounds seed cotton, or 50 to 70 bushels of corn, and 10 to 20 bushels of wheat per acre, and only two overflows in fifty years, this county is destined to become one of the first counties in Arkansas—as it is the geographical center of the State. TOM BOWLING.

True Democrat
Wed, Jul 21, 1858 ·Page 1

Green Grove, July 14, 1858.

Mr. EDITOR—Permit me to say through your valuable paper, that the new steamboat called Conway, now six miles below Lewisburg, in Conway county, will be ready to ply between Little Rock and Fort Smith by the 1st November. It is well constructed for low water, not exceeding more than 12 inches draught light, and will not fail to render all the comforts and accommodations to passengers and shippers that can be done under the circumstances of a low water boat. A. GORDON & CO.

True Democrat
Wed, Jul 21, 1858 ·Page 3

MRS. H. HATHAWAY'S SCHOOL FOR MISSES AND YOUNG LADIES,
LEWISBURG, ARK.

THE fall session of this School will commence on Monday, the 27th of Sept. Scholars from abroad will here be enabled to pursue their studies free from the interruptions of a large town, while no pains will be spared by the teacher to thoroughly instruct those committed to her care in any of the branches pertaining to a finished education. Care will be taken to avoid all useless show and to so train the girls that they may go forth with clear heads and earnest hearts to the arduous duties of woman's life.

Every pupil will be expected to cheerfully submit to the order and discipline of the school and carefully shun all habits that will interfere with their progress.

Lewisburg is one of the most healthful locations in the south-west and all that can be desired in morals.

TERMS PER SESSION OF 21 WEEKS,

TERMS PER SESSION OF 21 WEEKS,
Payable at the middle of the session.

Primary branches.......................$10 00
Intermediate branches.................. 12 00
Higher   " 15 00
French, Spanish, Italian, each........ 10 00
Music.................................. 25 00
Use of Instrument...................... 5 00
Map Drawing............................ free.

Pupils charged from time of entrance and no deductions made except in cases of protracted illness.

Good board can be had for $8 per month.

Application can be made to the teacher, or to
A. GORDON,
WM. L. MENEFEE,
F. W. HERVEY,
T. F. HENRY,
Sept 29, 1858.   5m   R. WELBORN.

True Democrat
Wed, Sep 29, 1858 ·Page 3

FEMALE SCHOOL AT LEWISBURG.—The citizens of Conway county ought to be rejoiced at the establishment of a school for girls at Lewisburg under the control of so accomplished a teacher as Mrs. Hathaway. A friend writes us that the school will be all that is claimed for it in the advertisement, which may be found in our paper to-day.

True Democrat
Wed, Sep 29, 1858 ·Page 2
Circus Coming
to Lewisburg, Oct.21;
and Potts Inn Oct. 20 1858

G. N. ELDRED'S
GREAT ROTUNDA
SOUTHERN MENAGERIE AND CIRCUS.

FIRST appearance in LITTLE ROCK, on *Monday* and *Tuesday*, 25th and 26th of October, 1858.

Complete New Outfit,

Just received from *New York*, at *Little Rock*—new and splendid water-proof Pavilion, Seats, and all the appurtenances necessary to give splendor and effect to the performances of this wonderful and popular troupe. This mammoth Pavilion is capable of seating 2,000 persons comfortably, and was constructed for Mr. G. N. ELDRED, by *the most celebrated Pavilion Maker in New York.*

Horses, Ponies, Educated Mules,

WILD ANIMALS, among which are Lions, Tigers, Leopards, Lama, Zebras, Black Tigers, California Tiger Cats, Monkeys, Birds, etc., together with the greatest curiosity now shown in any exhibition, being a *Baby Monkey*, the off-pring of one of the Mamozets, which nurses and tends to it with all the care and affection of maternal solicitude.

The Troup of Equestrians,

Clowns, Acrobats, Men of strength and agility, grace and athletic power, is unequalled by any that ever before traveled in the South, North, East or West, and challenges any company traveling, to contest with them the palm of superiority and excellence.

THE CLOWNS.

JIMMY REYNOLDS, *the Jester of the Poets*, whose world-wide reputation causes thousands daily to flock and hear his laughable witticisms and well-turned epigrams and repartees, assures the inhabitante of Little Rock, that his emporium of speeches, jests, jokes, hits at the times, and fancy funniments, shall be forthcoming, for their amusement and especial edification, on the 25th and 26th.

MIKE LIPMAN, the singing Buffo and Joker, will dance, talk, tumble, say good things, and make unusual sport and merriment.

MISS ALBERTINE E. ROBERTS,

The young, fascinating, and beautiful Equestrienne, Danseuse and Vocalist, will appear in her novel and graceful act, entitled

THE ÆRIAL NYMPH,
Or, the Fairy Triumph.

Miss Roberts will also execute some of the favorite dances which have rendered her so popular, as well as sing many of the popular burlesque songs of the day.

THE TROUPE OF EQUESTRIANS

comprises gentlemen of unrivalled talent, in every grade of the Profession, making such a combination of Acrobatic and Equestrian ability, as always insures the satisfaction and delight of the immense audiences, that daily and nightly, crowd the Rotunda Pavilion, of the

Great Southern Circus.

Among the more distinguished members of the Troupe may be found

MONS. LA THORNE, the Man of prodigious strength—*the Great Iron Globe Hurler*—Puller against Horses, etc.

Mr. THOMAS WYETH, the Great Seminole Rider.

MASTER SAUNDERS, the Equestrian prodigy, whose wonderful act upon a bareback horse, astonishes every beholder.

The extraordinary Patagonian brothers, JOHNSON and LOWLOW, in their startling feats upon a chair, on the top of a pole, 60 feet high.

Masters EUGENE and DE LORME, in their graceful and startling performances upon the corde de la trappeze.

Mr. MOSE LIPMAN, the great Vaulter and 2-Horse Rider.

MASTER LA ROIX, the Infant Equestrian and Acrobatic Prodigy.

LITTLE HARRY, the infant Tumbler, Vaulter, etc.

Wonderful Performing Horse Champion, instructed and performed by G. N. ELDRED. The United States is challenged to produce his equal, for beauty, intelligence and training.

Educated Performing Fighting Ponies, MORRISSEY and the BENICIA BOY. *Comic Mules*.

BAND led by DICK WEBBER, and comprising musicians of well known merit.

☞ Admission only 50 cents—children and servants 25 cents.

☞ It will be remember that the price of admission is only that charged for a Circus alone, the Animals may therefore be considered a FREE EXHIBITION!

Company will exhibit at LEWISBURG, 21st Oct. MOUTH CADRON, 22d October. BENEDICT'S,   23d   "
Oct. 20, 1858.

True Democrat
Wed, Oct 20, 1858 ·Page 3

W.L. Menefee of Lewisburg
Selling Land at Lewisburg & Cadron

For Sale.

THE Cadron property, thirty-six miles above Little Rock, fronts the Arkansas river two miles in a compact body, and can be divided into three or four farms, giving to each a desirable *River or Hill residence*.

This tract includes the Cadron Mills and Ferry —160 acres cleared and in cultivation, from five to six hundred deadened, spring, well and cistern water, with buildings sufficient to accommodate from 50 to 100 hands. Title unquestionable. If desired, I will sell with the place 100 head of cattle and as many hogs.

For richness of soil and convenience to market this place is unsurpassed by any lands in this country.

I will also sell *a magnificent tract of river land* fifty miles above Little Rock, fronting the river ¼ of a mile, containing 600 acres—125 in cultivation—150 deadened. For further particulars apply to the undersigned, at Lewisburg, Ark.

W. L. MENEFEE.

Oct. 23, 1858.   16—tf.

Weekly Arkansas Gazette
Sat, Oct 23, 1858 ·Page 3

Land for Sale in the Arkansas River Bottom.

WE the undersigned as executors of the will of A. Dowdle, deceased, offer for sale his former residence, lying four miles below Lewisburg, in Conway county, containing 880 acres, 120 in cultivation and 120 deadened. It has two wells of excellent water, gin house, negro cabbins, etc. We will also sell with the place the crop of corn, 12 head of mules, stock of cattle, hogs, etc., if desired. For further particulars apply to J. M. Dowdle on the farm.

J. M. DOWDLE,
W. M. DOWDLE,
R. A. DOWDLE,
R. A. TAYLOR.   *Executors.*

Dec. 15, '58. 4t.

Arkansas True Democrat
Dec 15, 1858, Page 3

Corn! Corn!! Corn!!!

THE undersigned has for sale, immediately upon the river bank, two miles below Lewisburg, Four Thousand bushels of corn, which will be shelled and sacked, or delivered in the husk, to suit the purchaser. Address me at Lewisburg, Arkansas.

Jan. 12, 1858. tf   STEPHEN RANKINS.

True Democrat
Wed, Jan 12, 1859 ·Page 3

For the True Democrat.

LEWISBURG.

MR. EDITOR—It is remarkably strange and yet it is a fact that public opinion will sometimes be founded on the very opposite basis of what is *reasonable*, *just* and *true*. Now as an illustration of this position, we see that the public sentiment of Arkansas is decidedly against the pleasant and quiet town of Lewisburg.— The very name of the place seems to excite and bring into action, feelings of a horrid and repulsive nature. And it is true beyond all dispute, that there is not a more peaceable, civil and agreeable town in the State; yet public sentiment is strong and bitter against it.

The citizens are clever, social and honest, and the community around are sober, temperate and industrious. Besides it is the healthiest spot on the Arkansas river, from its source to its mouth. The water that is furnished principally by wells, has peculiar mineral properties, which tend to invigorate the system and restore to health any whose misfortune it is to be on the list of invalids. There are very many travelers who can testify to this fact—indeed any one who has stopped at Lewisburg for a *few days only*, cannot fail to have noticed an improvement from the use of the excellent water there. The citizens are *always* healthy— you can seldom hear of a case of sickness there, and the physicians can testify that if all the world had as little use for physicians as the healthy and agreeable town of Lewisburg, there would soon be a hecatomb—yea a *"thousand and one,"* doctors turned loose, poverty stricken and *penniless* upon the world; and " pill-bags" without number would be placed away on shelves and packed up in corners to become the prey of moths and crickets.

I sincerely hope the time will come, (and I imagine it is already dawing) when the public sentiment of the State will undergo an entire change and a thorough revolution concerning Lewisburg.

It is true, that Lewisburg was at one time the den and the rendesvous of a *dark-minded, suspicious* and *bloody* clan. But that time has long since passed away, and now lives only in the memory of some of the old gray-haired citizens of the country. The bully no longer walks the streets with his high and haughty tread as if he was monarch of the world, to the annoyance of good and quiet people, and the assassin no longer with his dark and stealthy step creeps along with his dagger drawn eager to wet its glittering blade in human blood. These unhappy times are over. The curtain has dropped and bloody dramas will be played no more at Lewisburg.

A reformation has been at work for several years, and it now has a clever, hospitable, intelligent and enterprising population. It is improving rapidly and its extraordinary health will carry the improvements on successfully.— There is an elegant masonic hall in process of construction which will soon be completed.— There is also a large and commodious frame building now going up for a male academy, also another of a like nature for a female seminary, and in less than twelve months from this time, they will all be completed.

Then the town of Lewisburg will be inferior to none in the State in the way of educational advantages; and the great healthiness of the place will induce parents who have sons and daughters to be educated, to send them there. And I would seriously say to all who desire good health, to visit the town of Lewisburg, and then make it their home.

SPERO.

Springfield, Ark., Nov. 20th, 1858.

Arkansas True Democrat
Jan 12, 1859, Page 1

Administrator's Sale.

I WILL offer for sale, in the town of Lewisburg, Conway county, Ark. on the 26th day of February next, on a credit. until the 1st day of October next the following slaves (for life) viz: Clarisa, aged about 45 years, and her 2 children, Emeline. aged about 17 years and Ann, aged about 8 years, the purchaser giving bond and approved security.

A. G. GORDON. Administrator
of the estate of E. Gamble, dec'd.

Jan. 26, 1859. 4t. Cost of adv. $2 50.

True Democrat
Wed, Feb 16, 1859 ·Page 4

New College in Lewisburg?

For the True Democrat.
The New College Enterprise.

Mr. Editor.——

Many of the readers of your excellent paper and perhaps nearly all of them, are aware that strong exertions are being made in every part of the state for the purpose of raising a subscription to build a new college. This is the begining of a new and important era in Arkansas and shoutd awaken feelings of pride and pleasure in the bosom of every patriot within its limits. Only twenty-five years ago and this state was a territorial wilderness, uncultivated and uninhabited except a few sparse settlements along the borders of the White, Arkansas and Ouchita rivers, and school-houses were almost a matter of astonishment to the people. But now flourishing towns, cities, villages and shool-houses may be unnumbered, and the whole state presents the marks of cheering and rapid improvement.

Not only are school-houses growing more numerous, but there are a few energetic, and enterprising men who are making strong and successful appeals to the people for a new college, and from what I cyn learn there will certainly be no failure in this grand and important measure. And as success seems to be almost certain, it is now time for those who are interested to consider what particular spot would be most appropriate for the location of the institution.

And although I am not directly interested, I hope no one will think it arrogance on my part, to express my preference for its situation.

The situation of an institution of learning of high order, should be if possible in a healthy central and accessible locality. Parents will be more willing to send their sons and daughters to a healthy place to be educated, than to a place where they are in constant dread of disease. In fact students cannot learn with that facility they should when they are breathing an atmosphere that is loaded with poisonous miasmatic vapers. It has a tendency to inervate the physical, as well as the mental faculties. And if those who have a vote to locate the new college wish it to prosper and gather laurels on account of its merit. they should certainly consider long and well, before they cast their votes. For upon its location greatly depends its future success and prosperity.

For my part I think that no better place in the state of Arkansas could be selected for the situation of a college than the town of Lewisburg in Conway county. It is the healthiest place in the state, beyond a doubt, has a sober and moral community' and besides it is a very central and accessible point. And permit me to say that if I had a thousand votes to cast I should give them so all to Lewisburg. In regard to its health I refer you to the citizens of the place and surrounding country, as well as to the hundreds who have stopped as travellers there. I do not thus give my preference to Lewisburg, on account of any sinister motive. Not at all. I am not identified in any manner with the place. I own no land or property there, and consequently nothing but an honviction of what I really believe could induce me to write as I do. It is decidedly the best place I know of in the state for the location of a college, and I hope when the subscribers assemble for the purpose of bollotting for the location of the new colleg, they will cast their votes for *Lewisburg.* Yours, etc.

CLARENCE.

Springfield, Ark., Feb. 4, 1859.

Arkansas True Democrat
Feb 16, 1859, Page 1

Mrs. H. Hathaway's School for Misses and Young Ladies, Lewisburg, Ark.

Lewisburg, Ark., Feb. 26th, 1859.

Mr. Editor——I must ask of you a small space in the columns of your valuable paper, to say a word in relation to the above school.

I had the pleasure of attending the examination of this excellent school at the expiration of the first session on last Friday, and must say that every thing went off most admirably; the scholars all acquitted themselves with honor, and much credit to their worthy and accomplished teacher, Mrs. Hattie Hathaway. I do not believe that the progress of the scholars or thorough and sound knowledge, can be excelled in the State. I cannot refrain from mentioning particularly, the little family, which was altogether, with their teacher, they all acquitted themselves well. And again, I must mention the music, which was very select and well performed; more particularly Uncle Sam's Farm, which was performed on the melodeon by Miss Olivia Bentley, and accompanied with vocal music by Misses Olivia, Mollie, and Adda Bentley, and Kate Lewis and Miss Rachael Lewis and Miss Georgiana Gordon, all parts of which was most excellent, it was certainly the best thing of the season. This branch of the school deserves special encouragement. Also the compositions were all well composed and excellently written, as well as the map drawing which exhibited much taste in that branch. At the close of the examination,

branch. At the close of the examination, which lasted near half a day, without examining near all the pupils, the worthy teacher, Mrs. Hattie Hathaway, gave her scholars and the audience a most excellent lecture, illustrating and enforcing the practice and principles by which she admirably conducted her school; at the conclusion of which, Mr. S. S. Nord, esq., of Springfield, was called for, who responded in a short, neat and appropriate address.

The next session of this most excellent female school will commence on Monday the 14th day of March next, for five months, (for terms see previous numbers of this paper.)

Right here, allow me to say that this is one of the best conducted schools I have ever visited in the State, and I think is excelled by none anywhere. Parents and guardians having misses and young ladies to educate, could not do better than to send them to this school. It is situated in Lewisburg, Arkansas, which is famed for its healthy locality, and is almost directly in the geographical center of the State, and has become a very moral and quiet place, as much so as any little town in the State. So let us have a full and overflowing school next session. Good board, washing, lights, etc., can be had here in good families at from 6 to 10 dollars per month.

Yours,   G. A.

Arkansas True Democrat
March 16, 1859, page 3

Farm for Sale.

WE offer for sale the tract of land formerly owned by A. Dowdle, lying in Conway county, Ark., three miles below Lewisburg on the north side of the Arkansas river, lying within one quarter of a mile of the river, and running back one mile and a half, all high dry bottom land, entirely above overflow containing 880 acres, 125 in cultivation, and about the same quantity deadened, with splendid wells of water, a new gin house, negro cabins, etc., etc.

We will sell for cash or on time to suit the purchaser. For further particulars apply to J. M. Dowdel, Lewisburg, Ark.

J. M. DOWDLE, *et al.*,

True Democrat
Wed, May 25, 1859 ·Page 3

Valuable Arkansas River Bottom Land for Sale.

THE subscriber will sell at private sale, his plantation and other lands situated in Conway county, about three miles above Lewisburg, in the Arkansas river bottom; consisting of **two hundred and seventy-three** acres, (with the privilege of five hundred acres more adjoining if it suits the purchaser.) One hundred acres of this land is in a high state of cultivation, with a good dwelling and all necessary out houses, and a good well of water. Persons desirous of procuring a good cotton or stock farm will find this a most desirable location. For terms apply to Jonathan Wells, senior, Lewisburg, Conway county, Arkansas.   JONATHAN WELLS, Sen.

True Democrat
Wed, Jun 01, 1859 ·Page 3

Man Killed
at Lewisburg by a Runaway

Murderers and Runaways.

We have no doubt but the runaways and murderers referred to below, are the same who were arrested near this City as stated in the above article. The two who were not killed confessed that an attempt had been made to arrest them in some county south, that they fled, and got seperated from their companion. Bob, who carried a double-barrel shot gun, that they "heard a report of fire arms from the direction of Bob," and that they supposed Bob fired, but with what effect they profess to be ignorant.

On Monday the 20th ult., there was a man killed at or near Lewisburg, Arkansas, by a runaway negro in an attempt to arrest him. It seems, according to the statement of the letter, from which we make this extract, that the man who was shot did not see the negro who shot him, as there were two or three of them, and while arresting one, was shot by another with a double-barrel shot gun. The letter does not give any particulars more than above stated. It is thought that they are trying to make their way to the Cherokee nation. The citizens of the frontier are requested to keep a close lookout for them—they are all well armed probably oppose any attempt to arrest them. The letter says there will probably be a large reward offered for their apprehension. The unfortunate man killed was named J. W. Davison, living six miles west of Springfield, Ark.—We suppose, however, that these negroes will endeavor to reach their abolition brethern in Kansas.—*Arkansas Intelligencer.*

The Arkansian
Sat, Jul 02, 1859 ·Page 2

Steamboat For Sale
at Lewisburg

FOR SALE.

The A 1 New and Light Draught Steamer "*CONWAY*," DRAWING ONLY 15 INCHES WATER,

WILL be finished and at Little Rock, on or about the 8th August next, and will have immediate despatch for Memphis, Tenn.; when, if not sold, she will return to the Arkansas river, and during the *low water season* will run as a regular Packet between Napoleon and Fort

Smith. Merchants and Shippers may rely on shipments on the "*Conway*" having strict attention, as she is strictly an *Arkansas boat*, having been built and furnished in this river. The "*Conway*" will be very fast, and will not draw *over 15 inches water*.

For freight or passage apply to the undersigned at Lewisburg, Ark., or to Messrs. Rapley, Hanger & Co., at Little Rock, Arks.

A. GORDON.

Lewisburg, Arks, July 23, 1859; 3—3m.

Weekly Arkansas Gazette
Sat, Jul 23, 1859 ·Page 3

FOR SALE.

THE A 1 new and light draught steamer Conway, drawing only 15 inches water, will be finished and at Little Rock on or about the 8th August next, and will have immediate dispatch for Memphis, Tenn., when if not sold, she will return to the Arkansas river, and during the *low water season* will run as a regular packet between Napoleon and Ft. Smith. Merchants and shippers may rely on shipments on the Conway, having strict attention, as she is entirely an Arkansas boat, having been built and furnished in this river. The Conway will be very fast, and will not draw more than 15 inches water. For freight or passage apply to the undersigned at Lewisburg, Ark., or to Messrs. Rapley, Hanger & Co., at Little Rock, Ark.

July 27, 1859. A. GORDON.

True Democrat
Wed, Jul 27, 1859 ·Page 3

A VALUABLE tract of bottom land for sale, situated on Point Remove Creek, 5 miles from Lewisburg. The tract contains 600 acres, 100 acres in cultivation, 200 acres well deadened. Has on it a good steam saw mill and out-houses.

For terms apply to the undersigned at Lewisburg, Ark. JNO. H. CARROLL.

Aug. 31, '59 tf.

True Democrat
Wed, Sep 14, 1859 ·Page 4

MARRIED.

In Lewisburg, Oct. 13th, by the Rev. Wm. Binet, GRANVILLE WILCOX, Esq. Attorney at Law, Van Buren, and Miss JULIA HUBLY HAMILTON, of Lewisburg.

By the same, at the same time and place, OLIVER HAZZARD FISH, Lieut. of 1st Cavalry, U. S. A., and Miss ADELAIDE LOPEZ HAMILTON, of Lewisburg.

The Van Buren Press
Oct 21, 1859, Page 2

Dissolution of Partnership.

NOTICE IS HEREBY GIVEN, That the Partnership heretofore existing between JOSEPH C. ROGERS and THADDEUS TAYLOR, of the town of Lewisburg, in Conway county, Arkansas, as merchants and partners in trade, doing business under the firm, name and style of 'Rogers & Taylor, is dissolved ; and all the interest of the said Thaddeus Taylor in said firm has been purchased by the said Joseph C. Rogers, and all the business of said firm will hereafter be settled and arranged by said Joseph C. Rogers.

Given under our hands, on this, the 13th day of October, A. D. 1859.

JOSEPH C. ROGERS,
THADDEUS TAYLOR.
of the firm of ROGERS & TAYLOR.

October 22, 1859. 16—tf.

Weekly Arkansas Gazette
Sat, Oct 29, 1859 ·Page 3

Get Aboard Steamboat
"Little Rock" at Lewisburg

New Orleans and Arkansas River Packet
LITTLE ROCK,

Capt. JENKS BROWN......L. B. BROWN, *Clerk.*

WILL ply regularly during the season, and take freight and passengers for *Roseville, Spadra Bluffs, Norristown, Dardanelle, Lewisburg, Little Rock, Pine Bluff, New Gascony,* and all other landings on the Arkansas river. Orders entrusted to her will receive prompt attention.

For freight or passage, having unsurpassed accommodations, apply on board.

January 14, 1859. 28—

Weekly Arkansas Gazette
Sat, Mar 24, 1860 ·Page 4

Destructive Fire at Lewisburg.
Supposed to be the work of an incendiary— two cotton gins and a warehouse burned— loss estimated at $10,000.

The town of Lewisburg in Conway county, was thrown into intense excitement on the 8th inst., by the alarm of fire. About 8 o'clock A. M. the cotton gin of Anderson Gordon was discovered to be in flames, and so far advanced as to render all efforts to save it unavailable. The flames soon communicated to the cotton gin belonging to Mr. Thos. Henry, and then to the warehouse of A. Gordon. In less than an hour all these buildings were a smouldering ruin. There can be but little doubt but all this was the work of incendiaries, as the gins began burning at opposite ends simultane-

began burning at opposite ends simultaneously. A slow match is supposed to have been prepared by the villains and deposited among the combustibles of the houses. The lint rooms in each gin were first caught. Suspicion rests on two stage-drivers who had been ordered to leave the town the previous day for tampering with negroes, and trying to induce them to run away. A good and timely warning—let us keep a sharp lookout for we know not what may be hatching among us. The slow-matches having been applied, these two abolitionist incendiaries took their departure in the stage leaving behind them a token of their vindictiveness and treachery.

Anderson Gordon's loss amounted to near $6,000, Mr. Thomas Henry's loss about $4,000. Most of the merchandise in the warehouse was consumed and nearly all the cotton bales.

The Van Buren Press
April 13, 1860, Page 2

Fire in Lewisburg.
Lewisburg, Ark., April 9, 1860.

Messrs. Johnson & Yerkes—

Gents: I hasten to drop you a few lines of my own and other's misfortune; on yesterday morning (Sunday) about 8 o'clock my gin house in this town, containing some 50 or 60 bales of cotton was discovered to be on fire. As soon as the alarm was given, the citizens and some of the neighbors responded very promptly, and rendered active and valuable service. Soon afterwards the gin house of Mr. T. T. Henry, successor to Henry & Co., of this place, containing some 15 bales of cotton, was discovered to be on fire. Between these gins stood my large warehouse, which contained a large amount of cotton, beef hides, peltry and furs, together with a large amount of groceries and other goods—very soon it took fire from my gin, when all three of the buildings with nearly all of their contents were destroyed. The work was undoubtedly from an incendiary; and I think one George Crull, an overland stage driver did it, or knew who did—*we drove him off*. It seems that the fire was by a slow-match to each of the lint rooms of the gins, as they were both found to be on fire *near the same time*. By hard work we prevented the fire from extending to any other house.

My individual loss will be about		$5,000 00
Myself and R. B. Griffin	"	5,000 00
Dr. E. W. Adams	"	2,500 00
T. T. Henry	"	1,200 00
R. Weborn	"	300 00
T. W. Barber	"	500 00
Jno. Breedon	"	300 00
R. Simpson	"	150 00
N. S. Williams	"	100 00
Sundry other persons	"	250 00
Total loss		$15,300 00

There was no insurance on any of the loss unless it was on Mr. T. W. Barber's which

was in transportation. There was some 10 or 12 hundred dollars worth of cotton and other goods saved for various persons in a damaged condition. The citizens and friends—one and all—will please accept my most heartfelt thanks for their very extraordinary efforts to save the property.

Your friend,
ANDERSON GORDON.

True Democrat
Sat, Apr 14, 1860 ·Page 2

Democratic Meeting.

The democrats of Welborn township assembled at Lewisburg on the 7th day of April, for the purpose of sending delegates to the county convention at Springfield.

And upon motion of Dr. John H. Carroll, Dr. W. L. Menefee was called to the chair, and upon motion of A. Gordon, esq., Albert Brooke was appointed secretary.— The chairman explained briefly the object of the meeting.

When upon motion of Mr. H. Watson, that the American party and all others out side of the democratic, be invited to co-operate with us, provided they will give in their adhesion to the democratic party, which was unanimously adopted. Dr. Carroll then made a motion that we herein nominate all county officers.

The meeting then proceeded—Anderson Gordon was declared to be first and Dr. S. J. Stallings second choice for Senator. For Representative—Robert W. Harper was declared by a unanimous vote to be the choice of this township. For Sheriff— Mr. Cravey Harrison was declared first and Mr. Livingston second choice. For Probate Judge—Esqr. Russell Welborn was by acclamation declared to be the first choice. For County Clerk—Mr. Venable, upon motion of Dr. Carroll, was declared to be the first choice, and for Constable— Capt. Wm. Gordon was declared to be the first choice.

An amendment was then made to Dr. Carroll's resolution, that this meeting make no other nominations, but abide by the county convention.

Dr. J. H. Carroll, Dr. S. B. Sherman and T. J. Griffy, esq., were appointed delegates to the county convention to meet at Springfield on the 9th of April.

The meeting then adjourned *sine die*.

W. L. MENEFEE, *Chairman.*
Albert Brooke, *Sec'y.*

Arkansas True Democrat
April 21, 1860, Page 1

From Conway County.

Lewisburg, Conway Co., Ark.

Mr. Editor—The citizens of this county held a meeting in Lewisburg, on Saturday, April 7, and passed the following resolutions:

Whereas, There has been an effort made in this county by certain transient persons, whom we have good reason to belive are abolition emissaries, to interfere with our slaves, and persuade them to assumo an attitude of hostility to their masters; and whereas, we are determined to take action against all such, both vigorous and effective.

Resolved, That we hereby advise all suspicious men having no employment amongst us, and who are drifting about for the purpose of injuring us in the possession of our property, to cease from this day any intermeddling in our domestic institutions, else we pledge them and ourselves, that we will deal with them with the utmost rigor.

Resolved, That the chair appoint a committee of seven to wait on the agents of the overland and Fort Smith and Little Rock mail lines, and request the removal of all employees, except such as are known to be good southern men, and to engage no others.

Resolved, That the persons subscribing hereto shall constitute a vigilance committee, any five of whom shall have power to carry out these resolutions in spirit and effect.

Resolved, That the Little Rock papers be requested to publish these proceedings.

The chair appointed as the committee Messrs S. H. Nieman, R. Welborn, L. O. Breeden, A. Gorden, R. T. Markham, W. L. Menefee and R. W. Harper.

S. J. STALLINGS, *Ch'n.*

And Forty Others.

Arkansas True Democrat
Sat, Apr 21, 1860 ·Page 2

Abolition Emissaries amongst us—Destructive Fire.

Lewisburg, Ark., April 13, 1860.

Mr. Editor: I write this for the purpose of putting our people if possible on the alert—it really seems as if a lethargy had seized them that could not be thrown off. On Saturday the 7th of April, the democrats held a township meeting in Lewisburg, and then we learned for the first time the concerted operations of the overland and mail stage employees in our midst.—They had persuaded Dr. Menefee's negroes to revolt, and the project was nearly ripe for execution, when the affair was divulged to him by a trusty old negro woman.—One of the drivers acknowledged the facts as related to Menefee by the negro; and the Doctor I suppose in his anger and suprise forgot that the statute of our State would have dealt with him very severely. He told him to leave and he did so.

A citizen of our town overheard one of these men tell a negro that if he would wait until he made money enough stage driving, he would take him off where a negro is as good as a white man. He was whipped and told to leave, and he did not wait for a second warning. So hearing that there were two others left of the same sort, a committee of citizens was appointed to wait on them and ascertain the facts. We were not disposed to punish innocent men, and having nothing tangible to operate on, we merely read them the *"riot act."* In consequence of these proceedings, these men either in person or by proxy fired by slow matches the gin houses of A. Gordor and T. T. Henry, esq., which also consumed the warehouse of the first named gentleman, situated between the two gins. The loss to these gentlemen is very large, besides many others; back country merchants who had large freights stored in the warehouse. Estimated loss $20,000, and no insurance. We have heard of several other buildings being fired around the neighborhood; but believe the damage was inconsiderable compared with the above. These men are still running at large and the public should use due caution against all suspicious characters lurking in their midst.

We have determined if we cannot get our mail matter without having it brought by gin burners and negro stealers that we will dispense with it entirely.

VIGILENCE.

True Democrat
Sat. April 21, 1860, page 3

Horrible Murder at Lewisburg.—We learn the following particulars from a gentleman who arrived from Conway County yesterday. It seems that some four weeks since the gin and sixty bales of cotton, and a warehouse, belonging to Anderson Gordon, Esq., were burnt at Lewisburg, involving a heavy loss to Mr. Gorden, and gentlemen in the adjacent county who had goods stored in the warehouse.

On the 14th inst., Joseph Smith, Esq., was arrested, charged with having set fire to the gin and warehouse. Smith was taken to Lewisburg and tried on the 16th and 17th before Justices Wellburn and Harper, and acquitted. Strong demonstrations are said to have been made to shoot Smith before he left the room, but they were prevented. Smith eat his supper at the hotel, after which he started to the ferry landing, was fired upon, the shot taking effect in his arm above the elbow. Smith ran back to the hotel bleeding profusely. Medical aid was procured and his wounds dressed. He requested to be put in a room where he could not be hurt. He was placed up stairs, in a back room. About 2 o'clock that night some parties took ladders and ascended to the window of Smith's room—the head of the bed was next to the window—shot through the two extreme panes of glass, the shot taking effect in one of Smith's shoulders and his breast. He lived two hours after he was shot, protesting to the last his innocence of the charges againt him.

A Coronor's inquest was held next morning. Their verdict was that the deceased came to his death by gun-shot wounds.

Des Arc Weekly Citizen
Sat, Apr 28, 1860 ·Page

CONWAY COUNTY, June 25th, 1860.

EDITORS TRUE DEMOCRAT—

We have had abundant rains, and the crops of corn and cotton were never more promising at this season of the year.

The examination at the Lewisburg Male and Female Academy came off on last Friday and Saturday, and the result fully showed that the Rev. J. P. Russell, principal of the institution, is, in every way, well and truly qualified for the position he fills. The pupils exhibited a degree of proficiency rarely equalled if ever excelled.

After the exercises at the school-room, (and, by the way, we have a magnificent building for the purpose), the audience, numbering some 400, partook of a most bountiful and elegantly prepared dinner—gotten up for the occasion by the good ladies of Lewisburg and vicinity.

On Friday evening of the examination, the Hon. Jesse N. Cypert addressed the people upon the subject of national and state politics; and if an avowal of principles is a test of political orthodoxy, he is unquestionably the best Buchanan democrat that has shown himself in "these parts." He is for specific duties, the Pacific railroad, and denies the right of Congress or a territorial legislature to interfere with slavery, etc. He was particularly severe upon his competitor, Col. T. C. Hindman; reviewing his political course in the State, from his advent to the adjournment of the Dover convention; showing clearly and forcibly the disorganizing rule or ruin course of the latter. Cypert's speech had a telling effect upon his hearers, as was manifested by oft repeated and enthusiastic cheering. He will run " like a scared wolf in this neck of the woods."

Johnson's prospects for Governor are daily brightening, and he will doubtless carry Conway county, by a handsome majority, in August—the Old Guard is waking up, with bright hopes for the future, and are determined to vote for the nominee of the State convention; nor have they forgotten the man who has borne aloft, and *victoriously*, the democratic flag in every contest in Arkansas for the last eight years.

Yours,   L.

True Democrat
Sat, Jul 07, 1860 ·Page 4

DIED—Near Lewisburg, Arkansas, on the 6th of July, 1860, JONATHAN R. WELLS, after a lingering illness of many months, which he bore with christian fortitude, being a member of the Primitive Baptist church near 26 years. The deceased was born in Spartanburgh district, South Carolina, Sept. 1796, moved to Kentucky, and joined the Primitive Baptist church, in 1834, moved to Arkansas in 1838, and finally settled near Lewisburg, Arkansas. " Blessed are they that die in the Lord."

True Democrat
Sat, Jul 21, 1860 ·Page 3

To the People of Conway County.

Lewisburg, Conway Co., Ark.,
March 26, 1861.

Having been requested by a resolution passed at the mass meeting in Springfied a few weeks since, to canvass our county in advocacy of the secession of Arkansas, and having been induced by the subsequent development of circumstances to postpone our appointments, we beg leave to state to our fellow-citizens in this manner, the reasons by which we were governed, and to assure them that whatever of energy and ability we possess are dedicated to the delivering of Arkansas from the bondage of black republicanism.

The adjournment of the convention gave an entirely different complexion to our condition—as to the people was referred the question of "secession" or "co-operation," to be voted on in August next, and knowing this to be a busy season with a large majority of our citizens, we concluded that the necessity for an immediate canvass was obviated and hence the postponement.

It will afford us great pleasure, when your leasure will permit you to turn out, to present to you the considerations which have impelled us to the belief, that Arkansas should unite her fortunes with those of the Confederate States.

Our appointments will be duly advertised.   Your fellow-citizens,

W. L. MENEFEE,
R. W. HARPER.

True Democrat
Thu, Apr 18, 1861 ·Page 3

1,000 Acres of Choice Cotton Land for Sale.

SITUATED on the north side of the Arkansas river and has a front of one mile; six miles below Lewisburg, Conway county, with eighty acres in a high state of cultivation, and one hundred more well deadened, with a good frame dwelling and good out-houses, a good well of never failing water, etc., and the best of range for stock, summer and winter. Any person wishing to purchase would do well to examine my land before purchasing elsewhere. For terms apply to Jas. M. Gordon, at Lewisburg, or the undersigned on the pemises.   HARRIS CROSS.

May 9, 1861. tf

True Democrat
Thu, May 09, 1861 ·Page 2

From Conway County.

LEWISBURG, May 25, 1861.

MESSRS EDITORS: Our old and esteemed fellow citizen, the Hon. Geo. W. Lemoyne, of Dardanelle, addressed the Conway Mounted Rifles today at the Masonic Hall. A large assembly of ladies and gentlemen were present. His effort was enthusiastic, eloquent and intensely southern —few dry lids were to be found in the assembly. The women of '61 in Lewisburg and vicinity have been at work night and day making up the uniforms for the volunteers. Three cheers for the ladies—always true, always patriotic. At the conclusion of the address, the "soldier's response to Dixie," by Lemoyne was sung with telling effect. The Conway Rifles camped Monday at Lewisburg, and will be in readiness to join Col. Churchill on his way to Ft. Smith. May the God of battles prosper them. W. L. M.

True Democrat
Thu, Jun 06, 1861 ·Page 3

Lewisburg Mail Delivery Schedule
Aug. 24, 1861 to June 30, 1862

7812   From Little Rock, by Balam, Green Grove, Lewisburg, Galley Creek, Norristown, Russellville, Scotia, Pittsburg, Clarkesville, Horse Head, Ozark, Pleasant Hill and Van Buren, to Fort Smith, 190 miles and back, three times a week.
Leave Little Rock at 6 a m;
Arrive at Fort Smith third day by 11 p m;
Leave Fort Smith at 6 a m;
Arrive at Little Rock third day by 11 p m.

Arkansas True Democrat
Aug 08, 1861, Page 3

LEWISBURG, Sept. 3, 1861.

Messrs. R. S. YERKES & Co.—

Gentlemen: I thought you might like to know what we were doing up here about clothing our volunteers. We got word about the 20th ult., of our troops, under Col. Churchill of your city, getting their clothing and tents burnt, during the battle of Oak Hills, in Missouri, and in about 10 days the citizens of Cadron and Welborn townships have bought and made up some 300 garments, and on yesterday we started two 2 horse and one 4 horse wagon with them to the volunteers in Missouri. Messrs. R. W. Benedict, A. J. White, A. J. Lucas, Dr. T. W. Shore, Rev. J. Hargis Hogans and many others of Cadron township, contributed liberally towards clothing our unfortunate volunteers. The citizens of this place and Welborn township, done nobly towards rendering our brave volunteers both contented and comfortable. Up here we are all for prosecution of the war to the bitter end. Crops good—health fine.

Your friend, A. GORDON.

Arkansas true Democrat
Sept 12, 1861, Page 2

RICHMOND, Sept. 14.

The Examiner has the following letter from the postmaster at Lewisburg. Gen. Floyd had another engagement on the 10th. The federals had 600 killed, 1,000 wounded, and we took some prisoners. The report is reliable and was brought to this place (Lewisburg) by an officer who was in the engagement. The confederate loss was 1 killed and 8 wounded.

The Van Buren Press
Sept 25, 1861, Page 2

The telegraph line from here to Fort Smith is completed to a point beyond Lewisburg, in Conway county; say 60 miles; one-third of the whole distance.

True Democrat
Thu, Jan 16, 1862 ·Page 2

FOUR ESTRAY HORSES.

STRAYED from the river bottom in Perry county, near Lewisburg, Conway county, four horses of the following description. A grey mare, 10 or 11 years old, 16 hands high, branded, it is with W on the shoulder, supposed to be with foal. She had a 2 years old colt with her—light bay, white face and 2 or 3 white feet, well grown. A bay mare, 14 hands high, 12 years old, though she looks to be no more than 6 or 7 years old, heavy with foal, when riding she gives down in her shoulders, branded on the shoulder with W, and a gray speckled mare mule, 17 years old, good work mule, paces under the saddle.

I will give a liberal reward for the delivery of the above stock to me near Lewisburg, Conway county, Ark., or for information so I can get them.

JONATHAN WELLS.

March 6, 18__. 4t Cost of adv. $5.

True Democrat
Thu, Mar 06, 1862 ·Page 2

The telegraph line was completed and in working order to Fort Smith, but as the main army has left that region of country, it has been or will be taken down to Clarksville and perhaps to Lewisburg, and the wire taken to build a line to Pocahontas. The Yankees, in their advance on the latter place, built a telegraph line as they advanced. It is to be hoped when Van Dorn and Price march on to St. Louis that they will capture some of these lines and give us communication with Missouri.

Arkansas true Democrat
April 10, 1862, Page 1

Election Returns.

	RECTOR.	FLANAGIN.	RAINEY.
Richland, Jefferson co..	12	27	
Russellville, Pope co. ..	10	99	
Princeton, Dallas co....	11	98	
Lewisburg, Conway co...	21	54	
Austin, Prairie co......	19	164	5
Benton, & another township, Saline co.......	61	140	
Rockport, Hot Spring co..	15	126	
Arkadelphia, Clark co...	14	338	3
Camden, Ouachita co....	143	42	116
Tulip, Dallas co..	7	78	
Brownsville, Prairie co..	5	115	12
Clarksville, Johnson co..	113	117	
Des Arc, Praire co......	130	471	
Pulaski co.............	213	510	15

Stillwell is probably elected senator from Pulaski and Prairie. In this county, Fletcher and Pennington are elected representatives; Walker, clerk; Giles, sheriff.

True Democrat
Oct 08, 1862, Page 1

Brig General
Marched from Lewisburg

Gen. Marmaduke's Report.

HEADQUARTERS, 4TH DIV., 1ST CORPS T. M. D.,
Batesville, Ark., Jan. 13th, 1863.

COLONEL:—

In obedience to instructions from Maj-Gen. Hindman, I marched from Lewisburg, Ark., Dec. 31st, 1862, via Yellville, Ark., to strike the enemy in "rear and flank," with 1,600 men under Shelby, and 270 men under McDonald. Before marching I telegraphed to Lt-Gen. Holmes if it would not be best to move up the troops under Col. White to co-operate in the movement, to which he consented, and the order was given. Col. Porter with 600 men moved forward for this purpose.

En route in the Boston Mountains, Shelby attacked 60 tories and deserters—killed 12—captured 27. McDonald surprised, captured and burned Fort Lawrence, on Beaver Creek, Mo.—of its garrison—killed 10, captured 17 and routed the rest, about 250—captured 200 horses, 300 stand of arms, 10 wagons and a quantity of quartermaster and commissary stores.

Shelby captured and burnt the Fort at Ozark. The garrison fled. With Shelby and McDonald I attacked Springfield, Mo., and after eight hours hard fighting, driving the Yankees before me and into their strong holds, I captured one piece of artillery, (6 pounder) a stockade fort, a large part of the town, which the Yankees burnt as they retired. At dark the fighting ceased—the greater part of the town, fort and many of the dead and wounded federals in my possession. The federal force there was 4,200. My loss was 20 killed and 80 wounded. Yankee's loss much greater. I did not deem it best to renew the attack, and the next day marched towards Rolla. The federals scattered and fled before me. I burnt the forts at Sand Springs and Marshfield. After passing through Marshfield formed a junction with Porter, who had burnt the forts at Hartsville and Hazlewood.

All the forts burnt were well built works, generally large "block houses," with stockade and good earth works around, so strong that 100 brave men well armed could defy 1,000 infantry or cavalry.

After joining Porter I marched south-easterly, making my way towards Arkansas. At Hartsville I met, fought and drove in the direction of Lebanon, 1,600 infantry, 500 cavalry, under Gen. Merrill. The battle was desperate. My loss was 15 killed and 70 wounded, of the former was the brave McDonald, Lt-Col. Weimer, Maj. Keitley, and other brave officers and men. The federal loss was also heavy. The enemy sent in a flag to bury their dead. At this place I captured a caisson with ammunition, a number of small arms, and about 150 great coats, which the Yankees left as they ran off.

I continued my march and reached here to-day, will to-morrow morning commence crossing White river at this place and 12 miles below.

Both men and horses are worn out and need rest.

I will forward a detailed report of the expedition at the earliest moment.

Respectfully,
J. S. MARMADUKE,
Brig. Gen'l Com'dg.

To Col. R. C. NEWTON,
Chief of Staff, 1st Corps T. M. Army.

True Democrat
Wed, Feb 04, 1863 ·Page 1

RIVER NEWS.

—o—

The river at this point, since our last issue has been about stationary, until Thursday night, when it commence to rise, and still continues rising slowly. There is full two feet of water on Van Buren bar.

The J. S. Hall arrived from Little Rock on Tuesday and left for the same point on Wednesday morning.

The Ozark is laying up at Lewisburg, and is heavily freighted, and will await a rise to come up. By a notice in our advertising columns, it will be seen that she will make a trip to Cincinnati on the first rise in the river. Persons wishing to order goods from Cincinnati, will take notice.

The Van Buren Press
Feb 10, 1866, Page 3

For Sale.

THE tract of land on which I reside, on the stage road, 5 miles east of Lewisburg, containing 500 acres, 300 good tilable upland; good dwelling; out houses; stables; two good wells of excellent water; peach orchard; grass lots, etc.— Also 1,000 acres unimproved bottom land on Point Remove, 5 miles north-east of Lewisburg, immediately above Col. Carroll's—also 320 acres upland unimproved near Col. Hardin's. I will give any one wishing to purchase **one** or all of the above tracts for cash, a bargain not to be repented of— also for rent 150 acres river bottom, 3 miles above Col. B. F. Howard's; corn and bacon furnished purchasers at market price.

Feb 25, 1863. 3w*   T. W. HERVEY.

True Democrat
Wed, Feb 25, 1863 ·Page 1

TRIBUTE OF RESPECT.—At a meeting of Lewisburg Lodge, No. 105, held on the 4th day of March, 1863. resolutions were adopted expressive of their regret at the death of brother THOMAS T. HENRY, who departed this life on the 28th of February, 1863.

True Democrat
Wed, Apr 15, 1863 ·Page 1

25 DOLLARS REWARD —Strayed from my residence on the 5th inst., a sorrel horse mule—said mule is about 12½ hands high, 9 or 10 years old, under teeth projects over the upper; had on when he left, a small bell, there was a brown mare mule left with him, that does not belong to me.

Any person delivering my mule to me at my residence, 2 miles north of Lewisburg, Ark., will receive the above reward.

LOUISA N. OWENS.

Lewisburg May 12th, 1863.   34—3t*

True Democrat
Wed, May 20, 1863 ·Page 2

$20 Reward.

STRAYED from my residence, 3 miles north-east of Lewisburg, Ark., a dark brown Mare, 3 years old, 14 hands high, left eye out, white spot in forehead, sore back. I will pay the above reward for her delivery at my residence.

Lewisburg, May 27, 1863 4w*   J. D. STOCKTON.

True Democrat
Wed, May 27, 1863 ·Page 2

☞ We are indebted to Mr. ANDERSON GORDON of Lewisburg for New Orleans papers of Monday evening the 26th ult. He passed up to his home yesterday from that city.

Weekly Arkansas Gazette
Sat, Apr 07, 1866 ·Page 1

Steamboat "J. S. Hall" and "American" Schedule at Lewisburg

Little Rock and Fort Smith PACKET COMPANY.

Regular Weekly Tuesday Packet,

For Van Buren and Ft. Smith, Steamer

J. S. HALL,

W. M. REASONER, *Captain.* | J. W. WILLIAMS, *Clerk.*

WILL LEAVE LITTLE ROCK EVERY TUESDAY, as long as Navigation will permit, and

Arrive at Portland, Wednesday,	5 A. M.		
do.	Lewisburg,	"	9 a. m.
do.	Gally Rock,	"	12 m.
do.	Dardanelle,	"	4 p. m.
do.	Spadra Bluff,	"	12 night.
do.	Roseville, Thursday,	6 a. m.	
do.	Ozark,	"	8 a. m.
do.	Van Buren,	"	8 p. m.
do.	Fort Smith, Friday,	6 a. m.	

Returning,

Will leave Fort Smith, Saturday,	6 a. m.		
do.	Van Buren,	"	8 a. m.
do.	Ozark,	"	1 p. m.
do.	Roseville,	"	2 p. m.
do.	Spadra,	"	4 p. m.
do.	Dardanelle, Sunday,	6 p. m.	
do.	Gally Rock,	"	8 a. m.
do.	Lewisburg,	"	10 a. m.
do.	Portland,	"	12 m.
Arrives at Little Rock,	"	5 p. m.	

Passengers and shippers will please take notice, that every Boat in this Line has the old style, safe and reliable Double or Two Flue Boilers. No others are now considered safe.

May 31, 1866. tf   W. H. FULTON, *Supt.*

Little Rock and Fort Smith PACKET COMPANY.

Regular Weekly Friday Packet,

For Van Buren and Ft. Smith, Steamer

AMERICAN,

W. B. NOWLAND, *Captain.* | LOU. BROWN, *Clerk.*

WILL LEAVE LITTLE ROCK EVERY FRIDAY, as long as navigation will permit, and

Arrive at Portland, Saturday,	5, a. m.		
do.	Lewisburg,	"	9, a. m.
do.	Gally Rock,	"	12, m.
do.	Dardanelle	"	4, p. m.
do.	Norristown,	"	4, p. m.
do.	Spadra Bluff,	"	12, night.
do.	Roseville, Sunday,	6, a. m.	
do.	Ozark,	"	8, a. m.
do.	Van Buren,	"	8, p. m.
do.	Fort Smith, Monday,	6, a. m.	

Returning,

Will leave Fort Smith,	Tuesday,	6, a. m.	
Arrive at Van Buren,	"	8, a. m.	
do	Ozark,	"	1, p. m.
do	Roseville,	"	2, p. m.
do	Spadra,	"	4, p. m.
do	Norristown, Wednesd'y	6, a. m.	
do	Dardanelle,	"	6, a. m.
do	Gally Rock,	"	8, a. m.
do	Lewisburg,	"	10, a. m.
Arrive at Little Rock,	"	5, p. m.	

Passengers and shippers will please take notice, that every Boat in this Line has the old style, safe and reliable, Double or Two Flued Boilers. No others are now considered safe.

A word to the wise is sufficient.

May 31, 1866. tf   W. H. FULTON, *Supt.*

Daily Arkansas Gazette
Fri, Jun 22, 1866 ·Page 3

RAILROAD SPEAKING.

We on last week published a list of appointments for Railroad meetings along the line of the Des Arc, Dardanelle and Fort Smith Railroad. The friends of the Road thinking that sufficient time was not given for them to gain publicity, have made a new list, which are as follows:

Hickory Plain, Monday, September 17th.

Austin, Tuesday, September 18th.

Peach Orchard Gap, Wednesday, Sept. 19th.

Green Grove, Friday, September 21st.

Lewisburg, Saturday, September 22d.

Springfield, Monday, September 24th.

Dardanelle, Wednesday, September 26th.

Dover, Friday, September, 28th.

Handbills will be printed and sent along the proposed route of the road as far as Dardanelle.

Des Arc Citizen
Sept 01, 1866, Page 3

Little Rock and Van Buren Stage Company.

THROUGH IN 44 HOURS.

O. TULLER & CO., Proprietors.

THE Proprietors of the above line have placed upon the road good passenger coaches, fine stock and careful and experienced drivers; and every means will be taken to secure the comfort of passengers. The Stages pass through the towns of *Ozark, Clarksville, Norristown and Lewisburg.*

Leave Van Buren, every Monday, Wednesday and Friday morning at 9 a m.

Arrive at Van Buren, Sundays, Wednesdays and Fridays, at 6 a m.

Stages connect at Van Buren, with the lines to Ft. Smith and Fayetteville, the same morning of their arrival without unnecessary delay.

oct. 4.'66   HIRAM BRODIE, Agent.

The Van Buren Press
Nov 23, 1866, Page 1

1867 Season Arrangement. **1867**

Little Rock and Fort Smith Packet Co.

Regular Weekly Tuesday Packet,
FOR
Van Buren and Fort Smith.

Steamer American.

E. B. NOWLAND,   J. W. MOORE,
Captain.   *Clerk.*

WILL leave Little Rock every Friday, as long as Navigation will permit, at 4 p. m. and

Arrive at Portland,	Saturday,	5 a. m.
do	Lewisburg,	"	9 " m.
do	Gally Rock,	"	12 m
do	Dardanelle,	"	4 p. m.
do	Norristown,	"	4 " m.
do	Spadra Bluff,	"	12 night.
do	Roseville,	Sunday,	6 a. m.
do	Ozark,	"	8 " m.
do	Van Buren,	"	9 p. m.
do	Fort Smith,	Monday,	6 a. m.

RETURNING.

Will leave Fort Smith,	Tuesday,	6 a. m.
do	Van Buren,	"	8 " m.
do	Ozark,	"	1 p. m.
do	Roseville,	"	2 " m.
do	Spadra,	"	4 " m.
do	Norristown,	Wednesday,	6 a. m.
do	Dardanelle,	"	6 " m.
do	Galley Rock,	"	8 " m.
do	Lewisburg,	"	10 " m.
Arrive at Little Rock,	"	5 p. m.

W. H. FULTON,
Superintendent.

C. G. SCOTT & CO., *Agents, Van Buren.*

march 29.

The Van Buren Press
March 29, 1867, Page 2

Railroad Meeting.

The Board of Directors of the Little Rock and Fort Smith Railroad Company met in this city on the 24th inst., and we learn as the result of their action, that a location of the road was ordered from Little Rock to Lewisburg, a distance of about fifty miles. As soon as the survey of this part of the road is completed, agents will proceed to New York for the purpose of contracting for the construction of twenty or fifty miles of the road, and negotiating for the necessary means.

We congratulate our readers and the people of Western Arkansas upon this action of the Board, and the hopeful prospects of the company, upon which depends in a great measure the prosperity of this whole valley. We now feel assured that a step has been taken in the right direction, and we hope the good work may go on to its early and triumphant completion. The projected consolidation with the Memphis and Little Rock road,

with the Memphis and Little Rock road, has in all probability received its quietus by the late sale of that road to the Memphis and El Paso company, an interest in direct antagonism to ours, or the Thirty-Fifth Parallel Route.

Resolutions were adopted to comply with the late act of Congress renewing the land grant, and accepting the late act of the General Assembly amending the charter of the company.

The Van Buren Press
April 26, 1867, Image 2

I shall locate at the beautiful and classic town of Lewisburg, in this state Here, I believe, we may have good reason to hope that the "beautifully undulating" face of nature will not be disturbed in our natural life time.

Weekly Arkansas Gazette
Tue, Jul 30, 1867 ·Page 3

Excerpt from State Mineral Report

We passed Lewisburg July 30th, and there camped under a pile of lumber pitched tent-wise. In this county we got into the sub carboniferous and the twists and contortions of the mill stone grit notified us that we were approaching the region of trappe rocks, silicious and quartzoze sandstone, slate, granite and novaculite. The range of ridges from above Palarm to this city and beyond into several counties south side the river, are full of quartz, and are undoubtedly more or less metaliferous.

Daily Arkansas Gazette
Sun, Aug 11, 1867 ·Page 2

Tribute of Respect.

At a special meeting of the Lewisburg Lodge No. 105, A. F. and A. Masons, held at their lodge room in the town of Lewisburg, Arks., on the 10th day of Nov. A. D. 1867, the following preamble and resolutions were adopted:

Whereas, It has pleased the Almighty Grand Master of the Universe to remove from the scene of his earthly labors our esteemed friend and brother, Milage A. Hargis; therefore,

Be it Resolved; That whilst we bow in humble submission to this inscrutable decree of Divine Providence, by the death of this, our beloved brother, cut down by the all devouring scythe of Time, in the strength of manhood, and when the craft might well have expected many long years of pleasant intercourse with him and valuable assistance from his co-labors here on earth, this Lodge and the Fraternity at large has sustained a most severe loss; the community has been deprived of a valuable and honorable member, and in the circle of his relatives and friends a breach has been made that is irreparable.

Resolved, That we recognize in this afflictive dispensation the warning so often repeated, "Be ye also ready!"

Resolved, That the members of this Lodge wear the usual badge of mourning for thirty days.

Resolved, That a copy of these resolutions be sent to the family of Bro. Jas. M. Moose, the nearest relatives of our deceased brother in this country, and that a copy be furnished the Weekly Arkansas *Gazette* for publication.

W. A. C. SAYLE,
R. T. MARKHAM, } Committee.
T. H. BAUM.

Daily Arkansas Gazette
Sun, Nov 17, 1867 ·Page 2

Lewisburg's "White Man's Club"
opposes newly proposed Arkansas constitution

THE CANVASS

Cols. Williams and Clark have addressed good audiences in the counties west, although but short notice of their appointments was given.

A correspondent writing from Lewisburg, Conway county, under date of the 12th inst says, these gentlemen spoke there that day to a very large audience; among those present were many ladies. They presented the negro supremacy features of the constitution, and referred to the infamous test oath by which every decent white man in the state is disfranchised; and exposed the system of office holding that it proposes to establish, the indefinite delegation of powers to their future legislatures to indefinitely ___ere-ate more, and the system of enormous taxation inaugurated under the pretext of free _______, etc. Their exposition of the loose and indefinite provisions in reference to the judiciary department, was satisfactory and quite to the point. They showed that the constitution delegates unlimited power of multiplication of courts to the legislatures.   While it creates a circuit court it makes no provision for a county or probate court or any court with similar jurisdiction; and we would have under this constitution a circuit court without any defined jurisdiction whatever, and our probate and county courts are wiped out until a legislature chooses to create them or define their jurisdiction. It is true it provides that inferior courts shall exercise the same jurisdiction they now do by existing laws, but be it remembered that there is no laws creating or giving jurisdiction to any court,   save only the court of chancery by virtue of the delegated powers in the constitution; and courts must be created to provided for and the jurisdiction defined by the constitution only. We have laws governing the proceedings in inferior courts under the present constitution, but not a line or syllable of law giving or defining the jurisdiction of any inferior court, except justices and the chancery court. If this constitution is ratified, at one fell swoop we wipe out the jurisdiction of all inferior courts, for two of them are not provided for and the other has no defined jurisdiction.

After the speaking was concluded some sixty persons enrolled their names in the white man's club. The county will beyond doubt roll up a good majority against the constitution. Very many persons who voted for the convention, have announced their intention to vote against the constitution.

transcribed from
Weekly Arkansas Gazette
Tue, Feb 25, 1868 ·Page 2

RIVER NEWS.

During the greater part of yesterday we had undoubted March weather. In the early part of the day particularly, the wind blew a gale from the southwest, and the clouds of dust raised were blinding. At noon a slight rain fell which was very serviceable in laying the dust. The sky was cloudy and threatening throughout the day.

The American arrived from below Lewisburg, on Thursday evening, with 303 bales of cotton. She was posted to leave for below yesterday, having been detained here by high wind. The Fort Smith also arrived late on Thursday evening, from Dardanelle. She brought out 516 bales of cotton, making the quickest and biggest trip of the season. She reports the river as having risen $1\frac{3}{4}$ inches at Dardanelle; and also says the late swell here was out of Fourche le Fevre and is about exhausted. She left the Van Buren aground at Vann's bar below Lewisburg, with 350 bales of cotton on board. The Fort Smith was posted to return to Dardanelle last evening.

The river still continues on a stand with two feet out to Pine Bluff.

Daily Arkansas Gazette
Sat, Mar 07, 1868 ·Page 3

Col. F. W. Schaurtie U. S. Mail Agent, arrived here on the steamer *Ozark*, he brought a half-dozen mails, found at Lewisburg, destined for this section of the country, which had been detained at that point by high water. The government have we think selected a vigilant and efficient Mail Agent in Col. Schaurtie.

The Van Buren Press
March 27, 1868, Page 2

DR. CAYCE'S CHILL REMEDY.

Editors Gazette—I see you advertise in your paper a chill remedy known as Dr. Cayce's Chill and Fever Remedy. This medicine has been sold in our place (Lewisburg) for sometime, and I have never heard of a single case that it has failed to cure; therefore, I can cheerfully recommend it to the public.

R. T. MARKHAM,
apr21dwtf   Sheriff of Conway co., Ark

Weekly Arkansas Gazette
Tue, Apr 28, 1868 ·Page 3

DISSOLUTION OF COPARTNERSHIP.

Notice is hereby given, That the firm of Baum, Breeden & Adams, heretofore doing a mercantile business at Lewisburg, Conway county, Arkansas, was dissolved on the 2d day of April, 1868, by mutual consent.

The business will hereafter be conducted by F. H. Baum and John Breeden, under the firm name of Baum & Breeden, successors to the old firm. All parties having claims against the dissolved firm are notified to present them at once to Baum & Breeden, and all those indebted to the same will settle with the new firm.

F. H. BAUM,
JOHN BREEDEN,
apr21d1m   E. W ADAMS.

Daily Arkansas Gazette
Wed, May 13, 1868 ·Page 1

Steamboats "Cora S."
at Lewisburg Landing

RIVER NEWS

The river has risen six inches in the last forty-eight hours, and is now at a stand. We have heard of no rains in this neighborhood, and are at a loss to account for the rise.

The weather continues dry and hot with clouds of dust impregnating the atmosphere, and rendering out door work intolerable.

ARRIVED.—The Fort Smith came in late yesterday from above; left M. Burns at Fort Smith; met the American at Frog Bayou and Cora S. at Lewisburg. River falling with scant three feet water above. The American will be here to-day. The Fort Smith will need a few days' docking, when she will be again ready for service,

ARRIVED.—The Fort Smith came in late yesterday from above; left M. Burns at Fort Smith; met the American at Frog Bayou and Cora S. at Lewisburg. River falling with scant three feet water above. The American will be here to-day. The Fort Smith will need a few days' docking, when she will be again ready for service,

Daily Arkansas Gazette
Tue, Jun 16, 1868 ·Page 3

Anderson Gordon
Sells 51 Subscriptions
to the Arkansas Gazette

THANKS.—We are indebted to Col. Anderson Gordon, of Lewisburg, Conway county, for a club of fifty-one subscribers to our weekly during the presidential campaign. We return our sincere thanks to the Colonel for this evidence of the appreciation of the good people of his county of the principles advocated by the GAZETTE, and hope others may emulate the good example of our Conway friends. As yet Conway stands in the front on our campaign list.

Weekly Arkansas Gazette
Tue, Jun 30, 1868 ·Page 3

At Lewisburg, Conway county, on the 27th day of June, A. D., 1868, JULIA, infant daughter of Col. and Mrs. N. B. Burrow, aged about three years.

Another household has been saddened. A few days ago the prattling lips and laughing eyes of the little Julia made glad the hearts of a kind father and an affectionate mother. Those lips have now ceased to move, and those eyes are dull and sightless. The cold and unfriendy grave hides all that was earthly of the sweet little babe; but her gentle spirit, released from its prison here, has winged its way to eternal rest. The cup of life contains at best a bitter draught—murmur not then that God in His mercy and kindness has willed that she should not drink too deeply of its potion. It is well.

R.

Daily Arkansas Gazette
Thu, Jul 09, 1868 ·Page 2

Riot
In Conway County
RIOT IN CONWAY COUNTY.

We learn through a reliable gentleman of Pope county, a gentleman of the highest respectability, that the most serious excitement prevails among the inhabitants of Lewisburg, in Conway county, and vicinity, occasioned by the threatening attitude assumed by the radical negroes of that section, incited by the white scoundrels, who seem careless of life or the peace of the community, if the success of their party can be achieved. It seems that the negroes of Conway are divided in sentiment politically, and that the most bitter and proscriptive sentiments are entertained by each of the opposing factions for the other. Report says that some ten days ago, three radical negroes called at the house of a democratic negro in the night time and called him out. While the latter was putting on his clothes to comply with the request, the dog barked and was immediately dispatched by a gun shot. Knowing from this what was intended, the occupant of the house kept in-doors, and those without fearing to enter, finally dispersed. A day or two later, the miscreants were brought to trial at Lewisburg, but in making up the jury of colored men, the radical negroes refused to sit with a conservative negro who was selected, whereupon a dispute arose, weapons were exhibited and the court was broken up. Fearing trouble, some of the prominent citizens of that place, among whom Dr. "Adams, Anderson Gordon, Esq., and others were prominent, disarmed the negroes, telling them to go home quietly and remain so, and their arms would be returned to them. Otherwise not. The negroes then retired, but provided themselves with more arms and collected in numbers a few miles east of Lewisburg. The citizens of that place, feeling insecure from known facts, and from reports constantly coming in, sent out Mr. Thomas Burchfield, and Mr. George Bently, to ascertain the extent of the occasion of alarm, and if possible, to induce the parties who had assumed the hostile attitude to desist from the execution of their threats. Meanwhile some two or three hundred persons had assembled at Lewisburg to defend the place if necessary. Burchfield and Bently left on their mission of peace at an early hour on the 25th, but when some three or four miles east of Lewisburg, on the Little Rock road, they were suddenly fired upon by a party of nineteen negroes, the volley wounding Burchfield, it is said by his physicians, mortally, and killing Bently's horse. Both of these gentlemen are old and reliable citizens of Conway county, and undertook the mission for the single purpose of bringing about a cessation of hostilities and to preserve the peace. Burchfield is a one-armed man and entirely inoffensive.—When the report of this occurrence reached Lewisburg, Dr. Menifee, and Messrs. Green and

Lewisburg, Dr. Menifee, and Messrs. Green and Hervey went out to take care of the wounded man and to see if anything further could be done to avert a collision. These gentleman met the negroes together and told them if they would desist from further carrying out their threats, they would pass over what had occurred, and they should go unharmed. All agreed to do so but three, who were sullen and reticent. During the conversation it was elicited. that the negroes had been told on what they affirmed to be good authority, that the white men of the county were about to take away their property and kill and drive them from the country. Dr. Adams was sent for and came to the spot and endeavored to disabuse them of the idea. They had sent for Hinkle (a prominent and unscrupulous radical) and other preparations were making to resist the reported outrages about to be committed upon them. After the last named gentleman had returned to Lewisburg, the report came variously corroborated, that all had refused to retire, and that reinforcemeets were expected from all parts of the country. So the matter stands—two or three hundred white men and friendly negroes at Lewisburg, all armed and reinforcements coming, and an indefinite number of white and black radicals in unknown places with reinforcements coming. What will come of it we do not know. We hope nothing more serious than a point gained in the coming state and national elections, for which the whole thing was gotten up.

Gibbons, the radical representotiev from that county, Hinkle, a prominent so-called union man, and others are the reputed instigators.

It is reported that Clayton is about to send up his mililia. If so we hope they will not go as reinforcements to the radical recruits..

In this connection we cannot forbear saying in all truth and candor, that the way out of this trouble is not through the sending of an armed negro militia into Conway county. Any, the slightest outrage committed by such a force will most likely be followed by terrible results. If Gen. Clayton thinks the interposition of an armed force is necessary, and is seriously desirous of preserving the peace let him call in the aid of the United States troops, and the people of Arkansas will continue, as they have done heretofore to yield implicit obedience to its authority. But the teachings of the union leagues, and the manner of its organization under cover of darkness has so roused the passions of his black militia that it is impossible that their presence in the vicinity of the troubles could do aught else but precipitate a conflict.

We also have it on the authority of our informant that Dr. Adams, Anderson Gordon and Eugene Henry have received a joint letter informing them jointly that they cannot be permitted to remain in the county. These gentlemen are all old citizens of that place, and reliable, responsible men. If these reports are true,

ble, responsible men. If these reports are true, and we are well assured they are, excepting unintentional inaccuracies that in haste may have crept in—and if this sort of proceeding is to be backed up by the radical authorities, there is little doubt that the 100,000 white men of the state and the better class of negroes who may cast their fortunes with such, may be compelled to find a more speedy way out of this political thralldom than any yet suggested, and in which test oaths will not be necessary.

Daily Arkansas Gazette
Fri, Aug 28, 1868 ·Page 3

Steamboat "Harper"
Departed With Governor Aboard
for Lewisburg &
River Level Report,
Weather & War "Joke"

RIVER NEWS.

The river is still falling opposite this place, and since our last issue has gone down seven or eight inches. There is now but thirty inches in the channel to Fort Smith, and four and a half feet to Napoleon.

The weather yesterday was hot and sultry.— The heat came down in flakes, and not a breath of air came to the relief of the sweltering people. The war excitement made things fiz. We inquired for the *seat* of war, and all we coul learn about it was that Mrs. Smith had assaulted her truant son in the rear. Dats all vat we knows bout de vight.

Departed.—The steamer Hesper departed yesterday for Lewisburg with an excursion party, gotten up under the auspices of the governor, without respect to color or previous condition. We hope they will keep virtuous and enjoy themselves.

Daily Arkansas Gazette
Sat, Aug 29, 1868 ·Page 3

Governor In Lewisburg
to Quell War in Lewisburg

THE WAR IN CONWAY.

The Governor Visits that Locality Accompanied by a Deputation of Prominent Citizens of Little Rock.

How they were received---The Facts.

The Hesper backed out from the foot of Main street on Friday last, at 5 o'clock, freighted with dignity, patriotism, ice, muskets, and champagne, to look after the reported disturbances in Conway county. Just at the hour of starting, as before stated, Clayton very wisely concluded to leave the "colored troops' behind, and take with him some of the old citizens of Little Rock. Messrs. S. H. Tucker, S. L. Griffith, S. C Faulkner, C. G. Scott, A. H. Garland and W. D. Blocher accepted an invitation extended for that purpose, and accompanied the expedition. Nothing worthy of note transpired during the trip, which was accomplished by 9 o'clock on the following morning. On arriving, the heights at Lewisburg were as quiet as in the palmiest of the peaceful days gone by, not a bayonet bristling and not so much as a single war-horse neighing—unless it might have been Clayton's Bucephalus who was hitched to the bow of the Hesper, and who had grown restless from the trip. The citizens were all engaged in their wonted avocations, and we could find nothing to remind us of the reign of terror that was reported to exist there. The reception of the parties was kind and hospitable, pleasant words of greeting were exchanged, and the hospitalities of the place were extended to the guests. The morning hours were consumed in receiving statements of the causes and circumstances attending the late troubles, which were really serious, and might have involved the whole country in anarchy. Our reporter was on the ground, and we give the substance of the intelligence gleaned by diligent inquiry. It seems that some time ago two negroes killed a dog belonging to a third. Whether it was from jealousy growing out of mutual admiration for a lady of color, and which finally resulted in the utter defeat of the white man Thompson, does not fully appear since it was not deemed necessary to call Nancy to the stand, but certain it was that this Thompson, when he came to represent the peace and dignity of the state in the capacity of state's attorney, manifested an over zeal to bring the black boy Toney to justice for killing the dog. The trial came off on the 15th, Col. Anderson Gordon appearing in the forum for the first time in defence of an old servant and a very worthy colored man. The jury acquitted the accused, but the wiley Thompson found means through some trifling technicality, to secure a re-hearing of the cause which commenced on the 21st. The trial not having been concluded on that day it was adjourned over to the morning of the next, at which time, by direction of this Thompson, a large number of negroes from the surrounding country appeared in town armed with shot-guns and pistols. The determination of the court was as before, and the accused was acquitted. But the diverse political preferences existing among the ne-

litical preferences existing among the negroes led to high words over matters connected with the trial, and the citizens fearing disturbance, disarmed three of the worst characters among the negroes, telling them to go home quietly and remain so, and their arms should be returned to them. On the night of that day some mischievous boys or young men went out a short distance from town and unwarrantably disarmed three more negroes. On Monday (24th) reports came in that the negroes had held a meeting on the day previous and that they had resolved to exterminate the white people of Lewisburg from the cradle up. This created great alarm, and by 10 o'clock on Tuesday armed white men had collected at Lewisburg to the number of 100 or more. Before day on the same night, nine young men were sent out to ascertain the proximity and extent of danger, and were fired on by seventeen negroes from the roadside at a distance of about 15 feet. This occurred some two or three miles east from the town on the Little Rock road. The volley, so sudden and unexpected, threw the party into disorder and those not placed *hors du combat* made all haste back to Lewisburg without particular reference to order of march. On arriving, two of the number were found missing, and their horses having been seen to fall, they were supposed to have been killed, while a third—a Mr. Burchfield—was wounded. The excitement, as may well be imagined, became intense, and it was with difficulty that a few of the more prudent citizens of the county restrained the indignant people from going out at once and visiting a just punishment on those in arms. But a few hours later the missing men came in and a party consisting of Dr. Adams, R. B. Griffin, Col. Eagan, Capt Gill (the last two late of the federal army) and two negroes were sent out to confer with the beligerant parties, and induce them, if possible to lay down their arms. It was with some difficulty that a hearing was secured, but it was finally effected without accident, and the negroes, on being informed that if they would cease hostilities and go home, the matter would be dropped, agreed to do so reluctantly; but it was not accomplished until the 27th, until which time the citizens' remained in arms at Lewisburg, and much excitement prevailed. All this trouble arose from evilly disposed white radicals, who have nothing to lose, but everything to gain in the way of plunder, and whose political prospects and the success of the party, it was thought, would be greatly enhanced by a bloody riot. Fortunately, the people of Conway had taken the matter into their own hands and quieted the disturbance so that when our expedition arrived the country was as peaceful as nothing had occurred. They did right. It certainly would be very silly to sit down under such circumstances and wait for protection to come from the capital; and the vast prepara-

come from the capital ; and the vast prepara
tions made here, under what would seem th
impression that the conservative people of th
county were either doing so, or waging a pit
less war on negroes, based, as the reports wer
on information received from the instigato
themselves, are absurd and unreasonable
say the least of them.

On Saturday evening the citizens collected
the Masonic hall and Gen. Clayton made the
a speech, wherein he counseled peace, and to
the people they should have a fair registratio
and that if they desired to change the gover
ment or laws they always had the right to do
through the ballot box. His remarks were we
received. Hon. A. H. Garland also addressed th
assemblage in his usual happy manner. W
will publish these speeches in full in our ne
issue. The trip was a very pleasant one ar
greatly enjoyed by all parties. Capt. Housto
and the officers of the Hesper were very poli
and earned the good will of all on board.

Daily Arkansas Gazette
Tue, Sep 01, 1868 ·Page 2

Arrived—The steamer Hesper with the governor, a delegation of citizens and a guard of
thirty men, traversed the windings of the Arkansas from here to Lewisburg and then came
back again—and there was nobody hurt ; ex-
hibiting to the satisfaction of all that peace
reigned within the realm, thus enacting a farce
in which there was nobody killed or married.

Daily Arkansas Gazette
Wed, Sep 02, 1868 ·Page 3

Ifs and Whys
of Conway County War

IFS AND WHYS

If Clayton Bucephalus is not a was horse, what makes
him have a silver main and tail, and why did Clayton
take him to the seat of war on the steamer Harper?
*[Note: Bucephalus, was is the name of Alexander the
Great's horse.]*

If the "colored troops" will do to bet on, why should
Clayton cover them up with tarpaulins!

If Clayton's "colored troops" will not do to bet on,
why should Clayton not be permitted to cover them up
in tarpaulins in he chooses to?

If the radicals want a war in Conway county for political purposes, why is it not constitutional under the
reconstruction laws?

If Clayton wanted to make an attack on Conway
by land and sea, why did not the land forces move up

promptly?

If Clayton desires to preserve the public peace and
tranquility, why does he not call out his black militia and
engage a flotilla for the season?

If Clayton wans champagne and ice at state expense
during war times, why does he not buy it with the con-
tengent fund?

If the radicals have failed in getting up a war in Conway county, why should they not get one up elsewhere?

If the governor-general proposes to preserve the
peace of this country and protect the innocent, why does
he not arrest the man who made the cowardly assault on
George Robinson?

If Hinds can go about the country with lying tongue
and stir up the worst passions of the negroes against the
whites with impunity, it there any offence against the
law, in the catalogue of offenses against the law, that
Hinds or any other radical may not commit with impunity?

If Clayton wants to meet out justice to the people of
Arkansas during the term of his regency, why does he
not do it?

If a man wants to be a man, why does he not be a
man?

THE CONWAY WAR

We promised, yesterday, to present our readers, this
morning, with the speeches of the governor general and
Col. Garland, at Lewisburg, during the recent raid of the
former into Conway county to suppress the little rebellion reported to be in progress there. Here they are:

SPEECH OF GEN. CLAYTON

Fellow Citizens: I have not come here in any partisan spirit, to stir up strive or add fuel to the flames of
discord which have threatened your country with such
disastrous results; my mission is a peaceful one. I am
here under the obligations of my office, to see that the
laws are respected and enforced, and that all persons
who may be acting without authority of law, desist and
return peacefully to their homes.

It is not my present purpose to fix the responsibility
of the outrages which have disgraced your county upon
the guilty parties; this is properly for the courts to determine. I am here to turn aside, peacefully if I can, the
disastrous results which mush overtake the people if
they permit such illegal and unauthorized proceedings
to continue, as have taken place in your midst within the
past few days. What little I have to say I shall say plainly.
I shall not cover up my meaning with honed words. I
desire you to know the attitude I occupy toward you in
my official capacity, and to impress upon your minds the
necessity of an obedience to the laws as they now exist
–– and not as some of you would have them be. I had
information that your county was in a state of insurrection.

– 84 –

It seems that a few days ago such was the case. I am rejoiced to find that better counsels have at last prevailed. I am sure that if the people properly understood the motives and intentions of the state authorities, no further trouble would exist. I am unwilling to believe that there is any considerable number of citizens who are disposed to set the laws at naught and engage in armed hostility to the state government. I trust that this outbreak can be traced to a few evil disposed and irresponsible persons, and that the great mass who have been engaged in it have been lead through misapprehension to do that which a little cool reflection would have prevented. It seems that during the excitement, brought on by a few individuals, a very erroneous opinion was entertained that the colored people contemplated violence against whites. Without investigating the facts, unauthorized persons proceeded to disarm the blacks, which at once led them to believe that the whites were disposed to commit outrages upon them. **I do not believe that the white people of this county are disposed to kill off the colored people; neither do I believe that the colored people, ever for one moment, contemplated the massacre of the whites.**

The history of the late war shows that the black man is not naturally bloodthirsty or revengeful; for did he not remain with and protect your families while you were fighting the battles of rebellion?

You would have had no trouble if instead of taking the law into your own hands, you had called upon the sheriff of the county for protection; when you thought that the negroes were organizing to attack you. He could have gone clothed with the authority of the law, and the truth would at once been made manifest, and all cause of trouble have been removed. –– Now I say to all, white and black, if you at any time apprehend danger, invoke the aid of the civil authorities. Look to them for protection –– you pay them to perform that duty. It will not do for us to interpret the laws to suit ourselves, or to assume the authority of their execution.

Such a course would lead to insurrection, and perhaps to civil war. We must accept the laws as they are, and not as we might wish them to be. A court of justice has been broken up by a mob, and one class have been disarmed by another. This is all wrong, illegal, and insurrectionary. That court must be reinstated, and allowed to proceed. The right of the citizen to keep arms is a constitutional right, –– one that no citizen can be legally deprived of. The arms that have been illegally taken from the colored men must be returned to them. I have the assurance that it will be done. When you, my colored citizens, receive your arms again, use them as good citizens should. To white and black I say that armed assemblies are illegal; therefore, when you assemble, for any purpose, do so peacefully and unarmed. If there is any person in this audience, who does not recognize the fact that the colored man possesses the same rights and

privileges, and immunities, civil and political, that the white man possesses; let him pause and reflect, for I say to him that such is the case –– and the colored citizen shall be protected in these rights.

I am informed that it has been charged that you are not to have a fair registration, and that this has caused much bad feeling. Now, let me say a few words in regard to registration. You shall have a fair registration, and a fair election, too. When I say this, I mean just what I say. Let no one misunderstand me –– the registration laws shall be enforced. So far as my authority goes, every man, who is entitled to register, under the law, shall be permitted to do so; and those who are disqualified, shall not. It is not for me to say who can register, or who cannnot; the law fixes the qualification of electors. I have no authority to interpret it to suit myself; neither have you. When the day of election arrives, every citizen, who is registered, can vote in accordance with his own judgment. –– Those who are not registered; cannot vote.

I understand that the militia law is distasteful to some. I have only to say that it is a law that will be enforced.

The militia force will be organized in this county, and throughout the state. The organization of the militia does not inaugurate a new principle of government. It is as old as the constitution itself. Every state has its militia, I am inclined to think that you do not understand this law. It is to preserve the peace, and is only to be used when the civil authorities are unable to enforce the law. To all good citizens, who are willing to obey the laws, the militia need give no alarm, but rather give assurance of safety. If there be any who intend to resist the execution of the law, they may well object to the militia. But I say to all, that so long as the civil officers can enforce the law there will be no armed force called into the service.

And how, in conclusion, I am for peace, and will in exhaust all peaceful remedies to preserve and execute the laws. When peaceful remedies fail, then I shall resort to force, – but this must be the aim.

Let us have peace. Have we not suffered enough from war? We are just now recovering from its terrible effects. Providence has helped us with abundant crops – the lap of nature is full – her face is smiling – she invites us to stretch forth our hands and enjoy her rich gifts. Let us turn our whole attention to peaceful pursuits. Let us gather all we have sown and built up our broken fortunes, and not, by reason of our political differences, plunge headlong into rebellion. For rest assured, that if we sow the wind, we may expect to reap the whirlwind. If the American people make political mistakes they will rest by them. Trust to peaceful remedies. Violent measures will accomplish nothing but ruin and desolation.

I have brought with me Col. Garland and other prominent citizens of Little Rock, of both political parties. The Colonel and myself disagree upon the political issues of the day, but I am happy to say, that upon the questions of peace and the observance of the laws as they exist, we both stand upon the same platform. He will address you. I thank you for your attention.

SPEECH OF HON. A. H. GARLAND
Fellow Citizens of Conway County:

Although I have been a citizen of Arkansas for thirty-five years – nearly all my life – and I have lived near your county for years, and I have addressed people in most of the counties of this state, yet, for the first time, I have the honor and pleasure of appearing before an audience in this county. And why is it now, as this time, and in so unexpected a manner, I am here?

Governor Clayton, who has just addressed you, has, in a great measure, explained why I am to speak to you. I will add some little to that explanation. A few days since we heard at Little Rock most startling accounts from this place: and from what we heard, we might have believed that you were killing and being killed here at most wonderful rates. Knowing of course – whether these reports were true in all their length and breadth or not – there was trouble here and that every high and worthy consideration required it should not continue, Governor Clayton, in devising means to reach the difficulty, and to quite matters, requested a number of citizens of Little Rock to accompany him here for the purpose of restoring order and quite, if there was disorder existing. With him and his friends, we have come to advise and counsel with you; and, as Governor Clayton says, his mission is one of peace; I say, from our hearts, so is ours. With him and his friends, I and old citizens of the state come to talk with you. We bring with us the veritable Arkansas Traveller himself (Col. Faulkner) who "has traveled this country all over" for years, unharmed and unmolested; also, Mr. Tucker, Mr. Griffith, Mr. Scott, and Mr. Blocher of the *Gazette*, who sits side by side with Mr. Price, of the *Republican*, taking notes to print them.

Now all these men have the greatest and highest interests here and their welfare is yours.

Though a stranger to you, yet I am not altogether unknown to you; for in days gone by, I have been honored by the people of our state with positions of trust, and for this reason my friends alluded to, thought my voice might weight something with you. It is true I am of you and one of you, and, as said before, I have been here nearly all my life, and if I could have had my way about it, I would have been born here; but I was not consulted or asked about this, to me, a very important matter.

Well, we got together and came here, we had a pleasant time. The Governor and his friends and ourselves drank together; and the Arkansas water not being healthy, we mingled some spirits with it merely for health; that all tasted well; we ate together, and slept all around on the boat in a miscellaneous pile together and reached here this morning, and "nobody hurt." I see all hands of us are gladly received and welcomed, and all is peace and quite here –– everything looks as calm as a May morning; and, really, I have been ashamed to tell

persons why I came, and would not have done so, but I was fearful they might think I was here to stir up law suits and litigation, which is about as ungrateful business as getting up riots.

I know very well that our wives are at this moment alarmed about us, and are well supplied with camphor and harishorn, to break the force of any ugly report they may hear of things here, and we are preparing bandages for our wounds when we shall reach home all mangled and torn. Now, my wife, who, by the way, thinks much of me, and is one of the best friends I ever had in my life, was astonished that I should come off up here with no arms except my walking stick, which I always carry to support me in my premature old age, brought on by early piety. And, as Governor Clayton says, he is here without arms, so am I, and so are all my friends; and I hope we all feel at home here. I do, just as much as if I had lived on this old red hill all my life.

In all that Governor Clayton has said, I fully and heartily concur. Before this meeting assembled, he approached me and stated what he expected to say, and requested me to speak, too. I replied that I agreed with him in what he said, and I would take pleasure in speaking if such were his views; and I am very glad to be able to say to you, that he has here spoken what he expressed to me, and I do not believe there is, in our state, a man that would not agree in all he has spoken.

With him, I say, exhaust all your peaceful and peaceable remedies first, and he has promised you here as the executive of the state that you shall be heard, and you shall be righted. –– It is, then, your duty to take him at his word, and not in advance determine he will not comply. He has said all of you, regardless of race or color, or party, shall be protected –– this is all you can ask. He has said boldly and frankly, that, as far as in him lies, you shall have a fair and impartial registration; and this, my fellow-citizens, is the great matter now. There is pending a presidential contest before this country, in which the life of the government and the liberties of the people are involved. –– No one can over-estimate its importance, and we want a fair and open field here, and do nothing, for Heaven's sake, to cripple your friends in this mighty struggle. Be patient, cautious and prudent, and see what the third day of next November shall bring forth. That day may bring you all you want –– and it may do otherwise; but if you are allowed your rights, as they are now promised to you here, and you lose, you must submit as men and patriots. If your rights are denied you, and the law will not or cannot give them to you, through its agencies you still have your right to appeal to force, which law does not give and which law cannot take away. You have that right, that last right which Governor Clayton and his friends cannot deny you' and if they did, the denial would be futile. That right is settled by your ability to maintain it, and out of that right was born all the liberty this country enjoys. Washington, failing in our revolution, would have been as our noble

Lee is, but he succeeded, and he was almost deified the world over. And I undertake here to say to you, on this very delicate occasion, if you are wise, and watchful of your rights, and will exhaust those remedies that the law gives, and you fail, and you are oppressed and ground down, your appeal to force will not be in vain; but it will be successful, and at that point, I should be prepared and ready to take my full share of the risk, responsibility and danger, but till you have gone that far, I cannot encourage it –– I cannot be with you.

Now, I shall deceive no man –– look to this matter steadily in the face; it involves all to you and myself, and to us all. Do not be alarmed at shadows; do not quarrel for trifles –– overlook many things but claim and assert your rights; you are promised by the executive you shall have them as far as he can give them. I believe he means all he says. Test it thoroughly –– then if it fails your duty is plain and well defined.

But riots and insurractions will not secure you any good. They always defeat the very end in view –– it is but another mode for suicide. They are easily begun, but it is difficult to quell them; and, I tell you, it is rare that those who begin them ever suffer; but the innocent and unoffending do suffer. I have witnessed two in my life, and they are the most terrible displays of force that we know of; storms, whirlwinds and the ____ of nature are trifles, compared with those popular outbreaks. They are the most dangerous agencies every employed by man. From momentary excitement, or from misguided judgment, these things are inaugurated – small and almost trifling in the beginning, may be somewhat ___ but they know and ____ until they become fearful, sad, and hear__ing; somewhat li__ those w__, I am told, get on sprees –– it is the funniest thing in the world to get don one, but to get off they ____________ trying ordeal.

All noble achievements of reason and intellect and civilization over force and animal nature, and over barbarism, have been won by the exercise of a cool and calm reflection; first, then if it must be, call on force to accomplish what reason and reflection cannot do. And I have confidence my friends, in the _____ __ ___, that they will do right. They may go here and there, and commit wrong after wrong for a while, but after all, I believe they will see the right, and march up squarely and fairly to it. I do not believe they intend for it even anarchy or despotism to dwell in this land of ours.

The government here in our state, be it good, bad, or indifferent, it is the government that controls us, and under which we live, and we must obey its mandates until we are relieved of it. In that we all agree. It is idle, and indeed it is madness bordering on insanity, for us to take law and vengeance in our hands, simply because our government does not suit us or the officers are not of our selection. Out of all my votes yet given, I never cast one for a man who was elected president, for no one who was ever elected to congress, and never voted for but one person elected governor of Arkansas; and indeed until I moved to Pulaski county, I never voted for one elected to our legislature. I have objected greatly to many laws under which I have lived, but for all this, it was not right or just that I should get up trouble, fight somebody, whip some one or get whipped. It will not do for us, as they say about horses, "to slip the bit and jump the fence." As long as we say vote, let us do it, and make the victory one of peace if possible. The teachings of law, morals and Christianity all say this, any other course brings no government but anarchy, and the world is agreed that the meanest government is better than no government.

Look for one moment, we are just out of a most sanguinary war, our people are impoverished –– around and about us, we are blessed with every advantage we can imagine, that nature can bestow, and our fields are promising an abundant harvest this fall. A collision now would scatter these prospects to the wind and we would then enter into a contest of desolation, if not annihilation itself. There is no necessity or occasion for ill-feeling between the negro and the white man. Their lots are cast together, and they are necessities here, one to the other. Therefore I say to our white friends, deal fairly and generously with the negro; and to the negro, work according to your contracts, and deal in all things with us openly and without suspicion, and all will be well here yet. Do not let bad and ignorant men, be they who they may, ____ with your engagements and understandings, one with the other. You and all of us have too much at stake to throw it away on a mere question or matter of neighborhood difference, or temporary excitement. Great questions are before us upon us, reaching far above and beyond, whether a carpet-bagger, saddle-bagger, or any other bagger shall rule or govern. And I desire you to know and understand these questions, and I have spoken to you plainly that you may not misunderstand me.

I am glad that the governor has come here, and I say to him now, that I will go with him to every county in the state, to use my small influence for peace and order, that he may see that we have a fair and open contest. –– I will make any and all sacrifices to this end. I would rather make peace any time than to hold the best office there is. The bible promises much to the peace-maker. And with the assurances that Gov. Clayton had given here today, I will vouch for our friends that they are quiet and orderly, and will raise no hand or arm to strike him or his friends, unless the law is to execute fails to give them redress; but failing in this, then heaven tells them to strike, and strike they will, but not till that time comes. And I will go further, being dealt fairly with, if they are defeated, they will either submit like men if they remain here, or they will hunt homes elsewhere. This is all that is asked and is all that could be expected.

In this matter,disagreeably and unfortunately in your county, I have not inquired who is in fault –– who struck first, and all these things as it is now ended, and we hope not to be revived. Let us counsel for the future.

The lamp that threw the light upon the waters behind the ship was of no use –– light ahead was needed. And let us look before us, and try to get light on the road we are now journeying upon. With this purpose we have come among you, and I speak thus for your benefit and for the benefit of myself, and for every man, woman and child in the state, and now let us forbear as we ask to be forborne with, and watch our rights and assert them, but according to the law, and resort to no force or violence till we are compelled; but let us hope and let us work with that view, we may not be compelled at all, but that through peace and law, we will establish our rights and secure to this great country its noble government in theory and practice for all time to come.

transcribed from:

Daily Arkansas Gazette
Wed, Sep 02, 1868 ·Page 3

THE SPEECHES AT LEWISBURG.

In our issue of yesterday we laid before our readers a full synopsis of the speeches made at Lewisburg by Gen. Clayton and Col. A. H. Garland, on last Saturday, in relation to the recent disturbances in Conway county ; but for want of space we made no comments on them.

The speech of Gen. C. is fair enough in general terms, but he may mean more in what he failed to say than in what he said ; as we noted yesterday, more may be implied than he expressed. All who were present, as we learn, approved the speech he made. Mr. Garland's speech is open and frank, and is based upon the promises made by Clayton in his speech, and Mr. Garland endorses what Clayton said, as he promised us we *"should be heard and should be righted,"* and that the voters should have a fair and legal registration. There can be no cavil as to Mr. Garland's meaning, and our friends, as we are satisfied, will approve his course and action in this matter. And as we interpret Clayton's remarks there can be no objection to the speech itself, although it might very well have been more explicit. However, as he has made even these general promises, we hope he will be true to his word, and we shall all see if he is. In this view of the matter, much good will result from the speeches, and the efforts of the deputation to settle the troubles in Conway. We will wait and see how far Clayton will carry out his promises, and in the meantime we urge our friends to be cautious, prudent and watchful, and to follow the excellent advice given them by Mr. Garland.

Daily Arkansas Gazette
Thu, Sep 03, 1868 ·Page 2

GOVERNOR CLAYTON.

Gov. Clayton, in his Lewisburg speech, pledged himself to have a fair registration and a fair election. Of course he must have meant to say that the registrars of his own creation should not, from mere partisan feelings, exclude those from voting to whom that privilege is left by the constitution. Even this is something. No such promise has ever been given by any member of the radical party here before; in assurance that the registration law was not intended to give the registrars unlimited power to return such results as they might please, or as they might be directed; precisely as they returned the constitution as adopted, when it is a part of history that it was voted down by 10,000 majority; making an election a mere insult and a mockery.

So far as we know the radical party here has never talked of fairness before. We are willing to do Gov. Clayton and all other men ample justice, and will, in no instance, refuse to any one merited praise for duty performed; and if Gov. Clayton shall rise to the consciousness that he holds his position, not to gratify the insatiable greed of a few men, but for the good, the quiet, the welfare of the whole people, that his mission is not to destroy but to build up the common fortunes of the people; to protect such liberties as they have even now left, and to enlarge them as opportunity offers, he will receive his first applause, all that is valuable to an honorable mind, from the people. Doubtless he may hear the fierce bark of discontented curs about the public kennel, but they would be drowned in a louder applause, in the consciousness of a higher honor achieved, and a good name left among men. These are considerations that it seems to us must prevail with an intelligent mind. Can he look forward to some years of rule with the hope of successfully and continually stifling the cry of the majority of the people for simple justice, and to the perpetuation of his own power amid the ruin of everything worth preserving? Does he not know that those who would use him for unjust purposes will at last be involved in the ruin which they invoke for others, or that if successful their aims can confer no honor, and that at the last, in their mercenary quarrels they will display the crowning vice of ingratitude, lay the blame on himself and exonerate themselves? In short, if he expects to live in the state, what interest has he, or ought he to have which would be hostile to that of the people, who, by a series of improbable events, are consigned to his control?

These reflections must occur to him. Partisan clamor cannot dispel them. Will he yield to them or will he keep up a hopeless warfare on the rights of the people? The road is plain that he *ought* to travel; its rewards are certain. Any other route is beset with difficulties which would appal any man having the slightest regard for justice, or for his own permanent interests. Whether he will be guided in the one by his own consciousness of rectitude, or whether he will be led into the other by ruinous advisers who squat in his pathway, time only will reveal. In the meantime, his pledge of a fair election must have awakened terror in the hearts of those who have purposed to make a farce of republican government, and to triumph, as they only could triumph by the downfall of the last fragment of the liberties of the people.

Here is Gov. Clayton's platform for the future, taken from his Lewisburg speech:

I am informed that it has been charged that you are not to have a fair registration, and that this has caused much bad feeling. Now, let me say a few words in regard to registration. You shall have a fair registration, and a fair election, too. When I say that, I mean just what I say. Let no one misunderstand me—the registration laws *shall* be enforced. So far as my authority goes, every man who is entitled to register, under the law, shall be permitted to do so; and those who are disqualified *shall not.*

Again:

But I say to all, that so long as the civil authorities can enforce the law, there will be no armed force called into the service.

Weekly Arkansas Gazette
Tue. Sept 8, 1868, Page 1

A Little Rock dispatch to the Democrat says Capt. Simpson Mason, president of the board of registration of Fulton county, was assassinated on the 19th by Ku Klux. One negro in Lewisburg and three in Columbia county have been killed recently, and several negro churches burned.

Weekly Arkansas Gazette
Tue, Sep 29, 1868 ·Page 4

DEMOCRATIC RALLY AT LEWISBURG.

We are requested to state that there will be a grand rally of the democracy of Conway and adjoining counties, at Lewisburg, on the 16th and 17th of October. In addition to speeches by eminent orators, both white and colored, there will be a barbecue and an old fashioned *Bran Dance.* Everybody from everywhere is invited and expected to attend.

Weekly Arkansas Gazette
Tue, Sep 29, 1868 ·Page 3

Report on
Democratic Rally at Lewisburg

SPRINGFIELD, ARK., October 20, 1868.
EDITORS GAZETTE:

I write in haste to give you a short description of the grand barbecue at Lewisburg; and to be short, there were over one thousand people present. Young ladies were selected dressed in uniforms to represent every state. A procession was formed in town with the representatives of the states in front. Gen. Fagan was selected as marshal of the day, but as he was not present his place was supplied. Capt. Duncan and Mr. Burrow were appointed assistant marshals. The procession then moved to a beautiful grove in the suburbs, where a beautiful banner, made by the ladies of Lewisburg, was presented to the Seymour and Blair club by Miss Georgie Gordon in the following touching and beautiful language:

Mr. president and gentlemen of the Seymour and Blair club: Having been delegated by my lady friends I have the honor of presenting you this banner as a token of our appreciation of the cause in which you are engaged. The government of our fathers is in peril. Despotism like a blind giant stalks over the land; the gray haired sires of our beloved and sunny south are robbed of their dearest rights; eight millions of our southern brethren are groaning under oppression the most galling that yonder sun in his transit shines upon. Your object is to remedy these evils through the ballot-box. May your patriotic labors be crowned with the most abundant success. May the day be not far hence when radicalism shall have been swept from this fair land of ours and a democratic administration shall return to us the constitution of our fathers, which can alone make us a free, united and happy people. I now present you this flag in behalf of these ladies, whose invocations daily ascend to the magisterial throne for the success of the two distinguished citizens whose names are inscribed upon its folds.

The flag was received in a very appropriate speech by Mr. Conley, as president of the club; after which Mr. Sol. F. Clark, of Little Rock, was called upon, but soon after taking the stand it began to rain, and the crowd repaired to the masonic hall, which was crowded to overflowing, when Mr. Clark concluded his speech, which was I doubt not the most masterly effort he ever made.

Those who could not crowd into the hall remained at the stand and took the rain to hear Harris, the colored orator; and although it rained all the time still the people listened with eagerness for nearly two hours. He is a natural orator, a fine speaker, and he dealt the radical party more heavy blows than I ever heard it get before. If the colored people would turn out to hear him he would soon make democrats of them all. I have not time to write longer, suffice it to say that we had a splendid time notwithstanding the rain; and if it had not rained we would have had the grandest affair that old Conway ever saw.

Yours respectfully,
DEMOCRAT.

Weekly Arkansas Gazette
Tue, Oct 27, 1868 ·Page 3

Horrible Outrage in Conway County—The Militia Deliberately Murder Two Citizens and Attempt The Lives Of Others—The Late Fire, Etc.

From the Little Rock Gazette.

We give the following account of the late revolting outrages committed at Lewisburg, by the Militia, just as we have it from the lips of an old and reliable citizen of that place.

It appears that on Friday night (4th inst.,) a party of men said to have been in disguise visited the house occupied by two negroes named Wash and Alvan Lewis, who were living with two white women, and killed one of the men, the other (Alvan) making his escape. On the day following, one Captain Mathews, with a company of about thirty negro militia, all armed, made his appearance at Lewisburg, for the purpose, as he said, of avenging the death of the murdered negro.— "These men had been talking peace, we would now give them war."— "They would shoot every G——d d——d ku-klux they could find." Proceeding a short distance from the place, Robert Perry and a Mr. Jackson, peaceful, quiet citizens, were in the road hauling cotton and both arrested. Perry was then taken into a thicket by a detail of negroes, placed with his back against a tree and informed that he must tell all he knew about the ku-klux or die. His assurance that he knew nothing about any such order was of no avail, and a shot grazing the side of the head and taking off one ear, convinced him that the negroes intended his murder, so he broke from the thicket and succeeded in making his escape. Jackson was taken out in a similar manner, threatened with death if he did not disclose what they insisted he knew about the matter, and finally knocked down with a gun, and shot through the head. He afterwards revived sufficiently to restate the details of his murder, giving the name of the negro boy who fired the gun. The wound proved fatal. Mathews then proceeded with his gang to the house of one Thos. Hooper, an old man of about sixty years, whom they arrested and placed in the hands of a detail of six negroes to be taken by them to Springfield, as asserted. On the following morning, Hooper was placed on a small mule, his feet tied together under the animal, his arms pinioned behind, and a rope fastened about his neck and tied to the horn of the saddle of one of his guard. In this manner he was seen to pass along the road, and on Sunday his lifeless body was found about midway between Portland and Springfield. His death had been caused by placing the muzzel of a gun close to the back of the head, the entire charge passing through, inflicting a most horrible wound, and causing instant death. The militia then returned to Lewisburg and proposed to arrest Col. Carroll and Messers Armstrong and Wilson, but through the influence of the citizens, seconded by prominent radicals, Mathews was induced to desist, and return to Springfield. Meanwhile a meeting of the citizens had been held and the sheriff of the county sent for. On arriving that officer assured the citizens that with their support he would cause the arrest of Mathews and his gang, and advised them to organize for protection, which has done and all is now quiet. It seems that Mathews started out with the knowledge of the sheriff, but was told to make arrests if circumstances warranted it by the usual process and turn over his prisoners to the justice of the peace having cognizance of the offence, for investigation. The matter needs no comments. It is one of the terrible results of the prejudices and passions aroused for political purposes. The public will be glad to see a thorough, impartial investigation and justice meted out to whoever may be at fault.

Our informant says there is no question about the origin of the fire which occurred on Saturday morning, alleged to have been the work of the ku-kluk. It originated in a cook room in the rear of the Gills house, and the property destroyed was owned by both parties, the socalled ku-klux being by far the heaviest losers. The murder of the negro occurred on the night previous, but the facts were not known to the citizens until the following day.

Fayetteville Weekly Democrat
Sat, Dec 19, 1868 ·Page 2

Fire in Lewisburg

Lewisburg, Ark., Dec. 4th, 1868.

Editors Gazette:

Yesterday morning about four o'clock Messers. Gill & Mathews' hotel was discovered to be on fire, which was totally destroyed with its contents ; also the storehouse of Burrow, Rankin & Co., was destroyed with its contents, except some one thousand or fifteen hundred dollars worth and that was nearly ruined with the rain and mud. Our smoke house with considerable bacon, pork, lard, meal, molasses, etc., etc., was totally destroyed. The saloons of R. T. Markham and Carroll & Bertram with nearly all their contents was destroyed. Our dwelling house was saved by great exertion and work of the citizens. The losses are about as follows:

Burrow, Rankin & Co.,	$8,000
A. Gordon,	1,500
Gill & Mathews,	——
R. T. Markham,	300
Carroll & Bertram,	300

Messrs. Burrow, Rankin & Co., and A. Gor-

Messrs. Burrow, Rankin & Co., and A. Gordon and lady, hereby tender their heartfelt thanks to the citizens generally for their great exertion in saving our property.

Your Friend,
ANDERSON GORDON.

Daily Arkansas Gazette
Tue, Dec 15, 1868

ANOTHER FIRE AT LEWISBURG.

For the past few days rumors of another conflagration at the little town of Lewisburg, in Conway county, have been frequent on the streets, but until to-day we had been unable to trace the matter to any reliable source. We are now in possession of indisputable evidence of some of the most horrible acts committed by the militia that has yet been laid to their charge. The following statement was made to us by a reliable citizen of Conway county, who is now in the city, a refugee from home.

It appears that on Wednesday night last, the 16th, about 8 o'clock, Gibbons, with four companies of militia, commanded respectively by Gray, Williams, Roane and Matthews—the company commanded by the latter are negroes —entered the quiet little village with demoniacal yells, shooting in every direction, and marched up to the store of Messrs. Breeden & Casey, fired a number of shots through the door and then set fire to the building by pouring out upon the floor a can of coal oil and setting it on fire The flames rapidly spread and soon communicated to the store house of Messrs. Howard & Wells, which, together with the former, was entirely destroyed. Colonel Eagan's store, adjoining, was saved by the almost superhuman exertions of the citizens, through the use of wet blankets placed upon the roof. During the burning, Mr. Casey, of the firm of Breeden & Casey, was shot down by some one of the murderous villains and his body thrown into the burning flames—his pockets rifled of money, watch, etc., and his trunk bursted open and entire contents appropriated. The militia, both white and black, while the fire was in progress, consumed the time in rifling the buildings of their contents, reserving such articles as they desired for their own use, and burning such as could not be used.

The town is now occupied by these ruffians who perambulate the streets shouting, shooting and cursing, and no one allowed to go outside without a pass. Previous to these occurrences the citizens had organized a company to keep the peace, were sworn in by the sheriff, who informed the authorities of his action, and assured them that he could execute the laws without military interference, but no attention was paid to these assurances.

These are the facts; and the whole matter just resolves itself into this: These outrages must cease, or every mountain pass in the state will be made a Thermopolæ, and 300,000 white people be terribly avenged.

Daily Arkansas Gazette
Sun, Dec 20, 1868 ·Page 2

Captain Gibbon's Report on the Fire

GIBBONS' REPORT.

Capt. Jno. J. Gibbons, commanding the militia at Lewisburg, submits the following report to the governor, concerning the late fire at that place:

HEADQUARTERS, LEWISBURG, ARK., }
December 18th, 1868. }

HIS EXCELLENCY, POWELL CLAYTON.

Sir: I have the honor to report that on the night of the 16th inst., a fire broke out in the store room occupied by Breeden, Billingsly & Casey, and before it could be arrested, their house, and also the house occupied by Howard & Wells, was consumed.

Old man Casey, one of the first named firm, was burned up in the building. It is thought that Casey was murdered for his money and the building set on fire.

On the morning of the 17th, I organized a court of inquiry for the purpose of investigating the first and last fires; and if possible discover who are the guilty parties in these lawless acts. I am in possession of sufficient evidence to show that Gill & Matthews were burned out because they were radicals. There have been about thirty-five witnesses examined relative to the fire of the 16th inst., and I am satisfied from the evidence produced, that P. O. Breeden and George Bentley (the former one of the partners in the firm of Breeden, Billingsly & Casey), are the guilty parties, as they have fled to parts unknown.

Bear with me patiently, for I hope to give you a sworn history of Lewisburg for the last few months. I think I can conquer the ku klux in a short time.

I am getting along with the organization of the militia briskly.

Respectfully,
JNO. J. GIBBONS,
Capt. Commanding.

We are in possession of some information relative to the points touched upon in the above which we have every reason to believe is true. Gill & Matthews, who are said to have been burned out "because they were radicals," owned two wooden buildings in a block built up nearly solid. Their loss is estimated at less than $2,000, including buildings and stock. The loss of those who were not radicals, and who could not have suffered from that cause was as follows:

R. T. Markham, saloon stock	$300
R. M. Johnson, building	300
Gordon & Rayburn, damage to goods estimated at	3,000
Burtram & Carroll	300
Col. Anderson Gordon, store	2,000
Stock	5,000
Smoke house	1,500
Total	12,400

This burning out then of Gill & Matthews cost the rebel democracy six times the amount of that lost by the persecuted, and it should be remembered that the property was so situated that the fire once set to Gill & Matthews' building, must inevitably destroy the balance, and it was by the merest chance that greater losses were not suffered by those accused of committing the crime, if the fire occurred otherwise than by accident.

What could have satisfied the captain commanding that "P. O. Breeden and George Bently (the former one of the partners in the firm of Breeden, Billingsly & Casey)" were the guilty parties in the last fire, we are at a loss to know. It really does not seem probable that Mr. Breeden would set fire to his own property, and the allegation of having "fled to parts unknown," is true of a greater portion of the people of that section. The truth is that the negroes knew of the proposed outrage of the militia, and, unwilling to see the suffering, told the white people *before the fire* what was to come.— Warnings were received in this way at four different times and from as many different servants. Capt. Gibbons fails to incorporate this evidence in his report.

Daily Arkansas Gazette
Tue, Dec 22, 1868 ·Page 2

LEWISBURG, ARK., Jan. 5, 1869.

EDITORS GAZETTE :

I wish to say a few words through your paper, in regard to a publication in the *Republican* of the 30th of December, by John Gibbons, relative to the second fire in Lewisburg. I do not know from whom you received the information, that Gibbons pronounces a slander, nor do I pretend to say it was true or false, but his assertion that I was, at the time, a fugitive from justice, is a malicious lie. I was in Little Rock at the time, on business, and when I learned that martial law had been proclaimed in that county, and that John Gibbons and Mathews were in command, I did not feel disposed to return, fearing that they might see fit to mete out *such justice* to me as they did to Mr. Hooper, Jackson and Perry—*tie me on a mule,* or carry me into a *cane-brake*, and murder me without a trial. This is the *kind* of justice that Mathews meted out to the above named gentlemen, before martial law was proclaimed, which will doubtless be investigated by the civil courts of the county. I have never fled from justice or tried to evade the civil law in any way. I am now at home, willing to be tried for any offense against the law.

It has been published to the world that I had broken up a civil court in this county, which is

also a lie. And I challenge an investigation of the case, in order to set myself right before the good people of the country.

All quiet. The squad of militia left here under Lieutenant Conley have conducted themselves very well. It is believed that Lieut. Conley will have justice done to all parties.

E. W. ADAMS.

Daily Arkansas Gazette
Fri, Jan 08, 1869 ·Page 2

Bogus Investigation—Withdrawal of the Militia.

MEMPHIS, Dec. 26.

The Avalanche's Little Rock special says that Generals Babcock and Porter, of General Grant's staff, left on their return trip to-night. It appears they are not authorized to investigate the militia outrages. All the militia except twenty are to be withdrawn from Lewisburg, and the citizens are to be allowed to raise a company to aid the civil authorities. The Conway county refugees are preparing to return home.

Fayetteville Weekly Democrat
Sat, Jan 09, 1869 ·Page 2

The executive has offered a reward of two hundred dollars for the apprehension of the murderer of James N. Casey, who, it will be remembered, was killed and his body burnt with the store house of Breeden & Casey, at Lewisburg, on the 16th day of December last, the night of the entry into that place of the "loyal" militia.

Daily Arkansas Gazette
Sat, Jan 23, 1869 ·Page 3

The Fort Smith *Herald* of the 13th says, the "*Board of Trade*," of that city, "have gone to work in earnest and have taken hold of the proposed telegraph line from Fort Smith *via* Ozark, Clarksville, *Dardenelle* and Lewisburg to Little Rock, in such a manner that we may look for good results." We wish our friends every success in the good work. In the meantime, if the "*Board of Trade*" will come over "some day," we will intercede with the Superintendant of the Railroad for them to have a free ride. And if our friends over the river, will reciprocate, we'll come over and take a ride on their telegraph. Come.

The Van Buren Press
Feb 16, 1869, Page 2

– 92 –

In referring to the proposed telegraph line from Ft. Smith to Little Rock and Van Buren, Ozark, Clarksville, Dardanelle and Lewisburg, in our issue of the 13th inst., we inadvertently omitted to mention Van Buren as one of the points included in the proposition. It was wholly unintentional. We did not mean to give our sister city the go-by to this matter. - *Herald*

Explanation satisfactory. Van Buren will not be behind in doing her part.

The Van Buren Press
March 02, 1869, Page 2

The Railroad is Coming!
Survey Crew 10 Miles Away

—We had the pleasure of taking by the hand yesterday, Capt. Geo. H. Meade, of the engineering force on the L. R. and Fort Smith railroad. He reports everything pogressing finely.. They have reached a point 10 miles south of Lewisburg. The numerous friends of Capt. Henry West will be pleased to learn that he is in fine health, and enjoys the camp life as in days of yore.

Daily Arkansas Gazette
Tue, Apr 20, 1869 ·Page 3

Railroad Survey Crew is Here!

—Capt. Henry C. West, of the surveying party of the Little Rock and Fort Smith Railroad, is in town. He is in fine health, and reports everything progressing finely. They have reached Lewisburg, fifty miles above here, and are proceeding rapidly with the surveys beyond that point.

Daily Arkansas Gazette
Tue, May 5, 1869 ·Page 3

Telegraph is Here!

Telegraph Line.

A few months since the Board of Trade of this city, set on foot, the construction of a Telegraph line from Little Rock to Fort Smith, with offices at Van Buren, Ozark, Clarksville, Dardanelle and Lewisburg. For a time the project worked well, and evidence, that at an early day the points mentioned; among the most important in the state; would be bound together by stronger ties, than those now uniting them; and the importance and value of Telegraphic communication, between those places, and throgh them with the outer world, were being felt and acknowledged.

At Litttle Rock a liberal amount was subscribed, headed by Maj. John D. Adams, president of the packet company, with $1,000, and followed with proportionate amounts by others not so much, nor so directly interested: Lewisburg promptly came up with a liberal amount, and fully contributed her share in the matter: Dardanelle, with the public spirit that has always characterized her business men, followed suit, and took hold with a vim: Clarksville remained passive, like a bashful youth, waiting to be urged or coaxed to put the butter on her own bread: and Ozark, laboring under misapprehensions which have since been removed, has, as yet, given no assurance that she desires to be relieved of the curse of slow and irregular mails, but will do so in due time.

Fort Smith Weekly Herald
Sat, May 08, 1869 ·Page 2

Railroad Survey Crew
is 20 Miles Past Lewisburg

LITTLE ROCK AND FORT SMITH RAILROAD.—Mr. Wheeler, one of the directors of this road, returned from the east on Monday. He reports everything cheering for the early completion of the road In addition to the hands that are now employed, a large number will be put to work as soon as Col. Ceuckla arrives from New York, which will be in a week or two. Capt. George H. Meade, of the surveying party, is in the city. He reports that they have reached Gala creek, about twenty miles above Lewisburg, and are rapidly pushing forward the surveys.—*Gazette* 26th ult.

Helena Weekly Clarion
Wed, Jun 02, 1869 ·Page 2

Gunfire
in Eagan's Store at Lewisburg

"On Saturday last a squad of five or six men rode into Lewisburg, dismounted, went into the store of Mr. Eagan and fired several rounds with their pistols, without doing much damage. They were arrested and tried—three of them committed to jail and the others released on bail.

Daily Arkansas Gazette
Sat, Aug 28, 1869 ·Page 4

Anderson Gordon in Town

PERSONAL.--Col. Anderson Gordon, of Lewisburg, passed through the city yesterday, *en route* home from the east where he has been purchasing his fall and winter stock of goods.

1200 pounds table butter, received to-day.
H. W. WILSON.

Daily Arkansas Gazette
Sun, Sep 19, 1869 ·Page 4

Shooting Was Caused by Whiskey

The shooting affray referred to in yesterday's paper, turns out to have been caused by an indulgence of all parties too freely in whiskey. One of the parties was arraigned yesterday before Justice Henneberry, but upon examination was discharged.

Daily Arkansas Gazette
Sun, Sep 19, 1869 ·Page 4

Dardanelle Man Threatening to Collect the Enslaved at Lewisburg

Serious and Bloody Disturbance at Dardanelle.

In the afternoon on Christmas, at Dardanelle, in Yell county, on the river eighty miles above here, a serious disturbance took place between some of the white citizens and some of the negroes of that vicinity, which has resulted in the death of a young white man of Dardanelle named Port Jones, from a pistol shot in the hands of a white man named Holland Musteen, on Tuesday, at the Dickens farm, three miles below Dardanelle. On Saturday, being Christmas, many negroes from the surrounding plantations as well as the white citizens of Dardanelle and vicinity, were celebrating the holiday in the usual custom,—"more honored in the breach than in the performance"—by drinking more or less whiskey and discharging firearms.

A young man named William Jones. but no relative of the deceased, was firing powder from his pistol, near the store of Andrew Chandler,(colored,)and remarked to Chandler, who was passing by him,that the negroes were getting drunk and disorderly, and that he (Chandler) had better take them home. Chandler, the colored man, not only owns the store, but also owns a part of the old Dickens farm,upon which he was employing most of the negroes alluded to. Chandler, seeing the young man with a pistol in his hand, and not knowing that he was only firing powder from it, and being himself in liquor, immediately fired, two Derringer pistols at the young man without hitting him, and fled. After being fired upon, young William Jones drew a revolver loaded with ball, and pursued Chandler, and being joined by a number of other young men, drove all armed negroes out of town, offering no threats or violence to those who were unarmed.

Chandler immediately sent for Holland Musteen, who killed Major Burt last spring and several other citizens since the war, and against whom there are several indictments for murder pending in Yell and Franklin circuit courts. Indeed, a few evenings before this Christmas scrape occurred, the constable of Dardanelle went with a capias for his arrest, summoning a posse, of which young Port Jones, the deceased, was one. He made his escape, but announced afterwards in several places that he would kill every man that was on that posse.

On Tuesday evening, having been sent for by Chandler, he was at Chandler's farm as Port Jones and George Stirman son of Dr. Jno. I. Stirman, neither of whom were participants in any part of the Christmas scrape, rode along the road by Chandler's yard, when they were stopped by Musteen, who asked Jones if his name was not Port Jones. Jones answered in the affirmative. Musteen then said : "You said the other night if you got me I would be your meat; and now you are my meat," and shot Jones through the body, killing him instantly. Stirman rode off rapidly and escaped, the negroes in the yard with Musteen firing upon him. Jones' body was then shot through several times and thrown down the bluff With Musteen and the negroes are also Walker and White, two noted desperadoes At the time our informant left the scene a perfectly reliable and christian gentleman, they were threatening to collect the negroes at Lewisburg, who were engaged in last spring's disturbances, and those along the river to Gala Rock, and to re venge themselves on all engaged in driving Chandler out of Dardanelle. The people of Dardanelle and surrounding country, knowing the desperate character of Musteen and his white associates, are very much excited, and are assembling in bodies, with a view to their defence and that of their families.

Daily Arkansas Gazette
Thu, Dec 30, 1869 ·Page 4

Dardanelle Threat
to Lewisburg Enslaved Continued

The Disturbance in Yell.

On Thursday last we published an account of the trouble in Yell county, which later advices confirm as substantially correct.

After young Jones was killed, his body was rifled of watch, money and jewelry, and thrown over the bank of the river. On receipt of the news of his death at Dardanelle, the excitement was intense. A party of about 20 mounted and 30 men on foot, all armed, started for the scene of the murder to recover the body. On arriving at Chandler's place the mounted men sent forward a white flag, but they were fired upon by Mustain's gang. They then fell back and waited the arrival of the men on foot, when they again went forward. They found that Mustain and his gang had retreated, and the body, much mutilated, was recovered. It was taken to town and buried on Thursday. A very great number of people were present at the funeral.

On Wednesday, a party started below to arrest Mustain, Chandler, etc., armed with warrants issued by Judge May, of the circuit court. Arriving at Chandler's place they found the quarters deserted, and all the wagons, mules, etc., gone, and a quantity of cotton, belonging to parties in Dardanelle, burning. The fire was extinguished and information sent to stop Mustain and his gang at Gala Rock, as they crossed the river. The deputy, M. S. Marshal, at Gala Rock, succeeded in stopping a large number, and five or six negroes against whom were warrants, were arrested and placed in custody. The rest of them proceeded to Lewisburg, where they all but a few were induced to deposit their arms. They reported that Mustain and his brother and two other white men deserted them below Gala

Rock, and had gone over to the Springfield road, with the intention of going into Franklin county. A party was sent to intercept him.

Some excitement was occasioned by these stragglers among the negroes on the river below Lewisburg, several of whom were induced to arm themselves. Two parties of them, armed, were fired upon by parties endeavoring to arrest Mustain's gang, and two are reported to have been seriously if not fatally wounded. This is much to be regretted, as the men who were shot were not of the band of rioters.

We have conversed with men of all parties on the ground at the time, all of whom agreed in saying that the affair did not grow out of politics, but originated in the use of mean whiskey on Christmas day.

We have already mentioned the arrest here, of Anderw Chandler and four others implicated in the disturbances. They were taken before county Judge Reeve on Monday and admitted to bail in $1000 each. We could not ascertain the charge upon which they were arrested, but concluded it was not *murder*, because title III, ch. 2, sec. 43, of the Code, provides:

"Where an arrest is made without a warrant, whether by a peace officer or private person, the defendant shall be forthwith carried before the most convenient magistrate of the county in which the arrest is made, and the grounds on which the arrest was made, shall be stated to the magistrate, and if the offence for which the arrest was made, is charged *to have been committed in a different county* from that in which the arrest was made, and the magistrate believes from the statements made to him on oath, that there are sufficient grounds for an examination, he shall by his written order, *commit the defendant to a peace officer to be conveyed by him* before a magistrate of the county in which the offence is charged to have been committed; or if the offence be a *misdemeanor only*, the defendant may give bail to appear before the judge of the probate of the county in which the offence was committed," etc.

Daily Arkansas Gazette
Tue, Jan 04, 1870 ·Page 4

Lewisburg Pledges
$300 to $500 to Telegraph Company

Mr. L. C. Baker, superintendent of the Western Union Telegraph Company, a short time ago, proposed to put this line up, with offices at Lewisburg, Dardanelle, Clarksville, Ozark and Van Buren, for a loan of $8,000, to be paid back in telegraphing—as "good as cash." We presume the same offer will be renewed whenever we are ready to "come," and all it needs is for some person of energy and influence in each community to go to work and raise the required amount— This is not wind, nor a subject for wind. Let us have the line up. Dardanelle will give $1,000, they say; Lewisburg will give $300 to $500. Little Rock did offer $3,500; and now what will Fort Smith, Van Buren, Clarksville and Ozark do?— Who will move in the matter? We will aid to get the matter in motion again; and we propose to say telegraph! telegraph!! telegraph!!! until we have a telegraph here from Fort Smith to Little Rock.— *Fort Smith Herald.*

We are advised that the telegraph company adheres to its proposition. Our citizens no doubt will make good their subscriptions, and we hope soon to see the work under way.

Daily Arkansas Gazette
Wed, Jan 05, 1870 ·Page 4

Advice Offered to
Lewisburg and Dardanelle

YELL.

The *Transcript* gives the people of Yell some excellent advice:

Let our people be quiet. Let every man abide strictly by the law. Let every one aid the civil authorities in enforcing the law. The moment any democrat violates the law, let us seize him and have him punished in accordance with the law. Let us pay promptly and cheerfully the enormous taxation. In this way we will leave these fellows who pant to distinguish themselves in militia expeditions. without excuse. We are satisfied that it has been concocted in secret conclave by certain fellows to avail themselves of the first disturbance to turn loose upon our innocent people, for purposes similar to that which the sun beheld in Sevier, in Woodruff, at Lewisburg and Monticello, a little more than twelve months ago. Let us, therefore, walk circumspectly, giving no offense, and then these fellows will be defeated in their plans. This is the way to whip them out. This is the way to de-

Daily Arkansas Gazette
Sun, Feb 20, 1870 ·Page 2

Steamboat Ozark at Van's Bar
Five Miles Below Lewisburg

The Ozark is on her way down, "double tripping" her cotton over Van's bar, five miles below Lewisburg.

Daily Arkansas Gazette
Sun, Feb 20, 1870 ·Page 4

Rail is Being Laid
Passenger Train to Begin Next July 4th

Little Rock and Fort Smith Railroad.

We have been rather reticent regarding this great line of road that is being pushed rapidly toward completion. Not for the reason of manifest interest in the progress of work, fearful that we might promise too much and give the people to understand they might expect more than the contractors would be able to accomplish. But the work is progressing so rapidly that we feel safe in referring to it, and in predicting great things within the next three months.

The first arrival of iron is spiked down, reaching out three miles from the river. One engine and twelve cars are now on the track, and the "steam horse" will commence to-day moving out the rails that arrived a few days ago. And by the time they are in place three or four more steamers will add to the supply, and the "laying down of the rail" will continue as fast as the rails can be taken to the front. Thirty miles are graded, and the ties down ready for the iron. The "section grades" now extend beyond Lewisburg, and to Dover in Pope county. Before the people at Van Buren and Fort Smith are aware of their close proximity to Little Rock, the iron horse will pay them a visit.

It is conceded by all that a passenger train will be running to Lewisburg by the Fourth of July next. Only think of it. If the anticipations of the contactors are realized, and there is no delay in the arrival of the iron for that distance. now on the way here. would not the fourth be a capital day to celebrate the great event. the completion of fifty miles of the road to Lewisburg? Our friends thereaway had better prepare for the coming of the grand jubilee.—Little Rock Republican.

Fayetteville Weekly Democrat
Sat April 9, 1870, page 2

Dr. Davis' Death

DR. M. E. DAVIS.

At a regular communication of Lewisburg Lodge, No. 105, of F. & A. M., the following was adopted:

WHEREAS, It has pleased God in his infinite wisdom to remove from our midst on February 12th, 1870, to the celestial lodge above our Bro. M. E. Davis: therefore, be it

Resolved, That in the death of Bro. Davis the community has lost one of its best citizens,—the church one of its most exemplary members,—the masonic fraternity one of its brightest ornaments.

Resolved, That we tender our sincere sympathy and condolence to the bereaved family; and that the members of this lodge wear the usual badge of masonry thirty days.

Resolved, That a copy of these resolutions be furnished to the bereaved family, and to the Little Rock *Gazette* and Memphis *Christian Advocate* for publication.

H. W. BURROW,
G. W. HOWARD, } Committee.
M. W. STEEL,

Daily Arkansas Gazette
Sun, Apr 10, 1870 ·Page 2

Tracks Are Being Laid

Northwest Border Railroad.

The South Pacific Railroad is being pushed forward with great rapidity: the track is now being laid from one to two miles per day, and in a few days the cars will be running through to Springfield. By the refusal of the Mo. Legislature to extend the time for the completion of the road, the work will be pushed through to the State line during the present year. The Little Rock and Fort Smith Road is also being pressed forward with a will that betokens business on the part of the contractors. This road will be completed to Lewisburg, on the Arkansas river, by the 4th of July next, and from present indications we are led to believe that the cars on that line will reach Fort Smith during the next eighteen months. The completion of this road will leave an open gap between Van Buren and the South Pacific road, a distance of only about one hundred miles. The interests of Northwest Arkansas demand that this gap should be closed, that another link should be added to connect the great chain of thoroughfare.

The question arises, can it be done? We answer emphatically that it can.

We want a LIVE, BUSINESS man to take hold of the enterprise. Books have already been opened and a considerable amount subscribed. Let one or two good agents canvass the counties along the proposed route and secure individual stock; the counties directly interested should, and of course will, subscribe liberally. Put this enterprise on foot; show to St. Louis and Memphis that we are in earnest; both cities are interested in securing the trade of Northwest Arkansas, and will each contribute largely.

We say put the ball in motion and keep it rolling! until the Northwest Border Railroad is completed.

Fayetteville Weekly Democrat
Sat, Apr 16, 1870 ·Page 2

PROSPECTS OF THE ROAD.

The first twenty miles were completed just in time to save the congressional land grant, the time expiring on the day of the excursion. We were informed by the officers of the road that if necessary the grading of the whole of the first eighty miles could be finished in one month from to-day. It is the intention to have the road finished to Lewisburg by the 4th day of July. By the 15th or 20th of May 10 miles more will be completed. The ties are all out for the road to Lewisburg, and the greater portion of the grading done. At present the company is waiting for iron, having only enough to lay about three miles. A thousand tons is expected within two or three weeks. Another locomotive, "POPE," and several passenger and other cars are in *transit*. No regular trains will be run till the road reaches Lewisburg.

Daily Arkansas Gazette
Fri, Apr 29, 1870 ·Page 4

RIVER NEWS

The *Importer* turned back from Lewisburg, after storing her freight there, to be re-shipped and left in charge of Mr. ROWE, the second clerk of the Boat, to come forward with, deliver and collect freights and charges. This is the last trip of the popular *Importer* from New Orleans this season. In the Fall, nothing unforseen occurs, she will again enter the same trade. The officers, we believe, leave us with the good will and best wishes, generally of every planter and merchant on the river.

The Van Buren Press
May 24, 1870, Page 3

Stagecoach Disaster
West of Lewisburg

Stage Disaster.

We learn from Mr. R. P. Bolling, general agent of the Northwestern Mutual Life Insurance Company, that he left Fort Smith for this place, on Wednesday last, on the stage. On arriving at the second stand, imagine the astonishment of the passengers when a wild, ungovernable mule was hitched to the stage. Immediately on being seated, and before the driver had time to gather the reins from the ground, away flew the horses, to the terror of passengers—all but Bolling, whose life was insured, and who leaped from the stage to save himself. Finally the team was conquered, and the stage proceeded to Lewisburg, where a heavy rain overtook them, and shortly after that the creeks and bayous were all found overflowing their banks. On reaching the Cadron Mr. Bolling requested the driver to take one of his horses out, go forward and learn the condition of the stream before attempting to cross. Without heeding the injunction, however, the driver moved forward with the stage, and soon plunged into fifteen feet of water. The passengers were compelled to take water and swim for dear life. The current carried the stage down the stream some fifty yards, where it lodged against a log, and under which the horses were drawn, and drowned.

Mr. Bolling lost his baggage, and says he does not intend to travel again in a stage coach until he has prepared himself for becoming the inhabitant of another world, and that he charges double premiums on lives going to and returning from Fort Smith by the overland route.

Daily Arkansas Gazette
Tue, Jun 07, 1870 ·Page 4

LITTLE ROCK AND FORT SMITH.

The grading to Lewisburg is completed, and there only remains Cadron bridge to be finished to have this distance ready for the rails. That will be accomplished in ten or fifteen days. Grading on the 5th and 6th divisions will also be completed during the present month, and the 7th and 8th by the 15th July, making the distance of 80 miles. Trains will run to Piney by the time the cotton crop begins to come in. A steamer is about leaving New Orleans with iron, and upon its arrival track laying will be pushed forward rapidly.

The Van Buren Press.
June 14, 1870, Page 2

Train Coming July 4th
No Doubt

L. R. & F. S. Railroad.

Col. A. P. Robinson, chief engineer, has addressed the following letter to C. G. Scott, Esq. president of the above road. We copy from the Van Buren *Press.*

LITTLE ROCK, May 16th, 1870.

SIR: It becomes my duty to call your attention to the terms of the contract, between your company and Mr. Warren Fisher, Jr., for the construction and equipment of this railway. By its provisions the company undertakes to procure subscriptions from the counties through which the road passes, to the extent of five hundred thousand dollars in the aggregate, payable in the bonds of said counties. Up to this date the only subscription obtained is, from Crawford county—amounting to one hundred thousand dollars.

Mr. Fisher has not hesitated to push the work with the utmost vigor, relying with certainty upon these subscriptions being obtained. Twenty miles of the road is now completed and in the most perfect order. The grading is in such a state of forwardness from that point nearly to the mouth of Big Piney, that the track laying may be prosecuted without cessation. The cars will be running to Lewisburg by the 1st of July, beyond a doubt. Under these circumstances it is natural that Mr. Fisher should feel some concern at the delay in procuring the county subscriptions and hesitate in his progress until they are secured. The completion of the grading on the first fifty miles has multiplied the forces on the next thirty five to such an extent that he is seriously embarrassed in providing work for them; but nevertheless is holding them in hope of an early vote on the subscriptions, so that he may distribute them on the line between Piney and Ozark, which is already surveyed and ready for construction.

I beg leave, therefore, that you will represent to the county courts, of the various counties interested, and to the people in those counties, the urgency of immediate action. No time should be lost. If these subscriptions be voted promptly, I can safely promise you that the entire cotton crop of Johnson county, for this year, may be brought by rail to this city, as soon as ready; and that the road will be completed to the western boundry of the state long before the end of 1871.

Daily Arkansas Gazette
Fri, Jun 17, 1870 ·Page 3

Waiting on Rail To Be Delivered

RAILROADS.—The line of the Cairo and Fulton road is now located about fifteen miles out. About five miles are cleared and two miles graded. Work is progressing as rapidly as possible. Additional force will be put on as soon as it can be obtained.

By Monday the entire distance on the Fort Smith road to Lewisburg will be ready for the ties and iron. Every day a steamboat loaded with iron is looked for from below, when track-laying will commence again in earnest.

Daily Arkansas Gazette
Fri, Jun 17, 1870 ·Page 4

1 Mile to 1 ¹/₂ Mile of Track Laid Each Day

L. R. & F. S. Railroad.

Track laying on the Little Rock and Fort Smith Railroad will recommence to-day, and progress at the rate of from one to one and a half miles per day. The company's steamer Colossal leaves New Orleans to-day with another shipment of iron for the track. She will be able to keep the working party fully employed. It is expected that the road will be running through to Lewisburg in thirty days. Should low water in the Arkansas render it difficult for the Colossal to bring full loads, she will go by way of White river, discharging her cargo at Devalls Bluff to be transported by the M. & L. R. R., to this place.

Daily Arkansas Gazette
Tue, Jun 28, 1870 ·Page 4

DISTRESSING DEATH.—News reached the city on Monday that Mr. Cunningham, contractor on the 5th division of the Fort Smith Railroad, had been murdered and robbed of a large sum of money—$14,000—above Lewisburg on Saturday. Direct information was received yesterday, contradicting the report of the murder, but confirming the death of Mr. Cunningham. His body was found lying in the road, with a slight wound on the temple, and all his money on his person. He was subject to congestive chills, and it being an excessively warm day, is supposed to have taken a chill on the road, fell from his horse and died before any assistance could be rendered.—*L. R. Gazette.*

The Van Buren Press
July 12, 1870, Page 2

Soon...
Little Rock to Lewisburg
in Two Hours!

HO FOR LEWISBURG!—In yesterday's paper we announced the arrival of the Colossal loaded with railroad iron for the Fort Smith Railroad. She left a portion of her load at Fourche Bar, and returns this morning for it. She brought up from New Orleans also as far as the mouth of White River a large barge loaded with iron, and will return in a day or two and carry it up White River. On Sunday last the steamers Minnie and Importer, each with barges in tow, all loaded with iron, arrived at the mouth, and passed on up White River. All these boats have about 2,000 tons of iron, enough to complete the road to Lewisburg. In less than a month we will be able to greet our friends at Lewisburg after a two hours ride.

Daily Arkansas Gazette
Sat, Jul 30, 1870 ·Page 4

Death of
Benjamin F. Evans

Tribute of Respect.

The following resolutions were come to at a regular communication of Lewisburg Lodge No. 105, in the county of Conway, and state of Arkansas, the 30th of July, 1870.

WHEREAS, It has pleased Almighty God in his infinite wisdom to remove from our midst, and this lodge here below, to that celestial lodge above, our worthy brother Benj. F. Evans, who had recently removed to Maysville, Benton county, of this state.

Resolved, That in the death of this brother the community has lost one of its best citizens, his family a kind member, and this lodge one of its brightest ornaments.

2d, That we tender our sincere condolence to the bereaved family.

3d, That the members of this lodge wear the usual badge of mourning for thirty days, that a copy of these resolutions be transmitted to the bereaved family, and a copy to the Little Rock GAZETTE for publication.

J. C. EATON,
J. D. McREYNOLDS,
G. W. HOWARD.   Committee.

Daily Arkansas Gazette
Wed, Aug 10, 1870 ·Page 3

Little Rock and Fort Smith Railroad.

Notwithstanding certain parties, i[n] prove every occasion to belittle and di[s] parage the work being done on th[e] Road, from the following, from the Litt[le] Rock *Republican*, it will be noticed th[at] the work is going on steadily to compl[e] tion :

Messrs. Carpenter and Stone, assista[nt] engineers, and Mr. W. S. Barton, of th[e] road, arrived in the city Tuesday ev[e] ning from the upper end of the wor[k] about eighty five miles from the city, a[nd] thirty-five miles beyond Lewisburg. Se[v] enty five miles is now graded and near[ly] ready for the ties. Considering the o[p] pressive heat for a month or so past t[he] contractors have done nobly in pushin[g] the improvement so rapidly forwar[d.] The rails are now down as far as Gol[d] Creek, and would have been down t[o] Lewisburg had not the sun heated t[he] iron so that the men could not hand[le] the rails ; but have distributed the ti[es] up to Lewisburg or near there. T[he] bridge-builders are now up to the sevent[h] division, near Russellville, and pushin[g] ahead. Every department of the wor[k] seems to be progressing notwithstandin[g] the difficulties attending work of th[at] kind in the summer season. Very littl[e] sickness among the laborers thus far, an[d] it is thought the same careful manage[] ment as heretofore exercised will enabl[e] the men to get through the season wit[h] nothing serious occuring. The me[n] speak very highly of the Chief Enginee[r] Mr. A. P. Robinson, and Messrs. Stac[e] & Youston, Contractors.

The Van Buren Press
Aug 16, 1870, Page 2

Railroad Coming in September... Not by July 4th

L. R. & F. S. RAILROAD.—Gen. F. C. Armstrong, who has recently been on a visit to our city, gives the following en couraging report of the progress of the above road, to the Fort Smith *Herald*:

Iron, sufficient to complete the road to Lewisburg, is now on hand, and will be placed as rapidly as possible, and beyond doubt, the road will be finished to that point in September. The road is graded to a point within 15 miles of Spadra, the clearing of the road progresses beyond that point; and the bridge on Piney creek is rapidly hastening to completion.

General Armstrong is now making preparations and arrangements to connect with the railroad at Lewisburg, with good and comfortable four-horse passenger coaches, so that the time to Little Rock will be reduced to about thirty hours or less.

this evening for Van Buren, to make a preliminary survey of the Arkansas Wes tern Railway, from Van Buren to the Missouri border.

Daily Arkansas Gazette
Thu, Aug 25, 1870 ·Page 4

It Is September... The Tracks Still 15 Miles Away

Little Rock and Fort Smith Rail road.

On Sunday last quite a number of our citizens, accompanied by Chief Engineer Robinson anp his staff, took a ride in one of the new passenger cars to the end of the track—$32\frac{1}{2}$ miles. The passenger cars are known as the Cummins car, manufactured at Jersey City, N. J., and are acknow ledged to be the best in use. The compa ny now have two more engines *in transitu,* called *Pope* and *Johnson.* There remains but sixteen miles of iron to lay to reach Lewisburg. Track laying is now pro gressing at the rate of a mile per day. On the 1st October regular passenger trains will run to Lewisburg. The con struction party is now in the neighborhood of Cadron, which stream will be crossed during the week.

Chief Engineer Robinson deserves the thanks of the people of Arkansas, the con tractors and all concerned for the energy he has displayed since he was placed in charge of this work. Less than a year ago he went out with his engineers and established the line—since that time, by the most determined energy and perse verance, he has overcome all obstacles and constructed a first-class road in every particular. For new work, it is said to excel any road in the west.

Daily Arkansas Gazette
Tue, Sep 06, 1870 ·Page 4

Tracks To Reach Lewisburg by October 5th

LITTLE ROCK AND FORT SMITH.

On Saturday thirty-five miles of this road were completed. The Cadron has been reached, and there now remains but fourteen miles of iron to be laid to put us in communication with Lewisburg. Track laying progresses at the rate of about a mile per day. The 5th of October, at the furthest, will find the party at Lewis burg, when regular trains will commence running. The road bed is completed

– 100 –

burg, when regular trains will commence running. The road bed is completed and the ties put down ready for the iron for eighty miles, and thirty miles more are under contract. This carries us one hundred and ten miles from this city. Iron is constantly coming forward, and the hope is entertained that there will be no more delays on that account.

Daily Arkansas Gazette
Wed, Sept 21, 1870 ·Page 4

Train Service In October?
No, But Maybe November

OUR RAILROADS.—The delay in the completion of the Fort Smith road to Lewisburg has been occasioned by detention in shipments of iron. Enough is now here to build the other five miles, which will carry the road to that point, and it will probably be completed next week. About seven miles of iron have been laid, without fish plates, and until they are received and placed down, the track cannot be run over safely. These plates will be shipped from New Orleans, at once, and will, no doubt, arrive in time to complete the road, and have trains running by the 1st of November to Lewisburg.

There are now three locomotives on the road, two more *in transitu* and three others ready for shipment. Grading is now progressing on the 10th, 11th and 12th divisions of the road.

The first twenty miles of the Cairo and Fulton road is graded and tied, ready for the iron, and twenty more being laid off by the surveyors. Track laying will commence in a short time.

Daily Arkansas Gazette
Thu, Oct 20, 1870 ·Page 4

Five Miles to Go

Gazette, of the 11th, that the track of the L. R. & F. S. railroad is laid to within five miles of Lewisburg.

Fort Smith Weekly Herald
Sat, Oct 22, 1870 ·Page 3

Methodist Pastor at Lewisburg:
Rev. Isham L. Burrow

Appointments of Arkansas Conference, M. E. Church, South, for 1870--71.

CLARKSVILLE DISTRICT.—John J. Roberts, P. E.

Clarksville, Nathaniel Futrell.
Spadra, Charles H. Gregory.
Dover, Wm. R. Knowlton.
Galla Rock, Isaac L. Hicks.
Lewisburg station, Isham L. Burrow.
Lewisburg circuit, Abel C. Ray, Stephen P. Farish, supernumarary.
East Fork, Coleman H. Ford.
Clinton, Wm. E. Whittenburg.
Dardanelle station, John F. Hall.
Dardanelle circuit, Wm. J. Dodson.
Danville, George F. Fair.
Bluffton, John M. Bewley.
Quitman Institute, Peter A. Moses.

The Van Buren Press
Nov 08, 1870, Page 3

First Train to Lewisburg
Will be at 9am Today!!!

—The Little Rock and Fort Smith railroad will be opened to Lewisburg to-day. An excursion party goes out at 9 o'clock, returning in the afternoon.

Daily Arkansas Gazette
Sat, Nov 12, 1870 ·Page 4

Lewisburg Says No
to $100,000 for Railroad

—A letter from Lewisburg inform us that the proposition to subscribe $100,000 to the capital stock of the Little Rock and Fort Smith railroad, by Conway county, is probably defeated.

Daily Arkansas Gazette
Sat, Nov 12, 1870 ·Page 4

First Little Rock Train Trip
to End of Tracks - Lunch at Lewisburg

Little Rock and Fort Smith Railroad.

On invitation of Col. A. P. Robinson, chief engineer, and in company with Messrs. J. H. Pratt, Warren Fisher, Josiah Caldwell, and several others of the Boston capitalists who are now on a visit to our state, and who are the real parties interested in the building of the Fort Smith and Cairo and Fulton roads, and a number of other gentlemen, we went on an excursion yesterday to the end of the first named road.

In addition to one of the elegant pas-

In addition to one of the elegant passenger coaches, we had in our train one of the new baggage and emigrant cars. These are elegantly constructed, and contain every modern improvement and convenience. Behind the Pulaski engine No. 1, we had a pleasant run to within a mile and a half of Lewisburg. Among the distinguished railroad men present all were unanimous in the expression that they never saw a better new road. All the work is of the most substantial character, and reflects great credit on the builders. The Boston gentlemen expressed themselves as very agreeably surprised both in the character of the road and the country it traverses. One of them remarked to us that he never witnessed better engineering than in the location of the line.

After arriving at the end of the track, an elegant lunch was spread, and all partook heartily, and then sallied out to witness the operation of track-laying. Some went up to Lewisburg. The precision and regularity of the movements of the hands in putting down and spiking the rails is perfectly wonderful. They move like clock work. By Monday night, it is thought, the road will reach Lewisburg. Regular daily trains will commence running on Monday week.

As soon as the track laying party reach Lewisburg, they will be taken off and put on the Cairo and Fulton road to put down the iron on the first twenty miles. The ties are already laid, and if they commence on Tuesday next, it is thought that it will not require over twenty days to complete it.

It is not too much to say that the engineers, builders and contractors of the Fort Smith road have proved themselves worthy of the support and co-operation of the whole people of the state. We are glad to know, too, that the gentlemen who are furnishing the capital for the construction of the Fort Smith and Cairo and Fulton roads, express themselves as highly gratified with their investment, and just as quiek as money, muscle and brains can accomplish it, both roads will be finished. There is nothing visionary about it—they mean business, as they have proved by their past acts. We understand that a reorganization of the Fort Smith company is nearly perfected, and it is the intention to complete the road by the last of May next.

The only regret we had on the trip was that some of our Van Buren friends were not along to enjoy it.

Daily Arkansas Gazette
Sun, Nov 13, 1870 ·Page 4

First Excursion Completed - Regular Service to Start Soon

☞The Little Rock and Fort Smith railroad is finished to Lewisburg, 54 miles, and trains will soon be running from Little Rock to that place.

Tri-Weekly Fort Smith Weekly Herald
Thu, Nov 17, 1870 ·Page 3

Regular Service to Start Monday

L. R. and F. S. RAILROAD.—As we have previously announced, regular trains will commence running to and from Lewisburg, on Monday next. The trains will connect with stages to Fort Smith. Parties in the city desiring to transact business at Lewisburg can go and return the same day.

Daily Arkansas Gazette
Fri, Nov 18, 1870 ·Page 4

Schedule - Train to Arrive Noon Daily Connect with Stagecoaches to Fort Smith

TRANSPORTATION.

Little Rock and Fort Smith Railroad.

Time Card.

ON and after Monday, November 21. 1870, a passenger and freight train will run as follows :

GOING WEST.

Leave—

Huntersville,	8:30 a. m.
Bartlett	9:08 "
Palarm,	9:33 "
Gold Creek	10:8 "
Conway	10:24 "
Cadron	11:00 "
Plummer's	11:31 "

Arriving at Lewisburg 12:00 m.

GOING EAST.

Leave—

Lewisburg	1:00 p. m.
Plummer's	1:29 "
Cadron	2:00 "
Conway	2:36 "
Gold Creek	2:52 "
Palarm	3:27 "
Bartlett	3:52 "

Arriving at Huntersville 4:30 p. m.

☞Stage Connection between Lewisburg and Fort Smith.

Coaches will also leave the principal hotels at Little Rock for transfer of passengers to and from the station at Huntersville.

For further information. inquire at the general office of the company, Real Estate Bank Building, corner of Markham and Commerce streets, up stairs.

D. W. C. BROWN, Gen'l Sup't.
LORING S. RICHARDSON,
Gen'l Ticket Agent.

City dailies copy.   11 13 dtf

Daily Arkansas Gazette
Fri, Nov 18, 1870 ·Page 4

—The first regular train to Lewisburg will go out and return Monday, and every day thereafter. Our good looking young friend, J. T. Jenkins, is agent. Omnibuses will call for passengers at any part of the city.

Daily Arkansas Gazette
Sun, Nov 20, 1870 ·Page 4

☞ The Little Rock *Gazette* of the 16th, speaking of the bright prospect of that city, says :

"Our railroad prospects continue to brighten. We are assured that the Memphis road will be completed within two months, when we will have at least one outlet to the east easy of access. On Monday, regular daily passenger and freight trains will commence running as far as Lewisburg, on the Fort Smith railroad, a distance of 50 miles. It is the intention of the contractors to finish the road by May next. To-day, track laying commences on the Cairo and Fulton railroad, and within twenty days the iron will be laid on the first twenty miles. The second twenty, we believe, is being graded, while the actual work south from here, we understand, is soon to commence"

The Van Buren Press
Nov 22, 1870, Page 3

☞ On Monday, the 21st November, the Little Rock and Fort Smith Railroad commenced running a passenger and freight train over the road to Lewisburg, as far as completed. Stages will connect Van Buren and all points between with the trains. See the Time table in our paper. D. W. C. Brown, is Gen'l. Supt., Lorenzo S. Richardson, Gen'l. Ticket Agent, Little Rock.

☞ We are now getting our Little Rock mails, by rail to Lewisburg, in about thirty hours.

The Van Buren Press
Nov 22, 1870, Page 2

Tracks from Little Rock to Fort Smith to be completed by January 1st, 1872

"LITTLE ROCK AND FORT SMITH RAILROAD

Is now open to Lewisburg, fifty miles, and has been running regular trains to that point since November 21. Fifty miles more are already graded, and the ties are down ready for the iron. This second division will be open ready for travel in February, and the entire road from Little Rock to Fort Smith will be completed on or before the 1st of January, 1872. The track, locomotive, passenger and freight cars are first class in every respect. Close connections are now made by stage from Lewisburg to all points from there to Fort Smith and Van Buren and points beyond."

Daily Arkansas Gazette
Thu, Jan 05, 1871 ·Page 2

DOUBLE HOMICIDE IN POPE COUNTY.— A correspondent at Lewisburg, writing on the 30th, says :

" The stage driver, just in from above, informs me that a shooting affray occurred in Russellville, Pope county, on the 28th, between Charles Wofford and Joe Burton, in which both were mortally wounded, and died a few minutes after. Both had families. Burton was the town constable."— *Gazette 1st.*

The Van Buren Press
Jan 10, 1871, Page 2

EXTENSION OF THE LITTLE ROCK RAILROAD.—A construction train left here yesterday to assist in extending the road beyond Lewisburg. The road-bed is ready for the iron to Russellville, and unless accidents prevent the contractors will put down one mile of rail per day. The grade is completed to within four miles of Clarksville, Johnson county. It is the intention of the Company to have the road to Clarksville ready for trains to pass over by 1st of April next.—*L. R. Republican.*

The Van Buren Press
Jan 17, 1871, Page 2

While the completion of train tracks to Lewisburg were highly anticipated, it spelled the doom of Lewisburg. Residents started to dismantle their homes and reconstructing them, plank by plank and log by log, one mile north to be close to the railroad tracks. As the months and years passed, Lewisburg faded and Morrilton grew.

This transition wasn't as fast as often assumed. As evident in these newspaper clippings, Lewisburg remained a thriving community for several years after the arrival of the railroad.

In the Daily Arkansas Gazette, on Nov. 11, 1871:

"Lewisburg is a thriving town, supporting some eight or ten stores, doing an average business of $75,000 with a steady annual increase. The business men, as a class, of Lewisburg, would be creditable to any town; they are men of means, energy and tact, and this, together with the natural advantages of the place, ought to make it a place of considerable importance in the next ten years. It is surrounded by an excellent agricultural country, and the cotton crop this year is larger than any since the war. The fall being late, all the bolls came out full, and the fall rains being late, there will be less stained cotton, so that, with the increase in price, the larger yield and better quality of the cotton, planters are feeling in excellent spirits."

Ten years later in 1879, Morrilton was incorporated with a population of 800, and Lewisburg had shrunk from 2,000 to only 356 people and a few remaining businesses. Families continued to relocate to Morrilton as that new town developed with the stimulus of the railroad.

Photo Taken at Little Rock
Source: Mike Hood, Civil Engineering Manager for the City of Little Rock

LITTLE ROCK AND FT. SMITH RAILROAD

Is now open to Lewisburg, fifty miles, and has been running regular trains to that point since November 21. Fifty miles more are already graded, and the ties are down ready for the iron. This second division will be open ready for travel in February, and the entire road from Little Rock to Fort Smith will be completed on or before the 1st of January, 1872. The track, locomotive, passengers and freight cars are first class in every respect. Close connections are now made by stages from Lewisburg to all points from there to Fort Smith and Van Buren and points beyond.

The Van Buren Press
Jan 17, 1871, Page 1

Mr. D. B. SICKLES, Financial Agent of Arkansas, furnishes the New York *American Railroad Journal* the following information in regard to our Railroad :

The Little Rock and Fort Smith Railroad, running up the Arkansas Valley from Huntersville to Lewisburg, is in an encouraging state of progress. Over ninety miles have been graded and made ready for the ties, and the track is being laid as rapidly as the iron is furnished. Fifty miles of track have been laid and trains are now running regularly to and from Lewisburg. The fifty miles beyond that place will be completed by the first day of May next if the material is promptly supplied. The road is in splendid condition and the management of the work of construction could scarcely be improved. The State authorities are much gratified with the condition and progress of the road, and all the requirements of the law have been faithfully complied with. An inspection of the work has recently been made by a distinguished civil engineer, and he pronounced it superior to that of any recently constructed road in the Southwest.

The company has recently been re-organized, and the Boston interest has secured the absolute control of the old corporation together with all its rights, franchises, etc., etc. At a meeting of the Board of Directors held in Little Rock a few weeks ago, Mr. John C. Pratt was unanimously elected President of the company, and Mr. Edward Adams Treasurer.

When completed the financial condition of the company will be as follows, viz :

150 miles railway valued at	\$3,500,000
1,000,000 acres of land valued at	5,000,000
1,500,000 State Bonds valued at	1,500,000
Total	**\$10,000,000**

The Van Buren Press
Jan 24, 1871, Page 2

Letter to the Editor: Trains Are Slow --- Butterfield's Stagecoaches Were Faster

" I think what you call a "train" on your road to Lewisburg must be something else. The supposition arises from the published schedule. Hanger & Howell's old rickety hacks used to make as good time : Butterfield's Overland a great deal better.

Daily Arkansas Gazette
Wed, Feb 08, 1871 · Page 2

THE LITTLE ROCK AND FORT SMITH Railroad is one hundred and fifty miles in length, and traverses a section of country generally of very great fertility, and offering every inducement to settlers. The western portion, especially, runs through a delightful country, blessed with one of the finest climates in the world, well watered, and abounding in delightful scenery. This road, when completed, is destined to be one of the greatest thoroughfares in the State, since it will open up the Indian Territory and the great Southwest.

PROGRESS OF THE WORK.

Fifty miles of this road from this city to Lewisburg, is now complete, and trains are passing over it daily. The line is cut out throughout the entire distance, the grading done with the exception of about seventeen miles, and nearly all the cross-ties cut and on the ground ready for use. Forty additional miles of iron is also here, and twenty more on the way from New Orleans. When this arrives it is the purpose to complete fifty miles more of road west of Lewisburg, which is promised before the 4th of July. About three hundred men are now at work, and the completion of the road is promised before the beginning of the next year.

THE ROLLING STOCK

Now owned by the company, and in use, comprises seven new locomotives named "Pulaski," "Conway," "Pope," "Johnson,"

"Franklin," "Crawford," "Sebastian;" three fine passenger coaches and about one hundred freight and platform cars.

COUNTY AID.

We regret to learn that the counties along the route have not subscribed aid more liberally. There certainly could not have been a due appreciation of the value of the enterprise on the part of leading men in the counties traversed. All the subscriptions thus far received are: Fort Smith, $50,000; Clarksville, $50,000; Crawford county, $100,000, and Sebastian county, $100,000, making $300,000 in all.

The Van Buren Press
April 18, 1871, Page 2

A SWINDLER.

A Horsethief, Whose Name is not Vance, with Religious Proclivities.

SHERIDAN, (Grant co.) Ark.,
Monday, April 10, 1871.

Editors Gazette—From a communication published in your paper, dated "Lewisburg, March 14, 1871," and signed "T. F. R.," I learn that a young man calling himself E. J. Vance has been arrested as a horsethief. The writer expressed it as his opinion that Vance has relatives living somewhere below the Rock. This is a mistake; he has no relatives in this portion of the state. This Mr. E. J. Vance came into this neighborhood as a common laborer, worked a short time for Mr. Hicks, joined the Methodist Episcopal church as a probationer, made application for license to preach, and being informed by the minister in charge that he must first become a member in full connection in the church and become recommended by the quarterly meeting as a suitable person, etc., he concluded that this was too slow a process. He then attached himself to the Baptist church at Liberty, made application for license as a preacher, obtained it, and left here as a *Baptist* minister. He was, during his stay here, employed to teach a public school in this immediate neighborhood, and through the influence of my father, was dishonorably discharged from the same. He left here without paying his just debts. My father is of the opinion that his name is not Vance, but a name assumed by him. He knows nothing of the Vance family, as to their geneaology, etc. He is regarded here as a "dead-beat," and unworthy to be admitted into respectable society. I hope that you will give this an insertion in your paper. Respectfully, your obedient servant,
E. H. VANCE, junior.

Daily Arkansas Gazette
Wed, Apr 19, 1871 ·Page 4

—Col. Anderson Gordon, of Lewisburg, is in the city en route east for the purpose of purchasing a spring and summer stock of goods.

Daily Arkansas Gazette
Fri, May 05, 1871 ·Page 4

It has been reported by malicious or misinformed persons that labor on the Little Rock and Fort Smith Railroad, has been suspended, and that the rolling stock and other property of the corporation has been seized for debt. It is with profound satisfaction we authoritatively announce that these statements are not supported by the facts. The company is regularly running trains to Lewisburg, (Conway county,) fifty miles from this city; and for fifty miles beyond Lewisburg the road is graded and ready for the iron, which is here awaiting shipment. This carries the enterprise to Clarksville, (Johnson county,) and the remaining portion of the road to Van Buren is being rapidly pushed forward to completion. The rails for this last section fifty miles from Clarksville to Van Buren, (Crawford county,) are now *en route* from New Orleans, and may be expected at the levee of this city daily.

The Van Buren Press
May 16, 1871, Page 2

Little Rock & Fort Smith Railroad.

CHANGE OF TIME.

ON and after Monday, September 11, and until further notice, trains will run as follows:

GOING WEST.

Leave Argenta at 8 a. m., for Bartlett, Palarm, Gold Creek, Conway, Cadron, Plummer's, and arrive at Lewisburg at 12 m.

GOING EAST.

Leave Lewisburg at   12:30 p m
Arrive at Argenta at   5:00 p m

Stage connection between Lewisburg and Fort Smith.   PEIRCE, STEACY & YORSTON,
August 31, 1871—tf.   Managers.

The Van Buren Press
Oct 03, 1871, Page 2

Methodist Pastor at
Lewisburg: Rev. N. Futrell
Pastor of the smaller churches
near Lewisburg: Rev. W. R. Knowlton
Rev. I. L. Burrow is serving
the Seminary at Lewisburg

The following appointments were read out by the Bishop:

DARDANELLE DISTRICT.
J. J. ROBERTS, P. E.

Dardanelle Station—E. J. Dawns.
" Circuit—W. J. Dotson.
Danville " to be supplied.
Gally Rock " I. L. Hicks.
Clinton " W. E. Whittenberg.
Cadron " J. F. Hall.
Dover " C. H. Ford.
Lewisburg Station—N. Futrel.
" Circuit—W. R. Knowlton.
East Fork—A. C. Ray.
Quitman Institute—P. A. Moses.
Lewisburg Seminary—I. L. Burrow.

The Van Buren Ppress
Oct 24, 1871, Page 2

Dr. R. T. McLean, of Lewisburg, is in the city. Dr. M. is proprietor of the popular hostelrie at Lewisburg, and knows how to keep a hotel.

Daily Arkansas Gazette
Sat, Oct 14, 1871 ·Page 4

BEDENGER—The funeral of Mrs. MIL-
DRED B. BEDENGER, wife of Solomon S. Bedenger, residing near Lewisburg, Conway
county, in this state, will take place at the
residence of J. W. Smith, corner of Rock
and Fourteenth streets, at nine o'clock this
(Friday) morning The friends and ac
quaintances of the deceased are invited to
attend.

Daily Arkansas Gazette
Fri, Nov 10, 1871 ·Page 4

Election Results, and
Great Description of Lewisburg

Lewisburg—The Election—A Few Notes by the Way.

Special Correspondence of the Gazette.]
LEWISBURG, Nov. 8, 1871.

Editor Gazette—Last Tuesday morning we left Little Rock by the Little Rock and Fort Smith railroad, and after a pleasant ride of three hours with the accommodating conductor of that line, Mr. Geo. Stacey, we arrived at the village of Lewisburg. Yesterday the municipal election came off in this village, when the following officers were elected for the coming year: Mayor, E. W. Mason; recorder, W. P. Egan; councilmen, J. M. Higgins, R. T. Markham, T. B. Stout, J. L. Wilson and G. W. Blakely; marshal, S. Collins. A ticket headed by James M. Gordon for mayor was also in the field, but neither party came out on a political platform. Still it was essentially a conservative victory, as there were two colored men on Gordon's ticket.

Lewisburg is a thriving town, supporting some eight or ten stores, doing an average business of $75,000, with a steady annual increase. The business men, as a class, of Lewisburg, would be creditable to any town; they are men of means, energy and tact, and this, together with the natural advantages of the place, ought to make it a place of considerable importance in the next ten years. It is surrounded by an excellent agricultural country, and the cotton crop this year is larger than any since since the war. The fall being late, all the bolls come out full, and the fall rains being late, there will be less stained cotton, so that, with the increase in price, the larger yield and better quality of the cotton, planters are feeling in excellent spirits. It is a great misfortune that the Fort Smith road can not be immediately completed. Col. Stacey informs us that four months' work would finish it, but the prospect is anything but encouraging for the work to go on. The road, so far as built, is the smoothest we have rode on west of the Mississippi, and does infinite credit to the contractors, Messrs. Pearce, Stacey & Yorston. HARDSCRABBLE.

Daily Arkansas Gazette
Sat, Nov 11, 1871 ·Page 1

Isham is Editor
of Lewisburg Paper

The Wide-Awake is the name of a neat new paper in Lewisburg. H. P. Barry is proprietor, with Chas. E. Isham as editor. The latter, in his salutatory, says:

It is our intention to keep "Wide-Awake" to the political as well as local interests of our people. We need good, honest men in office, and an entire re-modeling of the state and national governments. May the time be not far distant when the monster, radicalism, shall have given place to a party upon whose banners shall be inscribed, "Down with despotism and up with the primeval liberties of our country."

Daily Arkansas Gazette
Sun, Nov 19, 1871 ·Page 2

WE must say that the following is decidedly the meanest thing we ever saw from the pen of any journalist claiming even ordinary decency. We clip from the Fort Smith *Patriot*:

THE LEWISBURG WIDE-AWAKE—We have received the first number of this nasty looking, poorly printed, little eight by ten disgrace to southern literature, and will thank the publisher if he will not send us number two. Its editorials read as if they were stolen from some other paper, or were written two hundred years ago, in the reign of James the Second, by that old terror to justice, Lord Jeffries. We have burned the copy sent us, and trust you will have the good sense not to send us another. No, we won't exchange.

The truth of the matter is, the *Wide Awake* is small in size, but is gotten up neatly and printed in a very creditable manner, when we remember the difficulties under which the publisher labors. Its editorials are decidedly more chaste, elegant, courteous and argumentative than those of its critical neighbor. The *Wide-Awake* is edited and published by one man alone. He writes, sets type, sweeps his office, makes his fires, and, indeed, does everything connected with his paper, without one particle of assistance. The *Wide Awake* is a conservative journal, and of course is alone dependent on the people of the town of Lewisburg and of Conway county for a support. If the Fort Smith *Patriot*, which is the official organ for seven counties, had to depend in a like manner upon its own merits, it would not live a month. Mr. Charles E. Isham—a sober, industrious printer, and a man of decided ability, as the *Patriot* man will find out if he measures swords with him—is the editor and publisher of the *Wide-Awake*, and he deserves all praise for starting as he has done. The sentiments expressed by the *Patriot* scribbler are unworthy any gen-

Patriot scribbler are unworthy any gentleman, and more particularly of one who has stood at the case himself, and who should, if he ever imbibed any gentlemanly instincts, wish a fellow-craftsman God-speed in his endeavor to establish a business of his own, even if he does happen to enjoy the public printing himself, secured at the sacrifice of a principle, which Isham would blush to even think of.

Daily Arkansas Gazette
Sun, Dec 03, 1871 ·Page 2

GEN. PIERCE, editor of the Fort Smith *Patriot*, seems to have a better opinion of Mr. Chas. E. Isham, of the Lewisburg *Wide-Awake*, than his associate, Mr. Corwin. In an editorial correspondence to the *Patriot* from Lewisburg, he thus speaks of the *Wide-Awake*:

They have at last succeeded in starting a paper here, called the *Wide-Awake*, edited by Chas. E. Isham, formerly a typo on the Dardanelle *Chronicle*. It is a neat six-column paper, well printed and well gotten up. Mr. Isham is a young man, ardent and enthusiastic, and for the first time sits astride the "editorial tripod." He naturally strikes out from the shoulder, in his salutatory, upon the state and national administrations. This was to be expected in the *first* number, but we opine the *Wide-Awake* will deal more with the many advantages and points of attraction in Conway county than with politics. We heartily wish this new born child of journalism a wide-awake and prosperous future.

Daily Arkansas Gazette
Fri, Dec 08, 1871 ·Page 2

—We had the pleasure of a call on yesterday from L. O. Breeden, esq., of Lewisburg, Conway county.

Daily Arkansas Gazette
Sun, Dec 17, 1871 ·Page 4

HERE is what the *editor* of the Fort Smith *Patriot* has to say about an item which appeared in his paper during his absence, about the Lewisburg *Wide-Awake*:

We observe that the rather severe notice given to the Lewisburg *Wide-Awake* by the *Patriot* during our absence, has been the means of advertising our friend Isham and his paper very extensively. Every democratic journal is taking up the club in his defense as though they had a severe attack of the colic, and we hope this extensive and gratuitous advertising will have the effect to make the

Wide-Awake as rich as **Helmbold, and** will bring to its coffers untold sums of filthy lucre. Mr. Isham really **ought to** *thank* our associate for going **for him so** roughly, and we hope **great good may** accrue to him from it. We really hope our friends at Lewisburg will give Isham a liberal support, and keep him going. We care nothing for the politics of the paper, but if it is conducted with spirit and vim it will add much to the prosperity of that enterprising little burg.

Daily Arkansas Gazette
Fri, Dec 22, 1871 ·Page 2

A correspondent of the Lewisburg *Wide-Awake*, writing from Springfield, says Dr. Senator Thomas is again in possession of the clerk's office. How he came by it we are not informed. Why don't you tell us all about it, Isham?

Daily Arkansas Gazette
Tue, Jan 16, 1872 ·Page 1

River News.

The river is falling slowly here and above; three feet reported above Lewisburg, and four from there down. It commenced raining at two o'clock yesterday evening, and continued up to the time of going to press. If the rain is general, look out for a big river.

Daily Arkansas Gazette
Fri, Jan 19, 1872 ·Page 4

LITTLE ROCK & FORT SMITH RAILWAY.

CHANGE OF TIME.

On and after Monday, September 11th, and until further notice, trains will run as follows:

GOING WEST.

Leaving Argenta at ....8:00 a.m.
for Bartlett, Palarm, Gold Creek, Conway, Cadron, Plummers, and arrive at Lewisburg at ....12:00 m.

GOING EAST.

Leave Lewisburg at ....12:30 p.m.
Arrive at Argenta at ....5:00 p.m.

Stage Connection between Lewisburg and Fort Smith.

PEIRCE, STEACEY & YORSTON,
8 31dawtf   Managers.

Daily Arkansas Gazette
Thu, Feb 01, 1872 ·Page 3

We learn of a severe fire at Lewisburg, a few days ago, in which the losses will foot into the thousands.

Fort Smith Weekly Herald
Sat, Feb 17, 1872 ·Page 2

LITTLE ROCK & FORT SMITH R. R.

Time Table.

To Commence Sept. 11, 1871.

Leave ARGENTA at............................8:00 a m
Leave Bartlett at.............................8:45 a m
Leave Palarm at.............................9:17 a m
Leave Gold Creek at.......................10:09 a m
Leave Conway at...........................10:34 a m
Leave Cadron at...........................11:01 a m
Leave Plummer's at ....11:30 a m
Arrive at LEWISBURG at......................12:00 m

Returning.

Leave LEWISBURG at........................12:30 p m
Leave Plummer's at..........................1:09 p m
Leave Cadron at..............................1:35 p m
Leave Conway at.............................2:08 p m
Leave Gold Creek at.........................2:35 p m
Leave Palarm at.............................3:34 p m
Leave Bartlett at.............................4:10 p m
Arrive at ARGENTA at.........................5:00 p m

PEIRCE, STEACY & YORSTON,
Managers.

Arkansas Weekly Patriot
Fri, Mar 01, 1872 ·Page 2

L. O. Breeden, esq., of Lewisburg, arrived in the city last evening.

Daily Arkansas Gazette
Sat, Mar 02, 1872 ·Page 4

[From the State Journal of the 26th ult:

An Excursion to Lewisburg.

Quick Time and a Jovial Ride on the L. R. and Fort Smith Railroad.

Shortly after three o'clock yesterday afternoon a number of prominent railroad gentlemen now visiting our city, together with several well known citizens, might be seen wending their way to the depot of the Little Rock and Fort Smith railroad at Huntersville, bent on a ride to Lewisburg. From the appearance of the numerous baskets and packages that accompanied them, it required no vivid imagination to predict that the hours until their return would fly swiftly on pleasure's wings.

Among those present might be notic-ed Messrs Allen, Caldwell, Marquand, Wheeler, Denckley, Tate, Leonard, McDonald, Oliver, Stoddard, Page, Williams, Bisford, Hadley, Morley, Townsend, D. E. Jones, Montgomery, Dillon and our short hand, lever bond reporter

The whistle sounded and away the engine sped. "We are off," shouted Keno, standing firmly on his dilapidated boots, and the popping of several corks announced that the spirit of good fellowship was on the move as well as the train. Lewisburg, which is fifty miles from Huntersville, was reached in one hour and twenty-eight minutes — This was glorious and exhilirating running on an Arkansas railroad and the announcement of the time was responded to with praiseful shouts and vivas. — An hour for dinner and sight-seeing was spent at Lewisburg, when the order "all aboard for Little Rock," was shouted by the conductor. The home run occupied but one hour and thirty minutes, yet the spirit of the party traveled faster than the puffing engine as it pranced and thundered along on its firm track. On the return trip an informal meeting was organized at one end of the car. — We give brief sketches of a few of the speeches made, and regret the tired condition of our special reporter does not permit him to remember all the proceedings fully. Like all the rest aboard he flung dull care behind him, and was too happy to care to remember one-half of the strict instructions we gave him. He handed us the following rough notes and warned us, when we frowned, to give him a congratulatory hand-shake, since, he said, the reporters of the Gazette and Republican he was sure, were too happy to pay any attention to their duties.

TOASTS AND SPEECHES.

After partial silence was obtained Dillon's sylph-like form slowly rose from a back seat, and his rosy lips lisped forth the following:

May the iron rollers of progress and material development glide more swiftly and smoothly than the boxwood spheres of Plimpton, and may Allen and others who supply the grease, and who are here to set them in motion, never cease their labors in our beloved Arkansas until the whole State is an immense railroad skating rink. (Uproarious cheers and music by the rink band.)

Shout's for Allen, compelled him to advance and say :

Gentlemen—Your State is rich in

Gentlemen—Your State is rich in Heaven's smiles and all kind nature's fairest gifts. [Here some one muttered about corrupt officials and levee bond stealing.] She is "in her sons in her soil, in her station thrice blest," and is the desired highway for the best intercontinental route to link the Atlantic to the Pacific. By October next the iron steed will take the track at St. Louis, and make no pause until he snorts a triumphant arrival at the gates of the City of Roses ; and twelve months from to-day he will be at the service of the Postmaster General of the United States, and ready to carry the Evening State Journal through without stopping, by lightning express, to all its subscribers in Texas. In one year we mean to have the Cairo and Fulton Railroad completed, and in splendid working order from its initial to its terminal point. And here let me read for you what I published in this morning's Gazette. [We have not space for the communication ; but its substance is that if certain aid, in bonds and land, is given by the counties south of here, he will extend the Cairo and Fulton Railroad, and have the cars running thereon from Little Rock to Fulton, on the Red River, within twelve months from that date—probably in less time.] In my vocabulary, he continued, there is no such word as fail, and soon Missouri and Texas will feel the thrill of union, as Arkansas with a hearty bounding with the throb of her great railroad artery, extends a hand of friendship to each, and form a beautiful trinity of Southern sisters—tria juncta in uno.

The cheers that broke forth were so long continued that Mr. Allen, though evidently meaning to say more, sat down. And then was heard a Minstrel piping this refrain : "Fill the bumper fair, every drop we sprinkle o'er the brow of care smooths away a wrinkle." and three times three were given for the Cairo and Fulton and its President.

Several other speeches were made on the occasion, but we have not space to publish them.

The Southern Standard
Sat, Mar 02, 1872 ·Page 2

THE Lewisburg *Wide-Awake* says a prominent colored man in that place received a very loving letter from Gov. Hadley the other day. The *Wide-Awake* expresses some doubt about the governor writing the epistle, and calls on him to know whether or not he is the author. Of course the governor will furnish the desired information.

Daily Arkansas Gazette
Sun, Mar 10, 1872 ·Page 2

A radical paper is soon to be started at Lewisburg in the interests of the Arkansas Tammany thieves.

Fayetteville Weekly Democrat
Sat, Mar 16, 1872 ·Page 8

—We have before us the first number of the Western Empire, a new republican journal just started at Lewisburg. It announces its adherence to the state and national administrations, and although it has no chicken pie yet in the way of public printing, we have no doubt it will get its slice in a few days. The paper is published by Messrs. C. C. Reid, jr., and James Pears, and edited by the latter. Look out, Wide-Awake. We welcome the Empire to the newspaper world.

Daily Arkansas Gazette
Fri, Mar 29, 1872 ·Page 4

—The corner-stone of a new M. E. Church, South, was laid at Lewisburg yesterday by Rev. J. J. Roberts.

Daily Arkansas Gazette
Sun, Mar 31, 1872 ·Page 4

—Charley Isham, of the Lewisburg Wide Awake, was in the city Sunday, looking "as happy as a big sunflower."

Daily Arkansas Gazette
Tue, Apr 02, 1872 ·Page 4

River News.

River falling fast——four feet and ten inches by the gauge. The rivers are all rising at most of the principal cities. The weather has been quite changeable—sunshine, then cloudy and sprinkling rain, nearly all day. Levee business dull

The Jennie Howell arrived from New Orleans, and left for Fort Smith on arrival of the train from Memphis.

The Little Rock was momentarily expected from above last night, and will be found at the wharf this morning with a fine trip, she having passed Lewisburg yesterday at 12 m. Capt. Gere and Mr. Chas. H Conrad will be found aboard.

Daily Arkansas Gazette
Wed, Apr 03, 1872 ·Page 4

As we expected it would, the second number of the *Western Enterprise*, the new Minstrel fledgling at Lewisburg, comes to us this week as the official journal of five counties—Conway, Searcy, Marion, Perry and Yell. That's right, Guvvy; pay 'em enough, and why shouldn't they indorse the administration? The avidity with which men jump at the bait reminds us very much of the fellow who sold himself for a mess of pottage.

Daily Arkansas Gazette
Thu, Apr 04, 1872 ·Page 2

STATE NEWS.

CONWAY.

On Saturday last the corner-stone of a new church was laid, with great parade and ceremony, at Lewisburg. What followed that night is told by the Western Empire of the 31:

Mr. Barns, the contractor, had just succeeded in finishing the entire frame work of the church, when, on Saturday night about 10 o'clock, a heavy thunder storm arose in the southwest. The wind blew a terrible gale, and for some time we apprehended a hurricane. Sweeping up from the river, the wind-storm struck the frame work of the church broadside, and the whole structure, with one crash, went to the earth.

Daily Arkansas Gazette
Thu, Apr 04, 1872 ·Page 1

A serious accident occurred last week to two men at Lewisburg, while engaged at work on a church building, by a lot of the timbers falling on them. Their names were Williams and Johnson .

Fayetteville Weekly Democrat
Sat, Apr 06, 1872 ·Page 5

Extend Tracks 10 Miles North From Lewisburg?

We hear at this time there is talk of laying ten miles more of the track, by some means or other, to save the land grant, and stop. What is the point? Where is the good of this? Is it not child's play to talk of this, when confessedly the company does not, and it seems will not pay its debts, and this does not decrease the debts, but leaves them drawing interest, and the litigation with its bulk of costs still going on? Why run up in the woods ten miles from Lewisburg and stop and wait another year, with no debt paid and nothing settled or cleared away? It will cost something to lay the ten miles: there is then another debt. This swells up the already existing debt that can't be paid. This little addition of ten miles may aid bondholders to sell bonds at an increased price, which will come back at last to increase the debt and crush the whole enterprise.

Daily Arkansas Gazette
Tue, Apr 23, 1872 ·Page 2

CONWAY.

The Lewisburg Empire says :

At our Conway circuit court last week, in the case of G. W. Howell vs. Little Rock and Fort Smith railroad, the demurrer filed by the attorneys for the road was overruled, and a decree went in favor of Howell. This decision gives to all settlers upon the lands granted to this company, who have heretofore availed themselves of the benefit of the law, the right to purchase their homestead at $2.50 per acre.

Daily Arkansas Gazette
Sun, May 05, 1872 ·Page 1

—Great credit is due Mr. Steacey for the prompt and efficient manner in which he laid the ten miles of track west of Lewisburg. Inside of ten days he organized his force and put down the iron. Yesterday an excursion party, consisting of quite a number of railroad officials, took a ride over the new part, running at the rate of twenty-five miles per hour. The work is reported to be well done. What is a little singular, three obstructions were found on the track between here and Lewisburg, at different points. At one place a cross-tie was laid obliquely across the track ; at another a pile of rocks, and at still another two cross-ties. These were evidently put there by designing persons, for they are the first obstructions of any character ever found on the road. Fortunately they were all discovered in time to prevent any trouble. We trust now that the land grant is safe, the company will be enabled to pay off its debts and proceed with the work at once.

Daily Arkansas Gazette
Tue, May 07, 1872 ·Page 4

The Lewisburg Enterprise says the frame-work of Mr. Atkins' new house was totally demolished during the gale on Saturday morning.

Daily Arkansas Gazette
Sat, May 25, 1872 ·Page 1

The Lewisburg Wide-Awake announces the death of Col. S. S. Ford, an old citizen and prominent lawyer of the county.

Daily Arkansas Gazette
Sun, Jun 02, 1872 ·Page 1

Charley Isham, of that exceedingly Wide-Awake newspaper at Lewisburg, arrived last evening. He is a delegate to the convention which meets to-morrow.

Daily Arkansas Gazette
Tue, Jun 18, 1872 ·Page 4

Isham, of the Lewisburg *Wide Awake* is a spiteful and horrid old bachelor. Of late he has been boasting of the many handsome bouquets arranged by delicate fingers, he has received, and Frolich of the *Searcy Record*, to curb his vanity, told him he could not regard himself as a "favored mortal" until he could induce some one to marry him. Hear the "horrid brute's" wicked and slanderous reply :

How "favored" Brother Frolick ? With a broken head, a wrenched nose, a gouged ear, or a hairless scalp ? "Favored" with numberless snappings, and snarlings, frownings and poutings ? "Favored" with long bills for false curls, paint and powder, and expensive Dolly Varden dresses ? "Favored" by being ordered round and "hen-pecked ?" Oh, no, Brother Frolich, we had much rather remain single, and be contended and happy, than to be married and wedded, perhaps, to misery.

"Horrid brute," brother Isham, to prate that way about the "fair sex," the noblest work of God. You should be banished away to some uncivilized clime, where you would never behold the smiling countenance of a lovely woman. If you was down in this section, and should show any inclnation whatever, to "take some fair lady's hand, for better or for worse," you would get the "dead shake" so quick it would make your head swim.

The Southern Standard
Sat, Jun 22, 1872 ·Page 3

**Lewisburg Paper Receives a
Complement from the Southern Standard**

One of the most pleasant episodes in our late visit to Little Rock was a social gathering at the *Gazette* office, one aftternoon, of the Democratic members of the press of the State, in attendance on the Convention. We there met the clever and chivalric Sparks, of the Fort Smith *Herald*, the genial and jovial Frolich, of the Searcy *Record*, the quiet and clever Maxwell, of the Batesville *Times*, the stirring and enterprising Newman, of the Pine Bluff *Press*, the solid and staunch Dunham, of the Van Buren *Press*, the honest and blunt Barrys, of the Dardanelle *Transcript* and the *Monticellonian*, and last and least in size, Isham, of the Lewisburg *Wide-Awake*. These, with Woodruff, Blocher and Smithee, of the *Gazette*, who are the synonym of cleverness and hospitality, and the very soul of honor, constituted a coterie the like of which seldom meets in this world. Long may they all live to battle for the right, and may many more such re-unions take place, and we be there to see.

The Southern Standard
Sat, Jun 29, 1872 ·Page

WANTED—INFORMATION—Concerning a young man twenty years of age, who has absented himself from home for two years. His name is William Boulcott, from Mobile, Ala. Any information concerning him would be thankfully received by his afflicted parents. Dear son—Should this meet your eye, write to us at once, and send for what money you need to return home. Let the past be buried; write to us at once. I and your mother will be but too glad to send you funds. We know, from a gentleman in Lewisburg, you are in want of money. Wold some minister be so kind as to make inquiry? He is a member of the Episcopal church. Address Mr. DAWS, care W. Cottrill, Mobile, Ala.   7-11 dlw*

Daily Arkansas Gazette
Tue, Jul 16, 1872 ·Page 4

—While Senator Clayton was speaking at Lewisburg, on Monday, he desired to quote from Scripture the sentence, "Nothing good can come out of Nazareth," but forgot the name. Turning to Mr. Brooks, who is supposed to be familiar with everything connected with the sacred volume, he asked him what was the name of the place referred to in the Bible from which no good could come. Instead of saying "Nazareth," Mr. Brooks promptly responded, much to the astonishment of the senator and the amusement of the crowd, "The state administration."

Daily Arkansas Gazette
Wed, Aug 07, 1872 ·Page 4

The Lewisburg *Wide Awake* says :

"Colored men delivered speeches at the African Church last Monday. We learn that the Ku-Klux of the Union League was on hand, and strict orders were given by white negroes that were present, that no black negroes should be allowed to hurrah for Greeley. A negro, exercising the right of free speech, saw fit to hurrah for Geeley. Brittentine, a negro who was there to keep down any Greeley demonstration, told him to stop it. He yelled again, and Brittentine hit him a severe blow on the head. This happened, luckily, at a Radical political meeting of the negroes. If it had happened at a Reform speaking, the hands of the editor of the *Empire* would have been held up in holy horror, and with his imbecile pen he would heroically exclaim : 'Ku-Klux outrage ! Fiendish barbarity ! Colored men denied the privilege of cheering for Grant ! Our black people need protection in their rights.'"

The Southern Standard
Sat, Sep 28, 1872 ·Page 2

—L. O. Breeden, esq., of Lewisburg, announces his candidacy for representative, on the Hunter ticket, from the district composed of the counties of Searcy, Conway and Pope.

Daily Arkansas Gazette
Sun, Oct 06, 1872 ·Page 4

ISHAM, of the Lewisburg Wide-Awake, says :

We must acknowledge that politics are getting too muddy for our limited comprehensive powers to, in the least, fathom. Just as we had become satisfied that Hunter was to be the nominee of the liberal-reform party, and we had consigned the Brooks ticket to the oblivion of the case, and had prepared to enter into an earnest effort for his election, the report comes that he has declined, and we are "up in a balloon." We were for Hunter, but we don't believe we know who we are for now. We pause for information.

Daily Arkansas Gazette
Thu, Oct 17, 1872 ·Page 11

THE STATE ELECTION.

Dispatches from various portions of the state to the republican and reform state central committees, report majorities about as follows for governor. The vote for president is about the same :

	Baxter.	Brooks.
Jefferson	2,256	
Phillips	3,630	
Mississippi	450	
Randolph	75	
Pulaski		100
Independence	200	
Woodruff	200	
St. Francis		55
Jackson	40	
Arkansas	50	
Prairie		521
Crittenden	1,600	
Union	487	
Conway		500
Hot Spring		390
Perry	100	
White		1,100
Craighead		400
Cross		250
Bradley		400
Calhoun		200
Columbia		400
Dallas		400
Drew		700
Nevada		91
Saline		737
Van Buren		200

CONWAY AND POPE.

Col. Anderson Gordon writes us as follows from Lewisburg yesterday :

Our election is over, and we have carried the county for the conservative ticket, Greeley and Brown and Brooks, by five hundred majority. I learn that Pope county has gone conservative by a considerble majority.

Daily Arkansas Gazette
Fri, Nov 08, 1872 ·Page 4

By Mr. White: A joint resolution requesting the postmaster-general to extend the mail service on route No. 7524, from Little Rock to Fort Smith, Ark., and running through the cities of Lewisburg, Clarksville, Ozark and Van Buren, from a tri-weekly to a daily service. Read and ordered engrossed.

Daily Arkansas Gazette
Tue, Jan 21, 1873 ·Page 1

—The citizens at Plummer's station, twelve miles east of Lewisburg, on the Fort Smith railroad, have petitioned the post-office department to establish a post-office at that place. We trust they will succeed.

Daily Arkansas Gazette
Wed, Feb 05, 1873 ·Page 4

Steamboats Still Active on River

RIVER NEWS.

The river still continues to fall. It has fallen two inches since our last report, and now stands two feet seven inches by the mark.

The Fort Gibson, Capt. Jim Bowlin, with Mr. John S. Jones as chief clerk, was at Lewisburg yesterday noon. She will be found at the wharf this morning.

Daily Arkansas Gazette
Sun, Mar 23, 1873 ·Page 4

The Lewisburg Empire of Friday says: We understand the jail at Perryville, in Perry county, was broken open on the night of the 25th, and all the prisoners escaped. The inmates were charged with various crimes—murder, larceny, etc. Two murderers were sent from our county. It is high time that our jails should be so constructed that these murderers and thieves cannot escape at pleasure.

Daily Arkansas Gazette
Tue, Apr 01, 1873 ·Page 2

HIT 'EM AGAIN.

The legislature catches it from all the state press, regardless of politics. We have yet to see the first republican or democratic paper published in Arkansas that fully indorses and approves the course of the present legislature. Here is what the Lewisburg Empire, the editor of which is a clerk of the house, has to say in the last issue of his paper:

We honestly think if our friends in the lower house intend to do anything it is high time they were getting about it. The people are very desirous of seeing a finance bill pass, that will restore our state credit and pay the interest on the public debt; and in this connection we hope measures will be adopted prohibiting the further issue of scrip. After this, the school law needs a good ventilation. The expense attached to this branch of our internal government should be very materially reduced, and the circuit superintendency wiped out. The revenue law should be amended. A new election law should be provided, and in such a manner that a fair expression of the votes of the people can be had, well guarded against riots, intimidation or ballot-box stuffing.

The nuisance of the present system of county and probate courts should be done away with. There is no branch of our whole state government, executive, judicial or ministerial, that is so much abused or fallen in so low repute. There are many other essential measures to which we would like to call the attention of our legislature, but we have not the time. We are only afraid they will not do what we have already mentioned. Gentlemen, the people's eyes are upon you, waiting and watching anxiously to "see the salvation of the Lord," in the way of good and prompt legislation. The spring is upon you and it is high time the farmers were at home. We have a good governor, who will look after the interests of the entire state, and if you will make good and wholesome laws, we guarantee they will be executed to the very letter, so long as Gov. Baxter presides over the destiny of Arkansas.

Daily Arkansas Gazette
Tue, Apr 01, 1873 ·Page 2

A bill passed the senate yesterday removing the county site of Conway from Springfield to Lewisburg. The county site of Faulkner is Conway station.

Daily Arkansas Gazette
Sun, Apr 13, 1873 ·Page 4

STRAYED OR STOLEN.

$25 REWARD.—STOLEN, FROM THE undersigned, on March 9th, at his residence, near Lewisburg, one bay horse, six years old; few white hairs in forehead; lame in right fore foot when leaving home; 12½ hands high. One black pony mare, seven or eight years old; 12 hands high. One bay filly, two years old. The above reward will be paid for delivery of stock to Deputy Sheriff Counts, or liberal reward for any one of them.

4-12d3t* D. T. CULBERSON.

Daily Arkansas Gazette
Sun, Apr 13, 1873 ·Page 4

THE LEGISLATURE.

Synopsis of Acts Passed—The Boundaries of Howard and Dorsey Counties.

The fifty-first act repealed the act authorizing the county courts of the several counties to issue bonds to build courthouses and jails.

The fifty-second act removed the county seat of Conway county from Springfield to Lewisburg.

Daily Arkansas Gazette
Tue, May 06, 1873 ·Page 4

County Seat Back at Lewisburg

A friend writes from Lewisburg under date of the 20th inst.:

Everything is moving along quietly in old Conway, since the county seat has got back to this place. The farmers are very much in the grass, owing to so much rain, but they are hard at work and will soon be out of the weeds. Crops look healthy but small. We are planting more corn this year than last, and the prospect is good for us to have corn to sell another season instead of buying, as now. Our little town is still improving, with an opening for a good manufacturing establishment. Politically we are quite cheerful. Gov. Baxter has the sympathy of nearly everybody, without regard to party. He has nothing to do but stand firm in the defense of the people, and he is all right.

Daily Arkansas Gazette
Fri, May 23, 1873 ·Page 2

THE Lewisburg Empire closes an article as follows, in reply to a recent editorial in the Republican ridiculing the idea that any *quo warranto* proceedings were ever dreamed of by the political desperadoes of this state:

The time for ruling Arkansas with a rod of iron, and fastening on her already overburthened shoulders an increased load of debt, has passed. The people have an honest governor, and to him they will cling as long as his actions are governed by pure and honest motives. If being honest in an official capacity is turning the state over into "democratic hands," then, for God's sake, let her go. If honesty cannot be found in the republican party, let us seek a party where it is respected.

Daily Arkansas Gazette
Thu, Jun 05, 1873 ·Page 2

Says the Lewisburg Empire:

Within the last three months our town has given marked evidences of thrift. Fine dwelling houses have been erected, and stores and other buildings. A spirit of energy has fallen upon some of our people. Lewisburg can be, for it possesses the advantages, the second town on the Arkansas river.

Daily Arkansas Gazette
Sat, Jun 21, 1873 ·Page 3

—C. C. Reid, jr., has retired from the Lewisburg Empire. He is succeeded by Mr. E. B. Henry.

Daily Arkansas Gazette
Wed, Jun 25, 1873 ·Page 4

—One of the pioneers is Mr. Samuel Plummer, who was in our city yesterday. He has been *paying* subscription to the GAZETTE since 1827, and has lived in one house, near Lewisburg, for forty-two years. He is a widower; and a gentleman, that learned him the art of bear-hunting when a boy, says Mr. Plummer is looking for his affinity.

Daily Arkansas Gazette
Thu, Jun 26, 1873 ·Page 4

—The Little Rock Cornet band goes up to Lewisburg to-day.

Daily Arkansas Gazette
Fri, Jul 04, 1873 ·Page 4

$3 Fare to Lewisburg from Little Rock

—Considerable pleasure to-day. Three dollars and a quarter will take you to Arkadelphia on the excursion train; three dollars will enable you to see the eagle flap his wings in Lewisburg. A ball at Papa Geyer's and speeches under the auspices of the Sons of Ham and Sons of Honor will serve to amuse the stay-at-homes.

Daily Arkansas Gazette
Fri, Jul 04, 1873 ·Page 4

July 4th
Celebration at Lewisburg

FOURTH OF JULY FESTIVITIES.

How the Day was Spent at Lewisburg—Speeches by Gov. Baxter and Others—A Good Dinner—Pretty Girls—A Good Time Generally.

Surrounded Hill Celebrates—James M. Thomas Delivers an Oration—Pleasant Day—Good Dinner.

The Excursion to Arkadelphia—Three Coach Loads of Passen-

Three Coach Loads of Passengers—The Railroad Men's Dinner—Shooting Affray.

The Dullest Day in Little Rock for Years—The Colored People Celebrate—Dance at Papa Geyer's—No Fun, No Fireworks, No People, No Nothing.

AT LEWISBURG.

Those of our citizens who did not celebrate in other places went up to Lewisburg on the Fourth, where one of the pleasantest days of the year was spent. A commissioner of the GAZETTE, who was on the train, saw, among others, Gov. Baxter and two sons, Gen. McCanany, Capt. W. S. Davis, Gen. E. W. Gantt, Wm. E. Woodruff, sr., Col. Embry, M. Dotter and lady, Senator Thomas, Circuit Clerk W. F. Blackwood, L. Breeden, and others on the train.

After considerable detention at the depot in Argenta, the train finally started at 8:45. In a few moments it became known that Mr. J. C. Hale was in charge of the train, as he kindly invited all on board to come down with their tickets. The genial Sam. S. Hascall occupied the footboard. We rolled past Palarm, took water at Gold creek, went on past Conway, the picnic station, Cadron, Plummer's, and arrived at our destination at 12 o'clock. At the depot was a dense crowd of people, and vehicles of every description. On alighting from the train, Gov. Baxter was escorted into the depot, where he was cordially welcomed by Judge Mason. In reply to the welcome, the governor returned his sincere thanks in brief and fitting words. After this the governor was escorted to a hack by A. D. Mason, the mayor, in which also rode the aldermen, Blakeley, Higgins, Henry and Morrill. The city of Lewisburg is situated about a quarter of a mile from the railroad, and although it is in the woods, some of the teamsters are regular scalpers, having the cheek to charge fifty cents for transportation. The gentleman who drives the two mules, canvas-covered wagon with a hole in the top is deserving special mention. We were transported over the hill to M. W. Steele's grove, which proved to be indeed a delightful spot. A beautiful arbor of trees for an audience-room had been constructed, and the speaker's stand was appropriately decorated. To the right of the stand were arranged fourteen pretty girls, representing the goddess of liberty and the thirteen original states of the union. The following are the names of the ladies and the states they represented, also the name of the goddess of liberty: Maine, Mollie Levmore; New Hampshire, Mollie Stallings; Massachusetts, Liddie Gordon; Rhode Island, Alice Sleeper; Connecticut, Tillie Collins; New York, Alice Davis; New Jersey, Phebe Bennett; Pennsylvania, Mattie Webber; Delaware, Anna Gordon; North Carolina, Emma Wilborn; South Carolina, Jo. Welsh; Virginia, Amanda Wells; Maryland, Mollie Gordon. Miss Mattie Gordon, the goddess, and the representative of North Carolina, were regarded as the stars of beauty. Sheriff Benton Turner, of Faulkner county, was the grand marshal of the day, and all arrangements were excellently carried out by the following committee: Dr. Davis, chairman; A. Gordon, G. W. Blakeley, Isaac Black, C. C. Reid, jr., E. B. Henry, W. G. Gray, J. H. Carse, H. A. Russell and W. B. Gibson. The Little Rock Light Guards were placed on the front seat, while the seats in the rear were crowded with the citizens of Lewisburg, Clarksville, Dover, Galla Rock, Conway, Springfield and Norristown. On the speaker's stand were Gov. Baxter, Wm. E. Woodruff, sr., Gen. McCanany, Senator Thomas and Gen. E. W. Gantt; also the city officers and committee of arrangements.

The order of exercises was quite lengthy, and was opened by Col. Gordon, who welcomed Gov. Baxter, and tendered thanks on behalf of the city for his presence. The governor replied that it afforded him great pleasure to attend, but said he knew from the programme he would be called on again, and so he would refrain from saying anything, except to return his sincere thanks.

The programme was read, after which Rev. Mr. Brewer, of Lewisburg, offered up prayer.

Mr. E. B. Henry, of Lewisburg, was introduced, and stirred up the patriotism of the audience by reading the Declaration of Independence. He is an excellent reader, and at the conclusion was loudly applauded. The choir, assisted by the audience, sang the "Star Spangled Banner."

Rev. W. C. Stout, of Lewisburg, delivered an oration, prefacing his remarks by saying he felt inadequate to meet the requisite necessities of the occasion; that he had expected to address no such an audience. He said he felt and spoke the sentiments of his heart in saying by God's grace we have an honest governor. [Applause.] People think it is not much to be honest, but it is a great deal. It is a great thing for a public man to be honest in the midst of corruption, etc. [Applause.] His oration was, "The Declaration of Independence," and was listened to with profound respect. After the oration came music by the band.

Col. C. C. Reid stepped upon the stage, and said it was altogether out of his power to speak, either national, political or personal. He excused himself by saying he was not present at the meeting of the citizens; that he had been serving on committees, etc. He said he would name as a substitute for himself the friend of the people of Arkansas, a man who, against the storm, has stood erect—the governor of Arkansas—who last winter was offered thousands upon thousands of dollars to barter away your rights. He felt it a great honor to name such a substitute.

At the conclusion of Mr. Reid's remarks, Gov. Baxter stepped forward and delivered an eloquent speech, of which the following is a brief synopsis:

Ladies, and Fellow-Citizens of Arkansas—You have conferred too much honor upon me on this occasion. I will address you briefly, but do not think I can do justice to myself, as it is getting late. After referring to the freeing of the colonies, he said the people of Arkansas are and ought to be free, and so help me God they shall be free! He was willing to pledge his sacred honor, property and life to that end. He said his remarks might be personal in a way, but as God was his judge he had no feeling of animosity towards any one; did not intend to malign any one, but to vindicate the right. Eight years ago, the state passed through rebellion, but all good citizens buried the past, and those who opposed were not good citizens. In 1864 the people organized a state government, but the officers were without ability, although their purposes were honest. If the state had been let alone, the people would long since have been prosperous and happy. In 1868, by authority of congress, the people were required to reorganize and reconstruct the government, although everybody knows it was not the will of a a majority of the whole people of Arkansas. Arkansas was not represented by the will of the people in the convention which assembled for that purpose. Joe Brooks was the chief man there. Very few people believe the present constitution was legally adopted. Wh— —

few people believe the present constitution was legally adopted. Why submit to it? Because it has been foisted upon us by the action of J. L. Hodges, Joe Brooks and Thomas M. Bown, the commissioners appointed to count the votes on its adoption or rejection? He read a certificate signed by them as commissioners, that the new constitution was adopted. Every man knows that it was never adopted by a majority of the legal votes! This view was new doctrine with him. He proposed to examine what had taken place and what will take place. On the 5th of November an election for state officers was held. His friends called on him to be the standard bearer for governor for the republican party. He never sought the office, but thought it a solemn duty to accept, and now that he is governor, survive or perish, sink or swim, he proposed to correct the errors that have crept into the government. The law requires that the returns for governor be made to the presiding officer of the senate. So they were, and went direct to O. A. Hadley, the president *pro tem.* of the senate and acting governor. The result gave him a majority of 3,200 over Mr. Brooks. Whether there was fraud or not he was unable to say, but knew there were men in the republican party guilty of fraud, and capable of committing any crime or wrong possible. If there were any frauds in electing him he had no knowledge of them. He read a certificate signed by J. M. Clayton, president of the senate, and C. W. Tankersly, speaker of the house, showing him to be elected governor. He felt it his bounden duty to exercise the duties of governor. Joe Brooks presented a petition to the legislature to contest for the governorship. No one ever heard him (Baxter) say he opposed hearing the contest. Joe Brooks alleges that I, in connection with Secretary of State Johnson, manipulated the returns. This statement is an infamous falsehood. He had never seen the returns, although now in his care. Every assertion to the contrary is an infamous lie, from whatever throat uttered. When the petition of contest was presented to the house, it was not of sufficient interest to call him there. He never entered the house but once during the entire session. The petition was presented, and the vote stood sixty-three against receiving it, and nine for; twenty-nine of his partisan friends not supporting it. [He hoped the ladies would not think he was angry—he was not.] Joe Brooks and his friends complain that he did not receive justice in the legislature. Maybe so! He, as a lawyer, had often in practice demurred to the declaration or bill, and the case had been thrown out of court without a hearing—the court holding there was no case. He thought the

court without a hearing—the court holding there was no case. He thought the legislature said Brooks had no case, and so threw it out. He referred to the *quo warranto* application. which was so elaborately argued before the supreme court. The four honest judges declared there were no grounds for granting the application. The one dishonest judge thought there was. He is known as Poker Jack, and is editor of the Republican. He has played his last game! Poker Jack's back is broken, and he will never be himself again. The attorney general and Joe Brooks have gone into the circuit court and brought suit again.' Next they will go before a justice of the peace, and next into the backwoods of Van Buren county, on Devil's fork, where they will hunt up a justice of the peace and contend for a *quo warranto*. They may bring a *quo warranto* to him, but he will never submit to be ousted by any circuit court of the state. If this is any consolation to Joe Brooks and his friends, they can put it in their pipes and smoke it. Joe Brooks claims that I have usurped the office of governor. This I deny; I never desired the office, but inasmuch as I have been called to discharge its duties, it would be treason for me to yield it to another. Were I to do so it would sink me so low the hand of resurrection would never reach me. Men claiming to be friends of Mr. Brooks say I was counted in by fraud. If fraud had been committed, Poker Jack and others of the same ilk had more to do with it than anybody else. Respectfully protesting that congress has no right to interfere in this matter, nevertheless if an election could be held under the auspices of the general government, I would be willing to compete with Mr. Brooks for the office, and in case of his success would yield all claims to the position. But now Brooks must be patient, and bring his petition before the next legislature, which would be the first elected from the whole people since reconstruction. He read that portion of the law in Gould's Digest bearing on the matter, which says the contest must be decided by the legislature. If this is so, how can Mr. Whytock, or any other judge, decide it? Five years ago he retired from political life, disgusted with certain republican leaders; had heard of the great corruption of Poker Jack, but not the half. The first difficulty Poker Jack and himself had was in the Metropolitan hotel, in Little Rock. Poker Jack came to him and said, "*we* have got a little bill we desire to get through." He asked P. J. not to drive him to an issue on that bill. Shortly after he went home for four days, and the bill passed the house during his absence. He referred to an editorial in the Republican suggesting how suscepti-

the Republican suggesting how susceptible he was of taking a bribe. He said there was no man who was bold enough to offer him a bribe. He did find one or two men, however, who felt of his pulse to ascertain his position relative to bribes, Poker Jack has made the issue, and he and the ring must go to the wall. There is no compromise. He lucidly explained the senate election bill, with its proposed board of canvassers, one of whom was to be Lieut. Gov. Smith. The canvassers were to have the authority to appoint the supervisors, and they in turn the judges of election. Suppose the bill was a law to-day. No one except those whom Poker Jack favored would ever come into office. The metropolitan police bill received his attention next. The bill proposed to allow men to be arrested at any place and any time, without a warrant. If these bills had passed, Arkansas would not be fit to be inhabited. Opposition to

Daily Arkansas Gazette
Sun, Jul 06, 1873 ·Page 4

Gov. Baxter stated in his Lewisburg speech that it was well known the present constitution was a fraud—that is, was never adopted by a majority of the legal voters. Mr. Brooks says *he* received a majority of the votes for governor, although Mr. Baxter was declared elected. Now, then, why should we have a new election for the office of governor, and none on a new constitution? One is no more fraudulent or usurping than the other—and Mr. Brooks knows it. While he favors a movement he thinks would be for his own *personal* benefit, will he favor a movement for the benefit of the people —a constitutional convention and a new constitution? Baxter's is as much a legal state government as was Hadley's or Clayton's or Murphy's. In fact, it is better founded than either of these was. If Mr. Brooks was governor, would we have a legal state government? Could we have a legal state government founded upon a fraudulent constitution? We would be pleased to hear from Mr. Brooks on this subject.

Daily Arkansas Gazette
Sat, Jul 12, 1873 ·Page 2

Making Fun of the Governor's Speech at Lewisburg

☞ Elisha Baxter run up to Lewisburg, on the 4th, and read a little speech to the "dear people," telling them what a fine Governor he is, and of ever so many good things he is going to do! The people are tired listening to the fair promises of this fraud, unless he can show better cause than he has that he is not usurping the high office of Governor of Arkanaas.

Hush, little Elisha, on the house top,
When the wind blows, the cradle will rock,
When the wind lulls, the cradle will stop,
When the props fall, the cradle will drop,
And down will come Elisha, co-whoop and co-whop!

Fayetteville Weekly Democrat
Sat, Jul 12, 1873 ·Page 2

Hon. C. C. Reid, jr., of Lewisburg, arrived in the city last night on the Fort Smith railroad. He is as jolly as ever.

Daily Arkansas Gazette
Tue, Jul 29, 1873 ·Page 4

Mr. E. B. Henry has retired from the editorial management of the Lewisburg *Western Empire*, and is succeeded by Messrs. Kearney & Watson. The *Empire* is a wide-awake Democratic paper. We wish the outgoing editor that peace and quiet which is so seldom found in editorial life, and the incoming editors more than the usual amount of pleasure and profit in their new enterprise. -

The Southern Standard
Sat, Aug 16, 1873 ·Page 2

From an article published in the Lewisburg Empire of last Friday, we extract the following :

We have just received information from a reliable gentleman of Perry county, that Manes on Thursday went to his farm on the river and put his house in order for a bushwhacking campaign. He stated, as we are informed, that he witnessed the killing of Pigg, and that the two Gadds and Oglesby done the killing, and he intended never to stop until he had their blood; that he had a hundred men at his command, and he intended to avenge the death of Pigg. He graciously informed the citizens now annexed to Conway, but formerly of Perry, that they must not be surprised if he subsisted his men from their produce in the event he had to fall back from Perryville; that he would pay for all they took; that his aid-de-camp, Jim Brown, had been out for the last forty-eight hours gathering up men, and they would assemble at Rocky Cypress, that Hambright had gone to see Gov. Baxter to get authority to arrest all persons engaged in last Tuesday's raid, and if they got the authority it was all right, if not, they would assume the power and go in. We learn from other sources that a squad of the Manes faction is in possession of the court-house at Perryville.

Fayetteville Weekly Democrat
Sat, Aug 30, 1873 ·Page

—Thomas White, a noted horsethief, who confesses to have been one of the leaders of the gang for fifteen years, was arrested at Lewisburg, Saturday, and placed in jail. He gives the names of a number of officials in adjoining counties as members of the gang.

The Osceola Times
Sat, Sep 20, 1873 ·Page 2

—D. W. Mason, the worthy mayor of Lewisburg, died Friday.

—Cotton bales are becoming frequent on the streets of Lewisburg

The Osceola Times
Sat, Oct 04, 1873 ·Page 2

Gordon to Run For
State Senator

In obedience to a request of a large number of his fellow-citizens, Col. Anderson Gordon, of Lewisburg, has declared himself a candidate for the state senate, to fill the vacancy in the Fifth district, occasioned by the appointment of Senator Thomas as pension agent. Col. G. is one of the leading citizens of his district, and we confidently look for his election. The people of the district could make no better selection.

Daily Arkansas Gazette
Sat, Oct 04, 1873 ·Page 2

Prisoners Set Lewisburg Jail on Fire
and Escape

Says the LEWISBURG EMPIRE of Saturday:

About four o'clock Monday morning, the calaboose was discovered to be on fire, and the alarm being given, several of our citizens hastened to the spot armed with water buckets, and the flames were speedily extinguished. The door of the building was found to be almost entirely destroyed, there being but little left of it except the iron bars that cross at each side. There were two prisoners confined in it, Jim Sofe, a colored individual of the town, who was up for cutting scrape, and a white man who called himself Purkey, arrested last Saturday for larceny, he being allowed to take his valise in the calaboose with him and which among other necessary articles, contained a box of matches, with which, in the dead hour of night, he proceeded Guy Fawkes like, to kindle the devouring flames. In the carrying out of his scheme for liberty he was highly successful, for upon a sufficient aperture being obtained, the worthy couple "wrapped the drapery of their couch around them" and squeezed out through the fiery wreck into the darkness, and proceeded to put the mud of Lewisburg in their rear. Jim was captured before night, and has since made his escape again. The ingenious Purkey roams at will, far from the scene of his last exploit.

Daily Arkansas Gazette
Wed, Oct 08, 1873 ·Page 3

Says the Van Buren Press: Sidney Wallace, of Johnson county for whom $200 reward was offered, was arrested about seven miles from Lewisburg, by Polk Allnutt. marshal of Lewisburg, and Sheriff Stout, of Conway county on yesterday last, and turned over to the sheriff of Johnson county. Wallace is also supposed to be the Aug.... of Judge Mears.

The Southern Standard
Sat, Oct 18, 1873 ·Page 3

Election Results for
Conway County

Official: For Senator—Scott, 292: Gordon, 178; Hayes (col.), 133. Representatives—L. W. Davis, 300; H. W. Burrow, 249; J. P. Venable, 227; John McGehee, 133; T. W. Bennett, 124; C. E. Tobey, 9. Supervisor—Robert Simpson, 79; D. M. Allen, 19: J. W. Madison, 17. Municipal officers elect of Lewisburg: Mayor, J. M. M. Higgins; recorder, W. F. Conlee; marshal, C. L. Rayburn; treasurer, W. M. Scarborough; aldermen, J. P. Allnutt, William Kearney, S. R. Waller, J. B. Dilling and E. B. Henry.

Daily Arkansas Gazette
Thu, Nov 13, 1873 ·Page 1

Methodist Preacher
Appointed for the Coming Year

Galla Rock---W. J. Dodson
Point Remove Mission--to be supplied
Lewisburg---T. F. Brewer
Lewisburg Circuit----C. O. Steele
Springfield---W. R. Knowlton

Daily Arkansas Gazette
Sun, Nov 16, 1873 ·Page 6

Indian Treasure Found
1 Mile from Lewisburg
STILL DIGGING
Old Man Hightower in Search of
Gold in Other Directions

The Lewisburg Empire of Saturday contains the following:

"The old man Hightower, spoken of in hast Tuesday's Gazette as hunting treasure in Little Rock, has dug a large hole on Point Remove creek, about a mile from Lewisburg, where it was supposed valuables had been secreted by the Indians prior to their removal to their new reservation, and it is reported that he has been successful at this point. He was a wealthy man at the breaking out of the war, and still owns some valuable property in Yell county, and seems determined to make a final effort to live once more in luxury. The point near Lewisburg is peculiarly designed, by a clump of trees bearing evident traces of marks of the ax, and seemingly trained, while young, to grow together at the tops, as they grow to a center in an unnatural manner.

Daily Arkansas Gazette
Sun, Nov 16, 1873 ·Page 6

Lewisburg Woman Has Had
10 Husbands

☞ They are boasting of a lady in Lewisburg, Ark., who has had ten husbands, and survived them all, and yet she is only seventy three years of age. This is a very fair record, and does credit to the lady's taste and judgment. It proves that there is something attractive in matrimony after all, and is a complete refutation of the theories of Victoria Woodhull. It has been suggested that this frequently-married person was unfortunate in all her matrimonial adventures, and kept on marrying in order to find a really good husband; but this hint, of course, comes from one of that class of people who are forever picking flaws. If her husbands were bad no one of them could have troubled her for a very long time, for supposing her to have been first married at eighteen years of age, her husbands would have only averaged five years each. She finds it difficult to take into herself an eleventh sharer of her joys and sorrows, as the marriageable young men of the place give her a wide berth, and look ominously in the direction of her church yard when her name is mentioned. But a woman who has had ten husbands need never despair, and if she be at all superstitious she will pin her faith on the truth of the proverb that there is luck in odd numbers, and persevere until she adds one more to her list.

The Southern Standard
Sat, Nov 22, 1873 ·Page 1

Reads Like a Western Movie Script
Ned Wallace the
Outlaw Murderer Arrested
at Lewisburg

SID. WALLACE.

The Johnson County Desperado—Attempt to Break Jail.

The Failure—Two Men Wounded—Wallace Brought to the Penitentiary.

Most of the readers of the GAZETTE have doubtless heard of Sid. Wallace, of Johnson county. He comes of a good family, which was universally esteemed prior to the war, and has a large and wealthy connection. Various assassinations and murders have been committed in Johnson county since the war, and suspicion rested upon Sid. Wallace and his brothers. He has three brothers living, all of whom (except his brother William) are regarded as desperate characters. Another brother was killed in February last. In 1871 Sid. waylaid the road about a mile and a half east of Clarksville and attempted to assassinate, by shooting him from the roadside, a man named Dickey, a drummer from St. Louis. Dickey was riding out in a buggy accompanied by a young man named Turner, a clerk in a house at Clarksville; the only witness against Wallace. For this he was arrested and gave bond for his appearance before the circuit court at the ensuing term. At the meeting of court an indictment was found against him for assault with intent to kill, besides several other indictments for minor offenses. The cases were continued and he gave bond for his appearance at the next term of court. No court was held after that until March, 1873. In February, 1873, Sid. and his brother George, made an assault upon Turner in the town of Clarksville and attempted to kill him. Turner being the only witness against him in the Dickey affair. He was prevented from killing Turner by the interference of citizens, and made his escape into the country. A few days after this Sid. and his brother, George, came to town again hunting Turner, when the latter saw them on the street and shot and killed George. Turner was subsequently arrested and brought before county judge Meers, who discharged him. A few days after this Sid. Wallace accidentally shot himself in the foot, and was arrested. At that time those who had gone on his bond for shooting Dickey gave him up, refusing longer to be his bondsmen. Just before the commencement of court in March he made his escape, and the governor offered a reward of two hundred dollars for his arrest. From that time on he was

for his arrest. From that time on he was in and out of the county at intervals, but managed to elude the officers of the law.

On the 20th of August, at night, he rode into Clarksville, hitched his horse in the court-house yard, secreted himself behind the court-house fence and shot, and fatally wounded, R. W. Ward, a constable, who was sitting in front of W. P. Rose's drug store, opposite the court-house square. He then got on his horse and rode away.

Just one week after this, about half a mile east of Clarksville, Hon. Elisha Meers, the circuit judge, was shot and killed from a blind near the road-side, the particulars of which we gave at the time. The evidence developed at the coroner's inquest pointed to Sid. Wallace as the perpetrator of the deed. The governor offered a reward of five thousand dollars for the arrest and conviction of the assassin. About this time Deputy Sheriff Kline, with a posse, got on the track of Wallace and run him out of the county. Soon after this Wallace very leisurely rode through the town of Lewisburg, in Conway county. Hearing of the matter, Sheriff Stout, of that county, in company with another gentleman, followed, overtook and arrested Wallace, carried him to Clarksville and turned him over to the authorities of Johnson county, who placed him in jail. Court came on the 20th of October, Judge Withers having been appointed to the vacancy created by the assassination of Judge Meers. The grand jury found three indictments against Wallace—one for the attempt to shoot Turner, and one each for the murder of Ward and Meers. He was tried on the indictment previously found for the attempt to assassinate Dickey, convicted, and the punishment assessed at four years in the penitentiary. Next, he was tried for the murder of Ward, convicted of murder in the first degree, and sentenced to be hung on the 23d of December. This was the condition of affairs on Tuesday. Clarksville has no jail, and the prisoners of the county were confined in a three-story brick building, known as the Hershey block. The prisoners were in the third story. There were six of them—Sid. Wallace and his two brothers, Mat. and Tom, the two latter having been committed to keep the peace, having given bond at first, but were afterwards surrendered by their bondsmen. Another prisoner was named T. J. Cargyle, nicknamed "Alabama," under an indictment for larceny. Chas. Bray was another prisoner, confined pending investigation for letting prisoners escape. Charles Clark was another prisoner, who had been convicted and sentenced to ten years' imprisonment in the penitentiary for assault with intent to kill Thos. Payne, the principal witness against Sid. Wallace for the murder of Ward. All these prisoners were chained in the third story, except Tom and Mat.

Wallace. There were four guards in the building. On Tuesday afternoon one of the guards went after a bucket of water; another one went down stairs to let him out, while still another stepped into a back room, when Tom and Mat. Wallace sprang upon the remaining guard, took possession of the guns of the other guards, and told him to drop his pistol or they would kill him. The guard retreated down the steps, pistol in hand, and when at the foot of the steps fired off his pistol. As he retreated Mat. and Tom released Sid. and the other prisoners from their chains, and took possession of the four shot-guns of the guards. At the sound of the pistol at the jail, a number of citizens rushed toward the building, covering themselves by a building on the corner opposite. Thomas H. Payne and David Winters stepped out into the street, Winters firing at Sid Wallace, who was standing in the window of the third story of the jail, shot-gun in hand. Wallace returned the fire, the first shot wounding Payne in the side and Winters in the right arm, and the next taking effect in Winters' back. Both are seriously hurt, though hopes are entertained of their recovery. Several shots were then fired at the jail birds, one of which cut off a lock of Sid's hair. The citizens then undertook to charge the jail. The second story of the building was taken, and the crowd started up the stairway leading to the third story. Here they were met by the three Wallace boys and Clark, with guns cocked, who told them not to come any further, and the cap on one of the guns was snapped, but missed fire. The party retreated down the steps and surrounded the jail. Four or five citizens then obtained five kegs of powder, placed them in a box, securely nailing it up, and placed the box in the lower story. A trail was then laid for some distance outside, and the prisoners were given thirty minutes in which to surrender or be blown up. After parleying a few minutes they agreed to throw their arms out at the window, which they did, and six citizens, accompanied by the jailer, went up stairs, took possession of and chained all of them. Prior to this neither Mat or Tom Wallace had been chained. On throwing the guns out of the window one of them went off, shooting Mr. Nicholson through the coat sleeve, Mr. Downy through the pants, and grazing the leg of Mr. Woolam.

The next morning after the occurrence Sid Wallace was brought before Judge Withers, who sentenced him to the penitentiary for four years, in accordance with a former verdict. He had not been

Daily Arkansas Gazette
Sat, Nov 29, 1873 ·Page 4

☞ MR. SAMUEL T. WATSON, of the Lewisburg *Western Empire*, was in to see us a few minutes this week. He is an old brother Typo, and is as full of life and energy as he use to be when we worked together on the Little Rock *Republican*, past midnight hours. We wish SAM and his paper abundant success.

The Southern Standard
Sat, Feb 14, 1874 ·Page 3

Two Attorneys Quarrel, & Ends in Shoot Out & Death in Lewisburg Store

Fatal Shooting Affair.

From passengers down from Lewisburg, yesterday, we learn that Prosecuting Attorney C. C. Reid, jr., of the Sixth judicial circuit, shot and killed another lawyer, named Samuel Hill, on Tuesday The facts, as near as we could glean them, are these: Two gamblers had been arrested on Tuesday morning, charged with violating some statute, and taken before a justice of the peace. Mr. Reid appeared for the prosecution and Mr. Hill for the defense. During the progress of the trial some hot words followed between the two attorneys, and the court had to interfere to stop them. Mr. Hill remarked that he would see Reid after court. When court closed, Reid walked into the store of Russell & Thomas, and was followed by Hill. Here the quarrel was renewed, Hill picking up a couple of two pound weights, one of which he threw at Reid, missing him. Just as he was in the act of throwing the second weight, Reid pulled out a pistol and fired, the ball passing through Hill, inflicting a wound from which he died in a half hour. The second weight struck Reid on the side of the head, inflicting a severe wound. A coroner's inquest was held over the body, and a verdict of justifiable homicide returned.—*Little Rock Gazette.*

The Southern Standard
Sat, Mar 21, 1874 ·Page 2

Attorney Released

IN Lewisburg, Conway county, Ark., recently, C. C. Reid, Prosecuting Attorney, shot and killed another lawyer named Hill. The dispute which led to the killing arose in the court-room. Reid was discharged on the ground of justifiable homicide.

Fayetteville Weekly Democrat
Sat, Apr 04, 1874 ·Page 3

Lewisburg Man Starved to Death

We had a call last evening from Mr. Chapman, who resides about five miles above Lewisburg, and who was with Mr. Hoffman, who it was stated, a few days ago, starved to death, and he gives a very different version of the affair from that heretofore published. From what we can gather, Hoffman no doubt died for the want of proper attention; but that was his own fault, in not making known his condition. The people of Lewisburg knew nothing whatever of the man or his condition, and from our knowledge of them as a generous, open-hearted people, we know they are not lacking in benevolence and charity. Below we give two statements—first, that of Mr. Chapman, and also a letter from Col. Anderson Gordon, of Lewisburg. The statements of these gentlemen can be relied on as true:

STATEMENT OF G. W. CHAPMAN.

Hearing that two copies of the Daily Republican have published long statements regarding the death of Mr. Hoffman and child, six miles above Lewisburg, on the Little Rock and Fort Smith railroad, which statements reflect severely on the people of Lewisburg, and especially the Masons of that place, I wish to make a statement of facts in the premises, presuming I know more of them than the party who told the Republican reporter.

Since December, 1873, Mr. Hoffman's family have lived in a rented house on the plantation of J. W. Smith, of which I am the agent. Having business with some renters in the same house, I called, and for the first time learned of Mr. Hoffman's illness, and the child's death. His wife and another child were also ill. There was some meat and meal in the house, and I sent them such provisions as sick people would need, and sent for a doctor at Lewisburg; also, sent a woman to nurse and cook for them. At that time the Masons of Lewisburg knew nothing of their sickness, nor did they know that Mr. Hoffman was a Mason, he never having affiliated as such with the lodge at Lewisburg, or called for such assistance as he might reasonably have asked for. The merchants at Lewisburg sold the shrouding at cost on my request, which was this: that if Hoffman was not a Mason and had no means to pay for a Mason and had no means to pay for the goods they must put down the price, as I would pay the bill myself.

I make this statement in justification of the people of Lewisburg, who certainly were not to blame in any way for the sufferings of the Hoffman family. He certainly did not starve to death, nor has the family at any time been in a starving condition. That they lacked nourishment suitable for sick people I admit, but they certainly had intelligence enough to apply for the assistance of the Masons, and most certainly would have received it.

STATEMENT OF COL. ANDERSON GORDON.

LEWISBURG, April 7, 1874.

DEAR SIR: I see an article in yesterday's paper, which purports to be a truthful statement, saying that a Mr. Hoffman, who came to this county some three or four months ago, and his son had starved to death, within four miles of Lewisburg, Arkansas, which I think does this community great injustice. The facts in this case are about as follows: Some two years ago a German with a wife and two children, named Hauffman or Hoffman, came up here on the railroad, and settled out on Over-cup creek, some five miles from this place, in a place that no one who knew anything of the country would have thought of settling, as it was mostly surrounded by a swamp, but because he had been told by his friends (I suppose in New York) that it was fine bottom land, he would consult none of the old citizens, but settled on said place. When Mr. Hoffman settled there he represented to his neighbors that he had furnished a large portion of the money to build the Little Rock and Fort Smith railroad thus far, and had the bonds to show for it. Last summer the whole family took sick, and were sick for several months, during which time they were nursed and waited on by their neighbors, and but for that, perhaps, they would have all died. I understand that some families who lived near them took the two children home, and cared for them until they got well, and Mr. and Mrs. Hoffman got well. When the lady, who had the youngest, took it home to Mrs. Hoffman, she did not want to take it, saying she did not want it, or could not take care of it, whereupon the lady left it and went home. Some few months ago Mr. Hoffman left the place he first settled, having done nothing except build a house (such a house as it was), and clearing off a small garden patch, and moved up on the railroad, near Dr. A. D. Thomas', and a mile or so from Mr. John Kurtz and Maj. J. W. Smith's place, where Mr. Chapman lives. It is about six miles from this place, and perhaps they had neighbors even nearer than that. Here it seems Mr. Hoffman and his youngest child died, and Mrs. Hoffman and the other child came near dying. Mr. Hoffman seems to have been well off in this world's goods, at one time, as the family now, I under-

to have been well off in this world's goods, at one time, as the family now, I understand, has plenty of good house furniture, jewelry, etc., and eighty thousand dollars of the Little Rock and Fort Smith railroad bonds; and certainly a family thus situated could have realized enough to have lived on, if they had tried, and Mr. Hoffman must have thought so too, for he never tried to make anything to live on, except a little garden vegetables, since he came to the county, two years ago (that I ever heard of); and as for Hoffman being a Mason and the lodge refusing or failing to do anything for him— I know nothing myself, but my information is that, if Mr. Hoffman was a Mason he lived here within a few miles of a regularly organized and working lodge for near two years and never reported himself to the lodge. Hence the lodge could not be charged with dereliction of duty, and Mrs. Hoffman's case was not reported to the lodge until last Saturday night, some time after the death of the man and child, when steps were taken for her temporary relief. I have been living here over thirty-four years and have never known or heard of any one starving to death, or likely to be buried without shrouding, before.

Republican please copy.

Daily Arkansas Gazette
Fri, Apr 10, 1874 ·Page 4

Lewisburg Reports That Starvation Story Above is a Gross Exaggeration

INDIGNANT LEWISBURG.

The Hoffman Case—The Story about Starvation Pronounced a Base Slander.

From the Lewisburg Enterprise.]

In the Little Rock GAZETTE of the 5th, and the Republican of the 6th inst., we notice an article headed "Death from Starvation," which is a gross misrepresentation of facts, and a base slander upon the Masonic fraternity, and the citizens of Lewisburg and vicinity.

The article referred to alluded to the sufferings of the family of Mr. John Hoffman; the death of himself and child, as reported, from starvation. Whilst we would cast no reflections upon either the GAZETTE or Republican for the course they have pursued in this matter, it does seem to us that they have commented unnecessarily, and that without due consideration. Such articles, published in the two leading journals of our state, are not only calculated to do the people of Lewisburg and vicinity great injury, but reflects with dishonor upon the entire state. The publication of such articles, and that alone, has given to Arkansas a

and that alone, has given to Arkansas a name abroad that is anything but enviable. The term death is sufficient to arrest the attention at all times, and death from starvation shocks humanity, and awakens feelings of sympathy and commiseration in any noble and generous hearts, for that reason we know how to exculpate the GAZETTE and Republican for publishing the disgraceful story, but it is with a feeling of supreme contempt, mingled with loathing and disgust, that we denounce the author as a base perverter of truth and a vile slanderer. We became acquainted with Mr. Hoffman about two years prior to his death, and during that period he was a quiet, unobtrusive citizen of this county, residing on Overcup creek, about six or seven miles from Lewisburg. Here he continued to reside until about the first of last December, when he moved down to the Smith farm—managed, we believe, by one Mr. Chapman, at least, Chapman at that time was the accredited agent of Smith, in this county. At the time Mr. Hoffman moved to the Smith place he was in ill health, and had been for some time previous. Mr. John Kurtz, Mr. George Kuhn and other neighbors visited the family, and from time to time supplied them with such necessaries as they requested. We had a conversation with Mr. Kurtz this morning. He seemed highly indignant and very much hurt that it should be reported that one of his neighbors had died from starvation, declaring the whole story to be a base fabrication and slander, to which history furnished no parallel.

At the time of Mr. Hoffman's death he was living on a place pretty much controlled by Mr. Chapman. At the time Mr. Chapman visited the unfortunate family and found them in such great want and distress, to alleviate their sufferings as much as he could, why did he not pay Mrs. Hoffman the money he was owing her? Why did he not pay her for her stove, her fine table, her chairs, her china and her silverware? These were articles that Mrs. Hoffman had sold him when in her greatest need, without fixing any price upon them, trusting to the integrity of the man, and believing he would pay her at once their value; but up to Tuesday night (to use Mrs. H.'s expression) he had not paid her a single penny, only about two dollars worth of provisions. When Chapman visited Little Rock last week for the purpose of giving publicity to the slanderous story, Mrs. Hoffman requested him to purchase certain articles, thinking that he would pay for them with the money that he was owing her, and he came back with a few articles, but not such as he had been requested to purchase; and Mrs. Hoffman stated that she felt very much hurt when he told her he had begged them in Little Rock.

The Republican states that Mr. Chapman laid the case of the suffering family before the Masonic fraternity of Little Rock, and they "at once raised sixty or seventy dollars; and now, thanks to their

Rock, and they "at once raised sixty or seventy dollars; and now, thanks to their generous hearts, the mother and her two little children have every necessary comfort." What became of the money? Notwithstanding Mr. Chapman has visited Mrs. Hoffman since his return from Little Rock, up to a late hour Wednesday evening, she had not received from him one penny, nor had he up to that time paid her a cent of what he was justly owing her for the furniture which he himself purchased from her. "Oh, shame, where is thy blush!"

When the Masonic fraternity of this place ascertained the facts of the suffering condition of the family, they took such steps as they could to alleviate the wants and assuage the sorrows of Mrs. Hoffman and her children. Listen to the vile and slanderous charge of a base calumniator, and talk about the unchristian indifference of the people of Lewisburg. Her past history refutes the foul insinuation. A more magnanimous and liberal people, where charity is the object, does not exist. Lewisburg gives every year to charitable purposes, according to her wealth and population, more than any village, town or city we know of; and we believe the statistics will bear us out in what we say. Mr. Chapman doubtless had some other object in view besides slandering the Masonic fraternity and the people of Lewisburg when he gave publicity to the infamous falsehoods published in the GAZETTE and Republican—a motive we trust he will be foiled in; and in place of putting money in his pocket, his false and slimy tongue has forever damned him in the estimation of the community in which he lives.

We will further add that at the time of going to press—12 o'clock, Friday—no money has been paid by Mr. Chapman to Mrs. Hoffman.

Daily Arkansas Gazette
Sat, Apr 11, 1874 ·Page 4

W. G. Gray, Postmaster of Lewisburg, Ark., spoils a sensation item published in the Little Rock papers, about a man by the name of Anthony Hoffman starving to death near Lewisburg, in Conway county, a short time since. Mr. Gray says that Mr. Hoffman did not starve to death, but, on contrary, about a week before his death he was in Lewisburg looking quite well, and bought a considerable quantity of provisions, paying for them, and having money left. The whole story appears to have been a canard, except the death of Mr. Hoffman, and that he did not receive proper attention during his illness, but that was on account of its not being known, he living several miles from any other house.

The Southern Standard
Sat, Apr 11, 1874 ·Page 2

Grand Picnic at Lewisburg
Attracting Statewide Attention

SPECIAL NOTICE.

TRAINS ON THE LITTLE ROCK AND Fort Smith railroad change time, for one day only, to accommodate parties wishing to attend the

GRAND PICNIC

at Lewisburg, on Saturday, May 23d, 1874.

Leave Argenta	7:00 a.m.	
" Conway	9:15	"
" Plummer's	10:40	"
Arrive at Lewisburg	11:00	"
Leave Clarksville	7 15	"
" Russellville	9:15	"
" Atkins'	10:05	"
Arrive at Lewisburg	10:50	"

RETURNING.

Leave Lewisburg	3:30 p.m.	
Arrive at Argenta	7:00	"
Leave Lewisburg	3:20	"
Arrive at Clarksville	7:00	"

Half fare for round trip.

T. HARTMAN, Superintendent.

Daily Arkansas Gazette
Sun, May 24, 1874 ·Page 4

Headquarters district Lewisburg, Conway, Faulkner and Perry counties, Arkansas state guards.

LEWISBURG. Ark., June 11, 1874.
General order No. 3.

Under general order No. 9 from general headquarters, all men subject to military duty under the militia law of 1868, in this military district, are hereby ordered to report to the enrolling officers at the different voting precincts in said district, on the 30th day of June, 1874, for enrollment.

Persons disobeying this order will be dealt with according to law.

By order of Brigadier General

A. GORDON,
Commanding District.

Daily Arkansas Gazette
Sun, Jun 14, 1874 ·Page 4

RIVER NEWS.

The river is still rising rapidly. The gauge last evening showing six feet six inches.

The Danville passed Lewisburg at 10 o'clock yesterday on her way down.

The Mary Boyd is looked for from below hourly.

VAN BUREN, June 14.—The river has risen three feet and continues to rise slowly, with five feet in the channel. The Danville left this a.m. for below. Clear and pleasant.

Daily Arkansas Gazette
Wed, Jun 17, 1874 ·Page 4

—A correspondent at Lewisburg writes as follows: "Politically we have little or no excitement, nearly every body is for the convention, but it is believed that the radicals will vote against the convention. We will certainly send you a good man from our county as a delegate."

Daily Arkansas Gazette
Fri, Jun 19, 1874 ·Page 4

Dr. Crittenden was killed on Tuesday night last, about eight miles of Lewisburg. Conway county, by a young man by the name of Hill. He was at his front gate when he was shot by Hill, with a shot gun, his horse being killed by the same discharge. The difficulty is said to have grown out of a family quarrel.

The Southern Standard
Sat, Jun 20, 1874 ·Page 4

A correspondent at Lewisburg sends us the following:

EDITORS GAZETTE: The Little Rock Republican of the 23d contains a communication dated at Memphis and signed "Arkansas," which was evidently written in your city. The writer purposely does injustice to Gen. A. Gordon, of this place. The order was made simply with the view to economize time and labor, as at this season of the year the farmers can ill afford to lose two days labor. As the order was alone for enrollment, Gen. Gordon never for a moment thought of the false and contemptible construction which has been given to it by the enemies of our state. Such a construction could only be given to it by the foul and corrupt crew who daily sluice their slanders through the columns of the Republican on the best men in the state. Gen. Gordon is not, nor has been, a candidate for delegate to the convention. He has never engaged in the dirty work of "overaweing the voters at the polls," nor in any of the foul "appliances" heretofore used by the "Republican ring." Gen. Gordon can rest satisfied that the abuse of the Republican and its correspondents is the highest recommendation of his honesty and integrity, which could be given to the people of this state.

Our people are a unit "for convention."

CONWAY.

Daily Arkansas Gazette
Sat, Jun 27, 1874 ·Page 3

The Lewisburg Empire contains these items:

Last Sunday—negro boy—Gay's landing—swimming—ticket to another clime.

The corn crops with some of our farmers are like some of our chronic candidates for office —laid by.

Daily Arkansas Gazette
Tue, Jun 30, 1874 ·Page 3

Negroes Tricked Into Not Voting

BROOKS STRIKERS IN POPE.

ATKINS, June 30, 1874.

EDITORS GAZETTE: A Brooks striker from Lewisburg, whose name I have not learned, was among the negroes near Galla Rock, in this county, circulating a report to this effect: "Every colored man who goes to the polls and votes will have to join the militia." The darkies believed it. Many—indeed, as far as I can learn, all—hvae been kept from the polls by these threats. Now this is a positive violation of section 17 of the act of the general assembly providing for a convention, etc. Will the people of Lewisburg see that this fellow is brought to justice? His name can be obtained by writing to Galla Rock. I can produce witnesses in attestation of the foregoing. Fellow citizens, let all stand at the post of duty; our salvation depends upon it. For further information address BAXTERITE.

Daily Arkansas Gazette
Fri, Jul 03, 1874 ·Page 4

LOCAL PERSONALS.

COL. "SANDY" FAULKNER is spending a few days at Lewisburg.

Daily Arkansas Gazette
Thu, Jul 09, 1874 ·Page 4

—No rain above Lewisburg on the Fort Smith road yesterday.

Daily Arkansas Gazette
Fri, Jul 10, 1874 ·Page 4

CAPT. T. L. HILL, Col. Chas. C. Reid, Jr., and W. B. Gibson, merchant, came down from Lewisburg on the Fort Smith train yesterday.

Daily Arkansas Gazette
Sun, Jul 12, 1874 ·Page 4

As He Announced at Lewisburg
Governor Baxter
Has Worked to Free the Enslaved

ELISHA BAXTER.

If the people of Arkansas, without regard to party, are under lasting obligations to any one man it is to the present occupant of the executive chair. When he said in his Lewisburg speech that the people should be free, there were many who doubted either his intentions or his ability to bring about that result. But he did keep his promise and has brought about that result. From the momen he was seated in the gubernatorial chair he set to work for the purpose of sending the thieves to the rear and striking the shackles from the people of this state. He struck many blows in this direction when his motives were misconstrued, and he knew that would be the case at the time, but he bore up under all the charges brought against him, trusting to time to vindicate him. And it has done so splendidly. Baxter could have been governor to the end of his term, and the Clayton-Dorsey rule have been perpetuated ad infinitum. By one word he could have continued these people in slavery —but he set out to enfranchise the people, and right well has he performed his work. The convention which is in session to-day could never have been held without Baxter's consent. He brought it about. The people of Arkansas would not now be free if he had willed otherwise. While, as a rule, a public officer is entitled to no special thanks for performing his duty, in this case Gov. Baxter is entitled to the lasting gratitude of the people of Arkansas, and as an evidence that what he has done is appreciated by them, he should be re-elected to the position he now holds, if he desires to be so rewarded. The people of Arkansas have never been accused of being ungenerous—they have never been ungrateful—and at this time they would prove unworthy themselves were they to fail in acknowledging their deep indebtedness to Gov. Baxter and partially discharge that obligation by re-electing the man who has piloted them safely through their troubles. We love consistency in politicians, but there are some performances within the reach

some performances within the reach of human endeavor, that entitle men to the lasting gratitude of a whole people. Baxter has signally distinguished himself as a benefactor to his people, and in our opinion is worthy of as signal reward and recognition of his great and good action. This much is due him as a man, not politician—and we do not hesitate to say it as men, not politicians. Let the parties nominate whom they please for all other state officers save the governorship, should the convention order new elections in the scheme of government yet to be adopted. But in that one exception, let them leave a chance for once to rise above party and faction, and say if he is worthy of the benediction, "well done thou good and faithful servant." If Grant could be magnanimous, we certainly hould be generous.

One year ago—seeing his opportunity to become a friend and saviour to his people, and believing such to be the wish of his heart—without hint from him or any other man, through these columns we extended to him the friendly and willing hand, and offered him the assistance of our best endeavors. He accepted, and held out faithful to the end, as the ballots of 80,259 voters have just testified in thunder tones. We would be untrue to him who was true to the people, and under the contempt of all honorable men, were we to prove false to him who accepted our invitation; and, whatever the consequences to us, and without advice from him or any other man, we offer him our support—should he seek an indorsement of his acts from the people at the ballot-box.

Daily Arkansas Gazette
Wed, Jul 15, 1874 ·Page 2

THE HURRICANE.

Lewisburg Wrecked by the Cyclone of Monday.

The storm which visited this city Monday afternoon did great damage in the surrounding country. It visited, with terrific violence, Lewisburg, on the Fort Smith railroad. The wind blew with incredible power. The City hall was moved six or eight inches, and the glass of the front all broken out. The house was materially damaged. Mrs. Mason's store was blown down. The warehouse of Mr. J. M. Gordon was unroofed. A portion of the roof of the store of Rankin, Hill & Co. was blown away, and the whole building badly damaged. The drug store of E. J. Morrill was razed to the ground, and the property of nearly every person in the village was more or less damaged.

The following is very suggestive of the violence of the storm at that place:

LEWISBURG, July 27, 1874.
EDITORS GAZETTE: This evening at 3 o'clock Lewisburg was blown away by a storm, and went in the direction of your city. Any person finding such a town will please return it, with all the chickens, dogs and appurtenances thereunto belonging.   A SUFFERER.

Daily Arkansas Gazette
Wed, Jul 29, 1874 ·Page 4

LEWISBURG, July 30, 1874.
EDITORS GAZETTE: Yesterday's GAZETTE contains a very inaccurate account of the effects of the storm here on Monday last, which is calculated to do injustice to parties here. Five hundred dollars would cover the damage done. The buildings blown down were "old shanties," and some roofing blown off. Your correspondent was evidently on a "high wind" himself when he penned his communication. Lewisburg is all "right side up with care," and intends to roll up a big majority for ratification and the democratic candidate for governor.
                        CONWAY.

Daily Arkansas Gazette
Fri, Jul 31, 1874 ·Page 4

The democracy of Conway county, met in mass meeting, at Lewisburg, on Saturday, August 22, 1874, Col. H. W. Burrows, chairman; Maj. F. P. Hervy, secretary.

The chairman appointed the following persons as a county central committee, being one from each voting precinct in the county, viz: M. W. Steele, John Kurtz, Shade Jones, J. J. Massie, J. M W. Massengill, J. McClure, F. P. Hervy, L. Morse, J. Grey and A. J. Higgins.

Daily Arkansas Gazette
Tue, Aug 25, 1874 ·Page 1

W. J. Sharp, the man who was killed near Badgett precinct on the 13th, came from near Lewisburg. He was kicked while hitching, and lived but forty minutes after receiving the blow.

Daily Arkansas Gazette
Fri, Oct 16, 1874 ·Page 4

JOLLIFICATION AT LEWISBURG.

LEWISBURG, November 6, 1874.
EDITORS GAZETTE: The democracy of this place had a regular jollification last night, and fired one hundred guns in honor of the redemption of the American people. This year should be called in the future, the " year of jubilee.' Our mutual friend, the indefatigable and unconquerable Capt. W. B. Gibson was the chief in getting up the material for our jollification. We had considerable sport here at the election. The radicals had two tickets in the field for the legislature. One was for Bent. Turner for senator and Dan. Thomas and one Murtin for the house. The other was for Nat Moore for senate and Gill and Brashear for the house. Considerable feeling got up among the rads themselves, and both sides accused each other of various rascalities, and we believe both.

Speaking of Gibson and Dan Thomas, neither of whom are natives of the south, and who settled here about the same time, illustrates fully how the conduct of outsiders are considered by our people. Capt. Gibson has been no candidate for office and has never joined the enemies of the people in oppressing them, and he is to-day beloved and honored by the honest people of this county. On the other hand, Thomas' conduct will never be forgotten. We congratulate you on the glorious victories of last Tuesday. Grateful prayers should· be sent up daily to Divine Providence for His grateful interposition in behalf of a suffering people.
OBSERVER.

Daily Arkansas Gazette
Sun, Nov 08, 1874 ·Page 1

—In yesterday's GAZETTE we mentioned that W. B Gibson & Co., of Lewisburg, had gone into bankruptcy on petition. This was done, as we are advised, because one of their creditors, whose debt had been previously paid to their attorney (but the latter had failed to pay the amount over), instituted attachment proceedings against them, and they went into bankruptcy in justice to their other creditors.

Daily Arkansas Gazette
Wed, Dec 30, 1874 ·Page 4

—Mr. A. B. Van Dyke, connected with the Merchants' Dispatch Fast Freight line, whose arrival in the city was mentioned yesterday, has gone up to Lewisburg. Mr. Van Dyke is making settlement for damaged goods shipped by that line.

Daily Arkansas Gazette
Thu, Dec 31, 1874 ·Page 4

Lewisburg May Loose Status as County Seat & Courthouse

Mr. Venable presented the notice and introduced a bill repealing an act for the removal of the county seat of Conway county, which changes the seat from Lewisburg to Springfield. Read twice and referred to the committee on counties and county lines.

Daily Arkansas Gazette
Fri, Jan 01, 1875 ·Page 1

Lewisburg Keeps County Seat

[A message from the house announced the passage of house bill to authorize the treasurer of the state to issue scrip; also house bill to repeal an act removing the county site of Conway county from Springfield to Lewisburg; also, senate bill to regulate the collection of county taxes, with amendments.]

Daily Arkansas Gazette
Fri, Jan 15, 1875 ·Page 4

BOUNTY TROUBLES.

For some months past Col. C. C. Reid, jr., of Lewisburg, has been working up a number of supposed fraudulent bounty claim cases. During the visit of Maj. Gibson to this city, Noah Hayes, William Randolph and Elizabeth Erwin, all living near Lewisburg, came down to draw a bounty which Elizabeth claimed was due her, swearing herself to be the mother of a deceased colored soldier. Through the efforts of Col. Reid it was proved yesterday, before United States Commissioner Goodrich, that Elizabeth was the sister of the deceased soldier, whose mother is still living. Hayes and Randolph were convicted of perjury in swearing that Elizabeth was the mother. All the parties were bound over for trial before the United States circuit court, April term. Hayes was released on $500 bail. Randolph and Elizabeth only "felt so-so" last evening, being in custody of Marshal Mills, unable to give required bail.

Daily Arkansas Gazette
Tue, Feb 23, 1875 ·Page 4

—At a meeting of the creditors, yesterday, before Register Fay Hempstead. Mr. Thomas B. Stout was elected assignee of the estate of James M. Gordon, of Lewisburg.

Daily Arkansas Gazette
Thu, Mar 04, 1875 ·Page 4

—One hundred and fifty guns were fired at Lewisburg, and one hundred at Fort Smith, on receipt of the news of the adoption of the Poland report.

Daily Arkansas Gazette
Sun, Mar 07, 1875 ·Page 4

Shooting at Clarksville & Mr. Breden Killed at Lewisburg

CLARKSVILLE, ARK., March 25, 1875. EDITORS GAZETTE : This afternoon Dick Johnson shot and fatally wounded Fred Crisp, at Webb's grocery, about ten miles west of this place. I send you the circumstances of the shooting, as given me by an eye-witness, and the men who brought the prisoner to town.

The parties were playing a game of cards for the drinks. Crisp won, but Johnson didn't want to acknowledge it ; whereupon, Crisp gave him the game, and quit playing. In a few moments, some one suggested that they play a four-handed game, when Johnson remarked that "he would rather kill some one than play cards." Crisp supposed he was the person referred to, and said : "Dick, I am unarmed, and you know it ; but if you want to kill me, do so ; though I don't believe you will." Johnson picked up his double-barreled shot-gun, and, with the remark, "I'll show you, damned quick, whether I will or not," fired, the charge taking effect in Crisp's stomach, tearing his bowels almost completely out. Johnson then made for the woods, wading a creek, and concealed himself in a drift, where, after a short search, he was found, and brought to this place and put in jail. Crisp, at last accounts, was still alive, though he cannot possibly recover. Johnson killed a man named Breden a short time ago at Lewisburg, and has been considered a dangerous man.

This county has been given an unenviable reputation on account of the numerous shooting scrapes which have taken place within its limits ; but the great promptness with which the guilty parties are being dealt with, will soon inspire evil-doers with a wholesome dread of giving a loose rein to their murderous passions, and free the county of such characters. LEX.

Daily Arkansas Gazette
Sun, Mar 28, 1875 ·Page 4

—The remains of Mr. Fairburn, who died at Lewisburg, a few days since, were brought to this city yesterday.

—Mr. John Fletcher, jr., of this city, and bride, married at Lewisburg, Monday, arrived in town by the Fort Smith train

Daily Arkansas Gazette
Wed, Mar 31, 1875 ·Page 4

—Deputy Sheriff M. W. Hause, of Saline county, arrived in town Sunday with a prisoner named Bud Crockett, charged with horse-stealing. The officer left on the Fort Smith train yesterday morning for Lewisburg, where the theft was committed, and where Crockett will be tried.

Daily Arkansas Gazette
Tue, Apr 06, 1875 ·Page 4

—How is it that Lewisburg has elected a mayor who voted against the convention, against the constitution, and was on the bogus ticket with Benton Turner for the state legislature.

Daily Arkansas Gazette
Fri, Apr 09, 1875 ·Page 4

New Officers Elected
for City of Lewisburg

Lewisburg invites the forty-five citizens of Little Rock who voted against license to locate in that thriving village, where they can find "pleasant homes" and a "hearty welcome."

The following are the new officers of Lewisburg: Mayor, D. H. Thomas; recorder, J. J. Beavers; marshal, R. G. Gordon; treasurer, George Morrill.

Daily Arkansas Gazette
Tue, Apr 13, 1875 ·Page 3

Sheriff T. B. Stout, of Lewisburg, came down on the Fort Smith train last evening, on attendance at the United States court.

Col. C. C. Reid, jr., of Lewisburg, is in town.

Daily Arkansas Gazette
Tue, Apr 13, 1875 ·Page 4

New Newspaper
Starts in Lewisburg

WE have before us the first number of the Weekly State, a new paper just started at Lewisburg, Conway county, by Rev. W. C. Stout. The State is a sprightly weekly, and makes a fine start. We wish it every success.

Daily Arkansas Gazette
Tue, Apr 13, 1875 ·Page 2

—We have received the first number of the Weekly State, a neat seven column paper issued every Thursday at Lewisburg, Ark., with Mr. W. C. Stout as editor and publisher. We welcome the State to a place on our exchange list and wish it much success.

The Russellville Democrat
Thu, Apr 15, 1875 ·Page 3

—D. H. Thomas, esq., mayor elect of Lewisburg, was commissioned by the governor.

Daily Arkansas Gazette
Sun, Apr 18, 1875 ·Page 4

—The Sunday school pic-nic and May-day celebration will be held on Illinois bayou, at the mouth of Mill creek, about two miles from town. Other Sunday Schools from Dardanelle, Dover, Atkins, Clarksville and perhaps Lewisburg are invited and a grand time is anticipated.

The Russellville Democrat
Thu, Apr 22, 1875 ·Page 3

Lewisburg is Close Enough to
Little Rock to Benefit from its Growth

LITTLE ROCK.

The Lewisburg State, edited by Rev. W. C. Stout, contains the following clever mention of our city:

"Few of our readers in the country know how fast our state capital is putting on metropolitan airs. It is no more the gentle and quiet abode of the state officials and a few nice aristocratic families. We remember the day when a walk from the landing, or Merrick & Wassell's corner, to the state-house, could be taken without encountering a strange face. Now it is all changed. But how could it be otherwise, becoming, as it is, a great railroad center, on a navigable river, in the richest valley and the finest climate in America—if not in the world. If this past dash is a little extreme, remember we belong to 'old Arkansas.' We are going to express our opinion. It is that Little Rock is just about to enter upon a new career of advancement. To-day she has wholesale houses from which our citizens and merchants can buy goods and lay them down at home cheaper than if they order them from distant cities. The merchants, for some reason, have not taken pains to make this known to the country people. The city is about to enter upon manufacturing enterprises. There is no

ufacturing enterprises. There is no better place for a cotton factory than Little Rock. The same may be said in regard to an oil factory, the manufacture of farming implements, iron foundries and machine shops. We have the raw material and plenty of fuel to drive the engines. The mere matter of freights will give home manufactories a margin of profits that can not be ignored. We look to the city for examples which the small towns may follow. Our own little town is near enough to receive influences of good from the city."

Daily Arkansas Gazette
Sun, May 02, 1875 ·Page 4

—Notwithstanding the rain of the preceeding day and night, last Saturday was a pleasant day, and there was a good turn out to the Sunday school pic-nic. There was a goodly attendance from Lewisburg and Atkins and a few from Little Rock. Also a few from Dover. Everything passed off pleasantly and to the satisfaction of all. The grounds were high, well drained and dry.

The Russellville Democrat
Thu, May 06, 1875 ·Page 3

Lewisburg Voted Against Bars, Pubs, or Taverns
(Called *'Dram Shops'*) Serving Alcohol

Notwithstanding the people of Lewisburg voted against licensing dramshops. they continue to exist—and always will.

Daily Arkansas Gazette
Sun, May 09, 1875 ·Page 4

Train Off Tracks at Lewisburg

—The up train on the Ft. Smith road, ran off the track at the old switch at Lewisburg last Saturday and smashed up the passenger coach, and frightened the female passengers considerably. No one was hurt and the engine and mail car arrived at this place thirty minutes late.

—A laughable incident occurred when the train ran off the track at Lewisburg last Saturday. An old lady who was aboard, was so badly excited when the smash took place, that she completely lost her presence of mind and did not know that she was in danger —at least did not seem to realize it until she stood safe on terra firma, when she commenced to jump up and down and cry, "Save me! Save me! Take me off! Take me off that thing!"

The Russellville Democrat
Thu, May 13, 1875 ·Page 3

$50,000 Wager on Steamboat Race
9 hr 20 min Little Rock to Lewisburg

RIVER INTELLIGENCE.

A correspondent at Lewisburg sends us the following table of the progress of the two boats.

LEFT	MAMELLE.	HUGHES.
Little Rock......................	5 p.m.	5:05 p.m.
TIME TO	h. m.	h. m.
Natural Steps.................	2 20	2 30
Palarm..........................	Scared.	Gained 4m.
Codfish Mils...................	3 30	4 50
Powell's Landing...........	5 10	5 50
Mouth Cadron................	6 05	6 40
Breeder's Landing.........	8 50	9 55
Lewisburg.....................	9 20	11 03

The time of the two steamers, so far, is the fastest on record. At latest accounts from Galla Rock, the Hughes was gaining. The banks were covered with spectators, and it is supposed that something less than $50,000 will change hands on the result. ANDY JOHNSON.

A note from a passenger on the Mamelle says she reached Dardanelle at 8:20 a.m. on the 16th inst., in 15 hours and 20 minutes from Little Rock, having made eleven landings and stopped once to wood. The Hughes had not arrived.

LATER.——At 9 p.m., Sunday, the Mamelle was at Ozark, two and a half hours ahead of the Ella.

The Clarksville is in port, and will leave for Fort Smith this evening at 5 o'clock.

Daily Arkansas Gazette
Tue, May 18, 1875 ·Page 4

Lewisburg Newspaper
Proposes a Centennial Celebration

AS CENTENNIALS are just now the fashion, the Lewisburg State wants to know if Arkansas can't have one. It says :

It is three hundred and thirty years since DeSoto died in Arkansas. It is nearly two hundred years since Marquette visited the mouth of the Arkansas. One hundred years ago what happened? Perhaps the descendants of the old French families in Arkansas county can tell us of some tradition of their fathers.

If we can find out just exactly what did transpire at that time, we vote for a centennial celebration.

Daily Arkansas Gazette
Tue, May 18, 1875 ·Page 2

—Rev. W. C. Stout, of the Lewisburg State, is in the city, having returned from the Episcopal Convention at Pine Bluff.

Daily Arkansas Gazette
Fri, May 21, 1875 ·Page 4

A man named E. H. Huckaby violated the person of a ten-year old daughter of John H. Burnett, of Point Remove, about eighteen miles above Russellville, one day last week. He was arrested, indicted and tried during the week just closed and sent to the penitentiary for three years. That's the manner in which justice is administered in Arkansas now.

Says the Lewisburg State: "Dr. A. Davis has brought to our office a stalk of orchard grass, measuring forty-two inches. This grass was introduced from England, about a half century ago, we believe. We remember it for forty years. In the last few years it has come much into notice as a meadow grass. Its excellence is claimed to be in that it will grow as well under the shade of trees as in open fields. We do not think it is known by this name in England, but cannot say positively that it is the English rye grass, but suspect it is. Dr. Davis' grass shows that we can produce grass if we will."

Daily Arkansas Gazette
Tue, Jun 01, 1875 ·Page 1

Horrid Double Murder
in Lewisburg, Conway County

—The report of a horrid crime, perpetrated in the vicinity of Lewisburg, Monday, by as yet undiscovered parties, is published in another column. The murder of two women by assassins in ambush, is a crime that Conway county cannot afford to let go unpunished. No expense should be considered too great, and no effort should be spared, to ferret out the distardly perpetrators. The assassination of women is something unknown to our criminal records heretofore.

HORRID DOUBLE MURDER IN CONWAY.

LEWISBURG, June 8.

EDITORS GAZETTE : Our peaceful community was yesterday shocked by the report of one of the blackest crimes that has ever been committed in the county. About two or three miles south of here the widow of the late John B. Stone and her servant woman were shot from the roadside, and mortally wounded. Both, it is said by the doctors, must die. The perpetrator of this dastardly and devilish deed has not yet been brought to light, but will be, no doubt, in a few days. No community can rest supine when such deeds are done and men go at large. Who can do them? Although the hand that did the deed cannot be named to-day, there is no difficulty in fixing the responsibility so close that the criminal cannot escape detection. WHETSTONE.

Daily Arkansas Gazette
Wed, Jun 09, 1875 ·Page 4

Another Account of the
Horrid Double Murder in Lewisburg

LEWISBURG, June 8.

EDITOR GAZETTE: Some weeks ago Mr. Stover, a very wealthy planter, living on the south side of the river, about two miles from this place, died. His sons-in-law were appointed administrators of the estate, named respectively J. R. Snapp and W. H. H. Van Winkle.

It appears that Stover was married to a woman unlawfully and the heirs were anxious to get her off of the place, and were about to enter suit against her, but, in the meantime the personal property was appraised and sold. The said Mr. Stover had renters on his place he was to furnish with provisions, etc. He had the supplies at his residence at the time he died. They were appraised and left there. On the 1st of June, Mr. Snapp went to the house (then occupied by Mrs. Stover), and asked Mrs. Stover for coffee for the hands. She refused to give it to him. She then went in the house and locked the door, which Snapp demanded her to open. She refused and he kicked it open, and went and procured an ax and told her if she did not get the coffee he would burst the safe open; he then set the ax down and went in the house. No sooner had he entered than she shot him with a pistol loaded with buck-shot, one ball taking effect in the nose, and another in the shoulder. She (Mrs. Stover) was arrested, had a trial, and was bound over to appear before the next term of the circuit court. The wounded man is doing well.

On last evening Mrs. Stover came over to the farm after her household furniture, and after starting back to Lewisburg was shot from the bushes, and is not expected to live. There was a negro woman with her, who was shot also. The negro will probably get well. There has been no arrest made up to the present time. I have given you the full details of the affair. A. W. R.

Daily Arkansas Gazette
Thu, Jun 10, 1875 ·Page 4

Lewisburg State, 11th: "At 5 a.m. Wednesday, after great suffering, Mrs. Stover breathed her last. A poor old woman has died by the hand of an assassin. Sooner or later this terrible crime will press itself upon the public mind, and all the guilty parties will be brought to suffer the extreme penalty of the law. At the closing of our forms the coroner's jury is still in session. It is understood, however, that the crime has been uncovered, and the fiend is in custody and in irons."

Lewisburg State: "We have reason to believe that our article entitled "Gray Hairs," has awakened considerable interest among our old citizens. We trust it will not die out. Among our gray-haired citizens are the men who once made a state, and who are yet capable of regenerating a ruined one. Let public opininion call them forth from that obscuriy into which modesty, disgust or wrong drove them, and their wisdom will be as potent as was the vigor of their youth."

Daily Arkansas Gazette
Sat, Jun 12, 1875 ·Page 1

—The Lewisburg State says of the murder of Mrs. Stover: "At present we can only say, that the coroner's jury found that the women were shot by one W. B. Thompson, who came to this neighborhood about four years ago. He said he was from Kansas, and from time to time, has told some very hard things on himself."

Daily Arkansas Gazette
Sat, Jun 19, 1875 ·Page 4

—Rev. W. C. Stout, of Lewisburg, has gone to Fayetteville to deliver an address to the trustees and faculty of the Arkansas Industral nniversity.

—The good farmers and gardeners around Lewisburg are stuffing the Stout editor of the State with new potatoes. That is the way to build up a paper.

Daily Arkansas Gazette
Sat, Jun 19, 1875 ·Page 4

ORCHARD GRASS.

Col. B. F. Danley, one of the best farmers in the state, says, in a letter to the Lewisburg State :

From my own observation and experience, I am perfectly convinced that it has no equal either for grazing on, or mowing for hay, but when sown for the latter purpose it should always be mixed with red clover. They both bloom at the same time, and consequently are ready for mowing at the same time. They will turn out a larger crop of hay per acre than any of the perennials sown in this country and the hay possesses more nutriment than any other grass.

It must be borne in mind however, that for the production of red clover, the land should contain a small portion of lime in its composition. This is not the case with the orchard grass, it will grow very well on the poor uplands, where there is a total absence of lime. Add a little lime, and sow red clover with it, and any of the poor uplands, not too sandy, will yield a fine crop of hay, and afford abundant pasturage, all through our mild winters, and in the early spring.

The advantage of orchard grass over blue grass, or any other grass known in this country, is its rapid growth, its great durability, and its great capacity to withstand the drought. It should always be pastured close, otherwise, it will grow in tussocks.

It will grow more in one day than blue grass will grow in a week. Neither cold nor heat injure it in this climate. Our farmers would hazard nothing, and derive great benefit by its culture. Urge them to try it.

Daily Arkansas Gazette
Sat, Jun 19, 1875 ·Page 2

VALUABLE
FARM FOR SALE

I OFFER FOR SALE THAT VALUABLE farm on Point Remove creek, Conway county, heretofore known as the Armstrong place; 778 acres in the tract, 320 acres cleared and in high state of cultivation. Gin-house, tenant houses and other buildings.

This is one of the most desirable farms above Little Rock. It lies between the Little Rock and Fort Smith railroad and the Arkansas river—one half mile from the former, and one and a half miles from the latter. There is a fine cypress brake at the upper end of the place. This farm will be sold upon very reasonable terms.

Apply to W. D. Blocher, Little Rock, Col. Whitthorn, A. Gordon, Lewisburg, or myself.   B. J. BROWN,
721‡   Van Buren, Arkansas.

Daily Arkansas Gazette
Sat, Jun 26, 1875 ·Page 1

Lewisburg Paper's Editorial
Protests Treatment of Indian Nations

THE INDIAN COUNTRY.

We are glad to see the interest the exposure of the plans of the Indian ring, in respect of the Sioux and the Indian territory, has aroused throughout the state. The Lewisburg State has an excellent editorial on the subject, from which we extract below ; and we give also a most interesting communication from Clarksville, which advances some views that are new to some, but are well worthy of being carefully considered. In reading this communication, it should be remembered that a large portion of the present Indian territory once composed a part of the territory of Arkansas, but it was cut off and assigned to the Indians by the federal government against the earnest protest, and to the serious pecuniary injury of many citizens of Arkansas.

We give first extracts from the editorial of the State; next the communication

"The semi-civilized tribes of Cherokees, Creeks, Choctaws and

"The semi-civilized tribes of Cherokees, Creeks, Choctaws and Chickasaws, with fostering care and wise legislation on the part of congress, might have been speedily brought to that state that they might have been safely, with their own consent, incorporated into a state. With the infusion of a fair portion of our frontier population, very soon all traces of barbarism would have disappeared." But "not only has there been a want of good influences applied, but there has too much of the application of positively evil influences."

These have been in the denying of the liberties, granted in the treaties made heretofore with these tribes : in the unrestrained and unlimited exercise of power by the officers and agents of the federal government. And worse than all, a threatening of the stability of their institutions by introducing new elements of barbarism. Small and broken tribes wandering on the borders of Texas, have been located in a part of the Chickasaw lands. Arapahoes and other savages from Colorado and Kansas, have been placed south of the Arkansas. And now there has been a persistent effort made to get the Sioux, the most savage of the Indians, in all our broad domain, to leave their wilderness haunts and accept homes west of Arkansas.

Now, is it justice or humanity to subject the Cherokee or Choctaw, the Creek or Chickasaw, to the savage influence and the irritating and disturbing neighborhood of these wild tribes?

It is taken for granted that there is no desire to do anything *good* for the Sioux. If *that* were so, civilisation might be *carried to them in their own homes* But this is not the object. It is to get them out of the way of the *northwestern* people, to get great Indian jobs in lands, reserves, contracts, removals, and all the well known ways by which a mercenary clan prey upon the public treasury at the expense of the honest laboring people. And, in carrying these purposes, there is no risk or care for the poor, ignorant Indian. Not only are they to be dragged from their homes and sent into strange lands, with all the attending miseries that pertain to the forced removal of nations, but the civilization which has been so long fostered by the kind neighborhood influence of the south is to be put in danger to satisfy this cursed thirst for public plunder.

We believe that it is the duty of the whole southern press, and all the honest newspapers in the nation to protest vigorously; and support earnestly any protest that our neighboring Indians may make. From childhood we have known the Cherokees, and we have heard good things of the other nations, and, from our heart, we sympathise with them, in the wrongs that are likely to be heaped upon them in this matter. These southern Indians are indeed a portion of our own people. As such, all who know them, are accustomed to regard them. And we believe that the whole southern people will regard as an outrage against civilization any attempt to swamp their hopes of the future, by this move of barbarism. No, give them a state government, with all the reserved rights of the states, under the constitution of the United States. They are, in the mass, an hundred times fitter for republican citizenship than the millions to whom false philanthropy and bad statesmanship did not hesitate to grant it full, without the least preparation.

Daily Arkansas Gazette
Sun, Jun 27, 1875 ·Page 2

Family Near Lewisburg
Poisoned by Centipede in Coffee Pot

Dardanelle Independent: We learn from Dr. Flower, of Peryville, that an entire family, consisting of father, mother and five children, living six miles below Lewisburg, on the river, were poisoned last Saturday by a centipede getting into the spout of the coffee-pot. It was boiled with the coffee, and killed the entire family. The father, mother and two of the children were found dead sitting upright at the table, and the other three children were found dead near the door in the yard.

Daily Arkansas Gazette
Sun, Jul 18, 1875 ·Page 1

Lewisburg State : Lift up your hearts. The rains have come : the crops are made : God be praised. No more starvation, no more want. The country abounds, and will abound, with bread.

Daily Arkansas Gazette
Tue, Jul 20, 1875 ·Page 1

P. O. Breedin, of Lewisburg, has clover forty inches high. It strikes us that that does pretty well for a c.untry not adapted to clover raising.

The Southern Standard
Sat, Jul 24, 1875 ·Page 1

– 137 –

In Support of Law & Order

TOO TRUE.

"It is now felt that there is far more consideration for the red-handed assassin, than for the rights, lives and general safety of the whole innocent community. The apprehension of a murderer does not mean the punishment of crime, but the taxing of the people a thousand or more dollars to get up a dumb show."

This is an extract from an editorial by Rev. W. C. Stout in the last issue of the Lewisburg State. It is a damaging statement, but it is too true to deny. We have, more than once spoken of this matter ourself. We feel it to be our duty to do so, although we know it is greatly detrimental to our country that such a state of affairs should exist. This is a serious matter and there is no use trying to dodge the issue. We must meet it, and with a voice that shall be heard and felt, demand that justice shall not be put to shame. We are now trying to build up our shattered fortunes and rehabilitate our state. We are inviting immigration and capitalists to our country; but let us say right now, that just so long as an old citizen of the state, who loves Arkansas and yearns for her prosperity, is forced by the slack enforcement of the laws, or the incompetency of officials, or the corruption of courts—and it is one of these three causes that produces the condition of affairs complained of—to come out with such a declaration as this, we will make no progress.

No matter how foul the crime, it appears that there are always those who are ready to become apologists for it, and who go to work immediately to manufacture public sympathy for the red-handed murderer. And strange to say, this vicious influence too often seems to be sufficient to secure the acquittal of the most hienous offenders. This shows clearly that there is not stamina sufficient in our courts to brave the vicious and corrupted morals of the class, who are ever ready to apologize for crime. We say this is strange, because we believe that those who compose this class are but a small proportion of our population. But small as they are, they seem to carry their point. The great majority of our people, we believe, are for law and order and justice; but they are unfortunately too indifferent in the premises. Indeed, they seem to be actually afraid to speak out and demand that the courts shall execute the laws against criminals. A false delicacy seems to have taken hold of them and they see crime after crime committed and are silent spectators, fearing to demand that just punishment be visited upon criminals lest they should be accused of prejudice against an unfortunate wretch. We have no hesitation in saying that all such conduct is discreditable, foolish, unmanly and a curse to our country. We must change public sentiment in this respect. We must make public sentiment so strong against crime that there will not be one chance in a hundred for a criminal to escape punishment.

We appeal to the press of Arkansas, who are in favor of law, order, and the punishment of crime, to come out and take a bold stand in favor of a strict enforcement of the laws. Until this is secured it is useless to expect that flow of good steady, industrious people to our country, who are so much needed. Let us hear from the press on this subject.

The Russellville Democrat
Thu, Jul 29, 1875 ·Page 1

Independent: J. W. Pollard brough us a fine stalk of cotton on Friday last, measuring 5½ ft. in hight, well branched, having 209 bolls and squares, many of the limbs are over 3 ft in length, it was raised on sandy land, on the Barry farm.

Fayetteville Democrat: Will. J. Stout has cotton breast high —[Lewisburg State.

The Russellville Democrat
Thu, Aug 05, 1875 ·Page 1

— Telegraph offices have been opened at the following stations on the Little Rock and Fort Smith railway: Argenta, Conway, Lewisburg, Russellville, Clarksville and Altus.

Daily Arkansas Gazette
Thu, Aug 05, 1875 ·Page 4

Brigade Reunion.

[Hot Springs Telegraph.]

We publish the following call for a reunion of Cabell's brigade on the 20th of October, at Lewisburg, on the Little Rock and Fort Smith railroad. By Cabell's brigade is meant the brigade. The best part of any brigade consists of the soldiers, the boys that "did the work," really. And, therefore, both rank and file are expected to be present. We hope to be there. We are persuaded that nothing but death will keep "Old Tige" away. The noble town of Lewisburg tenders its hospitalities, and the hospitable doors of its citizens will be wide to all who attend.

LEWISBURG, ARK, August 8.

To the officers and soldiers of Cabell's brigade, of the confederate service:

Having a desire to meet again all our old army friends, officers and soldiers, it is desired that we have a reunion of our old brigade (Cabell's) at some convenient point, in October next, where we can, we are assured, be met by our old commander, Gen. W. L. Cabell, and have an interchange of feelings, etc. and stir your minds by way of remembrance. We would suggest, therefore, that the meeting take place on the twentieth day of October next, at Lewisburg, Ark., and that all of the officers and soldiers be invited, and especially requested, to participate in said meeting. The hospitalities of our friends here are hereby tendered on that

friends here are hereby tendered on that occasion. Come all, and let us have a reunion indeed.   A. GORDON,
    S. SLEEPER.

Daily Arkansas Gazette
Fri, Aug 20, 1875 ·Page 1

A gentleman at Lewisburg, this state, in giving in his "experienc" at a Temperance meeting, said that his mother-in-law broke him from drinking whiskey. Vow let each county in the state be well supplied with mothers-in-law.

The time of the re-union of Cabell's old brigade has been fixed for the the 20th of October next, and Lewisburg selected as the place of meeting.

Fayetteville Weekly Democrat
Sat, Aug 21, 1875 ·Page 2

—Messrs. A. Gordon and S. Sleeper, of Lewisburg, have issued a call for a reunion of the surviving members of Cabell's brigade at that place Oct. 25th, 1875. All the officers and soldiers who survive are invited and the hospitalities of the place are tendered to those who may attend.

The Russellville Democrat
Thu, Aug 26, 1875 ·Page 1

Old Soldiers.

The surviving members of Cabell's brigade will observe the call for a reunion. This is not, as we understand it, to rekindle the old war spirit, but to renew those personal relations, that became so dear in the dark and bloody days when they were established. It is to strengthen the links of friendship's chain.

The old poetry of the Scandinavians had this sentence:

"If thou hast a friend visit him oft"

"The road becomes over-grown with bushes and brambles if it be not travelled." Lewisburg will do her best to entertain men, who meet as friends.—[Lewisburg State.

The Osceola Times
Sat, Aug 28, 1875 ·Page 2

At Methodist Conference Mention Made of the "Lewisburg Institute"

Conference Proceedings of the M. E. Church South--- Convened in Russellville, August 12th, 1875.

The Dardanelle District Conference convened at Russellville, Ark., on Thursday August 12th, 1875. Religious exercises by the Rev. B. H. Malone. of the Lewisburg Institute. C. H. Gregory, P. E. present and presiding.

The roll being called, six ministers and fourteen laymen answered to their names. Several circuits not being represented.

The Revs. B. H. Malone and S. A. Mason, of the M. E. Church South, and Rev. H. Smith, of the Cumberland Presbyterian church, were introduced to the conference.

Reports were then made by the preachers of their several charges.

The Sunday School interest is on the increase throughout the district, and our lesson papers and catechisms are meeting the demand, and have been adopted by most of our schools.

Financial report not good.

Membership increasing and in many localities there have been revivals of religion. Prayer meetings generally well attended.

An opportunity was given to Prof. Hooper and Rev. Malone to present the interest of their respective schools—Quitman and Lewisburg. The conference repledged itself to support Quitman Male and Female school.

Prof. Malone was recommended to the confidence and support of our people.

A. R. Winfield, D. D., was on hand urging the claims of the Arkansas Female College. His lecture was splendid, but his subscriptions small.

The Russellville Democrat
Thu, Sep 02, 1875 ·Page 1

Excerpt From Description of Excursion Through River Valley

MORRILTON,

about a mile from the thriving inland town of Lewisburg. Here the party was increased by the addition of that jolly, enterprising gentleman, Maj. W. B. Gibson, Col. T. B. Stout, Rev. W. C. Stout, editor of the Lewisburg B. Gibson, Col. T. B. Stout, Rev. W. C. Stout, editor of the Lewisburg State, Mr. D. S. Wolf, and Col. C. C. Reid, jr., and wife. Another spurt and we took the side track at Atkins, and awaited the arrival of the train for Little Rock, which passed us in a short time. Mr. Reynolds, the agent, showed us remarkable specimens of fruit grown in Col. Embry's orchard. Atkins is sixty-five miles from Little Rock, in the midst of a beautiful and picturesque country. Just north of the town, and visible from the railway for miles, is a ridge of mountains called the

CARRION CROW RANGE.

Near Mr. Potts' place, above Atkins, Mr. Lafferty, who had changed cars at the meeting place, and the other excursionists, ascended to the summit of the mountain, the height of which was full five hundred and fifty feet above the railroad track. The walk was long and tiresome, the ascent in some places being almost an impossibility, as the mountain side was almost as steep as the side of a house, and crowned with overhanging crags, frowning precipices rising in the air like turrets of a castle. The view from the summit was beautifully grand—was inspiring—and drew forth from one and all the praise so well

Daily Arkansas Gazette
Wed, Sep 08, 1875 ·Page 1

—Col. T. B. Stout, of Lewisburg, has just shipped to Col. T. B. Mills an enormous cucumber weighing sixty pounds. It was raised at Lewisburg by Mr. J. T. Hamford.

—We regret to learn that Major W. B. Gibson. of Lewisburg, had his right hand badly crushed day before yesterday, while experimenting with a machine on the depot platform at Morrillton.

—About 10 o'clock Thursday night, while the Mamelle was tied up at Lewisburg, a child was born to one of the female passengers. It was proposed to name the brave little stranger "Mamelle," but it wasn't that kind of a child.

Daily Arkansas Gazette
Sat, Sep 11, 1875 ·Page 4

Lewisburg wants a tannery and good roads.

Cotton picking has commenced in Conway county.

Daily Arkansas Gazette
Sun, Sep 12, 1875 ·Page 1

—T. B. Stout of Lewisburg, has forwarded to Col. T. B. Mills at Little Rock, a huge cucumber, which was raised by Mr. John T. Hannaford at Lewisburg. The monster vegetable weighed sixty pounds.

The Russellville Democrat
Thu, Sep 16, 1875 ·Page 4

THE Hot Springs Telegraph endeavors to make it appear that Rev. Wm. C. Stout, of the Lewisburg State, was a radical member of the constitutional convention of 1864. This is too bad. We should hate to think Col. Harrell knows so little of Arkansas history as to believe his own assertion, if *he* wrote it; and we don't like to charge that he uttered it knowingly. Mr. Stout, of the State, was not a member of the convention of 1864. The Telegraph sins without light or reason, it is to be supposed.

Daily Arkansas Gazette
Sat, Sep 18, 1875 ·Page 1

Lewisburg Paper Encourages
Farmers to Plant Wheat This year
Wheat.

We are anxious for a large sowing of wheat this fall, because we think that it is the surest road to independence. We have taken occasion heretofore to say that few men can make the living of two years on one year's work. At the beginning of this year nearly every one was a year behind, owing to the unprecedented failure of crops. However good the present crop may turn out, it will take the greater part to pay arrears, so that few will have enough to live on another whole year. If, therefore, wheat be heavily sown this fall, by June next you will again begin to be in funds to meet your wants, whatever they may be. The quantity of land is unlimited to the industrious, for he who sows can clear this winter, and have a new field for culture next spring. By thus raising two crops in the year, one of which requires no culture, you will be able to get ahead, and wipe out this state of dependence, and we do not know of any other way to do it.—[Lewisburg State.

Daily Arkansas Gazette
Thu, Sep 23, 1875 ·Page 1

Miss Ida, daughter of Col. A. Gordon, of Lewisburg, died a few days since.

The first bale of new cotton was brought to Lewisburg by Will J. Stout.

Daily Arkansas Gazette
Wed, Sep 29, 1875 ·Page 1

Van Buren Press: How about the Gazette's cucumber, from Lewisburg, weighing sixty pounds?

Lewisburg State: Well, this is all we know about it: J. T. Hannaford raised it, T. B. Stout sent it to T. B. Mills & Co., and the Gazette made mention of it. It DID weigh sixty pounds, and when you have digested that, prepare to swallow another ten or fifteen pounds heavier that that! Hannaford has it. Let no one forget that Lewisburg is in Conway County; and that the State is published there; and the County is rather noted for big things.

The Russellville Democrat
Thu, Oct 07, 1875 ·Page 2

Lewisburg State : A joint-stock company has been formed and Lewisburg is to have a cemetery.

Daily Arkansas Gazette
Thu, Oct 07, 1875 ·Page 3

—The Arkansas Annual Conference of the M. E. Church south, meets at Lewisburg on the 24th of November.

The Russellville Democrat
Thu, Oct 14, 1875 ·Page 4

COTTON BOLLS.

Lewisburg wants pickers.

Parker & Co. transferred 146 bales yesterday.

Cotton-picking is a month behind in Conway county.

Daily Arkansas Gazette
Thu, Oct 21, 1875 ·Page 4

One thousand men can find employment within ten miles of Lewisburg.

Daily Arkansas Gazette
Sat, Oct 23, 1875 ·Page 1

Fiend to be Executed
December 17th at Lewisburg

—W. B. Thompson, the fiend who assassinated Mrs. Stover, sentenced to be executed on the 17th of December, was brought down yesterday, from Lewisburg, by Officer Ragland, and placed in the county jail for safe keeping.

Daily Arkansas Gazette
Tue, Oct 26, 1875 ·Page 4

S. H. WHITTHORNE,

ATTORNEY AT LAW,

LEWISBURG, ... ARKANSAS.

Will practice in the courts of Conway, Faulkner, Van Buren, Pope and Perry Counties and in the Supreme and Federal Courts at Little Rock.

☞ Office up stairs in the 'State' building.

[Sep26-tf.]

The Russellville Democrat
Thu, Oct 28, 1875 ·Page 4

The Wonderful Coolness of a Condemned Murderer--Smoking and Laughing While He Talks of His Doom.

Last evening a representative of the GA-ZETTE called on Thompson, the convicted assassin of Mrs. Stover of Conway, who is now confined in the Pulaski county jail, awaiting the day of execution, the 17th inst., when he is to be hung by the neck at Lewisburg, until he is dead! *dead!* DEAD! The doomed man is still resolute and defiant in conversation, although at certain times there is noticeable an involuntary twitching of the lips. At the time of the reporter's visit he was sitting on the rail of the veranda in rear of the jail, apparently enjoying a cigar, the blue smoke of which partially concealed his head from view. He was very cordial—the same spirit of coolness asserting itself as on former occasions. He is apparently better contented than a month ago, and says he receives visits from the sisters of mercy, Father Pat, and Revs. Tupper and Turner. In his button-hole were two withered roses, gifts from the sisters, which he prized very highly. When asked if his execution day, now so near at had, did not make him nervous and sleepless at nights, he replied: "No, indeed; why should it? I never did kill that woman, and will never confess. I didn't have a fair trial, and if they want to stretch—break my neck—its all right. I can't help it. Everybody has to go, and its my time now, and I reckon its all right. Hard luck is caused by the view the people took of the case, and the witnesses' testimony. Why didn't they arrest Snap, who jumped on his horse and left the country as soon as the woman was killed? Snap was Stover's son-in-law. Well, I must stop and wait 'till I see the governor; don't want to blow all my brains out now. I was an orphan and never had any care or education, and have been kicked and cuffed about the world all my life." The prisoner, a few days since, had eighteen photographs taken by Mr. Alford the artist, to send to distant relatives and give to friends. The officers at the jail report Thompson to be very quiet and orderly. Officer Ragland will take him to Lewisburg next week.

Daily Arkansas Gazette
Tue, Dec 07, 1875 ·Page 4

—Thompson, the murderer of Mrs. Stover, was hung at Lewisburg at 12 o'clock yesterday.

Daily Arkansas Gazette
Sat, Dec 18, 1875 ·Page 4

—Buck Thompson, the murderer of Mrs. Stover, was publicly executed at Lewisburg on last Friday- He seemed perfectly dead to all feelings of remorse for the dreadful crime he had committed, and met his terrible fate with that stolid indifference which so frequently has been manifested by condemned criminals

The Russellville Democrat
Thu, Dec 23, 1875 ·Page 1

—The crowd which assembled to witness the hanging of Buck Thompson at Lewisburg last Friday, is estimated at from 6000 to 8000---all to see a poor deluded wretch's neck broken.

The Russellville Democrat
Thu, Dec 23, 1875 ·Page 4

The man Thompson, who was hung at Lewisburg, Arkansas, on Friday, was as impudent a criminal as ever stepped upon the scaffold. The report says he smoked a cigar, and "kissed his hand to the ladies." just before swinging off. But what were ladies doing at such a matinee as that."

Daily Arkansas Gazette
Sat, Dec 25, 1875 ·Page 3

—Several of our subscribers have expressed a desire to see the confession made by Thompson, who was hanged at Lewisburg for the murder of Mrs. Stover. For their gratification we publish the confession in full in to-day's paper.

The Russellville Democrat
Thu, Jan 13, 1876 ·Page 4

THOMPSON'S CONFESSION.

From the Lewisburg State.]

The following is a full confession of Thompson, made before T. B. Stout and E. B. Henry, at Lewisburg:

In view of the certainty of eternity and knowing that my fate and destiny on earth will soon be ended, I make this statement, and, for the truth, God above knows that these facts are solemn truths.

In regard to the death of Mrs. Rebecca Stover, I have this to say: Soon after John B. Stover's death, I made the remark that the old lady Stover should be killed in the presence of all Stover's hands, viz: Lee, Wallace, Tom Stover, Scott, and others. I was out in the mule lot two or three days after the burying of John B. Stover, in the evening, and Jack Snapp and Tom Stover were with me, and asked me how much I would take to kill old Mrs. Stover, and whether I would take two hundred and fifty dollars and the best horse on the place. I then best horse on the place. I then said I had nothing against Mrs. Stover. They (Snapp and Stover) said, would I kill her for five hundred dollars and the best horse or mule? I made the same answer. They then commenced jeering and taunting me, by saying that I was afraid, and dare not do it. I asked them, if they wanted her killed, why they did not kill her themselves? They then said, that I had no interest here and that I could get on a horse and leave the country, but they had property here and could not do it, and that it would be all the same—that is, my killing her—and that I would be protected, and if I got into trouble, money should be at my command for lawyers; and that they would spend their last dollar for me. This took place before Mrs. Stover shot Jack Snapp. After Mrs. Stover shot Jack Snapp, I was the party that arrested Mrs. Stover and brought her back to Stover's house, and all the men on the place were afraid to go after her. I was very mad, because I loved Jack Snapp as a brother, and seeing him shot raised all the evil in me. I had full confidence in Jack Snapp, and believed that he would do the same if I was shot. I was so wrought up in my feelings, that I swore that I would kill her. I felt the same as if she had shot a brother. I also brought her over to Lewisburg to be dealt with according to law; but after she was brought over she was placed under such light bonds, that I was afraid she would get away, and pay the money on the bond; so I concluded to revenge myself, and never let her get away.

I have never asked, demanded, requested or insinuated that I wanted any money, property or any consideration whatever; all that I ever asked them, was to protect me, in case of danger by the law, and the offer they made me was by their own voluntary act, and without my making any demands whatever, directly or indirectly.

MY FATE.

I attribute my death to Jack Snapp and Tom Stover, who together concocted the killing and used me as a tool. Tom Stover need not put on the garb of innocence, as his hands are bloody, need not put on the garb of innocence, as his hands are bloody, and on the day of the killing had full knowledge of it. They have deserted, betrayed me; and left me to my fate—even had a dance, last night, the night before I was to be hung, and have refused to pay my council or even get me a decent suit of clothes to be buried in. I freely forgive their heartlessness and their treatment, and I regret that I have been too zealous to defend those, whom I once thought to be my friends, having too true a heart, and that I am a victim to hypocrisy and deceit. If they can stand to live with the curses of their fellow man upon their heads, I can bear to die, and expect to die like a man, and leave them and their part to the God, who judges all.

As to all witnesses against me, I have this to say: in regard to Mr. Tucker; the morning after Jack Snapp was shot, Tucker proposed to Snapp to kill Mrs. Stover for five hundred dollars in cash, and told me that if I killed her, he would say nothing about it; and proposed to divide the money, when I killed her. I told him no, that I was going to kill her for no money, but for friendship. He has made false statements and if his perjured lips feel, that in swearing away my life in falsehoods, has done him any good, I am willing to let it all pass.

FOR TOM STOVER AND JACK SNAPP:

I know where Mrs. Stover secreted her money, but as they have sold their souls for money, I shall die with the secret of where it is, in my own breast.

To Charles C. Reid, Jr., who worked up the case against me, and prosecuted me, I freely forgive, and ask that my friends do no harm to him, as was requested in letters written by me for that purpose. I wish to die at peace with all mankind and hope only the guilty will suffer; my part of it I pay by forfeiting my own life.

The world that has ill used me, I leave without any regret; my enemies I forgive. As for those who betrayed me, I hope that a guilty conscience may bring them to repentance. My true friends I love hope to meet in a better land. I desire to express my sincere thanks to Father Pat Raley for his incessant devotion to me, and the consolation I received. I can only give him my earnest gratitude. On the Sisters of Charity I invoke my last and dying blessing. My dying love I leave to Mr. and Mrs. Hornibrook; and return my thanks to sheriff Rottaken, Frank Botsford, Jim O'Neal and the turnkeys of the city prison, for the many acts of kindness during my confinement.

In conclusion, I know that John C. Geyer and Wm. King and Wm. Vanwinkle are innocent, and 1 hope the courts of the country will exhonorate them.

It is now ten minutes till one o'ciock, and in one more hour I shall be in eternity. I am done, —a long and eternal farewell.

WM. B. THOMPSON.

Daily Arkansas Gazette
Sat, Jan. 13, 1876 ·Page 1

The Lewisburg State furnishes the following Centennial specimen: "Here is our specimen man for the Centennial. His name is Isaac Sharpe; he is seventy-five years of age, wears a number forty-five coat, a number twelve shoe, a seven and three-quarters hat, is six feet high, weighs 211 pounds, has a son forty-nine years old, and one not quite a year old, and buys his goods from Bill Ragland, at H. W. Burrow & Co.'s.

Daily Arkansas Gazette
Thu, Dec 23, 1875 ·Page 3

The cotton gin of H. W. Burrow, near Lewisburg, was destroyed by fire last week. Thirty-five bales of cotton were destroyed.

Daily Arkansas Gazette
Thu, Dec 23, 1875 ·Page 3

☞ The Lewisburg *State* is bragging about a turnip that weighed 4½ pounds. We can inform our cotemporary of the *State*, that that was a rather small size turnip for this section of the State. Our old friend, Mr. Rodolph Randolph, of this city, presented this office on Monday last, with two turnips that weighed 16 pounds—one of them weighing a little over eight, and the other not quite so large.— The larger one measured thirty-two inches in circumference, and was perfectly sound and sweet.— Go away with your little old 4½ pound turnip. It takes old Clark to produce big turnips, big pumpkins, big corn, bigger babies and more of them, than other county in the State.

The Southern Standard
Sat, Jan 22, 1876 ·Page 1

Holders of Conway county scrip will take notice that scrip, presented for funding on or before the 1st day of February, 1876, will be funded in ten year bonds, all after that date in fifteen year bonds. "A word to the wise."— [Lewisburg State.

Daily Arkansas Gazette
Tue, Jan 25, 1876 ·Page 2

Hon. John J. Clendenin.

We are pained to announce the death of Judge Clendenin, who for many years presided over the courts of this county. He was a good man and had many friends. —[Lewisburg State.

It is with deep sorrow that we learn of the death of Judge John J. Clendenin, which sad event occurred at his residence in Little Rock on the 4th inst. He had been in bad health for some time, and his death was not unexpected.— [Fayetteville Democrat.

The death of Hon. John J. Clendenin, judge of the sixth judicial circuit, is announced in the GAZETTE of the 6th inst. as occurring on the 4th of July. A good man, an honest citizen and an upright and impartial judge has gone over the river. Peace go with him.— [Jacksonport Herald.

Daily Arkansas Gazette
Wed, Jul 12, 1876 ·Page 1

—We were favored with a pleasant call from Col. S. H. Whitthorne and Capt. Gordon, of Lewisburg, last week. They are both genial gentlemen and we shall be glad to have them call often.

—A boy by the name Cloar, who lived in the neighborhood some 3 or 4 miles southeast of here poisoned himself by chewing hemlock root last Friday. He was hunting ginseng and took the poisonous root for that article. He died in a few hours.

The Russellville Democrat
Thu, Jul 13, 1876 ·Page 4

In speaking of the recent overflow in the Arkansas river, the Lewisburg State says: "No plantation in this county has been overflowed. The damage was simply by backing into low places and submerging a few acres on a farm. The soil in these old sloughs or low places is very rich and they are planted with risk. The height of the water was variable at different places. At Lewisburg it was nearly two feet below the water of 1872, while at the Stout plantation six miles above it was only four inches below the rise of 1872, and lacked but eighteen inches of reaching that of 1866, which was higher there than in 1867, and the highest since 1844. We have obtained reports from about twenty-five plantations, on which there has been more or less damage, amounting in the aggregate to two hundred and one acres.

Daily Arkansas Gazette
Sat, Jul 22, 1876 ·Page 2

A lady named Humphrey, living some three miles from Lewisburg, fell dead on Saturday last. Supposed to be caused by an affection of the heart.

Daily Arkansas Gazette
Tue, Aug 08, 1876 ·Page 1

Capt. Gill and his deputy, Pomp Breeden, took charge of the post-office at Lewisburg on the 14th inst., Capt. Gray having been removed.

Lewisburg State, 18th: "John Phillips, the prisoner belonging to Washington county who is confined in our county jail, managed to remove a stone from the wall of the building, and would have made his escape, Monday night, had he not heard the voices of some parties near by whom he supposed to be guards."

Daily Arkansas Gazette
Wed, Aug 23, 1876 ·Page 1

PERSONAL POLITICS.

The following article from the Lewisburg State is so sensible and truthful, and the truth of it is so plain and striking that we think it may do our readers well to peruse it:

"If there is any one thing that more than another mars our peace, in a free government, it is the spirit of self-seeking that characterizes the professional politicians. It is honorable to hold office and it is worthy of regard to seek office, when the seeker is conscious of ability to discharge the duties of office for the good of the people, or when urged to do so by the judgment of friends. But, when there is a color of seeking office, only for the honor and enoluments, without special regard to the public good; and in doing so, war is made on as good, if not better men, the matter is different. At best, there are few men really capable of filling the higher places in State. Of the grade that usually seeks them, the number is fearfully great. Fearfully great, we say, because this kind, more or less, will, by dint of pertinacity, and the use of means that the most competent would never resort to, obtain the

would never resort to, obtain the places and as a result the public service will suffer.

We do not indeed think it strange that this kind of men should seek office, for of that sort have been so many that a party, of very inferior gifts and graces, might hardly be able to retain his self respect if he did not claim to be as fit, at least, as others have been. But there ought to be an end to all this. What is the remedy? There is none, until the average voter has a better sense of his duty and responsibility. And when will that be? Not for many a long day to come. The people must be better educated, better instructed, and more fitted to discharge the duty of electors. To this end, as one instrumentality, we need a higher, truer and more conscientious journalism.

But here we find ourselves about to travel around in a circle, for until the people will more liberally support the press, and more conscientiously discriminate in that support, we cannot expect to have a truly independent, fearless and efficient journalism. There is not a paper to day in our State, we believe, that has the patronage that would justify the proprietor to employ a competent editor, as he would wish to employ a schoolmaster or minister. The ablest men that drive the quill do it without reward and earn their living by other means. Still, it is to be hoped that all, who find themselves in the responsible position of mentors to the people, will not refrain from constantly keeping before the people the fact that, by their indolence and indifference, and to say it plainly, ignorance, they are mainly responsible for the efficiency of the public service, in state, county and municipality. We venture to say that the voters of not five counties in the state, at the last election, called forth their best men for office, but blindly voted for those who sought most diligently for their sugrages. Pray for the day when shall be realized that dream of the Know Nothings. 'The office shall seek the man.' "

The Russellville Democrat
Thu, Oct 19, 1876 ·Page 2

Murder of Methodist Preacher Rev. George Pledger by moonshiners who mistook him for a U. S. Marshal

A DASTARDLY, CRAVENLY CRIME.

A Fiendish Deed of Blood Which Cries Aloud for Vengeance.

Let the Murderers be Hunted Down and Brought to Justice.

On Wednesday evening, the 25th ult., a most foul crime was committed in our county, and once more the name of Pope county will be connected with stories of blood and violence. In last week's paper we said nothing of this crime, because our information was so meager and unreliable that we did not wish to give an erroneous version of the deplorable affair. And as we had been informed by a reliable citizen from the upper end of our county that a company of the best men of that section would visit the scene of the dreadful deed and institute a thorough investigation, the result of which would be furnished us for publication, we deemed it best to wait for their report. We now understand that no such investigation has been had, and as we have had no account of the affair as full and correct as the following which we find in the Independent Arkansian, we copy below the statement of the Arkansian's correspondent, "T. J. C." The crime is a horrible one and no stone should be left unturned to ferret out the authors of the devilish deed. Such outlaws and barbarians as they should be allowed to find no resting place in our county or state. The damage which one such character can and will bring upon our name is greater than can be counterbaianced by all that ten good men can do. Not being informed what steps our officials have taken in this matter we are not prepared to censure them with the fact that nothing so far as the public know, has been done to arraign the guilty parties. This much, however, we do say, and that is this: suspicion points strongly to a desperado by the name of Hughes, who, with a few

name of Hughes, who, with a few associates of like character, are generally believed to be the guilty parties; and if our sheriff, his deputies. and the constable of that township have not taken steps and measures to secure these suspected parties, they have been guilty of a most flagrant neglect of duty, a neglect for which there is no excuse. We think, also, that the citizens of that community are guilty of great indifference in this matter. Every law abiding man in that section should feel it his duty to aid, demand and HAVE an investigation of this matter, and purge their community of the foul imputation of harboring, countenancing, or even allowing such desperadoes to remain in their settlement. Who can tell us if this matter has been brought to the knowledge of the Governor? This should be done at once if it has not already been attended to. The following is as full an account of the deed as we have heard:

MR. EDITOR:—Our county is considerably excited over the attempted murdering of four Methodist Preachers, who were on their return home, from Yellville conference, on Wednesday evening last, at Douglas' Store, Pilot Rock Township, Pope county, Arkansas.

The Revs. Burton N. Williams, Ambrose Williams, his son; W. H. Matheny and George Pledger, were traveling in company. The two young men Rev. W. H. and Ambrose Williams being a little in advance of the elder Williams and Matheny, and when they arrived at Douglasville, they dismounted to rest, and to await the arrival of those in the rear. Mr. Pledger stopped over some 80 yards to a blacksmith shop open at both ends, and was conversing with the smith and cracking nuts, when the attention of young Williams was attracted by the report of a gun shot, and in looking towards the shop discovered his associate in the act of falling. He started to his assistance but was met by the smith who implored him not

to his assistance but was met by the smith who implored him not to go there, if he did, he would be killed. By this time Burton Williams and Matheny rode up and by the assistance of several of the neighbors, living about the place, carried the wounded man to the residence of a Mr. Wallace, and dispatched a messenger for a Doctor. After doing all they could for suffering humanity, Mr. B. Williams and Matheny, walked out of the house, some few paces off and informed a small squad of men, who had got together, who they were &c., &c. The citizens appeared to deplore the act and had started off to their respective avocations, when the report of two guns were heard and an acclamation from both Matheny and Burton Williams, I am shot, which proved to be true.

They got into the house in some way and awaited with suffering patience for the arrival of the Doctor who when he arrived commenced to examine the wound of Mr. Pledger. The ball struck him at the point of the hip—went through him and lodged in his backbone—no hope. The next was Mr. Williams, shot nearly in the same place but did not enter the hollow, went around under the skin and come out at the backbone, a frightful but not dangerous wound. The next was Rev. W. H. Matheny, shot in the right side, did not enter the flesh very deep but made an ugly place.

very deep but made an ugly place.

These men were all shot from the top of the mountain, Douglasville, being situate at the base.

The wounded made some inquiry as to why they were to be murdered, shot down like dogs, when they were strangers and had malice toward none. They were told by the citizens that those who had done the shooting would feel DEEPLY MORTIFIED when they should learn that they had fired upon inoffensive Prechers instead of the U. S. Marshal and his posse.

It appears that Deputy Cline and his posse had visited that section on several occasions, and taken in about 20 of the illicit distillers—some are now at the Rock in jail, others at home on bail, hence their bitter hatred toward every stranger who goes through that valley.

It is not my province to comment on this dastardly act, but trust the strong arm of the law may be brought to bear, and that "no guilty man escape."

The above facts I received from one of the wounded and is substantially true.

Revs. B. and A. Williams and W. H. Matheny, live in Johnson county, Rev. Mr. Pledger, I think in Logan county.   T. J. C.

Ewing Seminary, Johnson county, Ark., Oct. 30th, 1876.

LATER.—I have just learned that the Rev. George Pledger died on Friday, after the shooting on Wednesday.   T. J. C.

The Russellville Democrat
Thu, Nov 09, 1876 ·Page 4

Says the Lewisburg State, of Saturday: "A young man was brought to town under the charge of murder. His name was Spears; and we understand that, under the influence of liquor, he stabbed to death another by the name of Carpenter, a poor simpleton, at Plummer, a few days ago."

Daily Arkansas Gazette
Wed, Nov 22, 1876 ·Page 3

—We were pleased to meet in our office this week our former fellow-townsman, Robt. B. Wilson, Esq., now of Lewisburg. Bob is a good boy, and deserves good treatment wherever he may go.

The Russellville Democrat
Thu, Dec 14, 1876 ·Page 4

MARRIED.

BOURLAND—GORDON—On the 26th inst., at the residence of the bride's father, by the Rev. J. L. Burrow, Mr. D. L. BOURLAND, of Ozark, to Miss NETTIE, daughter of Col. Anderson Gordon, of Lewisburg, Ark.

Daily Arkansas Gazette
Sat, Dec 30, 1876 ·Page 4

—Our good looking friend Mr. D. L. Bourland and bride passed up the road yesterday a week ago. "Buck" has captured one of the choicest prizes in Arkansas, Miss Nettie Gorden, of Lewisburg, daughter of Genl. Anderson Gordon. The marriage took place on Tuesday evening, the 26th Dec., and we extend our hearty wishes for the perfect bliss and prosperity of the newly wedded pair during their voyage of life.

The Russellville Democrat
Thu, Jan 04, 1877 ·Page 4

—The Lewisburg State says that last week two of the convicts employed on the farm above here attempted to escape. One was killed, but the other succeeded in getting free.

Daily Arkansas Gazette
Tue, Jan 30, 1877 ·Page 4

Lewisburg State: "One of our worthy citizens came to town last week and took on too much tangle-foot. He lived on Petit Jean Mountain, and before he undertook the steep ascent he braced himself with a huge potation. He got along very well until he reached the top of the mountain, when the tangle-foot got the better of him and rolled him over a bluff some twenty feet high. The poor man was so hurt by his fall that he could not move, and for hours lay where he had fallen before assistance came to him."

Daily Arkansas Gazette
Thu, Apr 05, 1877 ·Page 2

THE excursion of the Odd Fellows, to Lewisburg, advertised to take place to-day, has, on account of the inclemency of the weather, been postponed until Thursday next, May 3, when all parties wishing to enjoy a May-day excursion can join. The tickets are only seventy-five cents for the round trip.

Daily Arkansas Gazette
Thu, Apr 26, 1877 ·Page 4

Big Show will be at Lewisburg October 31, 1876

ILLE DEMOCRAT. THURSDAY. OCTOBER 26. 1876.

BIG SHOW. BIG SHOW. BIG SHOW. BIG SHOW.

At Russellville One Day Only----Wednesday, Nov. I.

W. W. COLE'S
Great New York & New Orleans
ZOOLOGICAL AND EQUESTRIAN
EXPOSITION!
The Mammoth Show!!
The Model Show!!
Larger than Ever! Famous Everywhere!!

Emphatically the Largest of all Zoological Collections!!
GREAT HIPPODROME, MUSEUM, AND CIRCUS!!!
COMING BY RAIL. ALTOGETHER THIRTY-SIX RAALROAD CARS!

ITS LEADING FEATURES! ITS LEADING FEATURES! ITS LEADING FEATURES! ITS LEADING FEATURES!

PROFESSOR ERNESTE---THE GREAT CENTENNIAL AERONAUT,
Will Positively Make a Grand FREE Ascension each Day at 1 oclock, P. M.
WITH THIS COMBINATION, THE GRANDEST SIGHT OF THE YEAR 1876.

FOUR GREAT CLOWNS,
Sixteen Ladies! Fourteen Children

THE GRAND PROCESSION ON THE STREET DAILY, at 10 oclock, a. m. Live Lions Loose in the Streets. Monster Serpents! Den open, and exposed to view will pass through the principal Streets. First the Magnificent Band Chariot, "SUN" drawn by 10 horses afterwards the Monster Tableau Car, "NEPTUNE." the largest in the World, 30 feet long, 35 feet high. The Sea God seated on his throne surrounded by Water Nymps, who toy with real water as it spouts from fountains surrounding them.

THREE SEPERATE TENTS,
ONE TICKET ADMITS TO ALL

NEXT ROLLS THE CAR OF THE CONQUERER, drawn by ten dromedaries, and containing the King of Beasts, and other animals, crouching at the feet of their Master, Man, viewed through the secure bars that surround them. Thirty dens of Zoological Wonders! Embellished with Biblical and Historical Paintings. Afterwards Zingra is seen seated in his plate-glass den of Monster serpents, Anacondas, Pythons, Boa-constrictors. Following this procession, and distinct in itself is a parade commemorative of the Centennial Year. Commences the great

Car "LIBERTY," bearing the Goddess and our Glorious banner, surrounded by living figures of Army, Navy, Peace, Justice and a mounted Body Guards on Gray stallion, of Ladies and Gents in Continental Costumes of 109 years ago. In this procession appears the tableaux of "Washington Crossing the Delaware," "Putnam leaving the Plow" "The death of Warren," concluding with "Washington's Triumphal March on his return to New York at the close of the revolutionary war." Following this the resources of the HIPPODROME will appear upon the Scene.

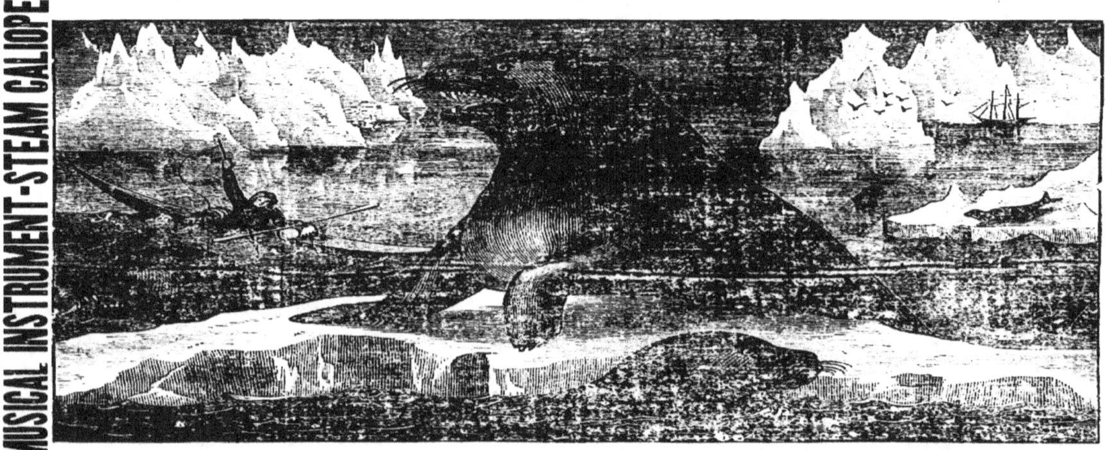

LADIES DRIVING (four horses abreast) CHARIOTS, LADIES DRIVING TWO HORSE CHARIOTS. MALE AND FEMALE JOCKEYS. MOUNTED ON their favorite steeds. Negro grooms leading Blooded Race horses, Boys riding Ponies, &c. The Grotesque figures in different Parts of the procession, will greatly enliven the Scene. The whole ending with the large musical Instrument, the Steam Caliope. Interspersed in the Procession in appropriate places the Elephants, Camels, Buffaloes, Elk, Zebras, will appear. The whole forming a gorgeous sight, never equalled. Never will be excelled. So don't miss it! See it, and bear in mind it will not overrate the merits of the Show upon the inside, for the SHOW has no equal on the Continent! this, the season of 1876.

Remember the date---Rain or Shine, we Show positively.
At Little Rock,	- - -	October 30.
At Lewisburg.	- - -	October 31.
At RUSSELLVILLE. -	Wednesday,	Nov. I.

The Russellville Democrat
Thu, Oct 26, 1876 ·Page 4

ODD FELLOWS EXCURSION.

The excursion of the Odd Fellows to Lewisburg, from this place, in commemoration of the fifty-seventh anniversary of the Order, took place yesterday, having, on account of the weather, been postponed from last week. The Lodges of this city, together with their families and other excursionists to the number of about 300 persons, left this city at 8 a. m., on the Fort Smith Railroad train, under charge of Superintendent Hartman, and were landed at Morrillton in good time, where a procession was formed and the members of the Order and the party proceeded to Steele's Grove, at Lewisburg, where they met the Clarksville, Ozark, Conway, Russellville and Lewisburg Lodges, swelling the party to about 500 persons. The visiting Lodges were received by E. G. Henry, N. G., of Eureka Lodge, Lewisburg, which was followed by prayer from acting Grand Chaplain C. W. Cox, after which the Ritual was read by Messrs. Albert Cohn and W. S. Davis. The Little Rock Glee Club then favored the multitude with some select music, which was followed by an excellent oration, made by Past Grand Master Peter Brugman, of Little Rock; then the excursionists enjoyed a basket dinner and the pleasures of the dance. In the afternoon addresses were made by Col. C. C. Reed, on behalf of Eureka Lodge, of Lewisburg, and L. C. Lincoln, of Center Link Lodge, Conway, which, with music and dancing, occupied the time very pleasantly until 5 p. m., when the Little Rockers started on their return trip, reaching home at 8 o'clock, fully impressed with the success of the first excursion sent out from the city this year.

Daily Arkansas Gazette
Fri, May 04, 1877 ·Page 4

MR. W. B. GIBSON, of Lewisburg, died yesterday morning. A casket for his remains was forwarded to that city by special train last evening.

Daily Arkansas Gazette
Sun, May 06, 1877 ·Page 4

—Atkins was well represented by our 3 meal brethren at the picnic given by the Odd Fellows of Lewisburg. The boys say they had a gay time drinking lager with those Little Rock girls.

—Rained nearly all day last Sunday and our boys were disappointed

The Russellville Democrat
Thu, May 10, 1877 ·Page 3

—Atkins can now boast of having a lawyer in the person of Col. Earle, of Lewisburg. We wish him success in his new field of labor.

The Russellville Democrat
Thu, May 17, 1877 ·Page 3

—Dr. Frank Gordon of Lewisburg was in town last Sunday and says he came up to rusticate. But we think he came up to see the latest styles.

The Russellville Democrat
Thu, May 24, 1877 ·Page 3

Road Notice.

Notice is hereby given that application will be made at the July 1877 term of the Pope County Court for opening a public road beginning at a point on the military road about half a mile from Atkins and running in a south-easterly direction through the "flat gap" by the farm of Mr. Kizer, thence south to intersect the Galla Rock and Lewisburg road at or east of the grave-yard lane at Wm. Reynolds' farm.

C. E. Tobey, George Byerly, Chas. Lewis.
May 31 1877 (9 times

The Russellville Democrat
Thu, May 31, 1877 ·Page 3

The Lewisburg *State* tells a story of three maiden ladies who lived in the vicinity of that place. They were considered poor, worked hard on their farm, and supported an imbecile brother. The three died in the last four years, and after the death of the last one, an administrator sold the effects, among which were one hundred and five calico dresses, nearly all new, and one thousand two hundred yards of calico that had never been made up. The sisters always dressed shabbily.

The Southern Standard
Sat, Jul 21, 1877 ·Page 2

COL. S. H. WHITTHORNE came down from Lewisburg last evening. He informs us that Conway County boasts of the finest crops she has ever yet raised.

Daily Arkansas Gazette
Fri, Aug 03, 1877 ·Page 4

—Our town boasts of the handsomest girls and the biggest fool boys in the state.—Lewisburg State.

Your town may boast away. We grant the latter but will dispute the former with you.

The Russellville Democrat
Thu, Aug 23, 1877 ·Page 1

LEWISBURG ins'sts on having a flouring mill. Situated as the town is, in a good wheat-growing county, the opportunity is a splendid one for an enterprising miller.

Daily Arkansas Gazette
Wed, Aug 29, 1877 ·Page 4

We clip the following from the Lewisburg State: "Messrs. Lewis & Thalheimer have commenced building a steamboat especially for the Perryville and Little Rock trade; their present steamer, Inspector, being entirely too small to fill the demand of increasing trade. The new boat will be 80 by 17 feet clear, capable of carrying 150 or 175 bales of cotton without barges. She will be able to make the round trip from Perryville to Little Rock in forty-eight hours."

Daily Arkansas Gazette
Wed, Aug 29, 1877 ·Page 4

—WE received a letter from friend W. F. Gray, at Plumer, yesterday, which reads as follows: "Our church was burned last night. We were in the midst of a revival. Messrs. Lucas, Wilkes and Rook say they put the lights out carefully. No further particulars." His letter leaves room for us to draw the inference that it was the work of an incendiary, but we hope however it is cendiary, but we hope however it is not so. The church was a handsome new building not long since completed, and was a credit to a place of such small population. We wish they may be enabled by the assistance of neighbor towns to rebuild, at an early day. If the firing was the work of an incendiary we hope he may be brought to speedy justice.—Lewisburg State.

The Russellville Democrat
Thu, Aug 30, 1877 ·Page 1

Detailed Lewisburg Description

SAXET ON HIS TRAVELS.

LEWISBURG, Sept. 10, 1877.

EDITOR DEMOCRAT: Although when I left you on Tuesday last I expected to remain at this place but one day, fate and circumstances seem to have decreed otherwise, and here I am in the pleasant little town of Lewisburg, with very agreeable surroundings, enjoying the full run of the State office, together with the companionship of the proprietor and the genial typos in his employ, all of which makes time pass smoothly on my hands. The State is a wideawake, spirited paper generally, and in the matter of locals has a rattle and a snap about it that wins approval from all readers. The proprietor is a young man of fine mental attainments and excellent social qualities. His avoirdupois is but little greater than that of your correspondent, though in the matter of good looks is all in his favor.

Lewisburg is situated on the Arkansas river, about 75 miles above Little Rock, and one mile from the Morrillton railroad station, 50 miles

Morrillton railroad station, 50 miles by rail to the State Capital. On the arrival and previous to the departure of each train hacks are in readiness to convey passengers to and from the depot. Lewisburg is one of the oldest towns in Arkansas, and some of the buildings bear the marks of age and of the primitive days when you and I were boys. Yet there are many buildings which present a newer appearance, showing that the town is not yet finished. It has a population of about 700, but with a rich farming country on the west, east and south to support it, the town cannot fail to increase in population and wealth as time rolls on and the lands adjacent to it are brought under cultivation. I find the people here very pleasant and hospitable, and always glad to welcome strangers who come amongst them. This is not only the outcropping of a genuine humanity, but is sound policy, taking the matter in only a business point of view, for a stranger in a strange land feels devilish strange (excuse this tautological and somewhat inelegant expression) if everybody looks at him without a sign of recognition.

The Masonic Academy began the fall session on Monday last with about 50 pupils in attendance. Mr. Mason, the principal, is a highly cultivated man, with the deportment and demeanor well calculated to fit him not only to instruct the youth in their various studies, but to inculcate in their minds a high standard of morality.

An amateur brass band is among the wide-awake and soul-stirring institutions of Lewisburg. For amateurs the members show a degree of proficiency which reflects credit

proficiency which reflects credit upon their efforts.

The Circuit Court opened here on Monday last—Judge Mansfield presiding with his usual dignity and urbanity, and J. P. Byers, Esq., Prosecuting Attorney, appearing as the energetic counsel for the State in all cases in which the State is a party. There was during the week a great number of attorneys from Little Rock and other places, besides the members of the bar residing here. Court adjourned on Friday morning to meet Monday afternoon, and Judge Mansfield, as well as the attorneys from other counties, have departed hence during the temporary adjournment. I will refer to the columns of the State for details of court proceedings during the week. Court will be continued this week, and as far into the succeeding week as may be necessary.

The termination of a state trial here last week induces me to indulge in comments which may provoke discussion. But no matter for that: I regard the law under which the conviction was had as a palpable absurdity. The case to which I allude was one wherein a man was indicted for hunting on Sunday, was convicted and a penalty of $5 assessed by the jury. Now it is all well enough to prohibit hunting on the Christian Sabbath, but it does seem to me that if the crime is so heinous in its nature as to require the intervention of a grand jury and to take up the valuable time of a Circuit Judge, it ought to call for some greater penalty than a fine from $5 to $25. In my humble opinion all those offences which are punishable by a fine less than $100 ought to be left to trial by Justices of the Peace. The punishment of Sabbath breaking ought to involve a much heavier penalty than it does, or else all cases for a violation of the law should be triable by Justices of the Peace.

Crops in this county are reported good, and the people are looking forward to more prosperous times when their crops are taken to market and disposed of.

As I found in Pope county, so I find in Conway county, many handsome ladies. Indeed pretty woman seem to be a natural outgrowth of Arkansas, for in all parts of the State I find numbers of them. Although I am in the sere and yellow leaf, I am still appreciative of female loveliness, and although nearly all the ardor of youth has passed from me, I am still susceptible.

My next may be from Little Rock, but more likely from St. Louis or Louisville. No matter where fortune may direct my steps, I shall have good words to say for Pope county and its hospitable people.

SAXET.

The Russellville Democrat
Thu, Sep 20, 1877 ·Page 1

LETTER FROM SAXET.

LEWISBURG, ARK., Sept. 24, 1877.

EDITOR DEMOCRAT: I am always glad to see a copy of your excellent paper, but the issue now before me which speaks so distinctly on the finance question, has a clear ring of defiance to your assailants that enlists my warmest admiration. I am not sufficiently versed in the intricacies of this financial problem to give me the right to pronounce a positive opinion, and I am only recording my approval of the clear and distinct manner in which your views are given to the public—presenting, as you do, the figures upon which you base the faith that is in you. Your tables amount to a direct challenge to those of contrary views, and if those who assail your position cannot prove that you are wrong, it will not be for the lack of an opportunity to do so. This is a mode of warfare that meets my approbation. A man's words may be misconstrued or distorted, but not so with his figures. They cannot be laughed out of existence. There they are: if correct, they proclaim the truth; if in error that error can easily be proven. You have taken the right way of demonstrating the correctness of your theory, and your manly stand for the right will give the DEMOCRAT a stronger claim to public good will and general approval.

I went out to the Carroll farm on Sunday to inspect that semi-State institution. I found Mr. J. C. Ward in charge as agent for the lessee. He has about one hundred convicts at work, and cultivates some eight hundred acres of cotton, which Mr. W. thinks will yield a bale to the acre. The convicts give evidence of being humanely treated, while being made to labor in atonement for the damage they have been to th State.

This immense field of cotton is a sight well worth looking upon. It is as clean and free from weeds as could be desired, and the admirable manner in which the farm is conducted is creditable in a higher degree to Mr. Ward. It is a source of

gree to Mr. Ward. It is a source of congratulation to all that the State is relieved of the expense and trouble of feeding, guarding and clothing its five hundred convicts, and that the lessee has a prospect of reaping a handsome reward for the large outlay he has made and the great responsibility he has taken upon himself is no less a source of satisfaction to his friends. Mr. Ward informs me that he expects soon to have one hundred and fifty more convicts from Little Rock, and that he has rented six hundred acres of land (in addition to that he now has) for cultivation next year. The health of the convicts is generally good. One of the number, however, (a colored man named Morgan) died of congestive chill early Sunday morning.

Now, Mr. Editor, notwithstanding the amiability which generally animates me, I am not free from dislikes, and you must pardon me if I "growl" a little. I don't mean to hurl my anathemas in your direction especially, but it is against the press of Arkansas generally. Although I respect public, I believe that opinions are neither criminal nor virtuous, and I desire to express what may prove to be an unpopular opinion; yet I hope the dear good public will give my protest respectful consideration. I therefore protest against the practice of using the names of ladies as freely as they are too often used in Arkansas newspapers. How often de we see something like this· "Miss Prudence Poppinjay, one of the reigning belles of Gumboville, arrived in town yesterday, and for the next fortnight will be the guest of the Misses Mc-Flimsy." My own opinion is, sir, that the name of a lady is something

that the name of a lady is something too sacred to be bandied about by the multitude, as it will be in bar rooms and street corners when the simple fact that one of the fairest of creation has seen fit to visit friends in town is seized upon by the ambitious reporter of the local paper. To mention the fact that Mr. So-and-so and his wife or daughter have arrived might do, but the mentionioning of young ladies' names promiscuously and without reserve, I regard as in exceeding bad taste and wholly unjustifiable. The time was when the mention of a lady's name in a saloon or in the hearing of a promiscuous gathering on the street was followed by a blow direct from the shoulder. It may be said that the young ladies are delighted with such public use of their names. Perhaps it does feed the vanity of some, but I doubt it, for I cannot think that a lady of characteristic modesty and proper training would care to have Tom, Dick and Harry know all the particulars of their movements. When visiting friends it is to be supposed that such as are worthy to make their acquaintance will be presented to them. If a young lady comes to town to visit friends it is a matter that concerns no one but her and her friends––it is in no respect a public matter. It is none of the public's business whence she cometh or whither she goeth. If you think I am wrong, consult your lady friends on the subject, and if they do not say I am right I will own up that I don't understand woman's true character and native instincts.

SAXET.

The Russellville Democrat
Thu, Oct 04, 1877 ·Page 1

WE are indebted to the young gentlemen of Lewisburg, Conway County, for an invitation to a grand calico hop, to be given in that town Friday evening, November 9, by the Lewisburg Terpsichorean Association.

Daily Arkansas Gazette
Fri, Oct 26, 1877 ·Page 4

Conference Appointments, M. E. Church South.

LEWISBURG DISTRICT—J. HARALSON, P. E.

Lewisburg Station, R. M. Tidings.
Lewisburg circuit, ————
Springfield Circuit, T. A. Graham; N. R. Knowlton, supernumerary.
Clinton Circuit, J. L. Massey; H. W. Burns, supernumerary.
Russellville Circuit, W, H. Corley.
Mt. Vernon Circuit, A. C. Ray.
Dardanelle Station, W. J. Dodson.
Dardanelle Circuit, J. J. Roberts.
Point Remove Circuit, J. W. Huffaker.
Perryville Circuit, ————
Shoal Creek Circuit, H. Puckett.
Opelow Circuit, J. E. Dunaway.
Quitman, T. J. Smith.
College, J. A. Peebles.

The Russellville Democrat
Thu, Nov 08, 1877 ·Page 1

MUCH ADO ABOUT NOTHING.

Strange as it may seem, the business men of Lewisburg, Dardanelle and other towns on the upper Arkansas river are not alive to their own business interests. The Little Rock and Fort Smith railroad in its greed and selfishness imposes upon the business interests to such an extent in the way of freights and the shipment of cotton that it is a burning shame to the management of the road. Only a short while ago the rates from this place on cotton to New Orleans were placed at four dollars per bale, shortly after this the river with a good rise alarmed the Shylocks and cotton rates were reduced to two dollars per bale to New Orleans. Since the river has fallen, up go the rates again.

Are the business men so dead that they cannot see that the aim of this corporation is to drive out steamboat navigation and destroy their trade when the river is in good boating stage? We ask our business men to patronize the steamboats because they are the means of bringing the railroad down to living rates and our merchants who do not know enough about business to give them a liberal share of their patronage stand in the light of their own interests. If forty business men in Dardanelle, Lewisburg, and other towns on the river, would consolidate and form a joint stock company a light draught steamer could be built and the trade wants supplied, freights be made reasonable and the investment made profitable. Will the Immigrant and Arkansian agitate this question and find out if there is not life in the old land yet. Talk it in public; talk it in private; talk it in your business circles and agitate it in your columns. We are certain to meet you half way.—Lewisburg State.

The Russellville Democrat
Thu, Dec 06, 1877 ·Page 2

Fight in Lewisburg

—Lewisburg State: There was a difficulty at Morrillton, Wednesday, between Mr. J. W. Gill and Carroll Armstrong, in which the former was seriously, if not fatally wounded. Armstrong was appointed as receiver for the Carroll estate at the last term of court and attached the crop of Gill for rents. Gill meeting him in Lewisburg last week knocked him down with a stick, and from rumors it is said that he intended doing the same thing every time he met him. So on Wednesday at Morrillton Gill and Armstrong met with the above results. There being so many accounts given of the affair we refrain from giving any particulars. We think this justice to all parties concerned.

The Russellville Democrat
Thu, Dec 06, 1877 ·Page 4

—The Lewisburg State misunderstands us when it supposes we are opposed to river towns putting in a light draught boat. We have not the slightest objection. We merely expressed our belief that as an investment it would not pay its owners. No doubt it would be a good thing for the planters and the towns on the river, and if they want it, let them go in.

The Russellville Democrat
Thu, Dec 13, 1877 ·Page 2

Child Burned to Death
CONWAY.

Lewisburg State, 8th: A negro child was burned to death below town last week. Left alone, it is supposed it had been playing in the fire and caught, burning to death before any assistance came.

Large crops of wheat are being sowed in this county.

Daily Arkansas Gazette
Sun, Dec 16, 1877 ·Page 2

Mr. J. J. Stout retires from the editorial department of the Lewisburg *State*. He made the *State* a lively paper. Who is to be his successor is not stated.

The Southern Standard
Sat, Jan 12, 1878 ·Page 2

Notice

Is hereby given that application will be made to April term 1878 of Pope County Court for an order for the appointment of viewers to view and report upon the utility of changing the road leading from Dover to Lewisburg, so as to move said road about four hundred yards west of where it intersects the wire road in Wilson township in said county. January 7, 1878.
J. M. BELL.

The Russellville Democrat
Thu, Jan 17, 1878 ·Page 3

—The Russellville Democrat man in speaking of the scarcity of suitable matters for the country editor to expostulate upon, suggests that right at this season mud throwing would be a nice avocation. He says, however:

We have the advantage of the State, for his mud is all clay and is not so easily handled as ours. No doubt it would hurt like the mischief to catch a wad of that clay, and the sting would be Felt(by)us a long time. So we won't try the State.

No, we don't want to sling mud at you, Jim, but if you will "come to see us," we can put a brick in your hat so much so that the Batten(d)field would be left to somebody else.—Lewisburg State.

All right, Edd, just wait until next June and we will see you and "go you a bean better."

The Russellville Democrat
Thu, Jan 24, 1878 ·Page 3

—The Lewisburg State says Supt. Hartman, of the L. R. & F. S. Ry. is laying off a new town on Railroad lands some 7 or 8 miles west of that place.

The Russellville Democrat
Thu, Mar 07, 1878 ·Page 3

—The Lewisburg State has just completed its third year. The State was started only a short time after the DEMOCRAT made its appearance, and we esteem it almost as a twin brother. For three years it has done good service for Conway county, and has, no doubt, been far greater benefit to the county than he has received pay for. We trust its fourth year may be the best and most prosperous one it has yet seen, and that the people of its county may rally round it with a rousing support.

The Russellville Democrat
Thu, Mar 28, 1878 ·Page 2

Masked Ball in Lewisburg

WE acknowledge the receipt of an invitation to a mask ball, to be given at Lewisburg, by the Terpsicorian Association, Friday evening, April 26.

Daily Arkansas Gazette
Wed, Apr 24, 1878 ·Page 4

—Henry T. Gordon is now connected with the Lewisburg State as Assistant Local Editor.

—The town was overflowing with people last Wednesday to see the balloon ascension.

The Russellville Democrat
Thu, May 23, 1878 ·Page 3

Wife Shot Dead by Husband

On Thursday evening about 8 o'clock the quietude of our town was disturbed by the firing of a gun and some one screaming. Upon investigation it proved to be the wife of Gus. Jamison, who was shot by her husband because she had expressed an intention of going to a dance that night. She is not dead at present, though there is no chance for her recovering. Her husband is now in jail awaiting trial and asks a speedy trial as he is innocent and dislikes the idea of staying in jail. It is the opinion of every one that he is guilty, and from rumors it will be proved on him.— Lewisburg State.

Daily Arkansas Gazette
Tue, Jun 11, 1878 ·Page 3

WE are pleased to learn that our young friend J. J. Stout, late editor of the Lewisburg State, was nominated for the Legislature by the Democracy of Conway County. He is one of the rising young men of the State, and will some day make his mark. Now, with Col. Anderson Gordon in the Senate, Conway and the district will be well represented.—[Van Buren Press.

Daily Arkansas Gazette
Fri, Jun 28, 1878 ·Page 2

Description of Russellville
by Lewisburg Editor

—We have to thank our near neighbor, the clever and wide-awake editor of the Lewisburg State, for the following handsome notice of our town and our paper:

"It was our pleasure last week to visit our neighbor city, Russellville, one of the most thriving towns in this section of Arkansas. The location of the town is very desirable. The streets are being graded after the most advanced manner at a considerable cost, showing the thriftiness and pride of the citizens. The commercial trade is large, and prices on all articles of barter compare favorably with those of Western cities. The town boasts of a first class school, in charge of Prof. Doggett, a gentleman of culture and learning. Russellville has always boasted of a good school. The leading institution of public interest is the DEMOCRAT printing office, in charge of B. F. Jobe, an excellent master printer and experienced publisher. The editorial department of the DEMOCRAT is under the control of Jas. E. Battenfield, one of the most true and sterling writers in the State. Will Miller, a rattling typo, does the honors of the composing rooms with good grace. Withal, the DEMOCRAT office is first class, the managers and attachees are clever gentlemen; and their paper one of the best. We will not hesitate to say that we believe the DEMOCRAT has done more to build the town than any other agent employed and at the least cost to the people. It is well worth being proud of.

The Russellville Democrat
Thu, Jul 25, 1878 ·Page 2

THAT GREEN B(L)ACK LIE.

The most infamous lie we have ever seen in print was "R.'s" communication to the Evening Post of August 8, in regard to Mr. Jake Lasker being kidnapped and tied to a tree to be shot at. On the day of the negro excursion from Little Rock, "Mr. Jake Lasker" (as "R." calls the dirty negro) was lawfully arrested for committing a disturbance, by a lawfully deputized constable, and was being carried to jail, with the assistance of Mr. Frank Yonley, who had been called upon by the officer to assist him, and the negro, by his cowardly blubbering, gained the mercy of the officer, and they, feeling sorry for a poor negro who was among strangers, and knowing that if tried he had no money or friend to pay his fine (although he valued his kinky head at the ridiculously low sum of $15), and would consequently have to lie in jail at the county's expense, released him after he promised to disturb the peace no more. Then the ungrateful wretch went and spread his filthy lies about being "kidnapped." He ought to be hung too high for the buzzards to reach him. We don't know who "R." is, but would take him and his darling Lasker to be "birds of a feather." And as for a crowd of white and "colored" (is black more of a color than white?) rowdies breaking up their dance in Lewisburg, that is another of "R.'s" lies, and not the least particle of it true. Now, as regards the "regular bulldozer, with uplifted revolver," we would inform him that the said B.-D. was promptly arrested (which "R." fails to mention) and, after being released on bond, he appeared with a D.-B. shotgun, and was again arrested; the consequence of which was that the B.-D., with his D.-B. s.-g., appeared no more until he was brought before the Magistrate, where he was released only upon paying a heavy penalty for his misdemeanors.

ors.

We think that "R." is a member of the Green B(l)ack party, and because the citizens of Morrilton and Lewisburg are not of his stripe, he did all in his power to show them up in the worst light possible. If "R." can't go abroad able to make a truthful statement of facts coming under his observation, he had better stay at home, which ought to be in the State Penitentiary. Yours, etc.

T. H.

Morrilton, Ark., August 12, 1878.

The Russellville Democrat
Thu, Jul 25, 1878 ·Page 2

The steamer Rose City, Capt. James Bowlin, went up the river last week as far as Lewisburg, where she met with a slight accident to her supply pumps, of such a character, however, that Capt. Bowlin returned to this city for repairs.

Daily Arkansas Gazette
Tue, Aug 27, 1878 ·Page 4

Aunt Sally Steamboat in Arkansas City, Kansas, 1878.

The Aunt Sally, Capt. H. Lewis, is making up a trip for points above as far as Lewisburg, and will leave to-day.

Daily Arkansas Gazette
Tue, Sep 03, 1878 ·Page 4

FOURTH CONGRESSIONAL DISTRICT.

There was a political discussion at Lewisburg a few days ago between the rival candidates for Congress in the Fourth District. The State speaks as follows of Col. Gunter and his speech :

Col. Thomas M. Gunter opened with a thrilling address, doing himself credit. He reviewed his labors in Congress and treated of the leading political issues in such a manner as to command the esteem of all present. Judging from the sentiment manifested, no man in the district could possibly be stronger than Gunter. He has made an honorable record and in the opinion of many, has been the most faithful Representative the State has had in the National Congress. The sense of the county has been taken and the people still say "Honest Tom, first, last and all the time." It is quite a compliment to the gentleman to know that his course is so heartily indorsed by his constituency and that they will not consent to lose his services. All honor to Thomas Gunter, say we.

The speech of Col. Gunter at Lewisburg on Thursday was not only logical but with such effective force and earnestness that carries conviction. The vote of Conway County will be solid for Gunter for Congress.—[Morrilton Plebian.

Daily Arkansas Gazette
Wed, Sep 11, 1878 ·Page 2

The Lewisburg *State* says, many, no doubt, will be surprised to learn that Henry M. Stanley, the great African correspondent of the New York *Herald*, was a Confederate soldier and served with the Arkansas troops. He was a captain in the regiment of Col. Anderson Gorden, of Lewisburg, Arkansas.

The Southern Standard
Sat, Sep 14, 1878 ·Page 2

REV. R. M. TYDINGS, in charge of the Methodist Church South at Lewisburg and Morrillton, sends from his congregation thirty dollars for Merchants' National Bank here to forward to the sufferers at Memphis.

Daily Arkansas Gazette
Wed, Sep 18, 1878 ·Page 4

—Edw. H. Feltus, Esq., editor of the sprightly Lewisburg State, came up on last Monday's train, and crossed over to Dardanelle on a visit to his old home and friends.

The Russellville Democrat
Thu, Sep 19, 1878 ·Page 3

Mr. W. D. Allnutt, revenue officer at Lewisburg, arrived by last evening's train.

Arkansas Democrat
Tue, Oct 01, 1878 ·Page 4

The Overworked Farmer of the frozen North, and the Farmer of the West, can shake off his Grasshoppers and Chinch Bugs, and seect for themselves

Beautiful, Cheap and Fertile Homes.

These Lands are in the Prosperous counties of Pulaski, Faulkner, Conway, Johnson, Perry, Pope, Yell, Logan, Franklin, Crawford, and Sebastian.

BEAUTIFUL CITIES

Dot the Entire Length of the road, among which are Little Rock, Conway, Lewisburg, Atkins, Russellville, Clarksville, Ozark, Mulberry, Van Buren and Fort Smith.

The company owns and offers for sale—

In Pulaski county, about	78,500 acres,
In Faulkner county, about	88,100 acres.
In Conway county, about	100,100 acres.
In Perry county, about	118,400 acres.
In Pope county, about	106,700 acres.
In Yell county, about	51,600 acres.
In Johnson county, about	181,800 acres.
In Madison county, about	11,500 acres.
In Franklin county, about	135,100 acres.
In Logan county, about	118,700 acres.
In Crawford county, about	132,500 acres.
In Washington Co., about	5,000 acres.
In Sebastian Co., about	45,800 acres.
In Saline county, about	4,500 acres.
In Van Buren county about	2,600 acres.

For further information address

W. D. SLACK,
Land Commissioner, Little Rock, Ark.
JOSEPH JAGEMAN,
Gen'l Agent, Covington, Ky.

Arkansas Democrat
Tue, Oct 01, 1878 ·Page 3

—The Lewisburg State is going to be published hereafter at Morrilton; Lewisburg not coming up to the support of the State as she ought to—or at least sufficiently to justify a continuance of the paper there. In losing Feltus Lewisburg has lost a good citizen and a good newspaper man. Success at Morrillton, Edd!

The Russellville Democrat
Thu, Oct 03, 1878 ·Page 3

DR. FRANK GORDON, of Lewisberg, who came down to visit the "Colonel," is still in the city. Of course, we won't say that Lewisburg owes her health entirely to him, but we can truthfully say that the place is no sicker on his account.

Daily Arkansas Gazette
Thu, Oct 24, 1878 ·Page 4

THE Lewisburg State is the cheapest weekly newspaper in Arkansas—only sixty cents a year—and a live, sprightly paper at that. The Arkansas DEMOCRAT at five dollars, is the cheapest daily in the State, and in fact, in the South, and always has the latest and most reliable news.

Arkansas Democrat
Thu, Dec 05, 1878 ·Page 2

—Mrs. C. C. Reid, of Lewisburg, has twice been elected Enrolling Clerk of the Arkansas General Assembly, and received a vote of thanks for the faithful and skillful manner in which she executed her clerical duties. The Gazette understands that she will be a candidate for the same position before the next Legislature, and commends her to the favorable consideration of the delegates elect.

The Russellville Democrat
Thu, Dec 05, 1878 ·Page 2

ESQ. JOHN GYER died at his residence near Lewisburg, of pneumonia, on the 8th inst. He was a good citizen.—[Morrillton Dollar.

Daily Arkansas Gazette
Fri, Dec 13, 1878 ·Page 4

The gin house of Mr. W. E. Green, five miles below Lewisburg, was burned last Tuesday. Loss, $1,060.

Arkansas Democrat
Thu, Jan 30, 1879 ·Page 4

—The DEMOCRAT returns thanks for an invitation to attend a select ball to be given by the Lewisburg Terpsichorean Society on the night of the 28th inst. The committee is Messrs. E. H. Feltus, Jack Gordon, G. W. Bennett, W. H. Robinson, S. R. Woller, J. H. Coblentz, F. G. Gordon and Waiter Wells.

Arkansas Democrat
Thu, Feb 20, 1879 ·Page 4

**First Reference to Lewisburg having a
"Dead" Commericial Center
Because of Morrilton's Growth**

"GERRYMANDERING."

PERRYVILLE, ARK., Feb. 24, 1879.
Editor Arkansas Democrat:

I noticed, in the Gazette of the 20th, an article from the pen of the Hon. J. J. Stout, Lewisburg, Ark., upon gerrymandering. The gentleman seems to be very much alarmed for the safety of the Democratic party, especially in the county of Conway. I presume you have heard the story of the boy and the wolf; well, sir, I look upon the cry of Mr. Stout in the same light, and if any go to his rescue it will only be to be laughed at.

Now, Mr. Editor, for facts: As we (Perry county) do not look upon this matter as a political issue, and I presume Mr. Stout knows how that territory was wrested from Perry county, and if he is so anxious for right, justice and party salvation, let him commence at the foundation and correct the original injustice, and all will be well with the party, this territory was taken from Perry unconstitutionally (and at a time when it was almost impossible to get justice in any of the courts,) making her less than required by the Constitution for a county. Now sir the members elected from Perry, Conway, Faulkner and Pulaski counties, are well aware of three facts and I know of none *elected* that were *pledged* to any course of action in regard to county lines. (I cannot say as much for some that were defeated in that political race.) The great secret of all this fuss is, there are two factions in Conway county, one desires (majority) to move the county site and the other (minority) desires it to remain at Lewisburg—now sir, Lewisburg as a commercial center, is dead, the entire business having gone to Morrillton. Our Representatives and Senators are willing to do right, hence thebill which in justice should carry. "Tell the truth and shame the Devil." Yours respecfully,
JAS. A. BRAZIL.

Arkansas Democrat
Thu, Feb 27, 1879 ·Page 1

**Conway County May Loose Land
on South Side of River**

THE Lewisburg State would like to see Governor Miller veto the bill taking away certain territory from Conway county. It says:

Governor Miller has twenty days from the time of the adjournment of the General Assembly to consider the bills not yet passed upon. Among the batch is the bill depriving Conway of her territory on the south side of the river. Let a pin be stuck here. If he approves that bill he sanctions the making of a Republican county. If he does not, why, then, he is a level-headed Democrat and an upholder of constitutional rights.

Arkansas Democrat
Wed, Mar 26, 1879 ·Page 2

New School to Start
in Lewisburg Courthouse

THE CONWAY NORMAL IN-STITUTE.

We have received the announce ment of the Conway County Normal Institute, Prof. W. S. Speer, Con-ductor. The institute opens Mon-day June 30th 1879, and will hold in session four weeks. This Normal Institute is one of the modern im-provements, or rather auxiliaries, to aid the teacher to step up higher in his profession, and is next to the Norman School in the work of mak-ing teachers what teachers ought to be. We quote the programme as follows:

FORENOON SESSION.

Time.	First 2 weeks.	Sec. 2 weeks.
8:00 to 8:45	Didactics	Didactics.
8:45 to 9:30	Orthography & Reading	Arithmetic
9:35 to 10:20	Arithmetic	English
10:25 to 11:10	Eng. U.S. History & Physiology	
11:15 to 12:00	Geography	Geology, Civ. Gov't
12:05 to 12:50	Book-Keeping	Book-Keeping

AFTERNOON SESSION.

4:00 to 5:00....Writing and Drawing............

EVENING SESSION.
(8 o'clock.)

Thursday.......................Weekly Social
Friday................................ Lecture

And the objects, aims and expens-es are thus stated by the announce-ment before us:

The Normal Institute has become a recognized power in the advance-ment of educational interests. Next to the Normal School it affords the very best means to teachers for the advancement of their calling to the dignity and position it deserves. The three and four day sessions are valuable for interchvnge of views and general discussions; but they lack time. The Conway County Normal appreciating the necessities of the vast body of teachers, will give a month of drills, of model teaching, a month of drills, of model teaching, and of discussion of the mechanism as well as the science of education. Live teachers will find in their own experience with the trying duties of the schoolroom, in their failure to make the practical reach the aims of the theoretical, the supreme value of such a course. The committee feels that the plan of the Institute needs but to be known to be appre-ciated. Teachers will be incalcula-bly benefitted by this month of vig-orous review and new inspiration; advanced students in ordinary schools will find the academic work alone worth a term of school. All will be cordially welcome.

MANAGEMENT.

The Committee takes much pleas-ure in expressing its confidence in the announcement herein made, feel-ing assured from the lengthened ex-perience of the Conductor as County and City Superintendent of Schools, and Principal of Normal and Train-ing Institutions, that this gathering of teachers will be found the most enthusiastic and profitable meeting ever held in the State. Able as-sistance will be had, both of Instruct-tors and Lecturers, providing work for all who may enter the Institute. Make your preparations beforehand to attend. Everybody can afford the expense. Board one month will cost you from $8 to $12, your Insti-tute fee will be $5 in advance. Text books will cost you nothing. Subjects, not books, will be discuss-ed. Bring your own books for con sultation. Your entire expenses need not exceed $15 for the month's work.

For information, address Col. Gor-don, Secretary, Lewisburg, Ark., or any member of the Executive Com-mittee.

The Russellville Democrat
Thu, Apr 10, 1879 ·Page 2

SCHOOL MATTERS.

Should sufficient encouragement be given, a normal school for teachers will be opened in this city, commencing June 16, and continuing four weeks. The instruction will be confined to the work of the public school teachers of the State. It will be found of vast importance to private school teachers who contemplate going into the public schools. It will be conducted by Hon. J. M. Fish, Prof. R. H. Parham, Miss Ida J. Brooks, Miss Hattie L. Meyer, Mrs. Mary B. Brooks, with lectures by Rev. J. L. Denton, State Superintendent.

A normal institute will be opened in the Masonic building at Lewisburg, on the 30th of June. The Board of Instruction embraces several of the leading educators of the State.

Arkansas Democrat
Mon, May 05, 1879 ·Page 1

Lewisburg High School Picnic

A PICNIC given by the Lewisburg high school last Saturday, is spoken of by the people of that town in the highest of terms. Miss Vena Lee, principal of the school, is a graduate of this city.

Daily Arkansas Gazette
Wed, May 07, 1879 ·Page 8

"Miss Minnie Ward, accompanied by her sister, Mrs. Fatherly, is visiting Mrs. John C. Ward."— [Lewisburg State.

Arkansas Democrat
Tue, May 27, 1879 ·Page 4

DEP'T OF PUBLIC INSTRUCTION,
LITTLE ROCK, May 10, 1879.
COL. A. GORDON, Lewisburg, Ark.:

DEAR SIR: Your favor to hand and considered. I am truly gratified to learn that a Normal Institute is in contemplation in your town. I sincerely trust that the project may not miscarry. It has my hearty approval, and shall have my cordial co-operation. Teachers in the surrounding counties should avail themselves of this opportunity for improvement. Familiarity with the latest and best methods of teaching, is indispensable to efficiency in the school-room. Wishing you success, I am yours very truly,

JAS. L. DENTON,
State Sup't Pub. Inst.

The Russellville Democrat
Thu, Jun 05, 1879 ·Page 2

—Miss Vena Lee, of this city, who has had charge of the Lewisburg school, returned yesterday evening. Miss Lee is one of the most accomplished young ladies in the state, and as an educator has won a name of which the Little Rock High school, of which she is a graduate, should feel proud.

Daily Arkansas Gazette
Wed, Jun 11, 1879 ·Page 8

—As a matter of importance to Teachers we give in to-day's paper the course of study and order of exercises to be pursued at the Conway County Normal Institute, which opens at Lewisburg on June 30th, to continue four weeks. We have devoted considerable space in placing before the Teachers of this and adjoining counties, the entire 30 days course, and it has required considerable extra labor for us, but we intend to publish such matters as are of importance and interest to the people, we will not mind the expense if the public is benefited thereby. We have always believed that such labors will meet with the appreciation which they deserve. We are not one of those who believe the public to be destitute of the proper appreciation of enterprise and pluck in county newspapers.

The Russellville Democrat
Thu, Jun 12, 1879 ·Page 2

THE Lewisburg academy closed its exercises last week, and Miss Vena Lee, the principal, returned to her home in Little Rock on Tuesday. She made many friends while here who regret her departure.—[Morrillton State.

Daily Arkansas Gazette
Wed, Jun 18, 1879 ·Page 8

—A report is current here that Col. C. C. Reid, jr., of Lewisburg, died day before yesterday, of cholera morbus. He was a well-known lawyer and politician.

Arkansas Democrat
Wed, Aug 13, 1879 ·Page 4

—C. C. Ried, Jr., of Lewisburg, died very suddenly at his home on Monday night last. His remains passed up the road Tuesday for interment at Clarksville.

The Russellville Democrat
Thu, Aug 14, 1879 ·Page 3

Description of Morrilton
and Declining Lewisburg
– List of Town Leadership –

A RACY LETTER.

Luscious Fruits—Fine Crops—Good Country—Personal Notes—Politics, etc.

MORRILTON, August 19, 1879.

Editor Arkansas Democrat:

Fruit is truly plentiful up in this part of the vineyard, and as luscious and tempting as that which Eve gave unto Adam—this I will not assert from personal observation, i. e., as far as Eve's apple is concerned—as to the exquisite ambrosial qualities of the peaches here, it makes the saliva in my mouth grow protuberant at the thought of the subject. It makes me even think of the "peach and honey" that we'uns and yo'uns used to prepare for—our grandfathers, whilst they were chatting of the times when Cornwallis surrendered at Yorktown. Well, peaches can be had here almost for the asking. An old darkey was selling real nice, juicy ones, at fifteen for five cents. Other fruit equally cheap and savory.

Crops were never better; cotton looks like it would make two bales to the acre, and I am glad to observe that my friend Colonel George Miller, is a farmer this year. I want him to make a fortune. He is a whole souled, courteous, honorable gentleman. Conway ought to send him to the legislature. Corn is plentiful also, and I heard a well posted gentleman, Mr. H. A. Nations, say that he believed corn would be worth only about twenty-five cents at gathering time. Mr. Nations is the old county clerk, a man well liked, honorable in his dealings, and has a kind heart. The immigrant ought to make a note of this twenty-five cent corn, also should they bear in mind that this town has a house wherein immigrants are welcome free of cost, until they can procure homes. The house is in charge of Mr. M. Brown, who will gladly give you all the information as regards lands, etc.

Looking around the town I find too very good looking hotels—both well kept. Mr. Williams keeps one and Mr. Speer the other. The "printing office" is easily seen, but the editor never *felt us*. I tried to shake him by the hand, but he has been "shaking" a little of late, and wouldn't award me that privilege. The State is a sprightly paper, and its editor, Mr. Feltus, a clever, accomplished gentleman. Hope he will yet make a fortune. Looking around town I see the sign of L. Sleeper. Now here is where a name will fool you. He is one of the wide-awake men of the town. J. T. Hannaford, R. A. Irving,

Rosewater & Gross, J. C. Holcomb, Wm. Howard, Niles & Rankin, Rankin & Goodman, all deal in general merchandise and seem to share the good will of the people. D. A. Thomas has a hardware and machinery depot. In the drug line the signs of W. M. Scarborough and W. D. Allnutt can be seen. The latter is all nut, but by no means a hard one, for I believe him a good-hearted gentleman. The legal profession is represented by O. F. Bentley, and W. D. Allnutt. The Justices of the Peace for this township are that clever soul L. O. Breeden and J. B. Dillon. When people settle their cares by compromises they generally go and "smile" with George Morrill, sometimes with Earl & Gill, and at others with Waller & Nilson. When the commercial representatives want to go out to Lewisburg or some other seaport town, they generally go and call on G. B. Wilbanks. He keeps a good livery stable. Lewisburg is not as much of a burg as it "used to was," nor has it any longer a burgomaster, unless Col. Eugene Henry would act in that capacity, or young J. J. Stone, both good lawyers; or, perhaps, my young friend W. F. Conlee, County Clerk, or Capt. D. B. Russell, Sheriff, would like to play that part.

Morrillton seems to be improving right along; saw several new buildings in process of erection, and the people expect still greater improvements this fall. Everybody talks business and precious little politics. Occasionally some

little politics. Occasionally some man will say "I like Jim Jones for Governor," or, "that he wouldn't object to seeing Tilden nominated;" but as for a regular political chat you could only accomplish that by first lassoing your man and then haul him to you. They also object to newspapers forcing them to read column after column of abuse of a man they voted for so lustily in '76, whom they helped to elect, but was cheated out of the victory. They can't see how it is that men in our party can support a man heartily in one campaign, and as the next appproaches, turn in and abuse him as do Radicals our men, for no earthly cause either. They can account for Radicals abusing Tilden and not wanting him for President, because he "goes for" thieves and robbers, but when it comes to Democrats borrowing Radical thunder for the destruction of known, true and tried Democrats they stop and scratch their head. Looks wrong. Radical argument in a Democrat's mouth makes sweet milk turn to clabber quicker than in a thunderstorm. The milk in the political cocoanut is this: Tilden carried New York when no other man could—he carries it whenever he is put on the ticket and always leads it. New York has 35 electoral votes. Who can carry these —Tilden. Because he carried them when it was boasted that he could not. Now put up a doubtful man, and lose New York; that would put 35 votes against us, or equal to put 35 votes against us, or equal to 70 for us to place us where they left us. Where can we get 70 votes from in the North or West, to make up for the loss sustained in New York. Echo promptly answers "Nowhere!" We had better keep our good horse, one that we know has crossed the political quagmires, and is ready to cross still more.

I shall fill my pockets full of Conway county peaches, and stone the first man that starts me on politics again.   *

Arkansas Democrat
Fri, Aug 22, 1879 ·Page 3

THE whooping-cough, says the State, is prevailing in Morrillton and Lewisburg.

Daily Arkansas Gazette
Tue, Oct 28, 1879 ·Page 8

MARRIED.

On Thursday, Nov. 13th in Lewisburg Ark., by Rev. J. D. Boone, Mr. Ellis Tobey, of Pope County, to Miss Mary Talkington, of Lewisburg.

The Russellville Democrat
Thu, Nov 27, 1879 ·Page 3

Conway County

This county has always been spoken of in the highest terms as possessing superior advantages for stock raising, but as yet little has been said for it in an agricultural point of view. This, perhaps, is due to the fact that, like all new counties, developments must first be made before we can properly put a just estimate upon their agricultural worth

In the southern portion of the county, along with its western limits, we find the Point Remove Creek, a beautiful living stream, with a magnificent body of rich bottom lands, extending twelve miles from the north in south, and averaging from two to five miles in width, covered with a medium growth of fine timber, principally over-cup oak of large dimensions, white oak, white ash, and white hickory in large quantity, together with all the different kinds of timbers, cypress, red oak, elm, sweet gum, etc., some of which are very valuable for manufacturing purposes.

The timber in this section is a good as an evidence as we could wish for to convince us of the fertility of the soil. These bottoms are covered with a luxuriant growth of grass, which completely covers the surface, and in many places attains to the height of from three to four feet. This affords a magnificent abundance of fine grazing for stock during the winter months.

Our description of Point Remove Valley is equally applicable to the Cadron Creek Valley, which forms the eastern boundary of Conway County, with nearly the same quantity and quality of soil.

These streams afford a sufficient water power for mills and manufacturing purposes.

North of the line of the L. R. & Ft. S. R. R., for eight miles, and extending along this line for fourteen miles, embracing about four townships, is a beautiful valley of fine uplands slightly rolling and very productive. Cotton, corn, rye, barley, oats, fruits, vegetables, and every product raised in a temperate climate, grow to perfection.

This valley is dotted with numbers of fine farms newly fenced, new buildings, new improvements of every description, presenting to the view, in every direction, the rapid progress and prosperity of this new country. Passing through this valley, we reach the mountains, the most prominent of which is the Pigeon Roost. This forms a magnificent plateau, presenting from its base, the appearance of a stupendous pile of rocks, diversified with some of natures most beautiful scenery, and presenting many curiosities in the way of natural architecture.

From the summit, we see stretching out in all directions, as far as the eye can reach, a magnificent body of rich lands.

Here the soil is exceedingly fine and well adopted to the growth of small grains such as wheat, rye and oats.

For fruits of every variety, it has a high reputation, and is destined some day to be a great fruit growing center.

Transcribed from: Hot Springs Illustrated Monthly, Thu, Jan 01, 1880 ·Page 12

LEWISBURG, ARKANSAS. Photo. by Clary.

Lewisburg

Lewisburg, this place of which our artist gives a beautiful birds-eye view, is the county seat of Conway County. It numbers among the oldest towns of the State, having been founded and laid off as a town by Stephen D. Lewis and Thomas S. Haynes, between the years 1830 and 1832. From the former it derived its name. Located in one of the most fertile and extensive valleys in the South, it became a prominent trading point.

In the building of the Little Rock & Fort Smith Railway, the citizens, through shortsightedness, failed to make reasonable overtures to the company, and the railway passed it to the north about three-fourths of a mile distant. At this point sprang up Morrilton, the present metropolis of the county, which has sapped the very life-blood of this old town. But one small business enterprise is carried on there, and it is no longer counted as a town. It constitutes a portion of the suburbs of Morrilton as it were. Lewisburg is situated on the Arkansas river, three-fourths of a mile south of Morrilton.

Transcribed from:
Hot Springs Illustrated Monthly,
Thu, Jan 01, 1880 ·Page 12

Morrilton

Morrilton is in Conway county, fifty miles west of the city of Little rock, on the line of the Little rock and Fort Smith Railroad, and three-fourths of a mile north of the Arkansas river.

Three years ago it was only a station on the line of the road, and had at that time three houses, being only three-fourths of a mile from the old town of Lewisburg.

From its meager beginning it has in this short period grown into a busy bustling town, having at this time thirty-five business houses, seventeen of this number representing dry goods, groceries, drugs, agricultural implements, saddlery and harness, stoves and tinware, etc., with two hotels, six saloons, one livery stable, blacksmith and wagon shop, meat market, restaurant, and bakery.

MORRILTON, ARKANSAS.   Photo. by Clary.

There is in course of erection a magnificent brick convent, and two churches, the Baptist and Presbyterian, both of which will be good structures. There is also an immigrant's home, which has just been built by the citizens, and an immigration society formed, M. Brown, Prest.

The town is situated on a beautiful site for building, with a sandy alluvial soul, finely adapted to the culture of fruits and vegetables, with good water, and an inexhaustible abundance of timber. The population is estimated at from five to eight hundred.

Most of the *(Lewisburg)* merchants who have their business entirely absorbed by Morrilton, and there is at this time only one business house open in that place *(Lewisburg)*.

Town property has advanced 100 percent, in the last two years, and the business of this season has been almost double that of the last.

We cannot remember when it has been our fortune to meet with a class of people so free from care, and whose faces wear that cheerful expression produced by a happy prosperity of business.

We are told that in the string, the railroad company will remove their present depot at this place, and supply its place with a handsome brick building' This will add materially to the town; and, as the business of the place is increasing so rapidly, their new building will no doubt be built with a view to meet the demands of an increased trade.

...Mr. Beers things there will be at least 6,000 bales*(of cotton)* shipped the present season of 1879-80.

Our large engraving of Morrilton was taken at a point east and south from the business center of the town. It takes in a number of the business houses on the north side of the railroad, showing the depot and trains of the Little Rock and Fort Smith road, and the cotton receipts at this point awaiting shipment. The new brick building to the right is the one just built by Dr. A. W. C. Sayle and occupied by the popular firm of Rosenwater & Gross, adjoining this building, Mr. J. T. Hannaford will build a handsome two-story brick business house in the spring, which he will occupy himself. The foreground takes in the lumber interests and coal sheds of Mr. M. Brown, the land agent of the L. R. & Ft. S. road.

Transcribed from:
Hot Springs Illustrated Monthly, Thu, Jan 01, 1880 ·Page 12

New Convent

This handsome brick edifice is now in course of erection and will soon be completed. Our engraving is a correct representation of what the building will be when finished. It is being built by the Very Rev. Joseph Colony, and, as soon as finished, will be placed under the management of the sisters.

The building is 96 by 42 feet, with basement, two stories and attic — with mansard roof. The convent is delightfully situated on a commanding elevation with a natural drainage on all sided while the grounds are covered with a fine growth of forest shades.

Transcribed from:
Hot Springs Illustrated Monthly, Thu, Jan 01, 1880 ·Page 12

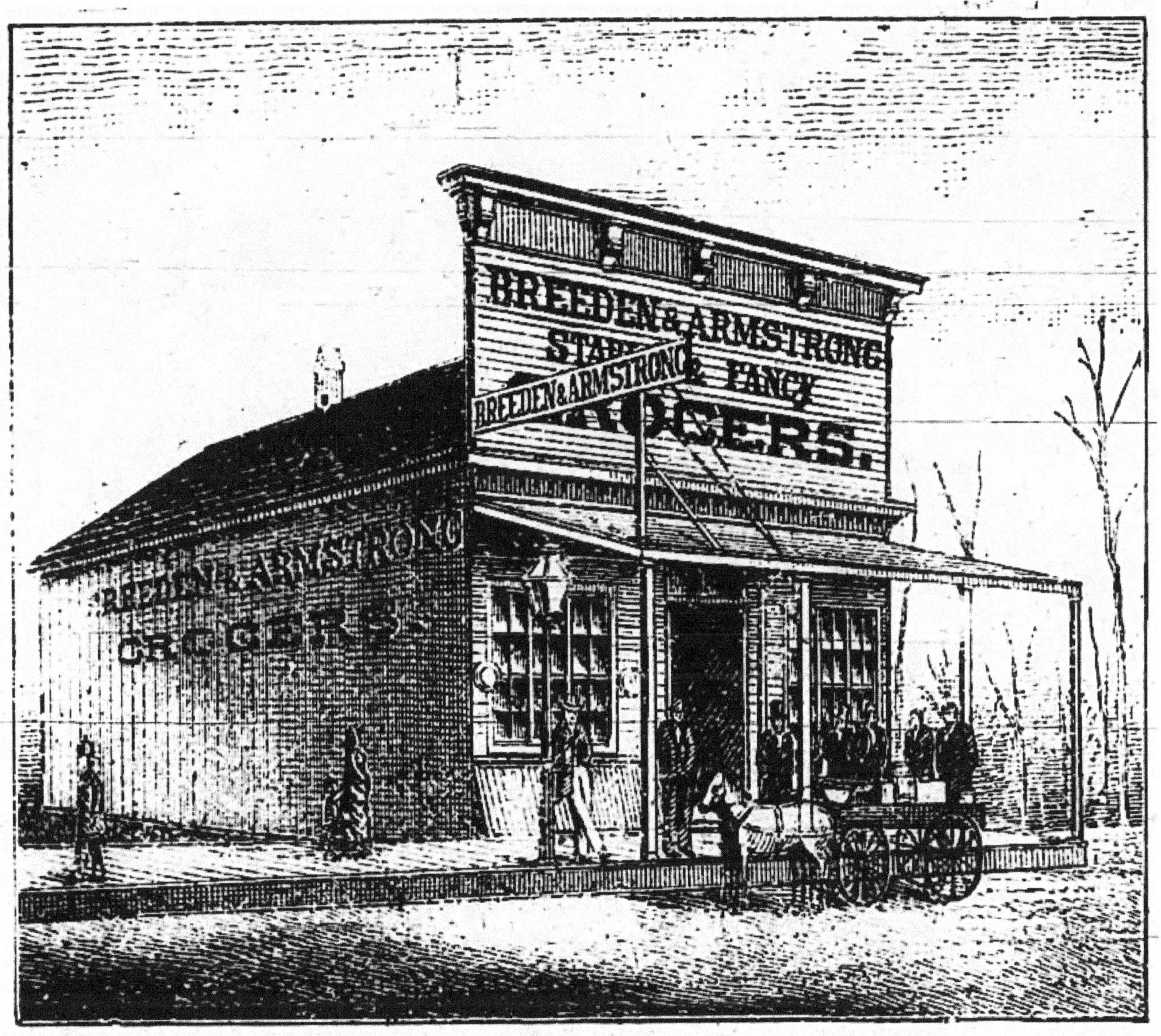

BUSINESS HOUSE OF BREEDEN & ARMSTRONG, MORRILTON, ARK.

Breeden & Armstrong
Staples & Fancy
Grocers

Breenden & Armstrong are the popular grocery merchants of this young and growing city.

Their stock is replete with every article carried in a first-class retail grocery business, and their extensive acquaintance and fine business standing is predictive of a bright and prosperous future.

Transcribed from:
Hot Springs Illustrated Monthly, Thu, Jan 01, 1880 ·Page 12

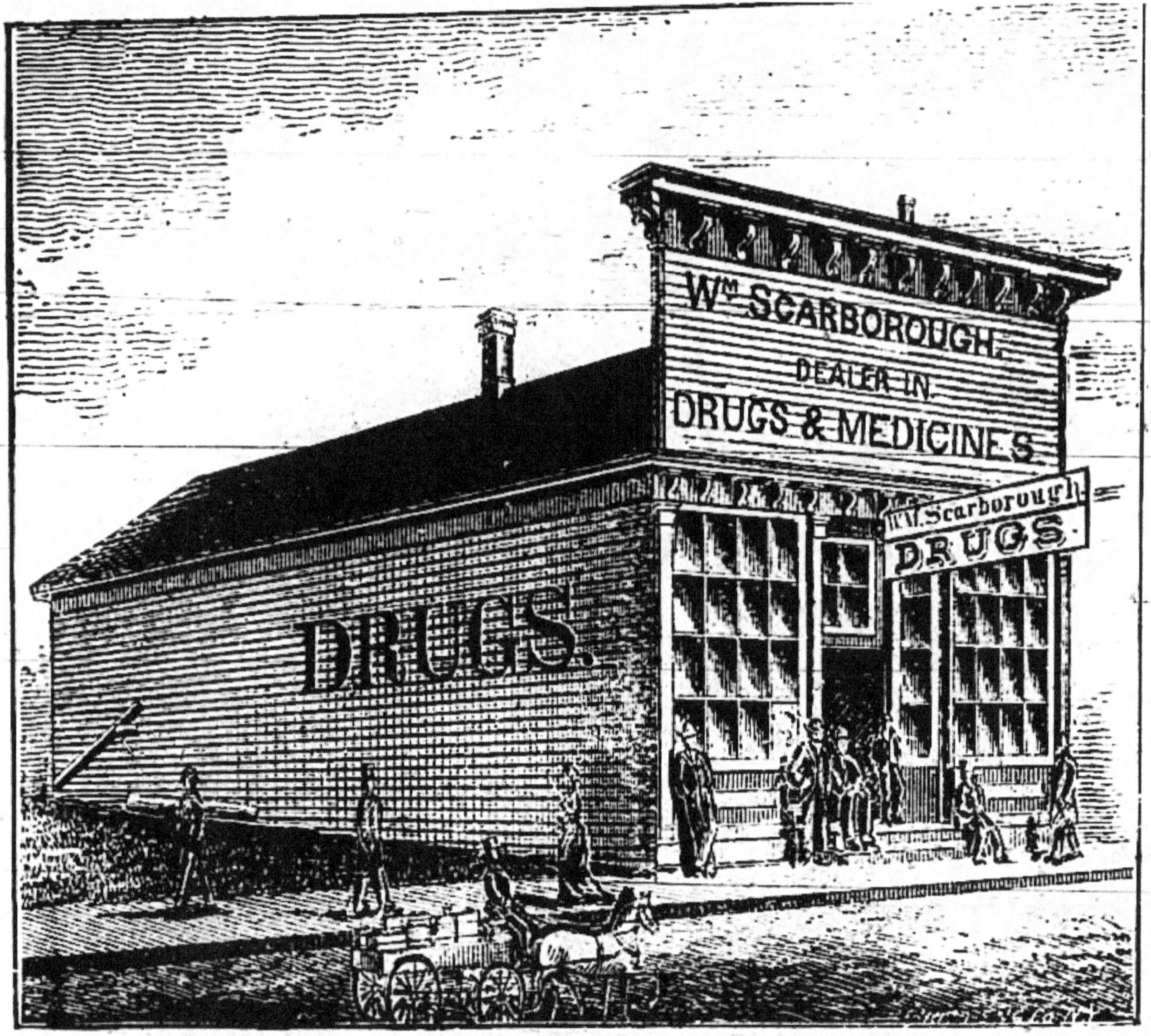

DRUG STORE OF DR. W. M. SCARBOROUGH,
MORRILTON. ARK.

Dr. Wm Scarborough,

DEALER IN

Drugs & Medicines

An old and most highly esteemed practitioner of Conway County, is in the drug business, and has one of the handsomest and most tastefully arranged drug establishments in western Arkansas.

His stock embraces everything to be found in a well appointed business of this description, and receives the personal attention and supervision of the doctor.

Transcribed from:
Hot Springs Illustrated Monthly, Thu, Jan 01, 1880 ·Page 12

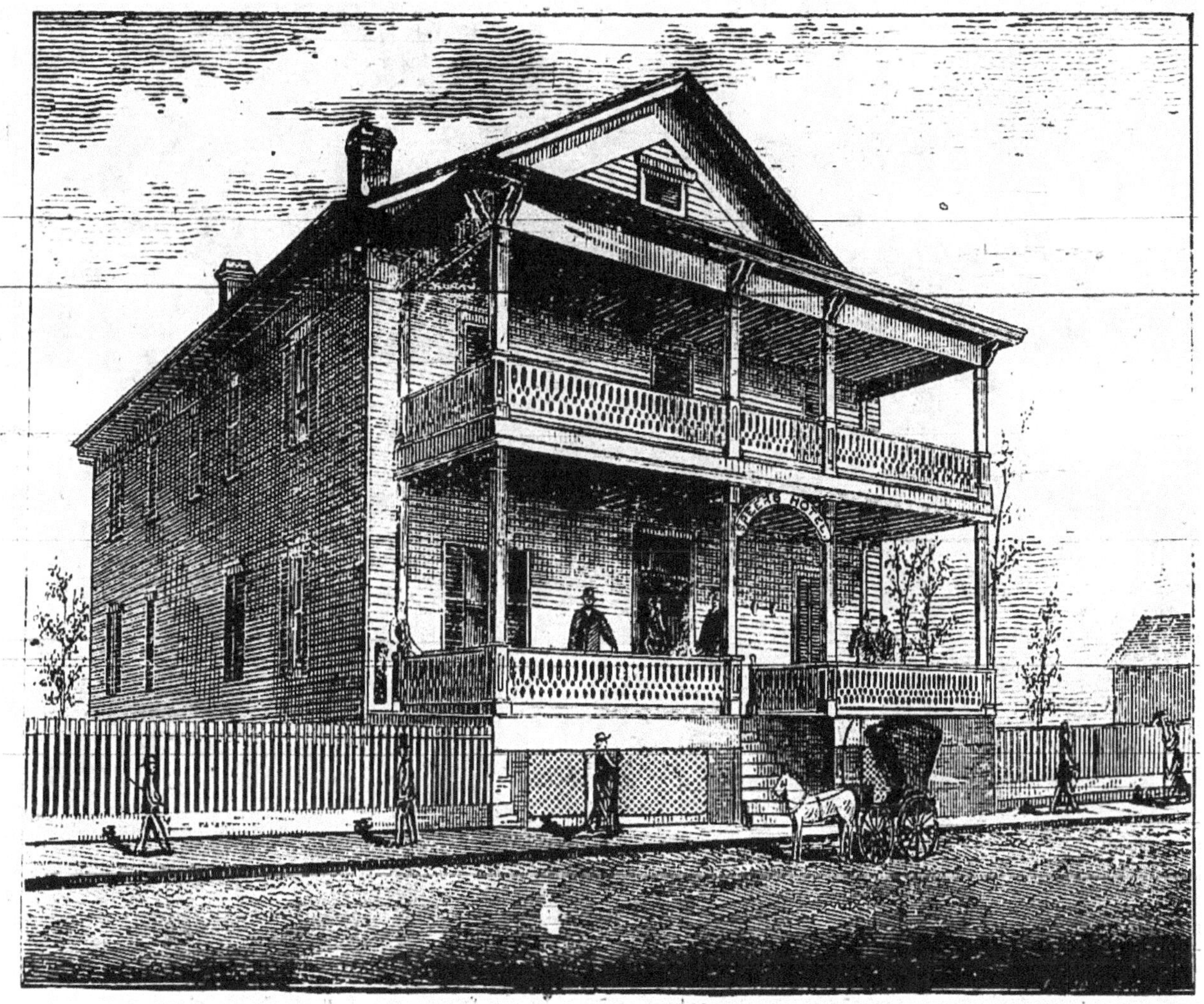

Speer's Hotel

Our engraving of this new and elegantly arranged hotel is a correct illustration. It was built by Mr. S. F. Speer, formerly of Conyers, Georgia, and was open for the reception of guests on the 6th of February in the present year.

The building is three stories high, and contains twenty rooms which are all newly and elegantly furnished. The cost of the building and furniture amounted to $7,000.

Mr Speer is a model hotel man, and is thoroughly conversant in all the arts necessary to make one's stay most pleasant and comfortable. The cuisine of this establishment and the well ventilated and nicely kept sleeping apartments have won for this house a high reputation and is daily making fresh additions to its now already large and prosperous patronage.

Transcribed from:
Hot Springs Illustrated Monthly, Thu, Jan 01, 1880 ·Page 12

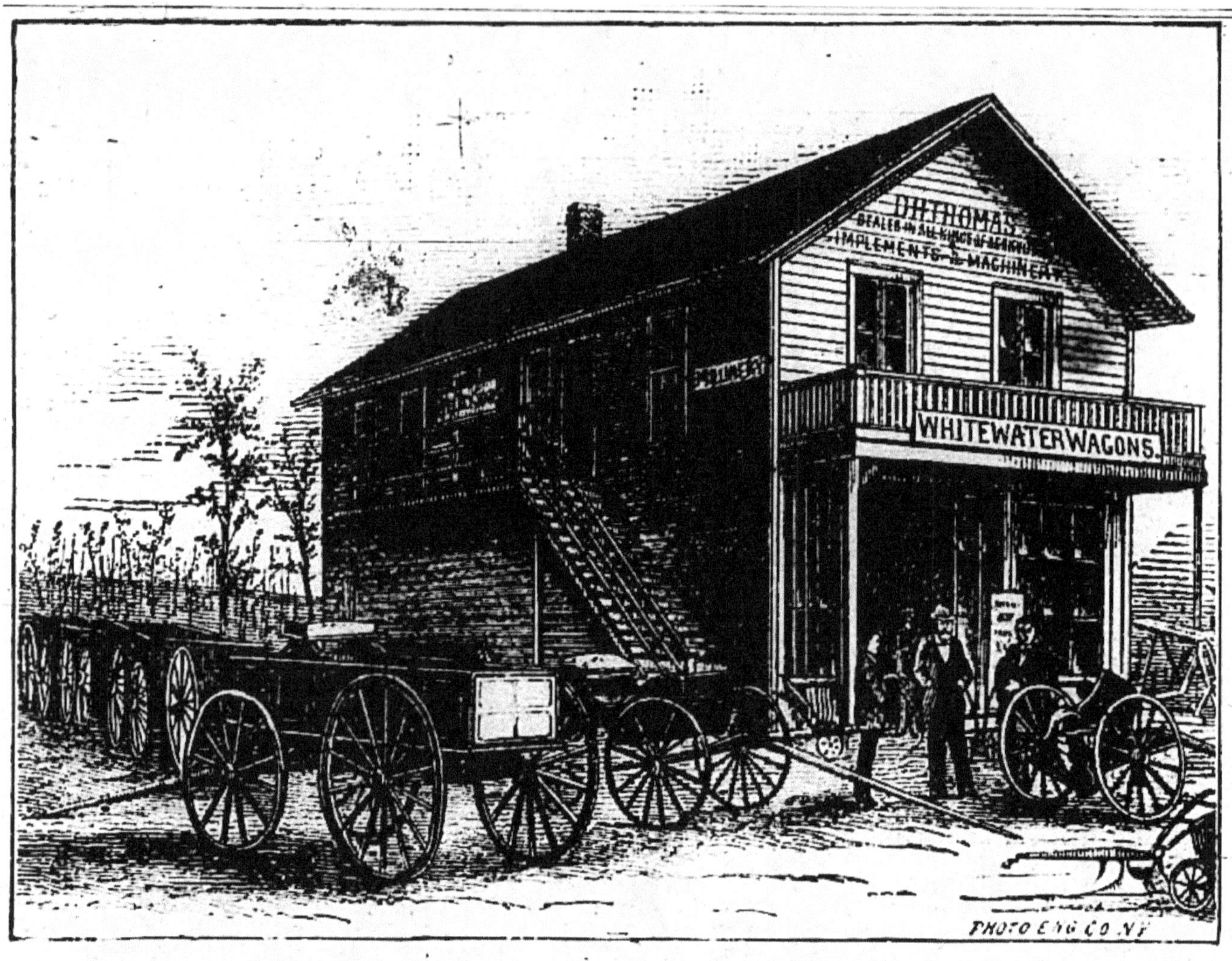

BUSINESS HOUSE OF D. H. THOMAS, MORRILTON, ARK.

D.H. Thomas

DEALER IN ALL KINDS OF

Agricultural Implements, Machinery & Whitewater Wagons

One of the leading and most enterprising of Morrilton's business men is engaged in the sale of machinery and agricultural implements.

Mr. Thomas has a wide and most popular acquaintance all over western and southern Arkansas, having been engaged in the business for a number of years in the old town of Lewisburg, at which place he was also postmaster.

During this time be built up a large and profitable trade which has been steadily increasing. About one year ago he moved his extensive stock of machinery to his present place of business, having previously built a large two story business house - the first two story building put up in Morrilton.

The first story is occupied by Mr. Thomas, whilst the second contains the office and press rooms of the "Weekly State" newspaper, and the millinery departments of Miss Ellis of Tennessee, who has recently embarked in this branch business at this place.

Transcribed from:
Hot Springs Illustrated Monthly Thu, Jan 01, 1880, Page 2

Mr. J. T. Hannaford is another one of Morrilton's active wide-awake business men, and is carrying one of the finest and most select stocks of Dry Goods, Groceries and general merchandise. Mr. Hannaford was one of the first to cast his fortune with the future of Morrilton and has never had cause to regret the step. His stock averages about $12,000, and he

SAYLE BLOCK, MORRILTON, ARK.

tells us that his sales for the present year will amount to $50,000, this being an increase of $10,000 over the past year which he attributes to the success of the cotton crop and the advance in the price of this staple.

The Weekly State is a twenty-four column sheet, published every Thursday, by Mr. E. H., Feltus, who is the editor and proprietor and who has ever used his best efforts in advancing the interests of this town and county.

Transcribed from:
Hot Springs Illustrated Monthly, Thu, Jan 01, 1880 ·Page 12

Rosenwater & Gross
The Sayle Block

This fine brick building, built by Dr. W. A. C. Sayle, one of Conway county's highly respected and eminent physicians, has just been completed. It is two stories, the first being fitted up into large handsome storerooms, whilst the upper story is arranged for offices.

The well-known firm of Messrs. Rosenwater & Gross have just removed their immense stock of Dry Goods, Groceries and general merchandise into this new building, which they have leased of Dr. Sayle, where they will be pleased to meet their many friends and old customers in the future.

Transcribed from:
Hot Springs Illustrated Monthly, Thu, Jan 01, 1880 ·Page 12

The next town that demands anything like attention is Morrilton. To any one who knew this country two years ago this improvement is not only surprising, but suggestive of the incredulous. When the railroad ran through this country, there was not a house to serve as the peg to advancing civilization. Lewisburg, a mile and a half distant, was the only place of collected residences. Soon the people began to see that it was necessary to live near a railroad. Store-houses were erected at the nearest railroad point; dwelling-houses were put up, and after a while the place became known as Morrilton. And this town now is one of the most prosperous in the state. Fine brick buildings stand up and stare the train in the face, and just back of the long commercial line which stretches itself along the railway, an almost completed convent shows itself. This building is a splendid structure, and one that reflects beam upon beam of credit upon those most instrumental in its construction.

Daily Arkansas Gazette
Tue, Jan 20, 1880 ·Page 8

The residence of John Wells, at Lewisburg, was destroyed by fire last week. Cause — stovepipe. Loss, $4,000.

Arkansas Democrat
Mon, Mar 01, 1880 ·Page 3

—We republish the following from the Lewisburg State in regard to the arrest of Bell as mentioned in this paper last week!

On Saturday, City Marshall Alnut arrested the man Bell referred to above, on the down morning passenger train, on authority of a telegram from Capt. John Quinn, Deputy Sheriff of Pope county. Deputy Sheriff Quinn, Arthur Erwin and Col. Hill came down on the afternoon frieght, and accompanied by the parties City Marshal Alnutt started to Russellville late that afternoon, when within two miles of Atkins, but leaped from the wagon and made good his escape. The posse ran him all night, firing several shots at him. Ward's blood-hounds were secured and put on trail, but to no avail. John Quinn and J. P. Alnut distinguished themselves by a famous bareback ride in a ten mile heat.

The Russellville Democrat
Thu, Jul 01, 1880 ·Page 3

MARRIED.

Dr. Frank Gordon, of Lewisburg, was married this morning at 7 o'clock to Miss Susie Sullivan, at the residence of Mr. J. P. Riley, in the east end. The marriage service was performed by Rev. T. C. Tupper, and after the nuptial knot was tied the couple started for Lewisburg, where the honeymoon will be spent. Dr. Gordon and his handsome bride are both well known in Little Rock, and the best wishes of many friends are with them in the new matrimonial enterprise.

Daily Arkansas Gazette
Thu, Dec 23, 1880 ·Page 4

". S. MAIL.

Regular Upper Arkansas River Packet Co.

For Lewisburg, Dardanelle, Ozark, Van Buren and Fort Smith.

Steamer DOVE

.............Master
W. C. GHRIEST,......Clerk

Will leave for Fort Smith and all way landings every Saturday at 12 m.

Str. JOHN G. FLETCHER

H. HENNEGIN.......Master

Will leave for Fort Smith and all way landings, every Tuesday at 12 m.

For freight or passage, apply on board or to NIEMEYER & DARRAGH, Agents.

Daily Arkansas Gazette
Tue, Jan 25, 1881 ·Page 4

—There is one W. S. Partain living out on the Lewisburg road a half mile from town, since last fall has hauled 457 loads of wood to town at fifty cents per load; eighty-three bales of cotton to Russellville at 75 cents per bale; made two trips to the Boston mountain; two to Big Piney and one to Atkins, and his team is in good condition. If you hear any one saying that W. S. Partain will starve you can just inform your folks that there is a mistake in the print.

—A few items from the long ago days of Pope county might be of some interest to some one. The first transfer of real estate in this county was executed by Joseph Mays and Lurtier, his wife, to Jonathan Clark, consisting of a grant of 320 acres, and to be located in the "county of Lovely, territory of Arkansas," now Pope county, and was executed on the 15th day of July, 1828, and recorded in book "A," page 1. In the same book is recorded the last will and testament of David Brearly, one of the framers of the constitution of the United States, a delegate from the state of New Jersey, and father of Dr. J. H. Brearly, of Norristown.

The first marriage on record was solemnized between James Whitson and Miss Jinney Davis, by A. E. Pace, J. P., on the 16th day of April, 1830. At this time Yell county, a good portion of Johnson, and a part Conway belonged to Pope with the seat of government at Norristown. The settlement given is verbatim as had at the January term 1831, to-wit:

"CHARGES.
"Jesse L. Cravens, sheriff to Pope county, Dr.: To three merchant licenses, $60.00; to one ferry license, $2.00; to six ferry licenses, $18.00; to one peddler license, $20.00; to 4 merchant licenses, $80.00; to fines from Justice Brown, $5.00; to fines from Justice Bollinger, $5.00; to fines from Justice Heck, $5.00; to 5 peddler licenses, $100.00; to county taxes $288,-50; to amount due from county of Crawford, $17.22½. Total, $600.72½.

"CONTRA.
"By 6 peddler licenses returned, $120.00; by 3 ferry licenses returned, $9.00; by amount of certificates taken in, $30.60; by amount of scrip taken in, $140.99¾; by error on ferry licenses, $1.00; by per cent for assessing property, $13.80; by delinquent list $15.81¼; by per cent. for collecting taxes, $19.81; by per cent. on licenses collected, $4.20; total credits, $355.31. To balance due the county on settlement at the January term 1831, $245.41½."

Property assessed for taxes in Pope county for 1840: Persons liable to pay a poll tax, 363; acres of land taxed, 16,550; val. $83,557; town lots, 18; val. $3,186; slaves, 109; val. $50,583; horses, 616; val. $32,460; mules, 8; val. $591; jacks, 1; val. $400; cattle 1417; val. $17,-385; capital invested in merchandise, $8,201; money at interest, $661; total

$8,201; money at interest, $661; total valuation, $109,171; county tax, $995.45; state tax, $248.96; total state and county taxes for the year 1840, $1,254.81. The aggregate increase of taxes for ten years $644.09.

County tax for 1850 was $1,718.63; state tax, $1,052.63; total tax, $2,771.26; increase of taxes for the next decade, $1,526.45. John Hickey, sheriff, and as shown by settlement was defaulter about $1,520.82 and was by the bondmen William L. Witt, Thos. J. Barnes, J. A. Hearren, J. H. Brearly, Darling Love, J. T. Sillman and C. B. Darneel, paid over.

Settlement of T. J. Linton, sheriff, for the taxes of 1860: Total state and county taxes, $5,421.44; increase of taxes $2,650.18 for ten years.

Pope county is still here, and though progress may seem slow, never give up in despair, for there is a faster day coming.

Settlement of James F. Clair for the county revenue alone (state tax not known) for the years 1869-70 together was $25,336.39.

But don't we swim now though—two-forty on a plank road—go 'long.

SCRAP.

The Russellville Democrat
Thu, Mar 17, 1881 ·Page 3

Hanging to be at Lewisburg
May 27, 1881

—A murderer is to be hung at Clarksville on the 20th inst.; and another, James Burcham, will be hung at Lewisburg on the 27th inst.

The Russellville Democrat
Thu, May 12, 1881 ·Page 2

A. C. Wells has moved his new store house from Lewisburg to Morrilton.

Arkansas Democrat
Mon, May 16, 1881 ·Page 4

Remembering the
1868 Burning of Lewisburg
and the criminal Matthews
excerpt from a larger article

J. L. W. Matthews was a native of Perry or Yell county, Arkansas, and during the war was a lieutenant in the

THIRD ARKANSAS CAVALRY,

called by many the "bloody third," though I believe that such is the epithet earned by many other detached commands during the bloody war, on both sides. After the war was over he settled in Conway county at Lewisburg, only one-half mile from where our flourishing little city of Morrilton now revels in healthy, peaceful progress. In 1868, if I am informed correctly, Matthews was appointed by Governor Clayton as captain of a company of negro militia to control this county of Conway, then under the blight of martial law. His senior officer was John J. Gibbons, but the murders, intimidations, arsons and plundering that followed are laid principally to J. L. W. Matthews and an ebon fiend named Enoch Payne. The town of Lewisburg, county seat of Conway county, was

BURNED DOWN,

while villainous robberies were the order of the day. An old citizen by the name of Casey, having nothing to do with politics or war, or offense to any one, was murdered because he had money.

A negro was living with a white woman as his wife not far from Lewisburg, and some person or persons sought to set the matter right by committing another great wrong; the negro was killed and the militia captains proceeded to retaliate according to the code of murderous barbarity. Three men were

SINGLED OUT FOR DEATH

without trial and without evidence. Joseph Jackson and Robert Perry were riding on a load of cotton and were met by Matthews and his squad. "Get down and come along with us," was the order. "What do you want?" they asked. "We are going to kill you," was the answer. "Then kill us here!" they replied. "Run for the canebrake!" was the next order. They ran, and Jackson fell dead, pierced with many bullets. Perry miraculously escaped, though badly wounded. The third victim was Mr. Hooper, also murdered in cold blood. For this last outrage Matthews, in 1877, nine years after its perpetration, was arrested and brought to Lewisburg to be tried for his life. Change of venue was had to Yell county, and the trial came off; but time had removed important links in the evidence,

important links in the evidence, and, as some reliable citizens state, by the jokes of Milt. Rice he missed conviction. The case was nolle prossed and Matthews was again at large.

Arkansas Democrat
Tue, Jul 26, 1881 ·Page 3

J. T. Goede, of Conway county, who died recently, was buried at Lewisburg.

Arkansas Democrat
Mon, Feb 13, 1882 ·Page 3

Mr. G. W. Griffin, of Conway Co., who was indicted for malfeasance in office, was tried at the recent term of the circuit court at Lewisburg and acquitted. The event was the signal for a grand jolification by Mr. Griffin's friends, who fired one hundred guns in honor of his vindication.

The Russellville Democrat
Thu, Mar 30, 1882 ·Page 1

END OF NEWSPAPER CLIPPINGS

By 1884, Lewisburg "gave up its life" for Morrilton... its now only "crumbling ruins."

Daily Arkansas Gazette, Fri, Sep 26, 1884 ·Page 2

THE TOWN OF MORRILTON,

the county seat of Conway county. Lying but fifty miles to the west of our capital city, and in the midst of one of the richest sections of the Arkansas valley, it is recognized as one of the most important stations along the line of the Little Rock and Fort Smith railway. But a few short years ago it sprang into existence, growing up about the railroad depot to which it clung as its natural support. We have seen it gathering strength with the years, each year extending its borders further out into the surrounding country, and each season seeing it gather within its warm embrace an increased number of

THRIFTY CITIZENS.

The town of Lewisburg, but a short distance away on the banks of the river, gave up its life to nourish the young one. As a hen broods its young, it sheltered its sturdy sons until they left it for better fields, and then deserted by all, it sank peacefully from existence leaving nothing to mark its resting-place, but a few crumbling ruins. The new city soon advanced to that stage of existence which makes the active period of youth, numbering among its citizens some of the best blood of Arkansas, and much which attracted from other countries, had settled there, recognizing its many advantages.

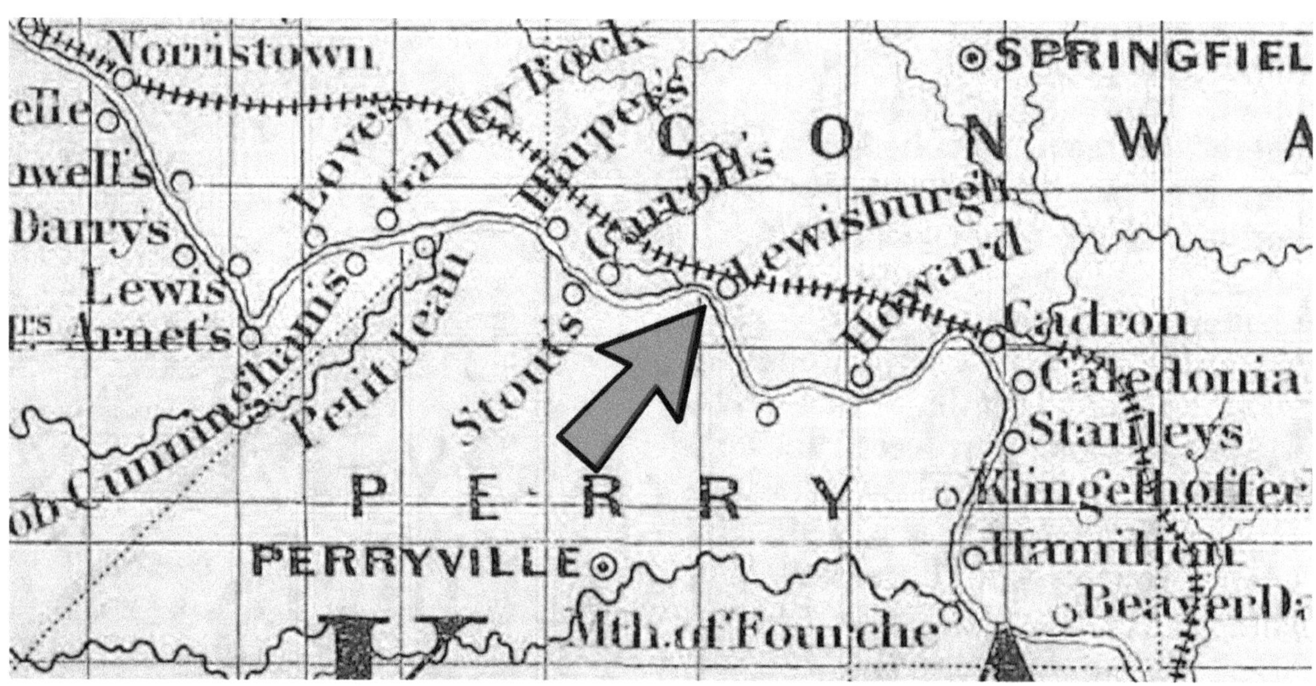

1874 Map of Arkansas, by Asher and Adams
showing the names of the Steamboat River Landings
above and below the Lewisburg landing.

Photographs

1817 Cherokee Boundary Marker

In 1936 this historic marker was placed on the corner of Jackson and Cherokee Streets in Morrilton, Arkansas.
In 1828, the Cherokee were removed farther west into Indian Territory, now called Oklahoma.

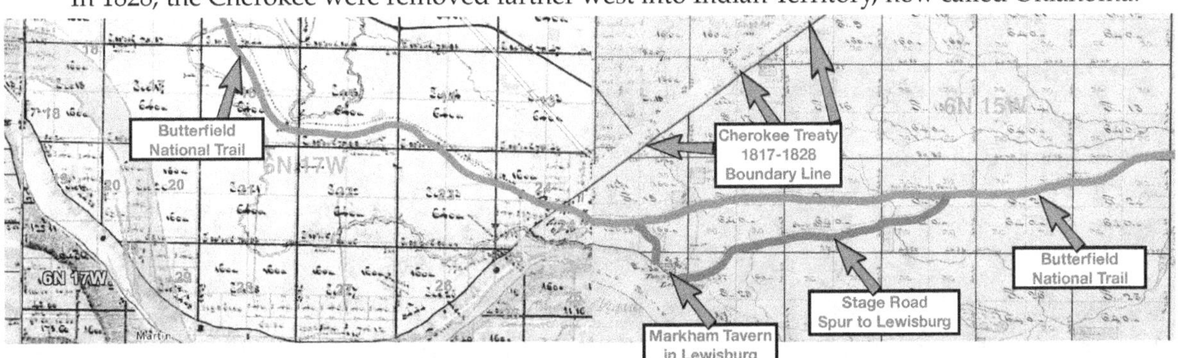

1858 Survey Showing the 1817-1828 Cherokee Boundary & Butterfield National Historic Trail
From the corner of Jackson and Cherokee Streets, Morrilton, AR
In 1828, the Cherokee were removed farther west into Indian Territory, now called Oklahoma.

"City of Lewisburg 1852" by Susan Gordon, ca. 1860
This image was made before the painting was cleaned by a professional art restorer.
Image courtesy of Conway County Historical Society Museum

Reproduction of Susan Gordon's "City of Lewisburg 1852"
Modern copy by D. Imhauser, 2008

"Old Lewisburg, Arkansas" photo by Grissom
This image is on a 1907 photo-postcard from the collection of Sharon Hamilton.
The post card was mailed from Morrilton on March 25, 1907, addressed to Atkins, Arkansas.
Image courtesy of Sharon Hamilton

The Town of Old Lewisburg, photo by Grissom
Close up of the above postcard's upper left corner.
Retired Corp of Engineer employee, Jack Johnson, reports: *"Lewisburg, like Ozark Arkansas,
never flooded because it was on high-ground overlooking the Arkansas River."*
Image courtesy of Sharon Hamilton

The Arkansas River Ferry Crossing Site at Lewisburg ca. 1900
Image courtesy of Conway County Historical Society Museum

Lewisburg Ferry, *ca. 1900*
Image courtesy of Conway County Historical Society Museum

Lewisburg Ferry,
ca. 1917
Will Hardin (left) and Frank Robinson, who was the father-in-law of Charles Isely
Image courtesy of Conway County Historical Museum

Road to Morrilton from Lewisburg Ferry, *by Thos. H. Jerome, ca. 1900*
The Lewisburg community, with several hundred residents, is now on the south side of today's Morrilton. Only one or two of the homes look like they might have existed in 1858-1861. In the 1870's many of the Lewisburg residents disassembled their houses to relocate them one mile north to be near the new railroad depot in Morrilton.

Sulphur Spring, *ca. 1900*
"Located near the Morrilton City Park on East Broadway."
Image courtesy of Conway County Historical Society Museum

LEAP YE LAME FOR JOY.

THE Weathersfield Sulphur Springs, midway between Lewisburg and Springfield, Conway county, Arkansas. They are not inferior to any in the State as many can testify, being situated on the main road between the above places. The proprietor would invite the attention of the public to them.

Sept. 25, 1755 4w   ELI EATON.

True Democrat
Tue, Oct 09, 1855 · Page 4

St. Paul A.M.E (Methodist) Church, *ca. late 1800's*
Image courtesy of Conway County Historical Society Museum and Ophelia Wells, whose great grandmother, Annie Wells, is identified in the picture.

In 1876 the St. Paul A.M.E (Methodist) Church was organized at Lewisburg Landing to provide free slaves a place to worship. A few years later, the congregation relocated to Morrilton on land donated by David Anthony, Henry Dunlap and Phyllis Cool of Conway County. In Morrilton, a small frame building was constructed at the present location, and later a parsonage for the pastor's family was built north of that location. The parsonage no longer stands.

The present building, as shown here, was built in 1922-23 by members of the church. Some of the lumber from the old Lewisburg church was incorporated into this structure.

Image courtesy of Conway County Historical Society Museum

Crowd gathered at the Lewisburg ferry landing for a baptismal service. *date unknown*
Image courtesy of Conway County Historical Society Museum

Statement from one of the Lewisburg stores, dated June 14, 1867, now on display at the Conway County Historical Society Museum.

Steamboats Dardanelle and Copin at the Lewisburg Landing. *date unknown*
Image courtesy of Conway County Historical Society Museum

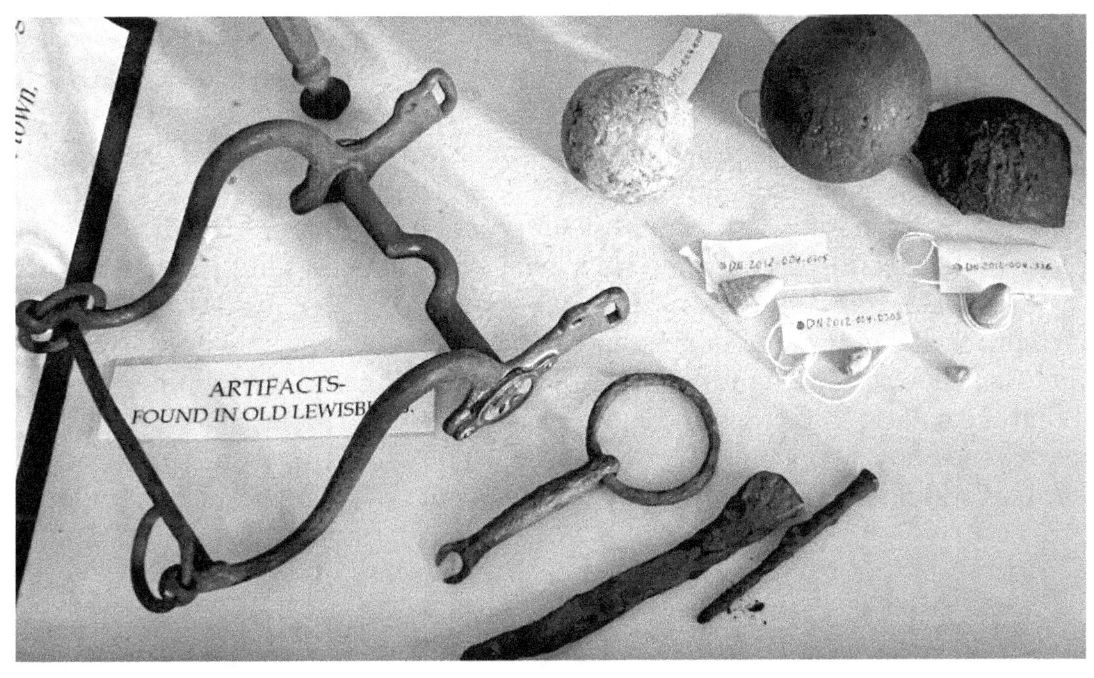

Artifacts found at the site of old Lewisburg, now on display at the Conway County Historical Society Museum.

Steamboat "Rapids" at Lewisburg Landing
"Reminiscent of the days gone by is one of the old ferry boats which churned the waters
of the Arkansas River before the modern steel bridge south of Lewisburg was constructed.
Otis L. Massey operated one of the early steamers. The boat pictured above carries a load of
baking powder for the Plunkett-Jarrell Grocery Company."

THE EXCURSION
May 15, 1896

The local lodge of the Woodmen of the World gave an excursion up the river last Thursday on the steamer 'City of Little Rock,' one of the slowest crafts afloat. There was a large crowd on board, and had the boat made reasonable time and the river had more water in the channel, a splendid time would have been had by all, but such conditions did not exist and all drew a sigh of relief when the gang plank was lowered at the wharf here on the return trip.

The boat left the wharf here about 9 a.m., and after stopping at every landing possible, succeeded in getting some twenty odd miles up the river by 4 p.m., when a sand bar was struck and the boat stuck. After backing and going forward a few times the captain decided that it was impossible to go farther and the return was begun, and about 9 p.m. the familiar banks of Lewisburg showed up and the crowd quickly landed, heaved a sigh of relief and went home.

It must be said that the gallant Woodmen did everything possible to make the trip pleasant, and had the boat crew made any arrangement for the crowd, a pleasant trip would have resulted. To the gentlemanly Woodmen we say, try it again next year, but do not allow the boat to carry freight.

This newspaper clipping is now on display at the
Conway County Historical Society Museum,
located at the railroad depot in downtown Morrilton.

The Lewisburg Cemetery

The Lewisburg Cemetery contains 102 graves dating from John Ewing McClure (1790-1835) to the most recent, Carl E. Dickson (1938-2018).

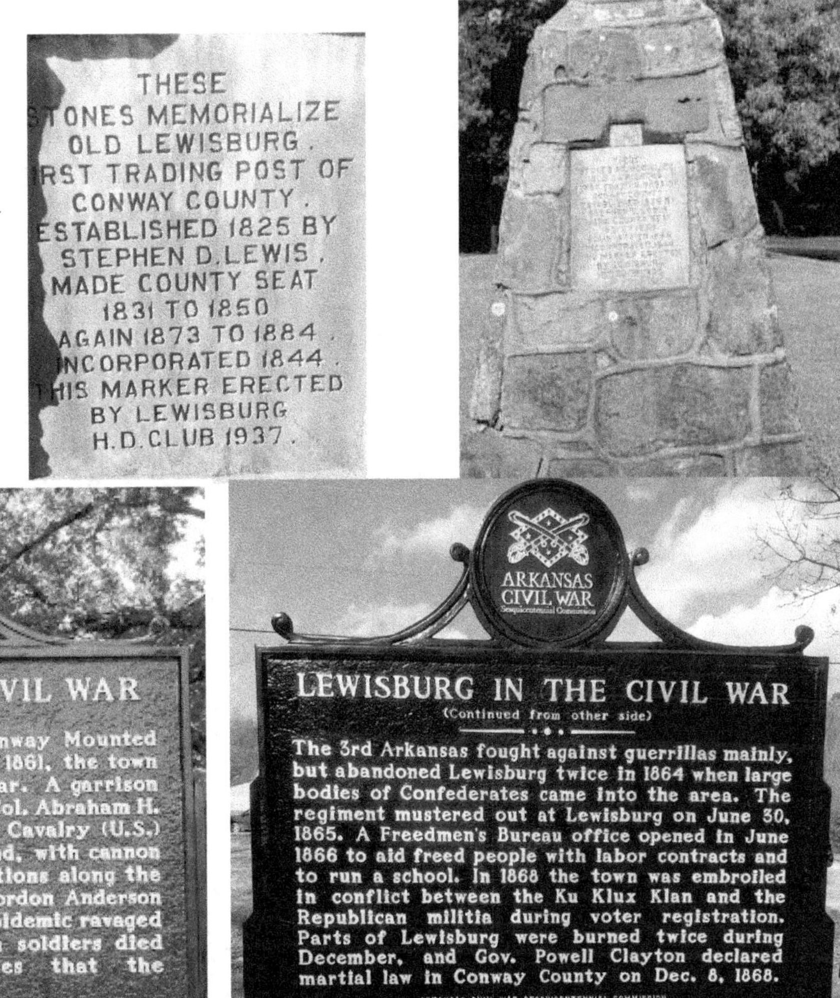

The Old Lewisburg Cemetery

These two images were taken at the second cemetery at Lewisburg. It contains 37 graves dating from Harriet B. Lewis Menefee (1803-1828) to the most recent, Sarah M Krueger Weckwerth (1897 - 1996). The Old Lewisburg cemetery overlooks the Arkansas River.

This map of Lewisburg is a portion of the
"Map of the City of Morrilton,
Conway County, Arkansas,
in the township 6 north - range 16 and 17 west."
Prepared by Rufus Haydon, surveyor.
Drawn by Joan M. Pulliam.
November 1956.

Street Layout of Old Lewisburg

Current streets and highways are shown with dotted lines in the background.

Where in Lewisburg Was the Markham Tavern Located?

Markham Tavern & Butterfield Stage Station

This photo was taken after James Miles Moose *"reconstructed"* the Markham Tavern *"log by log and plank by plank"* one mile north on 711 Green Street in Morrilton in 1866. After photo was taken, Moose *"enlarged and enhanced"* the tavern. This structure that housed the Reuben T. Markham Tavern, was originally built about 1835, close to the banks of the Arkansas River in the community of Lewisburg. *Photo courtesy of the Morrilton Depot Museum*

Where Was the Markham Tavern Located?

Markham Tavern served as the swing station for the Butterfield Overland Mail Co. stagecoaches between September of 1858 and March of 1861.

Exactly where was the Markham Tavern located in the town of Lewisburg, Arkansas?

Local historians report that the Markham Tavern was located very close to the Gordon home.

A trip was made to the Conway County Clerk's offices in August of 2024, to find the deeds of any lots in Lewisburg purchased by the Gordon's or by Reuben T. Markham.

The deeds found, are reproduced on the following pages.

Some years after the above photo was made, the structure was *"enlarged and enhanced,"* adding a two-story portico entrance and rooms in the rear of the home. This home is still standing at 711 Green Street in Morrilton, Arkansas.

This is the deed of R. T. Markham purchasing ½ of lot 2 (adjoining lot 1), in block 3, (being the eastern half, or the half adjoining lot #1 in block 3; divided by a line commencing on Main Street running through to the center of said lot, back to an alley) at Lewisburg from R. & Sanai (wife) Welborn, on August 18, 1858.

Conway County Clerk, Book H, pg 69-70.

This deed of conveyance made and executed at the Town of Lewisburg within the County of Conway in the state of Arkansas this the 18th day of August in the year our Lord one thousand Eight hundred and fifty Eight, in and from R. Welborn and Sinai Welborn of the County and State aforesaid of the first part hereto, unto and with R. T. Markham and John Hadlock party of the second part hereto.

Witnesseth that the said party of the first part, for and in consideration of the sum of fifty Dollars by the said party of the second part at and before the ensealing and delivery of these presents unto them in hand paid, the receipt of which is hereby acknowledged, have bargained and Sold, aliened and Conveyed, and do hereby bargain and Sell, alien and Convey and forever quit claim unto the said party of the second part the following described Lot, Tract or parcel of Land lying and being situate in the County of Conway and known as the One half of Lot No Two (2) in Block Three (3) being the East half or the half adjoining Lot No One, in said Block, divided by a line commencing on Main Street running through to the center of said lot Block to an alley. Together with and Singular the appurtenances thereto belonging To have and to hold to the said R. T. Markham and John Hadlock their heirs and assigns forever hereby covenanting with them that we will and that our heirs and assigns shall forever Warrant and defend the same unto the said R. T. Markham and John Hadlock their heirs and assigns against the lawful claims and demands of all persons claiming by through or under us But against none other. And the said Sinai Welborn wife to the said R. Welborn for and on her part and behalf doth hereby freely and fully relinquish and release unto the said party of the second part, all her right and claim to Dower in and to the aforesaid granted and bargained premises.

Witness our hands and Seals at Lewisburg this the 18th Day of August A.D. 1858

Signed and sealed in presents of E. N. Adams
Wm L Menefee

R. Welborn (Seal)
Sinai Welborn (Seal)

Where was this ½ lot that Reuben T. Markam purchased in August 18, 1858?

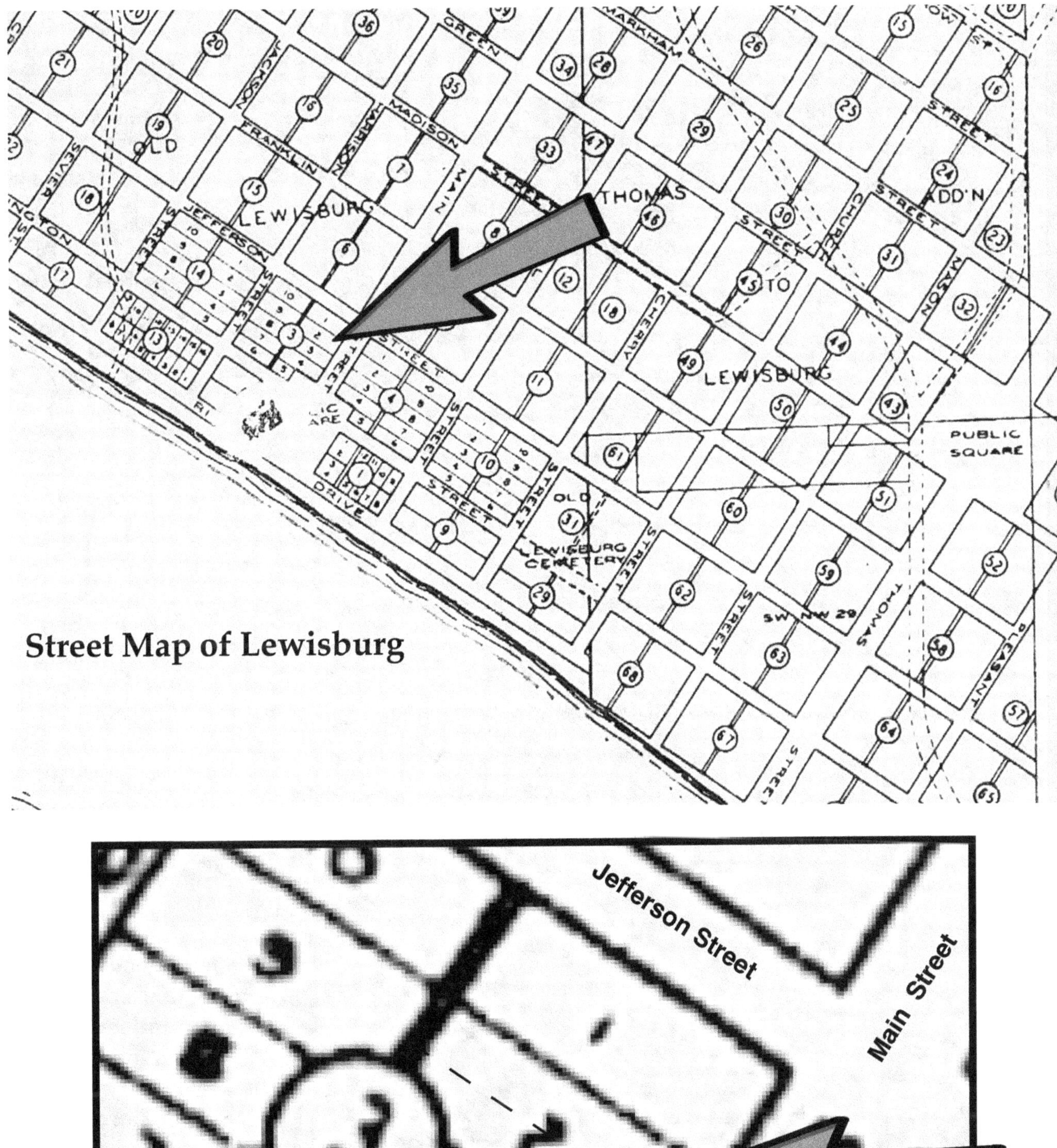

**Reuben T. Markham bought ½ of lot 2 in August, 1858 on Main Street.
Is this where Markham's Tavern was located?**

Local historians report that the Markham Tavern was very close to the home of the Gordons.
So, where did the Gordon's own property?
This is the deed of James M. Gordon and Anderson Gordon, who on March 3, 1849 purchased from Michael & Lorence (wife) Whisler, lots 3 & 9 in block #3 in Lewisburg, Arkansas. *Conway County Clerk, Book D, pg 83.*

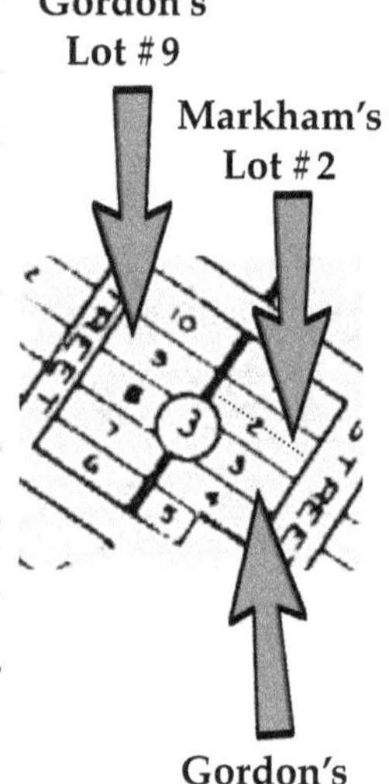

Was Reuben T. Markham's Lot #2 the location of Markham's Tavern, OR was Reuben's home on lot #2 ?

Deeds show that Lot #2 was indeed close to lots owned by the Gordons.

This Deed of Conveyance Made and Entered into this Twenty Third day of March Eighteen hundred and forty nine (1849) by & from Michael Whisler and his wife Lorence Whisler of the City of Camden County of Ouachita, & State of Arkansas, of the first part, and James M Gordon, & Anderson Gordon of the second part, of the County of Conway and State of Arkansas, Witnesseth that the said parties of the first part, for and in Consideration of the Sum of Six hundred dollars to them in hand paid at and before the delivery and Sealing of these presents by the said parties of the Second part, (the receipt whereof is hereby acknowledged) have granted bargained & Sold, aliened and Conveyed and do by these presents grant, bargain and Sell Alien and Convey unto the said parties of the Second part, the following described Lots in the Town of Lewisburg County of Conway State of Arkansas, Known in the Corporate & Surveyed limits of the aforesaid Town of Lewisburg as Lots No Three & No. Nine, in Block No Three, Together with all the rights and appurtenances thereunto belonging, To have and to hold the above Granted Lots unto the said parties of the first part and their heirs and assigns forever,

And the Said parties of the first part and their heirs and assigns, will Warrant and forever defend the Same unto the said parties of the Second part their heirs and assigns.

In witness whereof the said parties of the first part have hereunto set their hands and affixed their Seals at the City of Camden the day and year above written

Signed Sealed and delivered in the presence of

M Whisler {Seal}
Lorence Whisler {Seal}

From the Oct. 7, 1915 issue of the *Log Cabin*, Conway, Arkansas:

Wife of Reuben T. Markham After Leaving Lewisburg

Pioneer Woman Reaches 80 Years

"Mrs. Burilla T. Markham of Conway, one of the pioneer women of Arkansas, resident of this section of the state for more than three score years, is today celebrating the 80th anniversary of her birth. She is bearing lightly the weight of her years, is still active and strong and shows little loss of the unusual energy which has characterized her long life. *[She died Jan. 2, 1920, age 86]*

Long before the town of Conway was thought of, before Arkansas could boast of a mile of railroad or telegraph line, Mrs. Markham came to this state. Born near Memphis, TN, Sept 30, 1835, she was married, before she was 17, to Dr. R. T. Markham, at Hernado, Miss., April 12, 1852. The young couple left at once to carve their fortune in the wilds of Arkansas. They first settled at Jacksonport, Jackson County, but after living there only about a year moved to Lewisburg, near the present site of Morrilton, then the only settlement of importance between Little Rock and Dardanelle.

Lewisburg was a well known trading post, a regular stop for steamboats and stagecoaches plying between Little Rock and Fort Smith. Dr. and Mr. Markham for more than 20 years kept the inn and stage stand at Lewisburg, but when the railroad was built in the early 70's, Lewisburg was off the line and a new town was established and called Morrilton.

The rapid decline of steamboating and the passing of the stage line sounded the death knell of Lewisburg, and the Markhams moved to the newly established village of Conway, where they continued in the hotel business. Dr. Markham died about 25 years ago , but it was only two or three years ago that Mrs. Markham retired and disposed of her hotel here. *[Log Cabin, Oct. 7, 1915, p.2]*

The Markham Hotel was established in Conway in 1879, west of the railroad tracks at 116 West Oak St.

After the Markhams, Joe Rosa bought the building and renamed it the Rosa Hotel.

Upon the 80th birthday of Burilla Markham, wife of Reuben T. Markham, the Log Cabin newspaper *(Conway, Arkansas)* ran the story above that gives us interesting details on the Markham Tavern.

This article reports that Reuben and Burilla moved to Lewisburg about 1853 as a young married couple. It also reports that *"for more than 20 years kept the inn and stage stand at Lewisburg..."* In the 1870's, they moved to Conway, and continued in the hotel business there. According to the article, Reuben Markham died about 1890.

The Jan. 3, 1920 issue of the *Arkansas Gazette*, reports that Burella Markham died Jan. 2, 1920, survived by three sons, R. T. Markham, Chester Markham, and Thomas Markham all of Conway.

MRS. BURILLA T. MARKHAM.

Special to the Gazette.

Conway, Jan. 2.—Mrs. Burilla T. Markham, aged 86, a pioneer of Conway, died at her home here this afternoon. Mrs. Markham formerly conducted an inn near Morrilton and for 30 years she conducted a hotel in Conway. She is survived by three sons, R. T. Markham, Chester Markham and Thomas Markham, all of Conway, and several grandchildren and great-grandchildren.

Daily Arkansas Gazette Jan. 3, 1920, Page 9

History of Conway County can be found at museum

Arkansas Democrat Gazette
by Carol Rolf, August 18, 2013

Dorothy and Carl Imhauser stand in front of the Morrilton Depot Museum and Genealogy Research Library.
The museum is open from 10 a.m. to 2 p.m. Fridays and Saturdays and by special appointment.

MORRILTON — The Morrilton Depot Museum and Genealogy Research Library is dedicated to the history of Conway County.

"That pretty well sizes it up," said Carl Imhauser, president of the Conway County Historical Preservation Association, which owns the building and operates it as a museum, staffing it with volunteers. Volunteer members of the Conway County Genealogy Society staff the research library and help with the museum.

Imhauser said the museum is 35 years old. The Missouri-Pacific Railroad closed the passenger depot in 1954, and sometime after that, the preservation association purchased the building in order to preserve it.

"The railroad caused Morrilton to be formed," Imhauser said. Union Pacific Railroad, which merged with Missouri Pacific in the early 1990s, continues to operate the rail line through Morrilton. "Union Pacific has been a big help to preserve this building. I can't thank them enough. They have helped us monetarily."

"We have many things that have been donated, and continue to be donated," said Carl's wife, Dorothy Imhauser, a member of the Conway County Historical Preservation Association Board of Directors and a volunteer tour guide, especially for groups of schoolchildren. "Our job now is to get everything documented and put into the computer so that we might become an accredited museum."

Among the earliest exhibits at the museum are Native American artifacts found in Conway County.

There is also an exhibit about Lewisburg, a town on the Arkansas River just a few miles from Morrilton. Lewisburg was founded as a trading post and steamboat landing in 1825. It was the site of a skirmish during the Civil War and suffered its final demise when the railroad bypassed the town in 1875 and built its train stop in Morrilton.

Lewisburg was not only a river port but also a stagecoach stop between Pottsville and Fort Smith, and a part of the Indian removal along the Trail of Tears.

One of the highlights of the exhibit is a copy of the painting The City of Lewisburg, done in 1852 by Susan Gordon, whose family lived in the area. Another highlight is an Arkansas Civil War Sesquicentennial Commission plaque featuring two Conway County soldiers — Pvt. James N. Garvin, 31st Arkansas Infantry Co. G, and Sgt. James W. Carter, 31st Arkansas Infantry Co. C — who received the Southern Cross of Honor medal.

Carl said Morrilton was incorporated in 1884 and continued to thrive. In those early days, there were many businesses, including several hotels and an opera house. Morrilton was also the site of two colleges — Harding College was established there in 1924 on the site of the current Southern Christian Home but moved two years later to Searcy, and the Morrilton Male and Female College was built in 1890 but served as a college for only a few years before the building became part of the South Conway County School District.

High school class pictures can be seen on several walls of what was the ticket office of the depot.

"The oldest is 1908," said Carl, noting that former students often come in to view the photographs.

There is also a space dedicated to the late Gov. Winthrop Rockefeller, who moved to Petit Jean Mountain in 1953 and served as governor from 1967 to 1971.

"We want to enlarge this exhibit to include his son, Winthrop Paul," Carl said.

Outside in the garden, there is a large statue of the younger Rockefeller, who served as lieutenant governor of the state from November 1996 until his death in July 2006. He also maintained a home on Petit Jean Mountain.

Work continues at the museum to expand space for more exhibits and to create a larger space for the genealogy research library.

"We have received some grant money that will help with the renovations, but I do a lot of the work myself," said Carl, who is retired as superintendent of maintenance at Little Rock Catholic High School. The museum also accepts donations.

The Morrilton Depot Museum and Genealogy Research Library is open from 10 a.m. to 2 p.m. Fridays and Saturdays and by appointment.

For more information, call (501) 354-4347 or email morriltondepotmuseum@yahoo.com.

Conway County Historical Society Museum
In Morrilton, the old railroad depot located at 101 East Railroad Avenue,
is now the home of the Conway County Historical Society Museum.
The museum is open, free of charge, Friday and Saturday from 10:00 am to 2:00 pm.

Additional Reading

"Butterfield's Overland Mail Co. STAGECOACH Trail Across Arkansas"

This full color 266 page book tells the story of the Overland Mail Company stagecoaches which carried passengers and mail west from Memphis and St. Louis to San Francisco through Arkansas. The Overland stagecoaches and stage wagons traveled day and night, completing the 3,293 mile journey is less than twenty five days.

This book pays special attention to each of the twenty Overland Mail Company stations spread across Arkansas. The stations were typically located about fifteen miles apart. The stagecoaches or stage wagons would stop for ten minutes at each station for the quick change of horses. Twice a day the stage would stop at a station for about forty minutes, allowing the passengers to have a moment of rest and purchase a quick meal while the driver obtained a fresh team of horses or mules.

Butterfield's Steamboat, *Jennie Whipple*
from the art collection of Bob Crossman

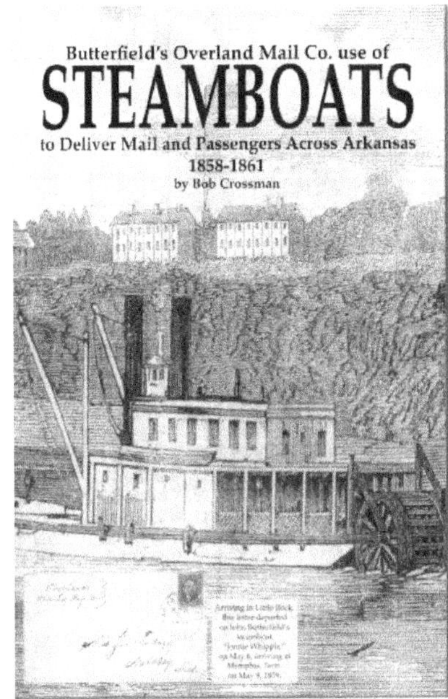

"Butterfield's Overland Mail Co. use of STEAMBOATS to Deliver Mail and Passengers Across Arkansas 1858-1861"

This 460 page book explores the untold story of John Butterfield's use of STEAMBOATS to carry the Overland Mail over portions of the Fort Smith to Memphis route of The Butterfield Overland National Historic Trail.

While the purpose of my research of the Overland Mail was to satisfy my personal curiosity, hopefully this collection of my research will also make a contribution to the efforts of officially recognizing the route of Butterfield's Overland Mail Co. as a National Historic Trail.

"Butterfield's Overland Mail Co. as REPORTED in Arkansas Newspapers of 1858-1861"

In this 632 page book, the newspapers of Arkansas do an amazing job of covering the news around Butterfield's Overland Mail Company. Frequently the newspaper editors would draw their information from their exchange of newspapers across the country to bring to their subscribers the most accurate and comprehensive description of facts as possible.

In this book I have let the newspaper reporters tell the story in their own words. It has been difficult, but I have limited my interpretive comments to the brief title I've assigned each article. In this way, today's reader can immerse themselves into the world of the citi-

"POSTAL HISTORY of John Butterfield's Overland Mail Co. on the Southern & Central Routes including Butterfield's Pony Express 1858-1864"

This new full color 354 page book reports on the mail carried by Butterfield's Overland Mail between September 1858 and March 1861 on the Southern Ox Bow Route, and beginning in July of 1861 on the Central Route. Also, to include additional information and artifacts from US transcontinental mail carried immediately before and immediately after the existence of Butterfield's Overland Mail Co.

In most instances within his previous three books on Butterfield's Overland Mail Co., Dr. Crossman focused primarily on the Arkansas route. This volume, by contrast, expands to focus on the entire route of the Butterfield. Also, by contrast, this volume focuses on Butterfield's presence on the Southern Ox-bow Route and later on the northern Central Route. In addition, this volume covers the entire time period of the Overland Mail Company's contract with the postal system: 1858 to 1864.

While the purpose of this research of the Overland Mail was to satisfy his personal curiosity, he is hopeful that summary of Butterfield Postal History will also make a contribution to Butterfield's Overland Mail Co. new status as a National Historic Trail.

"PASSENGER DIARIES & STORIES across Oklahoma, Arkansas and Missouri"

In this 460 page book, you will read stories of Butterfield's Overland Mail Company stagecoaches rolling across Oklahoma, Arkansas and Missouri one hundred and sixty five years ago as they connected with San Francisco.

Now that Congress has named the route **"The Butterfield Overland National Historic Trail,"** it seems appropriate for the Butterfield passengers to tell us about their experience on the trail. This book contains reminiscences and interviews of first person observers in their own words.

In most of the chapters of this book, the author only included portions of each original document that focus on passage through Missouri, Arkansas and the Indian Territory.

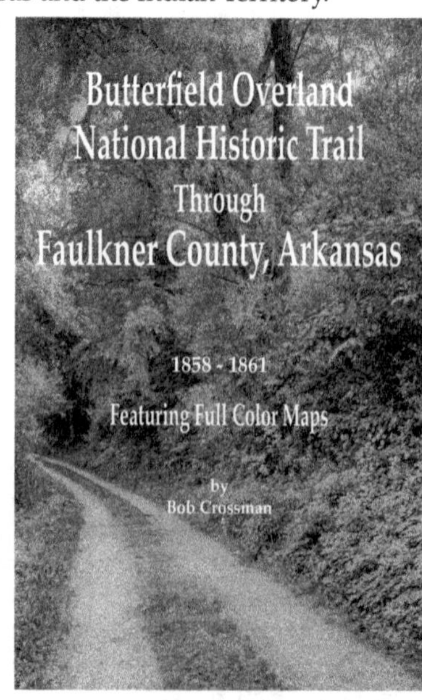

Some of the original source documents are hundreds of pages long and include details of passage through Texas, New Mexico, Arizona, and California that are not included here. Several of the source articles were brief enough, *[such as Henry Everett, J. W. Farwell, Warren Baer, Thomas M. Johnston, and the speech by Waterman L. Ormsby]*, that the author included their full remarks concerning the entire route from San Francisco to the Mississippi River.

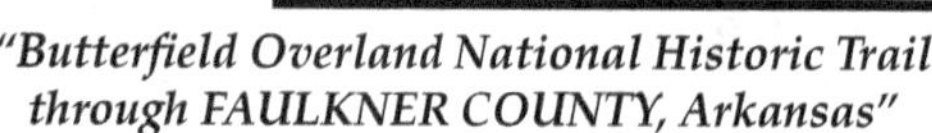

"Butterfield Overland National Historic Trail through FAULKNER COUNTY, Arkansas"

After twenty years of effort by the Heritage Trail Partners, and Arkansas Senator John Boozman, legislation was signed into law Jan. 2023 establishing **The Butterfield Overland National Historic Trail.**

That historic decision brings up the task of determining exactly where that trail crossed Faulkner County.

This full color 144 page book outlines the two year process Dr. Crossman followed to determine the exact route of **The Butterfield Overland National Historic Trail** across Faulkner County, Arkansas.

*"Butterfield Overland National Historic Trail
through Arkansas' POPE & CONWAY Counties"*

In this new full-color 236 page book, you will find a report of the author's four year search through Conway and Pope counties as he explored the disappearing route once taken by the Butterfield Overland Mail Company stagecoaches as they sped from Memphis to San Francisco.

Why, you may ask, is this search worthy of such an effort? From September of 1858 to March of 1861, Arkansas was a vital link in the longest stagecoach line in the world. The importance of this route is reflected in the January 2023 decision of the U. S. Congress and President Biden to declare this route "THE BUTTERFIELD OVERLAND NATIONAL HISTORIC TRAIL."

This NATIONAL HISTORIC TRAIL played a vital role as it drastically improved communication and transportation between California and the east coast.

This book includes survey maps of the 1828 Old Military Road, and reveals the old trail my overlaying that route on current road maps.

Also, enjoy these You Tube Videos by Bob Crossman

Open YouTube and search for the following titles produced by the Oregon-California Trails Association:

"Authentic letters from the Butterfield Overland Mail"
"Butterfield Trail Arkansas Ferry"
"The Butterfield Trail across Arkansas"

You may order copies from your favorite local book store, or Barnes & Noble, Books-A-Million, Wal-Mart, Target, Amazon, Thrift Books, or Abe Books.

OR, to order signed copies from the author send funds through PayPal to: Bcrossman@arumc.org OR by mailing a check to: Bob Crossman, #8 Sternwheel Dr., Conway, AR 72034

THE BUTTERFIELD OVERLAND NATIONAL HISTORIC TRAIL STORY:

USE OF STAGECOACHES	USE OF STEAMBOATS	POSTAL HISTORY	NEWSPAPER ARTICLES	PASSENGER DIARIES	FAULKNER COUNTY	POPE & CONWAY COUNTIES
$30 SOFT	$30 SOFT	$40 SOFT	$40 SOFT	$30 SOFT	$30 SOFT	$30 SOFT
$40 HARD	$40 HARD	$50 HARD	$50 HARD	$40 HARD	$40 HARD	$40 HARD

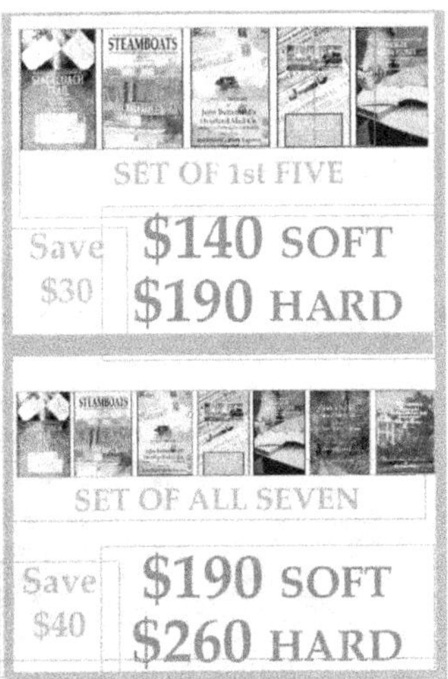

SET OF 1st FIVE	
Save $30	$140 SOFT
	$190 HARD

SET OF ALL SEVEN	
Save $40	$190 SOFT
	$260 HARD

Historical Marker at Tipton, Missouri

ABOUT THE AUTHOR:

Dr. Robert O. "Bob" Crossman has lived in Faulkner County, Arkansas since 1988, when he and his wife established Crossman Printing near downtown Conway's Toad Suck Square.

He is a member of The Butterfield Overland National Historic Trail Association, Faulkner County Historical Society, Arkansas Historical Association, Southern Trails Chapter of the Oregon-California Trails Association, Shiloh Museum of Ozark History, Faulkner County Museum, Fort Smith Museum of History, Old Colony History Museum, and numerous philatelic societies.

Dr. Crossman, and his wife of 52 years have two sons, and five grandchildren all living in Faulkner County, Arkansas.

After graduating from Russellville High School, Dr. Crossman received a B.A. from Hendrix College in Conway, Arkansas, and received graduate and post-graduate degrees from SMU in Dallas, Texas.

Bob Crossman is the author of seven books on the Butterfield:

- Butterfield's Overland Mail Co. STAGECOACH TRAIL Across Arkansas;
- Butterfield's Overland Mail Co. Use of STEAMBOATS Across Arkansas;
- Butterfield's Overland Mail Co. as REPORTED in the Newspapers of Arkansas;
- POSTAL HISTORY of John Butterfield's Overland Mail Co. on the Southern & Central Routes including Butterfield's Pony Express, 1858-1864;
- Butterfield Overland National Historic Trail PASSENGER DIARIES & STORIES Across Oklahoma, Arkansas, and Missouri, 1858-1861;
- Butterfield Overland National Historic Trail Through FAULKNER COUNTY, Arkansas; and
- Butterfield Overland National Historic Trail Through Arkansas' POPE & CONWAY COUNTIES.

Dr. Crossman has four published articles on the Butterfield including:

- *"The Butterfield Overland Mail Company: Faulkner County Connection,"* Faulkner County Facts & Fiddlings, Fall 2021, p. 24-32.
- *"Fort Smith's Connection to the Butterfield's Overland Mail Co.: Stations Between Memphis and Fort Smith,"* Fort Smith Historical Society Journal, Fall 2021, p. 25-43.
- *"I Lived on The Butterfield Mail Route for Decades and Didn't Know It,"* The American Philatelist, Jan. 2023, pp. 17-31. - Winner of the 2024 United States Stamp Society / Barbara J. Mueller Award.
- *"Faulkner County and Butterfield's Overland Mail Company Stagecoach Route,"* Faulkner County Facts & Fiddlings, Spring 2024.

The cemetery for the community at the old Green Grove steamboat landing is alongside THE BUTTERFIELD OVERLAND NATIONAL HISTORIC TRAIL in Faulkner County, Arkansas. Photo by D. J. Charles

I just couldn't resist including photos of my family.

Bob & Marcia Crossman

Paul Crossman & Louis Lefebvre

Owen, David, Cooper & Marlie Crossman

Jessica, Blake Charles and Grayson with Bob & Marcia Crossman

Fred Borck, Raquel Borck, Brooks Bachamp, Bailey Bachamp, Dylan Bachamp & Sherry Borck

Gracie & Maggie Mae Crossman

My Golden Anniversary Edition of the 1929 Model A